Hitler's Munich

This book is dedicated to my students, past and present, in the Hitler Studies seminar, part of the King's College London MA in Defence Studies at the Joint Services Command and Staff College, Shrivenham, United Kingdom

Disclaimer
The analysis, opinions, and conclusions expressed or implied in this book are those of the author alone and do not necessarily represent the views of the Joint Services Command and Staff College, the Ministry of Defence, or any other government agency.

Hitler's Munich

The Capital of the Nazi Movement

David Ian Hall

Pen & Sword
MILITARY

First published in Great Britain in 2020 by
Pen & Sword Military
An imprint of
Pen & Sword Books Ltd
Yorkshire – Philadelphia

ISBN 978 1 52670 492 4

A CIP catalogue record for this book is
available from the British Library.

Typeset by Mac Style
Printed and bound in the UK by TJ Books Ltd,
Padstow, Cornwall.

MIX
Paper from
responsible sources
FSC® C013056

Pen & Sword Books Limited incorporates the imprints of Atlas,
Archaeology, Aviation, Discovery, Family History, Fiction, History,
Maritime, Military, Military Classics, Politics, Select, Transport,
True Crime, Air World, Frontline Publishing, Leo Cooper, Remember
When, Seaforth Publishing, The Praetorian Press, Wharncliffe
Local History, Wharncliffe Transport, Wharncliffe True Crime
and White Owl.

For a complete list of Pen & Sword titles please contact

PEN & SWORD BOOKS LIMITED
47 Church Street, Barnsley, South Yorkshire, S70 2AS, England
E-mail: enquiries@pen-and-sword.co.uk
Website: www.pen-and-sword.co.uk

Or

PEN AND SWORD BOOKS
1950 Lawrence Rd, Havertown, PA 19083, USA
E-mail: Uspen-and-sword@casematepublishers.com
Website: www.penandswordbooks.com

Contents

MAP OF BAVARIA

MAP OF THE PUTSCH MARCH

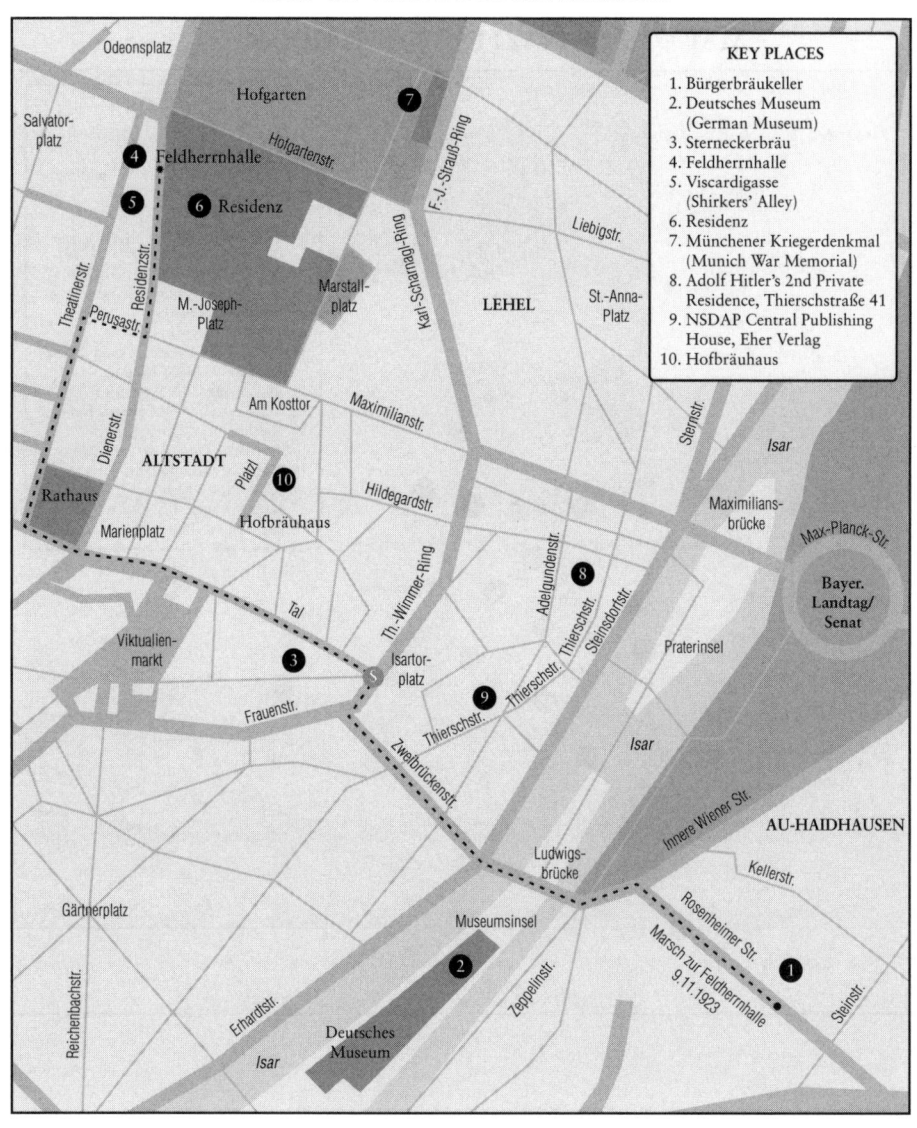

KEY PLACES

1. Bürgerbräukeller
2. Deutsches Museum
   (German Museum)
3. Sterneckerbräu
4. Feldherrnhalle
5. Viscardigasse
   (Shirkers' Alley)
6. Residenz
7. Münchener Kriegerdenkmal
   (Munich War Memorial)
8. Adolf Hitler's 2nd Private
   Residence, Thierschstraße 41
9. NSDAP Central Publishing
   House, Eher Verlag
10. Hofbräuhaus

MAP OF THE NAZI PARTY DISTRICT

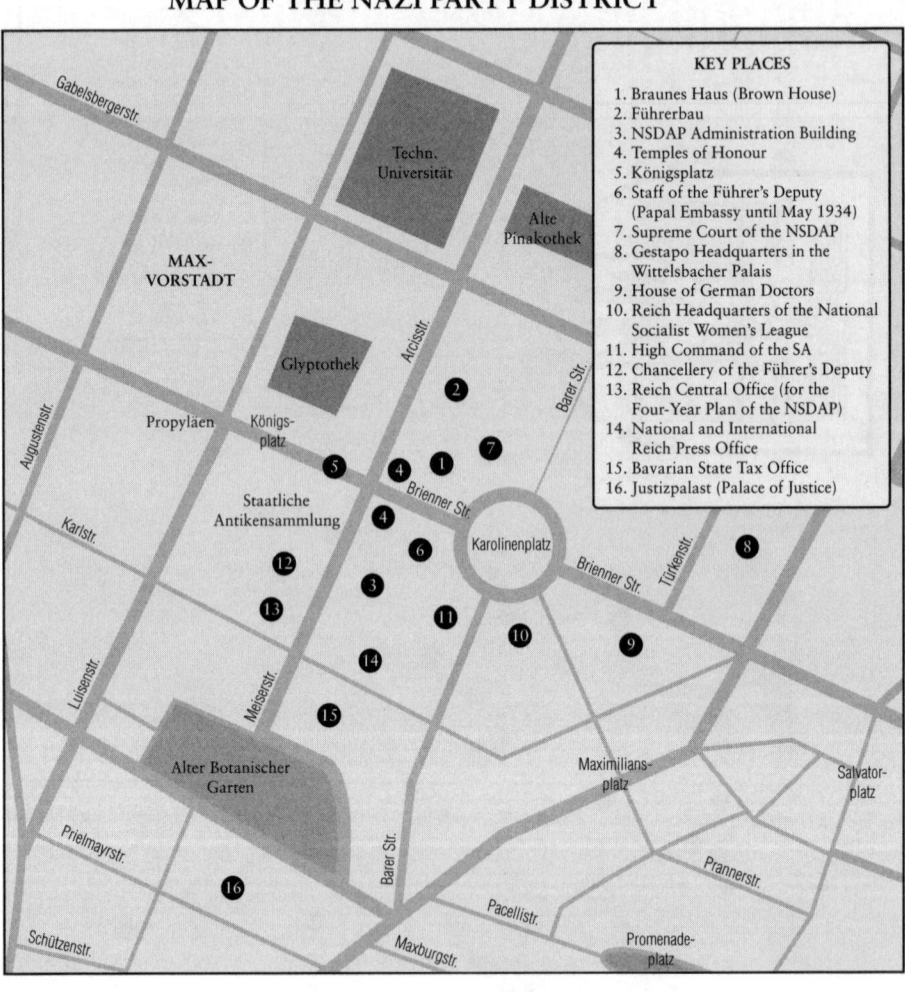

KEY PLACES

1. Braunes Haus (Brown House)
2. Führerbau
3. NSDAP Administration Building
4. Temples of Honour
5. Königsplatz
6. Staff of the Führer's Deputy
   (Papal Embassy until May 1934)
7. Supreme Court of the NSDAP
8. Gestapo Headquarters in the
   Wittelsbacher Palais
9. House of German Doctors
10. Reich Headquarters of the National
    Socialist Women's League
11. High Command of the SA
12. Chancellery of the Führer's Deputy
13. Reich Central Office (for the
    Four-Year Plan of the NSDAP)
14. National and International
    Reich Press Office
15. Bavarian State Tax Office
16. Justizpalast (Palace of Justice)

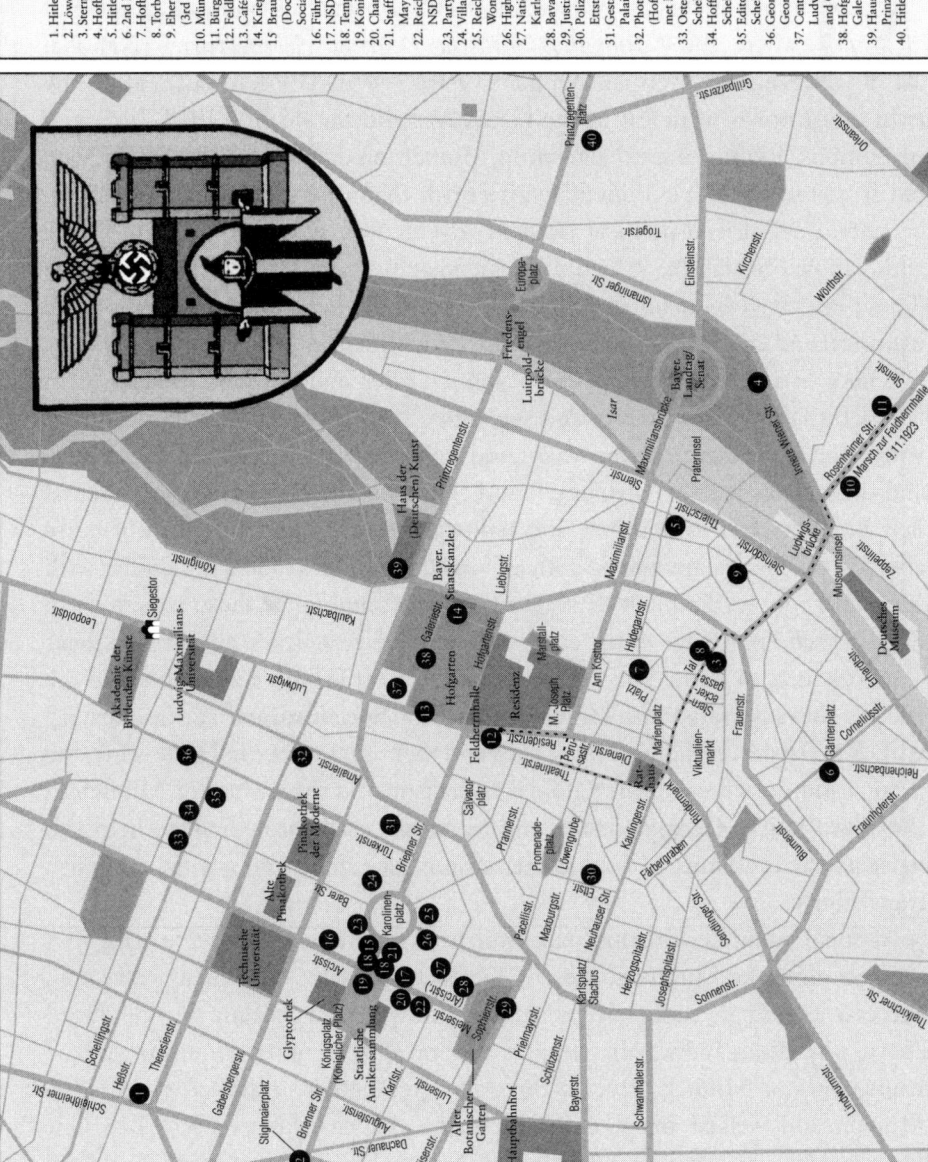

Preface

Munich is the city where Adolf Hitler began his political career, and where the *Nationalsozialistische Deutsche Arbeiterpartei* (National Socialist German Workers' Party, NSDAP) was born after the twin catastrophes of defeat in the Great War and the fleeting 1918–19 Soviet revolutions. Right-wing extremism in Munich predated the First World War, but it was in the war's immediate aftermath that a perfect storm of cultural, economic, social, and political factors converged to facilitate the rise of Hitler and National Socialism. Why did it happen and why did it happen in Munich? These are the two main questions this book answers through an in-depth historical and culturally-orientated study of Munich and its Nazi past.

There is no better way to learn about Hitler and National Socialism in Munich than to visit the city and see where it happened: where Hitler lived; where the Movement began; where and how the Nazis promoted themselves and their ideology. Nazi ideology found expression in Munich in monumental new buildings, art exhibitions, and political street theatre. The book you are about to read is designed to be both an introduction for readers unfamiliar with Munich's role in the birth of Nazism, and a stimulus for those who wish to deepen their knowledge of the city – its architecture, culture, and urban spaces – and its links to Hitler and National Socialism. It is both a guide book to the specific sites associated with Hitler and National Socialism, and a critical history with detailed descriptions of these sites and their importance in Hitler's life, the origins and development of National Socialism, and the history of Munich in the Third Reich. German names and terms are used throughout to help you navigate the museums in Munich because most exhibits do not have English translations.

My inspiration to write this book came from the students who were in my MA seminar on Hitler Studies at the UK Defence Academy. Over many years now, successive seminar classes have asked the same questions, mainly the ones listed above, why Hitler and why in Munich. Several of my seminar groups organized study tours in Munich. Over a three-day weekend we travelled together to Munich and walked many miles exploring the city's Nazi past. The new Documentation Centre on the history of National Socialism in Munich and the permanent exhibition on the *NS-Zeit* (NS-time) at the *Münchner Stadtmuseum* (City of Munich Museum) are the best places to start your study. They provide both historical context and visual material essential to a thorough understanding of how and why the city played a significant role in Hitler's political career and the rise of National Socialism. Many of the buildings and places where these events occurred still exist, and they are well worth seeking out to see and feel the impact they had in contributing to the tragedy that unfolded in Munich, spread throughout Germany, and ultimately had such devastating consequences for Europe and the rest of the world.

Munich is a culturally rich city, and it possesses a unique aesthetic allure and charm. How did it become a centre for ethnic-chauvinist nationalism and the Capital of the Nazi Movement? Visiting the city and seeing its buildings, monuments, and urban spaces offers a new perspective on the construction and evolution of NS-ideology and history through local culture and stone. There are a few guide books that identify and briefly describe a number of the main sites in Munich associated with Hitler and National Socialism. These include: Brian Deming and Ted Iliff, *Hitler and Munich* (1988); Steven Lehrer, *Hitler Sites* (2002); Maik Kopleck, *Munich 1933–1945* (2006); Joachim von Halasz, *Hitler's Munich* (2007); Colin Philpott, *Relics of the Reich* (Pen & Sword, 2016); and David Mathieson, *A Guide to Hitler's Munich* (Pen & Sword, 2019). All of them list approximately forty buildings and places of importance, and most provide a cursory descriptive narrative that links the site to Hitler and his political movement. At the opposite end of the historical spectrum are the main biographies on Hitler. The best is Volker Ullrich's two volume work, the second volume entitled *Hitler. Downfall 1939–1945* was published in English in February 2020. Other leading biographies include Ian Kershaw's extensive two volume critical assessment (1998–2000), Joachim Fest (1973), John Toland (1976) and Richard Evans' comprehensive three volume study on Hitler and the Third Reich (2003–2008). To obtain a picture of Hitler, his politics, and Munich's role in the rise and fall of the Third Reich the reader must digest thousands of pages just to begin to assemble a complex jigsaw puzzle that frustratingly lacks a number of key pieces.

Hitler's Munich: The Capital of the Nazi Movement completes the picture puzzle and fills a sizeable gap in the literature. It is a book that combines a short biography of Hitler and his 'Movement' with a history of the turbulent *NS-Zeit* in Munich. The aim is to enhance the reader's understanding through a virtual experience of seeing where the key events in Munich's Nazi past happened, treating the history as a living space and emphasising the experience of being there. Please take the book with you when you visit Munich as it also serves as a guide to where these events took place.

Employing a loose chronological structure, the book begins with Hitler's early years and his desire to live in Munich, the Bavarian capital renowned for being a liberal centre of art, music, learning and culture. The Great War and the four socialist and communist revolutions between November 1918 and May 1919 left an indelible scar on the people of Munich, and contributed significantly to the city's transformation into the spiritual centre of National Socialism and the Capital of the Movement. Hitler was instrumental in this process, but the city and its history exerted an equally strong influence on him, his politics, and the development of the Movement. The connection between the physical and political landscape of Munich and the cultural exploitation of the city by the Nazis deepened. Hitler and the Nazis used Munich, its structures and its traditions to create a 'new spirit' ostensibly harmonising the past with their ethnic-chauvinist nationalism and populist politics. The chimera of 're-birth and rejuvenation' ended in death and destruction. This book is a history of Hitler and his life in Munich. It also explains how and why Munich became the Capital of the Movement.

David Ian Hall
Oxfordshire
14 April 2020

I

Early Years, 1889–1918

Austrian Beginnings

At around 6.30 pm on 20 April 1889, Alois Hitler's wife Klara gave birth to a son on the second floor of the Zum Hirschen, a Gasthof owned by the Dafner family (after 1912 renamed the Gasthof zum Pommer[1]) in the upper Austrian town of Braunau am Inn on the Austro-German border. The infant's mother was 28 and his father was 51, and on Easter Monday he was christened Adolfus in the Stadtpfarrkirche St. Stephan, the same church where his parents were married on 7 January 1885. Hitler's birth house, at Salzburger Vorstadt 15, is just a few hundred metres from a bridge over the River Inn, linking Braunau with the Bavarian town of Simbach, an act of fate that Hitler later claimed was providential. 'For this little town,' wrote Hitler, in the first lines of *Mein Kampf*, 'lies on the boundary between two German states which we of the younger generation at least have made it our life's work to reunite by every means at our disposal.'[2] Other than being his place of birth, Braunau did not have much of a role in Hitler's childhood. Braunau was a short posting for his father, a customs officer in the imperial Austrian civil service. In 1892, Alois was promoted to senior customs official (*Zollamtoberoffizial*) and transferred to Passau on the Bavarian side of the border. It was in Passau that the young Hitler acquired the lower Bavarian dialect that proved to be very useful to him as a political agitator in Munich's beer halls during the early 1920s.[3]

The Hitler household in Passau was a comfortably middle class if somewhat unorthodox family. Alois's annual salary of 2,600 Kronen – roughly similar to a school principal in Austria at the time – enabled him to dress smartly, fund his hobbies (he was a keen beekeeper, and he enjoyed his beer and wine), and provide for his family. Between 1892 and 1894 the Hitler family consisted of six people: Alois and Klara (née Pölzl) his third wife; baby Adolf; Alois Jr. and Angela, two children from Alois's second marriage to Franziska Matzelsberger (Fanni); and Johanna Pölzl, Klara's younger unmarried sister, known as 'Hannitante' (Aunt 'Hanni') who helped out with domestic chores and the children. Adolf was the fourth (and first surviving) child of Alois and Klara, who had six children together. The first three all died in infancy.[4] Adolf's younger brother Edmund was born in Passau in 1894, but he died six years later of rubella in 1900. The only other child of Alois and Klara to survive childhood was Paula, who was born on 21 January 1896 in Hafeld, a small rural community about thirty miles southwest of Linz, where Alois had bought a farm of nearly ten acres the previous spring, and began his retirement after forty years of imperial service.

Alois's career in customs had entailed frequent changes in residence with each new posting, and lengthy periods of time when he was away from his family. Klara and the children also did not accompany him on every move, and until he retired there was a noticeable absence of paternal influence in the house. Despite this the Hitler children had a fairly normal and happy childhood. They spent long hours playing outdoors, enjoyed each other's company, and were well cared for by Klara and her sister Johanna. If young Adolf had a problem, it was an abundance of maternal attention and care. Klara spoilt Adolf, but her indulgence is entirely understandable given the enormous loss she suffered with the early deaths of her first three children. In the spring of 1895, the family were reunited briefly in Linz before they all moved into Farm Rauschergut, their new home in Hafeld. The contrast between a strict father, who demanded respect and obedience from his children, and an overly kind and uncritical mother could not have been more stark. It marked the beginning of a life-defining phase for young Adolf.[5]

Alois, now retired, had time to devote to his children's upbringing. Farming and parenting, however, were not endeavours that he either enjoyed or had much aptitude for, but he did have high expectations for his children. His own personal experience – leaving home for Vienna at age 14, teaching himself how to read and write, learning a trade but aspiring to much more in life, enlisting in the frontier guard, and ultimately pursuing a highly successful career in the civil service – had taught him the value of hard work and will power. What Alois had learnt the hard way, through hard knocks in the school of life, he hoped his children would acquire through a rigorously supervised education that emphasised practical skills, and equipped them with the qualifications necessary for a reputable career similar to his own. The Hitler children would not be allowed to drift through their childhood years indolent and intoxicated by fanciful dreams.

Six-year-old Adolf started school in May 1895, a small primary school (*Volksschule*) in Fischlham near Lambach, about an hour's walk from his family's farm. Adolf did well at school, the lessons were easy,[6] and he learned how to read and write very quickly. He and his half-sister Angela also made a good impression on the schoolmaster, who later recalled that both were attentive and orderly, further noting that Adolf was 'mentally very much alert, obedient, but lively'.[7] Alois Jr. was less interested in his studies. Once he skipped school for three days to finish building a model boat. His father was livid and punished him severely.

On 21 January 1896 baby Paula arrived. Tensions in the turbulent Hitler household and Alois's increasing irritability became too much for 14-year-old

Alois Jr. Following in his father's footsteps he left home never to return. Less than a year later Alois moved his family to Lambach, a small village of approximately 1,700 inhabitants, where he hoped to find some respite from the drudgery of the farm and his family in the pleasures of the town's inn, the Gasthaus Leingartner.

Despite the change of residence Adolf continued to excel at school. He attended a modern school run by the Benedictine monastery in Lambach until the spring of 1898, and in all twelve of the subjects he studied he was awarded the highest grades from his teacher, Franz Rechberger. Hitler also briefly served as a choirboy in the Junior Choral Institute, where he saw his first swastika. The *Hakenkreuz* was the most prominent feature in the monastery's insignia, displayed both inside the abbey and on the large stone archway in the main cloister. The swastika was also the symbol used by German-Austrian nationalists. Lambach, however, proved to be almost as dull to Alois as the farm so in February 1899 he moved the family again, this time to Leonding, a larger village of 3,000 inhabitants on the south-west outskirts of Linz.[8] Alois bought a modest house with a fine garden just across the road from the main cemetery. This house, at Michaelsbergstraβe 16, is where the Hitler family lived until June 1905.

The Leonding Volksschule was Adolf's third and last primary school. He continued to get excellent grades, found school work easy, and had plenty of free time to pursue other interests. Hitler impressed his classmates with sketches of the Bohemian military commander Wallenstein and the castle of Schaumberg, and he devoured the adventure novels written by Karl May. He also developed an interest in military history, reading books his father owned on the Franco-Prussian War and following the events of the Boer War. Writing about his time in Leonding years later in *Mein Kampf*, Hitler claimed that he 'became more and more enthusiastic about everything that was in any way connected with war or, for that matter, with soldiering'.[9] He also attributes to this period his growing sense of German patriotism, and his first pangs of uneasiness 'that not every German was fortunate enough to belong in Bismarck's Reich'.[10] Politically aroused, 10-year-old Hitler revelled in playing soldiers with his classmates and after school they re-enacted battles of the Boer War. Johann Weinberger, one of Hitler's schoolmates, later recalled these 'wars' between the boys of Leonding and those of Untergaumberg, telling the Nazi officials who interviewed him that 'we Leondingers, with Hitler for our captain, were the Boers while the Untergaumbergers were the English.'[11] Hitler enjoyed taking command, issuing orders, and leading his comrades in their playful battles. He had become 'a little ringleader', confident and with identifiable oratorical talents.

Hitler started secondary school in Linz on 17 September 1900. His father sent him to a Realschule, where he received a more practical and technical education, not a Gymnasium that emphasised the humanities and prepared students for university. Alois may have made his choice of school on an assumption that it was the best one for a career in the civil service like his own, but he may also have been concerned that his son, of relatively humble origins, might be stigmatised as a country bumpkin in a large liberal arts school that enjoyed much greater social prestige than a Realschule. Whatever the reasons were for sending young Adolf to the Linzer Realschule, it brought his happy childhood days to an abrupt end. From the first day onwards Hitler struggled. He was no longer the leader of his class, the other students tended to look down on him, he lost interest in his schoolwork, and he viewed most of his teachers with contempt. The only thing Hitler seemed to like was the long walk between his home in Leonding and his new secondary school in the Steingasse. Basically, he was overwhelmed by his new urban surroundings, became introverted and moody, failed mathematics, science, and French, and had to repeat his first year. His detractors said he was lazy and obstinate. One of his teachers, Dr Eduard Huemer, recalled that Hitler was 'definitely talented' but 'not diligent'. Huemer was certain that Hitler, 'with his undoubted gifts' should have done much better.[12] Deeply unhappy, often unwell, and lacking in confidence, is it really a surprise that his school work suffered?

Twenty years later Hitler claimed that his four difficult years at the Linzer Realschule were the unfortunate manifestation of a contest of wills between himself and his father. He wanted to be an artist, a painter, and his father, asserted Hitler, had insisted that he become a successful civil servant. To sabotage his father's intentions, Hitler claimed that he applied himself only to the subjects that gave him pleasure and which served his requirements as a painter. He excelled at drawing, geography, and even more so at history. Hitler's history teacher, Professor Leopold Pötsch, a pan-German nationalist, nourished the 'budding nationalistic fanaticism' in his young students with tales of old Germanic heroes, of Bismarck, and with more contemporary aspects of German nationalism that were at odds with the multi-ethnic Austrian state. Hitler began his lifelong worship of Richard Wagner at this time, particularly after watching his overtly Germanic opera *Lohengrin*. Wagner's music and storytelling aroused the strongest feelings of German nationalism in young Adolf, feelings and a love for Wagner's art that increased in intensity throughout his life. Even at a young age Hitler took his Germanness more seriously than most, something that must have added to the escalating tensions between himself and his father, who was a loyal defender of the House of Habsburg.[13]

Hitler's conflict with his father came to a sudden end on 3 January 1903. Alois died unexpectedly of a pleural haemorrhage while enjoying a glass of wine in the Wiesinger Inn in Leonding. He was buried two days later in the cemetery in St Michael's Churchyard just across the road from his house. His pension provisions enabled Klara and the children to remain in their house in Leonding, where they continued to enjoy a comfortable existence. Hitler's school reports, however, did not improve. He failed French again, and had to sit a supplementary examination in August. To his mother's delight he passed, and advanced to the fourth form, but only on the condition that he transferred to a different school. The nearest Realschule was in Steyr, some thirty kilometres away. Eager to fulfil her husband's last wishes that Adolf successfully complete his schooling, Klara enrolled her son at the *Staatsoberrealschule* (senior secondary school) in Steyr, and found him accommodation in the residence of court official Conrad Edler von Cichini. Hitler started his new school in September 1904, and predictably he was unhappy from the start. He detested the town. Steyr was red and black (socialist and clerical) whereas Linz was national and pan-German. One of his former teachers in Steyr remembered him as a pale boy who 'acted somewhat shy and cowed, probably because it was the first time he had been away from home'.[14] Unsurprisingly, his school work was poor. His report card in February 1905 recorded wildly unbalanced results. He was failing in German, French, and mathematics, and even in his favourite subjects, geography and history, he was only 'adequate'. He had also been 'absent without reason' for thirty days. Despite his disinterest in school, and his initial lack of application, his grades improved, and his end of term report records that he passed all of his subjects. Hitler celebrated by getting drunk with his classmates, only to be embarrassed the next morning when he was woken up on the roadside by a milkmaid. To graduate Hitler still had to sit his final examinations for the *Matura* (Austrian secondary school diploma), but the mere thought of this literally made him ill.[15]

Hitler had already suffered from a lung infection during his family's summer holiday with relatives in Spital. Back in Steyr, during the cold and wet autumn, he experienced further respiratory problems. One of his classmates remembered that 'he was plagued by coughs and nasty catarrhs',[16] and his drawing teacher, Professor Gregor Goldbacher, noted how unwell he looked.[17] Klara was so concerned about her son's poor health that she took him out of school and brought him to Spital where he was treated by Dr Karl Keiβ. Hitler's cousin, Anton Schmidt, later said that Adolf 'ate well, drank plenty of milk, and made a quick recovery'.[18] Free from illness and no longer burdened by the frustrations of school, 16-year-old Hitler returned to the family home, now in Linz. Klara had sold the house in Leonding in June 1905 and rented a flat in Humboldtstraβe 31. Only four members of the Hitler family lived together in Linz: Klara, Adolf, Paula, and Hanni. Angela, Hitler's stepsister, had just married, and now lived with her husband, Leo Raubal, a civil servant. Linz suited Hitler. He no longer had to undertake the long walk from Leonding into the city to enjoy the many cultural activities on offer at the opera, the theatre, or the city's libraries and museums. He was free to drift, the master of his own fate, pursuing his own interests, and enjoying a life that is best described as one of 'comfortable idleness'.[19]

Young Hitler in Linz

L inz is the state capital of Upper Austria, and in 1900 it had a population of just over 60,000. It was also an important railway junction between Austria and Bavaria, connecting Vienna and Munich. Serving as the main railway link between these two great German cities, Linz boasted a rich cultural life for a provincial city. During Hitler's time in Linz, which was renowned for being the hometown of the composer Anton Bruckner, the city enjoyed a particularly good period for music and opera. The regional theatre, the *Landestheater*, staged an impressive repertoire of first-rate operas, especially those of Richard Wagner. Linz's art galleries and museums, libraries, theatres, music and opera offered a broad and diverse cultural programme that appealed to 15-year-old Hitler, now no longer attending school and free from his father's control. For two years, between 1905 and 1907, Hitler indulged all of his own interests and pleasures. Later he recalled this time as being 'the happiest days of my life and seemed to me almost a dream'.[1] He spent most days drawing, painting, reading, and exploring Linz. He enjoyed long walks on the cultural mile, where many of the magnificent cultural institutions of Linz are located, walking along the Danube and down to the main train station in the city centre. Young Hitler was always well dressed when out on these walks, and he was often seen either carrying heavy bags overflowing with books to and from the libraries or more dandified strolling down the *Landstraße* twirling a black ivory handled walking stick and admiring the architecture. In the evening, he attended the opera, never missing a Wagner performance.[2]

Hitler led quite a solitary life in Linz, usually taking his daily walks alone, but he was never lonely. His mind was constantly churning over ideas for grandiose and fantastic projects, and his dreams of the future. His one close friend was August Kubizek, whom Hitler called Gustl.[3] They met by chance one night in the autumn of 1904 at the *Landestheater*, and soon discovered they shared the same enthusiasm for opera. Kubizek was the son of a decorator and upholsterer, but he too had a dream that one day he would be a professional musician. Together Adolf and Gustl attended almost every opera performed at the *Landestheater*. The two friends spent time together during the day too, walking the cultural mile or the enchanting Turmleitenweg footpath, or sharing a park bench overlooking the Danube. Often Hitler would speak about his future hopes and plans, recite a poem he had written, show Gustl a drawing for a new bridge or theatre he had designed for Linz, or sometimes he would paint. Their conversation centred on art and music, and on one occasion Hitler proclaimed that he was going to be an artist. Kubizek was not convinced. Hitler clearly had talent with watercolours but painting could not, Gustl reflected, satisfy the ideas and emotions that seethed inside him. Painting was one of Hitler's hobbies rather than one of his more serious aspirations.[4] It was art, however, that was the essence of their friendship, and both 'considered art to be the greatest thing in a man's life'.[5] This bond was strengthened further by their shared passion for Richard Wagner, to whom, Kubizek insisted, 'we had the highest devotion.'[6]

Enthusiasm for Wagner was common amongst many adults in both Germany and German-speaking Austria at the time. Thomas Mann, one of Germany's most famous authors, and slightly older contemporary of Hitler, wrote in 1907 that Wagner's art had to be experienced 'to understand anything about our age'.[7] Hitler's first Wagner opera was *Lohengrin*, which he saw at the Linz *Landestheater* when he was just 12 years old. 'I was captivated at once,' Hitler wrote in the opening pages of *Mein Kampf*. 'My youthful enthusiasm for the master of Bayreuth knew no bounds. Again and again I was drawn to his works.'[8] Wagner's art aroused intense Germanic feelings in Hitler, and fortified his conviction that Wagner's ideas and personal life struggles were a model both for his own and a united Germany's destiny. Kubizek recalled that Hitler behaved as if Wagner's ghost possessed him, and acted as if he were Wagner's mortal heir.[9] It was on a cold and wet January night in 1905 that Hitler revealed to his friend the special Wagner-inspired mission that would guide his future. They had just been to the Linz Theatre to see a performance of *Rienzi*, the story of a populist hero's rise to be Tribune of Rome and his subsequent downfall. When the opera was over, and without stopping for their usual after-performance critique, the two teenagers walked in silence up to the Freinberg heights overlooking Linz. It was here that Hitler told Gustl that his '*Rienzi* experience' was in fact a prophecy of 'a mandate which, one day, he would receive from the people, to lead them out of servitude to the heights of freedom'.[10] Kubizek was left dumbfounded by what he had just heard. Together, and in silence, the two friends walked back down into the city to Gustl's home where they solemnly shook hands. Hitler then returned to the mountain alone to ponder what his experience might portend. Kubizek said nothing more about it until August 1939, when he recounted the story to Winifred Wagner at a reception at *Haus Wahnfried* at the conclusion of the Bayreuth Festival. Hitler remembered. He too had shared the importance of this moment with his inner circle during his political ascent. He told Rudolf Heβ about his '*Rienzi* experience'. When they were incarcerated together in Landsberg Prison, after the failed Munich Putsch in November 1923, Heβ always called Hitler 'the Tribune'. Heβ even referred to him as the Tribune in his correspondence from prison to his future wife,

Ilse Pröhl. Albert Speer also recalled a conversation between Hitler and Robert Ley, Reich Minister of Labour, during the Nürnberg Rally in the summer of 1938, in which Hitler explained why he had chosen the overture to *Rienzi* as the introductory music for the Nazi Party rallies.[11]

Hitler read everything he could get hold of on Wagner: his autobiography, his diaries, essays, and letters, and all that had been written about his hero, including a substantial and critically acclaimed biography by Houston Stewart Chamberlain, a *völkisch* ethnic-nationalist pan-German editor and writer who married Wagner's youngest daughter Eva in 1908. Hitler could not have known at the time just how important Chamberlain and his interpretation of German nationalism would be to his early political career and his success in Munich. His greatest longing as a 17-year-old 'Wagnerian' teenager was to visit Bayreuth, and to see *Wahnfried*, the house where this incomparable German genius had lived.[12] Hitler's dream would be fulfilled beyond his wildest imagination once he was a politician, but in May 1906 he had to settle for a short trip to Vienna and performances of Wagner's *Tristan und Isolde* and *Der fliegende Holländer* (*The Flying Dutchman*) at the *Wiener Hofoper* (Vienna Court Opera) conducted by Gustav Mahler with sets designed by Alfred Roller. Hitler wrote four postcards to Gustl while he was in Vienna, marvelling about the contemporary interpretation of Wagner's *Gesamtkunstwerk* (total work of art), but also telling his friend about the galleries and museums, the Austrian parliament and town hall, and the exquisite architecture on the Ringstrasse.[13] When Hitler returned to Linz he immediately began planning his return to Vienna to become an artist.

Except for the customary summer holiday in Spital with Klara's relatives, Hitler stayed in Linz painting and reading. He was an avid reader, and remained so throughout his life. He read serious subjects such as German history, art and architecture, and military affairs, as well as popular books, newspapers, and pan-German pamphlets. The newspapers that appealed to him were generally conservative and ethnic-nationalist in terms of their editorial policy, and in Linz he read the Christian-Socialist *Linzer Post*, the *Linzer Fliegenden* (subtitled the '*Völkisches Witzblattl*' – folkish joke journal), and the *Alldeutsches Tagblatt*.[14] In October, Klara bought him a grand piano and he started taking piano lessons with Gustl's teacher. Hitler applied himself to his self-directed course of study, but his Bohemian existence of sleeping late and staying at home to draw, play the piano, and read, did not impress his wider family. Leo Raubal, Angela's husband and Klara's son-in-law, and Josef Mayrhof, the Hitler children's guardian, both insisted that Adolf should either complete his secondary school education or select a respectable occupation. Hitler urged his mother to ignore these arguments and allow him to return to Vienna and study at the Academy of Fine Arts. Klara was torn over what to do, but the dispute came to a temporary end in early January 1907 when Klara was diagnosed with breast cancer. A few days later, on 18 January, she had a mastectomy at the Barmherzige Schwestern hospital in Linz. Klara remained in hospital until 5 February, but once back home, and still recovering from the operation, she could not manage the three flights of stairs to her third-floor flat in Humboldtstraße. In May the Hitler family moved to a bright first floor flat in a smart new building on Blütenstraße 9 in Urfahr, a suburb of Linz on the north side of the Danube.[15]

Klara found her new three-bedroom flat very comfortable, but it did little to improve Adolf's overall disposition. His new neighbours, a postmaster and his wife, urged him to stop being a dilettante and get a proper job. They even suggested that he join the postal service. Hitler hated the idea. He would not contemplate a 'bread-and-butter' job, and he loathed the very idea of entering the civil service at any level. He was still committed to returning to Vienna to become an artist. In the summer, when his mother's health seemed to have improved, he implored her once more to let him go to Vienna to take the entrance examinations for the Academy of Fine Arts. Reluctantly, Klara agreed, and on 9 September 1907, Hitler left a tearful mother and younger sister behind to catch his train to Vienna.[16]

Hitler arrived at the Westbahnhof and found accommodation nearby, renting a room from Frau Maria Zakrejs, a Polish woman who owned a large flat on Stumpergasse 31. He spent the rest of September painting and reading, preparing for his examinations at the beginning of October. The entrance examinations were held over two days, 1 and 2 October, and 113 candidates sat the formidable three-hour compulsory composition session on day one. The themes for these compositions reflected the traditional ideas of the Academy and demanded a high degree of technical skill from the aspirants. Only eighty candidates including Hitler were invited back on day two for the second round of compositions and to show the admissions committee a selection of their works. Hitler was confident that he would be accepted, but he was not one of the twenty-eight candidates granted admission. Siegmund l'Allemand, the Rector of the Academy, told a dejected Hitler that his ability lay clearly in the field of architecture not painting. Hitler was stunned. His disappointment was made worse by his knowledge that without a secondary school diploma he lacked the basic prerequisite for admission to the Architectural School. The shock of not being admitted into the Academy plunged Hitler into a deep depression. He spent the next few weeks reading, aimlessly wandering the streets of Vienna, and attending the opera, until he received a letter from his neighbour in Urfahr, the postmaster's wife, telling him that his mother was gravely ill. On 22 October Hitler rushed back to Linz.[17]

Hitler immediately threw himself into caring for his mother and running the household. With help from Hanni, his aunt Johanna, he cooked, and cleaned, and helped his sister Paula with her homework. His friend Gustl recalled that during the weeks before Klara died Adolf had become a different person. 'Gone were the problems and ideas which used to agitate him so much,' noted Gustl, 'gone all thought of politics. Even his artistic interests were hardly noticeable.'[18] Klara was in constant pain, both from the cancer that had spread through her body, and the agonising iodoform treatments that were applied around her open wound almost daily. Despite all her suffering, Kubizek noticed how pleased and serene Klara was at having her son back at home and by her side. In the early hours on 21 December Klara died. Later that morning, Eduard Bloch, Klara's Jewish family doctor, came round to the Hitlers' flat on Blütenstraße to sign the death certificate. He tried to comfort Adolf, telling him that 'death had been a saviour' but Hitler was inconsolable. Recollecting that morning some thirty years later Bloch wrote: 'In almost forty years of practice, I have never seen a young man so utterly filled with pain and grief as the young Adolf Hitler.'[19]

Klara's funeral was held on 23 December in a local church in Urfahr, and then her body was taken to Leonding where she was buried beside her husband in the Catholic cemetery in St Michael's Churchyard. On Christmas Eve, Hitler and his two sisters, Angela and Paula, went to see Dr Bloch to pay the outstanding amount of their mother's medical bill. When the formal business was concluded, Hitler grasped the doctor's hand and solemnly declared: 'I shall be grateful to you forever.' Bloch was certain that Hitler kept his promise, extending favours to him and his family that enabled them safe passage from Nazi-occupied Austria to the United States in 1940.[20]

On New Year's Day 1908, Hitler visited his parents' grave. The year could hardly have started off any worse for 18-year-old Hitler. Both of his parents were dead, and his future prospects were somewhere between exceedingly bleak and at best uncertain. There was nothing left for him in Linz. He was, however, still set on becoming an artist. Standing alone in the damp and foggy churchyard, deep in contemplation, he resolved to move to Vienna. For the next several weeks he set about organizing his and his sister's financial affairs. He could not access their inheritance from their father, but Adolf and Paula could make use of an inheritance of 2,000 Kronen from their mother. Adolf's share was more than enough to pay his tuition and to live on for more than a year without having to work. Hitler packed up all of his things, said his goodbyes, and convinced the Kubizeks that they should let Gustl accompany him to Vienna so that their son could study music at the Conservatoire. Gustl helped his friend carry his heavy cases to the train station on 17 February. On arriving in Vienna, Hitler once again rented a room from Frau Zakrejs on Stumpergasse 31 in the Viennese district of Mariahilf. The very next day, Hitler dashed off a quick postcard to Gustl – 'Am already dying to get news of your arrival. Write soon ... All of Vienna is already waiting. So come soon. Will of course pick you up.'[21]

Vienna

Kubizek followed Hitler to Vienna five days later, arriving late in the afternoon on Saturday 22 February. Hitler, as promised, met his friend at the Westbahnhof and helped him carry his bags and cases to their room at Stumpergasse 31. After a rather sumptuous feast of cold roast pork, freshly baked bread rolls, cheese, and a flask of coffee – all provided by Frau Kubizek – Hitler took Gustl on an impromptu evening tour of central Vienna. Their first stop was the Court Opera. They went inside. The doors were open because the evening's performance had not yet ended. Kubizek was overwhelmed by the splendour of the entrance hall, the magnificent staircases, the marble balustrades, the thick carpets, and the gilded decorations on the ceiling, declaring 'I felt as though I had been transported to another planet.'[1] Next Gustl wanted to see the Stephansdom (St Stephen's Cathedral), but it was so misty they could barely see the spire. Finally they walked to Maria am Gestade, one of the oldest churches in Vienna and an impressive example of Gothic architecture, before returning to their room at Stumpergasse.

Over the next few days Hitler helped Gustl get settled, even convincing Frau Zakrejs to exchange her larger room for the smaller one Hitler had rented in order to accommodate Gustl's grand piano. Kubizek registered at the Academy of Music, passed the entrance examinations, and began his course of study. Over the next few months Hitler and Kubizek explored Vienna and repeated on a grander scale their cultural activities in Linz. Most nights they went to the opera, seeing Wagner's *Die Meistersinger* and *Lohengrin*, each one ten times or more. Hitler preferred a Wagner opera, even a poor one, to any other opera, but Kubizek did get Hitler to join him at symphony concerts. Hitler developed a fondness for the Romantics – Brahms, Bruckner, Liszt, Mendelssohn, Schubert, Schumann, and Weber. He also liked Beethoven and Mozart.[2] On fine afternoons, Hitler and Kubizek would wander through the grounds of the Schönbrunn Palace, or walk on the Ringstrasse and admire the splendid Imperial architecture. Vienna, however, was a city of stark contrasts. The façade of glitz and glamour in *fin-de-siècle* Vienna was exposed by widespread misery and poverty, shabby and overcrowded tenement buildings where many immigrants and the working class Viennese lived, ethnic hatred, and a sense of impending doom more than anywhere else in Europe. 'Everyone is waiting for the end,' wrote the Viennese satirist Karl Kraus, 'Let's hope the apocalypse is pleasant, Your Highness.'[3]

The capital of the Habsburg monarchy was a leading European centre for fashion, culture, commerce, and industry, but it was also a city of rising revolutionary tensions brought on by a toxic mixture of festering social injustices and racial prejudice. While Vienna was German in tradition, by the end of the nineteenth century it was an unhappy multicultural city of incongruous peoples – Czechs, Poles, Hungarians, Ruthenians, Serbs and Croats, and Jews. Vienna had the highest rate of immigration in Europe, and between 1880 and 1910 the population of the city doubled. One in five residents was a Czech, and just under ten per cent of the population were Jewish, many of them coming from the poorer eastern parts of the empire. The longer Hitler lived in Vienna, the more his revulsion grew for the foreign mixture of peoples whom he believed were corroding the German culture of the old state. Every time Hitler and Kubizek walked together in the Prater pleasure gardens they were confronted by the 'Viennese Babel' that not only distressed Hitler but tormented many other pan-German-thinking Austrians.[4]

Hitler was both familiar with and sympathetic towards the basic ethnic nationalist ideas of pan-Germanism from his Realschule days in Linz. He believed implicitly in the superiority of German culture, and like most other pan-Germans thought that everything that was wrong in Austria was the fault of foreigners and Jews. His beliefs were further entrenched through his reading of pan-Germanic newspapers and pamphlets, and the incendiary political climate in Vienna. Most days Hitler would go to a café where he could read the newspapers. He read the *Alldeutsches Tagblatt* (Pan-German Daily), which was produced not far from where he lived on Stumpergasse. He was also acquainted with *Ostara*, a racist journal founded by Jörg Lanz von Liebenfels, an eccentric former Cistercian monk whose real name was Adolf Lanz and who promoted the idea of an Aryan master race destined to dominate the world. Hitler read the anti-Semitic papers, but he was an avid reader with eclectic tastes. As a member of the Hof library he regularly borrowed books on German history and mythology, art and architecture, as well as literary classics and philosophy, including works by Goethe, Schiller, Schopenhauer and Nietzsche, to deepen his knowledge of the political and philosophical problems of the day.[5] He further supplemented his reading by regularly attending debates in the Reichsrat (Vienna parliament). The parliamentary sessions were conducted in all of the languages of the empire, the debates were long and often ill-tempered, and rarely did they resolve any of the issues that were being discussed. The dithering and unseemly conduct of politics that Hitler witnessed increased his fears of the de-Germanisation of the state, and filled him with contempt for the 'democratic parliamentary process'.[6]

Two politicians in Vienna that Hitler came to admire were Georg von Schönerer and Dr Karl Lueger. Schönerer was an extreme German nationalist who advocated German Austria's *Anschluss* (annexation) to the German Reich.

He was the founder of the pan-German movement in Austria, and the *Deutscher Schulverein* (German School Association) whose main aim was the 'preservation and spreading of Germandom'.[7] Lueger was the mayor of Vienna and the founder of the Christian Social Party. Initially Hitler was opposed to the Christian Social Party because of his own anti-clerical views, but he admired Lueger, 'the people's Tribune', for his oratorical skills, and his widespread popular support as Vienna's foremost 'German man'. Hitler also agreed wholeheartedly with Lueger's firm Germanophile policies. Hitler particularly liked the simplicity of Lueger's often repeated slogan 'Vienna is German and must remain German.'[8]

Hitler asserts in *Mein Kampf* that his *Weltanschauung* (political philosophy and world view) was forged in the hardest school, the five unhappy years of hardship and misery he suffered through in Vienna. It was in Vienna, he proclaims, that he fully realised the historical importance of the German people and the twin mortal threats of Marxism and Jewry to their existence.[9] Historians Brigitte Hamann and Timothy Ryback have shown that Hitler's account is an exaggeration of his political awakening in Vienna, a stylised version of his past that served his political agenda in Munich in the mid-1920s. Both historians agree that when Hitler lived in Vienna he fully embraced the pan-German aspiration of a united Germany free of foreign influences, but he was neither anti-Marxist nor anti-Semitic.[10] He did not join any political associations, clubs, or parties. He also did not share his political opinions and prejudices with those around him. 'Adolf was always very reserved,' Kubizek recalled, 'but within him everything was in a ferment and urged him on to radical and total solutions.'[11]

Kubizek noticed how irritable his friend had become, but he did not know why. Could it be politics, or was it the obvious social injustices of 'poverty, need, and hunger on one side', and the 'reckless enjoyment of life, sensuality and prodigal luxury on the other' which aroused in Hitler 'a demonical hatred of all that we saw around us'. He seemed to be angry with everyone and everything, as if the world was conspiring against him. Hitler was depressed. He lurched between phases of frenetic activity and periods of lethargy that declined into total idleness. Kubizek thought that Hitler had a lot of leisure time for a student, and on rainy days when they were both studying in their room on Stumpergasse they tended to get on one another's nerves. On one such day, when Gustl was practising the piano and Hitler was reading, they were arguing over Gustl's timetable at the Conservatoire when Hitler blurted out that he was not studying at the Academy. He had been rejected. He was not a student after all. The mystery behind Hitler's volatile mood had been solved. Less clear was what Hitler was going to do. For the time being he immersed himself in reading.[12]

Just before Easter, in early April 1908, Gustl received notice that he had to register for military service. He showed his call-up papers to Hitler, who could see how upset his friend was with the distressing news. Hitler urged Gustl to throw the letter away, further telling him that under no account should he serve in the Austro-Hungarian Army. He was a musician, not a soldier, and the moribund empire had no right to waste his artistic talent and turn him into worthless cannon fodder. Hitler then offered up a bold plan. He advised Gustl to report to the army medical board in Linz when summoned. If the board passed him fit, Hitler counselled, he should secretly slip across the border at Passau into exile in Germany where he could continue his musical studies. Gustl was stunned, both by the call-up notice and Hitler's plan to avoid military service. The next morning Gustl spoke with the Director of the Conservatoire about his predicament. The Director proposed a less radical plan. He advised Kubizek to join the reserves. Gustl would only have to do eight weeks initial training and later on three more training sessions of four weeks each. He would remain a student at the Conservatoire and not bring shame upon himself and his family by running away to Germany.[13]

Hitler thought little of the Director's plan, but over the Easter holidays Gustl discussed it with his parents back in Linz. They thought it was an excellent idea, and Gustl's father helped him draft a successful application to join the reserves. Gustl returned to Vienna relieved that his studies at the Conservatoire would continue with minimal interruptions. Energised and happy Gustl completed the spring term strongly. He passed his examinations with excellent grades, and he was selected to conduct the academy's end of term concert, a gala event that included a number of his own compositions and songs. Afterwards he was congratulated by both the head of the Conductors' School and the Director of the Conservatoire. Hitler was Gustl's guest at the concert, and in the artist's room after the performance he beamed with pride at his friend's accomplishments.[14]

Kubizek returned to Linz to spend the long summer vacation at his parents' before doing his eight weeks compulsory military training with the reserves in the autumn. Both he and Hitler agreed to keep their room at Frau Zakrejs'. Hitler did not have any confirmed plans for the summer other than staying in Vienna, and when he said goodbye to Gustl at the Westbahnhof in early July neither of them knew it would be more than thirty years before they would see each other again. They exchanged a few postcards and letters, and in mid-August Hitler told Gustl that he was going to see *Lohengrin* before making a trip to Waldviertel to visit his relatives. Part of the reason why Hitler left Vienna for Spital at the end of August was to look for a new source of income as his maternal inheritance was running out. He succeeded in getting a loan of 924 Kronen from his Aunt Hanni, but his half-sister Angela demanded that he get a real job, earn a living, and give up his share of the orphan's allowance for his 12-year-old sister Paula.[15] Hitler's refusal to abandon his dream of being an artist, and his way of life in Vienna, cut him off from his family. By the time he returned to Vienna, even Paula was annoyed with her older brother. Years later she recalled that 'while we were fond of each other, we often spoilt each other's pleasure of living together'.[16] There was little common interest or understanding between Hitler and his family. He never visited Spital again.

Hitler returned to Vienna in September and began his preparations for the entrance examinations at the Academy of Fine Arts. He drew and read and organized his portfolio of drawings and paintings, comforted by the knowledge that his finances were secured for another year. It was all to no avail. Hitler's application to sit the examinations was rejected. The drawings he had submitted were mainly of buildings, and the Rector allegedly asked him 'what architectural school had you attended' during an interview in which Hitler was told that his particular talents were not what they were looking for in prospective students at the Academy. This was a crushing blow, and it left Hitler in a considerable quandary. What was he going to do? How was he going to keep his orphan's allowance and avoid conscription into the army if he was no longer a student? Until he had the answers to these questions he was content to fall back on the activities that gave him pleasure: studying Vienna's architecture, reading, and going to the Opera.[17]

Richard Wagner's operas were performed at the Hof Opera on no fewer than 426 evenings during Hitler's time in Vienna. Hitler claims to have seen *Tristan and Isolde* some 'thirty or forty times, and always from the best companies'.[18] He paid two Kronen for a standing place on the promenade at the Hof Opera. How much he spent on his almost daily visits to the opera at less expensive theatres or a symphony concert is unknown, but it was a substantial amount of his fixed income, and quite a luxury for an unemployed young man living an otherwise frugal life in Vienna.

Opera was also an escape from the uncertainty of his current circumstances. Wagner's art, unlike any other opera, transported Hitler into a mystical dream world. Hitler identified with Wagner's heroes and could correlate his own misery with that of Tristan's, a tragic hero who longed for release from the passions that tormented him. Wagner drew his inspiration for *Tristan and Isolde* from his own ill-fated love affair with Mathilde Wesendonck and Arthur Schopenhauer's pessimistic philosophy. Schopenhauer's world-view held that man was driven by continued, unachievable desires, where the gulf between these desires and the possibility of achieving them leads to misery. Hitler was very miserable in the autumn of 1908.

Kubizek was due back in Vienna on 20 November. Two days before, Hitler moved out of Stumpergasse and into a small and cheaper room at Felberstraße 22, located near the Westbahnhof, slightly further out from the city centre. It was not far from his previous room at Frau Zakrejs', who was sad to see him leave. Hitler paid his share of the rent, said goodbye, but did not leave either a forwarding address or a note for Gustl. Hitler had already cut himself off from his family in the Waldviertel, and now from Kubizek and his previous life in Linz. He never explained the reason for abandoning his close friend, but the embarrassment of not being accepted by the Academy is likely to have been a large contributing factor. Hitler did not, however, disappear. He registered his new address with the police, as was required in both Austrian and German law, declaring himself a 'student'. Though unable to study at a specialised school for art or architecture, Hitler was resolved 'to continue his efforts as a self-taught man, and to go and settle in Germany'.[19] His new landlady, Helene Riedl, later attested to his studiousness, and his neighbours remembered him as being polite but distant. Hitler lived a quiet and solitary existence at Felberstraße, but Marie Rinke, a waitress at a nearby café, the Café Kubata, took a shine to him. She recalled Hitler as being 'very reserved and quiet, and would read books, and seemed very serious, unlike the rest of the young men'.[20] With his loan from Hannitante almost exhausted, on 22 August 1909 Hitler moved again to an even smaller and cheaper bedsit at Sechshauser Straße 58. He left it three and a half weeks later, this time not registering with the police, disappearing into Vienna's swelling underclass of the homeless and the forsaken poor.[21]

Hitler emerged from the shadows in November 1909, turning up at a large modern shelter for the homeless (*Asyl für Obdachlose*) in the district of Meidling, south of the Westbahnhof. When he arrived he was in a dreadful state. He no longer owned a heavy winter coat, he was hungry, tired, 'blue and frostbitten', wearing only a threadbare blue-check suit. Hitler was offered lodgings, consisting of a bed in one of the large dormitories, and soup and bread every night. The Meidling shelter provided temporary accommodation for approximately 1,000 of Vienna's indigent vagrants. On his first night in the shelter Hitler met Reinhold Hanisch (living under the alias Walter Fritz), a convicted petty criminal who originally came from the Sudetenland. Hanisch occupied the neighbouring cot. The two men talked about art and Germany, and quickly became friends. Hanisch had been through Braunau am Inn and easily followed Hitler's stories. He taught Hitler the words to the German patriotic anthem *Die Wacht am Rhein* (Watch on the Rhine) and was struck by how enthusiastic his new friend was about everything German. Each morning all of the residents had to leave the shelter, and they were not allowed to return until the evening. Hanisch and Hitler spent the day trying to earn a bit of money, shovelling snow, carrying passengers' bags at the train station, and even begging. Occasionally they made the long walk to St Katherine's convent, near Hitler's old room on Stumpergasse, for soup and warmth from the cold. Hitler often spoke about his ambitions to be an artist, and this gave Hanisch an idea that would enable them both to escape their unhappy predicament. Hanisch suggested that Hitler paint postcards, which he would sell in restaurants and taverns, with the two men splitting the profits. There was only one problem, Hitler had sold his paints and paint brushes. The resourceful Hanisch was not put off. He urged Hitler to ask his relatives for some money. Hanisch took Hitler to the Café Arthaber, opposite the Meidling station, where Hitler wrote a card to his aunt Hanni asking for money to buy art supplies. A few days later, a surprised Hitler received 50 Kronen from Hannitante.[22]

Hanisch urged Hitler to start painting immediately, but Hitler wanted a week's rest to find inspiration. He also pointed out that there was nowhere to paint at the Asyl. Hanisch soon lost patience with his recalcitrant partner, left the shelter, and took a job as a servant. Hitler, flush with the money from his aunt, bought himself a new winter coat, and on 8 February 1910 moved to more comfortable lodgings at the Männerheim on Meldemannstraße 27 in Brigittenau, an outer district in north Vienna. The Männerheim men's home was modern and offered its 500 residents more comfortable accommodation than the homeless shelter. Hitler had his own tiny room, and access to a number of common rooms, a library, and a small writing room where he sat by the window during the day drawing and painting. Hanisch joined him at the Männerheim a week later, and soon their partnership was thriving. Hitler painted two or three postcards a day, and Hanisch had no difficulty selling them in taverns and the train stations. Soon they both realised that there was even more money to be made with larger works, so Hitler began painting watercolours of city scenes and famous Viennese landmarks such as the Stephansdom and the town hall. He could paint one larger work in a day, but the work was monotonous, and sometimes he preferred reading the newspapers, or joining a political discussion in the reading room. Hanisch implored him to paint and not waste his time on idle chatter. He was selling the paintings much faster than Hitler could paint them, and by the summer the joint venture was increasingly strained because of Hitler's inability to keep up with the orders. Tensions increased when Hitler disappeared for the better part of a week with a Jewish friend and fellow resident at the Männerheim, Josef Neumann, who also sold Hitler's postcards in direct competition with Hanisch. Hitler and Neumann had talked about emigrating together and going to Germany, but instead they spent five days between 21 and 26 June visiting Vienna's museums and luxuriating in unaccustomed amenities at a proper hotel. Hitler's partnership with Hanisch broke down completely when Siegfried Löffner, another one of Hitler's Jewish friends and business associates, accused Hanisch of 'misappropriating' a large picture of the Parliament that Hitler had painted. Hanisch was arrested, sentenced to a week in jail for using a false name, and did not return to the Männerheim when he was released. Hitler now sold his paintings himself, primarily to two Jewish art dealers, Jakob Altenberg and Samuel Morgenstern, saving the commission he had paid to Hanisch and others, and earning a much greater return for his art by selling through reputable galleries.[23]

During the remainder of 1910, and the next two years, Hitler settled into a stable routine. He was admired and respected by his fellow residents at the Männerheim. He was their *Künstler* (artist). The quality of his painting also improved and he sold almost everything he completed. He continued to read widely, and during the evenings attended the opera or went to a symphony concert. Women were not allowed in the Männerheim, but Hitler did not appear to mind their absence, nor did he crave a close friendship with anyone. Nonetheless, those who knew him in Vienna, according to Karl Honisch, another resident at the Männerheim, regarded him as a 'friendly and likeable fellow' who 'showed an interest in others' while taking care 'not to get too close to anyone'. Hitler rarely revealed much about himself, though he did talk a lot about art, and his desire to move to Munich, a city he was becoming very familiar with through his reading. In this respect he was rather unique among the residents at the Männerheim, as Honisch recalled: 'we all lived pretty thoughtlessly through the days… Hitler was the only one among us who had a clear vision of his future.'[24]

In early February 1913, Hitler met Rudolf Häusler, a new resident at the Männerheim. Häusler was four years younger than Hitler and had recently been banished from the family home by his strict, civil servant father after being expelled from school. Häusler also liked to paint, and the two started to talk to each other while painting in the writing room. They soon became inseparable and called each other 'Adi' and 'Rudi'. Häusler's circumstances – a domineering father and a loving mother who surreptitiously provided him clothing, food, and money – reminded Hitler a little of his own. Hitler took Rudi under his wing, introduced him to Wagner's operas, and persuaded him to come along to Munich, a German city, full of opportunities for young artists, and where dreams come true. Their fantasy came closer to becoming a real plan in April when Hitler turned 24 and was eligible to claim his paternal inheritance. He applied to the Austrian District Court in Linz and on 16 May the court decreed that 819 Kronen and 98 heller be paid to the 'artist' Adolf Hitler in Vienna, at Meldemannstraße 27.[25] This was a considerable amount of money. It enabled Hitler to purchase a completely new wardrobe, and clean himself up so that he was a smart looking, well-presented young man. On 24 May, he went with Rudi to say goodbye to his mother. Ida Häusler liked and trusted Hitler. She gave them her blessing and wished them well on their new adventure. Hitler and Häusler notified their local police precinct that they were moving out of the Männerheim and listed their new place of residence as 'unknown'. The next morning Adi and Rudi set off for the Westbahnhof to catch their train. They were accompanied by Honisch and others from the men's home. Honisch recalled that they were sorry to see Hitler leave: 'we lost a good comrade with him.' Later, Hitler was philosophical about his departure from Vienna, writing in *Mein Kampf*, 'I had set foot in this town while still half a boy and I left it a man, grown quiet and grave.'[26] The train passed through Linz, arriving later in the afternoon at the Munich Hauptbahnhof (main train station). It was Sunday, 25 May 1913, the sun shone brightly, and the air drifting down from the Bavarian Alps was clean and fresh. Hitler had arrived in this most German of German cities.

Munich

The name of the city comes from the old German term *Munichen*, which means 'by the monks' or *München* (near the monks' place) and comes from the Benedictine order who ran a monastery in what later became the Altstadt (old town) of Munich. The monk in the centre of the city's coat of arms celebrates this early monastic origin. Until the nineteenth century Munich was little more than a small backwater situated north of the Bavarian Alps and straddling the River Isar. This unflattering image changed when Bavaria became a sovereign kingdom in 1806, and its Wittelsbach kings transformed their royal capital into a major European centre of *Kunst und Kultur* (art and culture). Ludwig I, who reigned from 1825 to 1848, aimed to build a capital fit for a king, declaring that he 'will make Munich a city that everybody who wants to know Germany must know'.[1] Ludwig's artistic tastes were classical, and he was an admirer of ancient Greece and the Italian renaissance. His legacy is a neoclassical cityscape of buildings, statues, galleries and art collections, royal boulevards and beautiful parks that by 1850 led to Munich being known as 'Athens on the Isar'.

Ludwig's son Maximilian II, who reigned from 1848 to 1864, continued to develop Munich as a cultural and educational city. Unlike his father, he preferred the romantic architecture associated with Gothic Revival, a style that combined new modern building technology with historical representation. The elegant Maximilianstraße soon rivalled the classical Ludwigstraße as Munich's most beautiful and impressive street. Maximilian II, however, was more like his father when it came to celebrating and promoting the unique character and identity of their people. He financed the study of local art, customs, dress, and language to accentuate a separate Bavarian identity in opposition to Prussian nationalism. His son, Ludwig II (1864–1886), continued this policy of Bavarian independence as well as an extravagant building programme and generous patronage of the arts. Ludwig II, the Swan King, was the devoted patron of Richard Wagner. By the end of his reign, Ludwig II had spent his personal fortune financing Wagner and building lavish castles and palaces. Two of his fairy-tale castles, *Schloss Neuschwanstein* and *Schloss Linderhof*, to the west of Munich, celebrate the romantic Teutonic legends set to music in Wagner's operas *Lohengrin*, *Tannhäuser*, *Tristan und Isolde*, and *Parsifal*. This was the high culture and *weiß und blau* (white and blue) Bavaria of the Wittelsbachs that the

Englishman Reginald Maxse wrote about in *Bavaria in a nutshell*, a guide for British and American tourists in 1910. He described Munich, 'the capital of Bavaria with about 600,000 inhabitants' as a carefree and cheerful city, and 'one of the finest and most beautiful' in Europe.[2] It was the Munich that Hitler knew from his reading – a city of exquisite architecture in a German kingdom that both promoted and revered art and culture.

Hitler's Early Years in Munich

The first thing that Hitler and Häusler did when they arrived in Munich on Sunday 25 May 1913 was find a place to live. They left the Hauptbahnhof (Munich's main train station) and walked north for about fifteen minutes, arriving at the Königsplatz, Ludwig I's impressive square attentively designed in homage to antiquity. Hitler marvelled at the great arch, the Propyläen on the western edge of the square, and the two classical temples to art, the Glyptothek and the Staatsgalerie on the north and south faces of the square respectively. This square would become the 'Acropolis Germaniae' during the Third Reich, and the central parade ground in Munich for the National Socialist Party's quasi-sacrosanct ceremonies, but on this spring afternoon in 1913 Hitler merely absorbed the majestic vista of the Königsplatz with admiration.[1] Hitler and Häusler continued their walk north to Schleißheimer Straße, 'an unpretentious thoroughfare' straddling the districts of Maxvorstadt and Schwabing, and where there was an abundance of 'lodging-houses with smallish shops on the ground floor'. At Schleißheimer Straße 34, the Popp Tailor Shop, Hitler noticed a handwritten advert stuck on the window: '*An soliden Herrn möbliertes Zimmer zu vermieten*' (furnished rooms to let to respectable man). Hitler knocked on the door. Anna Popp answered. Frau Popp directed Hitler and Häusler up a narrow flight of stairs to a room on the third floor. The room was small, five by two and a half metres, and minimally furnished. It contained a bed, table, sofa, and chair, and two oleographs hanging on the wall. There was also a large window facing west, from which can be seen the imposing tower of the Löwenbräukeller, close by on Stiglmaierplatz. 'The young man and I soon came to terms,' recalled Frau Popp. 'He said it would do him alright, and paid a deposit.' With great satisfaction, Frau Popp told her husband Joseph about the presentable young man who was their new lodger, pointing at the completed registration form: 'Adolf Hitler, *Architekturmaler aus Wien*' (architectural painter from Vienna).[2]

Hitler and Häusler may have gone out to eat at the Löwenbräukeller that first night. It was then, as it is now, one of Munich's great beer halls, serving generous portions of Bavarian favourites such as *Schweinsbraten und Knödel* (roast pork and Bavarian dumpling) and *Hausgemachte Wurst mit Sauerkraut* (homemade sausages with warm pickled cabbage), and refreshing beers in a Maß (one litre earthenware mug). Hitler had not renounced either alcohol or meat at this point in his life, and he enjoyed an occasional Münchner Löwenbräu (a new light-coloured beer) or the more traditional, dark and fortified, Triumphator. The Löwenbräukeller would become another important venue in Hitler's political career and the history of National Socialism in Munich, but before then it was a welcoming venue for traditional Bavarian *gemütlichkeit* (leisurely comfort) in a vast complex of dining rooms and festival halls capable of catering for over 4,000 guests on the south-western corner of Schwabing, the artists' quarter.[3]

Hitler arrived in Munich full of enthusiasm. One of his reasons for moving to Munich undoubtedly was aesthetic, as he later explained in *Mein Kampf*, asserting that it was 'my study which at every step had led me to this metropolis of German art'. He proclaimed that 'the city itself was as familiar to me as if I had lived for years within its walls', following up this personal affiliation with Munich with his own version of Ludwig I's claim that to know Germany one had to know Munich. One has 'not seen Germany if one does not know Munich,' Hitler declared, and 'above all, one does not know German art if one has not seen Munich.' Hitler was genuinely impressed by Munich's imposing architecture and its grand boulevards, amplifying his feelings about the visual splendour of the city by divulging that he was attracted to the city by its 'wonderful marriage of primeval strength and fine artistic sentiment', and noting the 'single line from the Hofbräuhaus to the Odeon, from the Oktoberfest to the Pinakothek'. He also claimed that he 'had left Austria for political reasons' namely that he 'did not want to fight for the Habsburg state'.[4] The latter point is consistent with the advice to avoid Austrian military service Hitler gave Kubizek in April 1908 when they shared a room in Vienna. Hitler should have registered for military service in late 1909, and been medically assessed for duty in the spring of 1910 just after his twenty-first birthday. The police in Linz had been looking for him. His file read: 'Illegally absent because whereabouts unknown.'[5] Avoiding compulsory military service carried a heavy penalty: up to a year in prison and a 2,000 Kronen fine.[6]

Hitler was blissfully unaware of the trouble he might be in back in Austria. Safely ensconced in Munich, he embraced the freedom and independence that characterised his new surroundings in Schwabing. His time was his own, and he did not have to conform to the rules of the men's hostel as he did when he lived in Vienna. He could come and go, paint, read, or be as idle as he pleased.[7] Munich was one of Europe's most vibrant cultural centres in the years leading up to the First World War. Schwabing, where Hitler chose to live, was the centre of artistic and bohemian life, attracting painters and writers from all over Germany and other parts of Europe. Pioneers of artistic innovation such as Wassily Kandinsky and Alexej von Jawlensky from the east, Paul Klee from Switzerland, and Franz Marc, Gabriele Münster, and August Macke formed *Der Blaue Reiter* (the Blue Rider) and revolutionised expressionist painting.

The Mann brothers, Heinrich and Thomas, lived and wrote in Schwabing, as did some of Germany's leading poets, Stefan George and Rainer Maria Rilke. Thomas Mann completed his novella on bourgeois decay, *Der Tod in Venedig* (*Death in Venice*), and Oswald Spengler, in a room not dissimilar to Hitler's, was writing the first volume of *The Decline of the West* in 1913, the year Hitler arrived. Schwabing's cafés and restaurants catered to the eccentric, combining an easy atmosphere of free thought with an air of feisty independence and rebelliousness in all matters of art and politics. Frank Wedekind, the German playwright and dramaturg, shocked audiences in Schwabing's pubs and theatres with his *Henkershumor* (hangman's humour) attacking middle class proclivities with his short routines and offensive songs. Weiß Ferdl and Karl Valentin, and his professional partner Liesl Karlstadt, were just beginning their careers as Munich's favourite folksingers, mocking the people of Munich and the Bavarian way of life with equally impertinent but humorous rather than vulgar cabaret acts and songs. A popular venue frequented by Schwabing's artists and literati was Café Stefanie, nicknamed Café Megalomania, on Amalienstraße, not far from the university (Ludwig-Maximilians-Universität). It was the most famous of Munich's *Größenwahn* cafés where intellectuals and nonconformists of all sorts indulged in their dreams and delusions of grandeur.[8]

Schwabing's residents who were more interested in revolutionary politics gravitated to Alter Simpl, a small restaurant on Türkenstraße, just north of the large military base, the Türkenkaserne (also known as the Prinz-Arnulf-Kaserne). Named after Munich's satirical magazine *Simplicissimus*, it was a favourite meeting place for the leading writers and illustrators of the magazine, and their most devoted readers. The iconic red bulldog, designed by the gifted caricaturist Thomas Theodor Heine, served as the logo for both the magazine and the restaurant. Heine provided many illustrations for *Simplicissimus*, appropriating the stylistic idiom of *Jugendstil* (Youth Style), the late nineteenth century German contribution to Art Nouveau that espoused new modern art in opposition to traditional academic art in buildings, interior furnishings, and painting. Ludwig Thoma was the editor. His weekly magazine provided biting criticism of the church and everyday Bavarian life, and lampooned the Kaiser and everything Prussian. On the occasions, and there were many, when Thoma's sarcasm forced the authorities to clamp down on the magazine, its circulation increased, reaching a peak of 85,000 copies before the war.[9]

Hitler visited Café Stefanie at least once in August 1913, but he did not mix with either the avant-garde café community in Schwabing or the political agitators on the left or the right. He never established contact with any political party or organization in Munich before the war, not even the Pan-German League that boasted the largest local chapter in Germany and had the publisher Julius F. Lehmann as one of its leading spokesmen. Lehmann would become a member of the ultranationalist and anti–Semitic Thule Society, an early and stalwart supporter of Hitler, and take part in the Beer Hall Putsch in November 1923, but he and Hitler did not meet each other until after the war.[10]

Hitler felt at home in the bohemian environs of Schwabing, but he preferred the small corner-cafés near his room on Schleißheimer Straße, where he could be alone, read the newspapers unnoticed and undisturbed, and take a break from his painting. He was not interested in the avant-garde, and he rejected the new ideas of the *Jugendstil*. He marvelled at the old masters in the Alte Pinakothek, and Ludwig I's private collection of art in the Neue Pinakothek. His favourite painters were Anselm Feuerbach, a German classicist, and the romantic symbolists Arnold Böcklin, Carl Spitzweg, and Moritz von Schwind, who drew on themes of chivalry, mythological figures, and folklore along with classical architecture. Hitler believed that true art was essentially classical, and he agreed with Schopenhauer's dictum that 'art should represent the nature of existence in such a way as to proclaim: Look! This is how life is!'[11] He further agreed with Schopenhauer that after music, the highest form of art was architecture, followed by sculpture and then painting.[12] Writing about Hitler and Art in a 1938 essay entitled 'Bruder Hitler' (Brother Hitler), Thomas Mann admitted that, with a large degree of pathos, his own idea of the true nature of art was basically in agreement with that of the Führer.[13]

As he had done in Vienna, Hitler painted architectural themes, especially the famous landmarks and well known tourist scenes in Munich. These included the Frauenkirche, Theatinerkirche, Feldherrnhalle, Sendlinger Tor, Asamkirche, Marienplatz and the neo–gothic Neues Rathaus, the Hofbräuhaus, and the Alter Hof (Old Residence) where Hitler used to wash out his brushes in the red marble fountain in the courtyard. Hitler also painted pictures of the Registry behind St Peter's Church and sold them to the brides and grooms.[14] His landlords, Joseph and Anna Popp, could see 'with their own eyes' that their lodger was a 'serious artist'. He painted most days and read all evening and night. Frau Popp asked Hitler once, 'What's all the reading got to do with your painting?' Many years later she recalled his reply as if it was yesterday: 'Hitler got up and smiled and took me by the arm. "Dear Frau Popp," he said, "does anyone know what is and what isn't likely to be of use to him in life?"'[15] Hitler derived more enjoyment from reading newspapers and his nocturnal studying than he did painting, but he sold enough of his work to make roughly 100 Marks per month, at a time in Munich when a bank clerk of the same age would have earned 70 Marks a month.[16] Hitler sold his watercolours and the occasional oil painting at some of the small commercial galleries in Schwabing and the Kunsthandlung Stuffle in the Maximilianstraße. He also sold paintings and negotiated commissioned work at the Löwenbräukeller and the Hofbräuhaus. Two of his more affluent Munich patrons included a doctor, Hans Schirmer, and a judge, Ernst Hepp. Hitler was trying to sell an oil painting in the Biergarten at the Hofbräuhaus when he met Schirmer. After a long night of drinking, the doctor did not have enough money to buy the painting so he asked Hitler to bring it to his home the next day. Hitler insisted that Schirmer take the painting, entitled *Der Abend* (Evening), and he would collect the money. When Hitler went to Schirmer's the next day to collect his money, the doctor ordered two additional works.[17] Ernst Hepp also bought a painting from Hitler at the Hofbräuhaus, and was so impressed with it that he invited Hitler to his Munich apartment for dinner. Hepp and his wife commissioned Hitler for a few more paintings, and in July 1913 they invited the young artist to spend a weekend with them at their country house in Wolfratshausen.[18] Once Hitler sold a painting he often received commissions for more work through word of mouth. Paul Kerber, a Munich jeweller, bought twenty-one of Hitler's paintings between the summer of 1913 and August 1914.[19]

Hitler's new life in Munich came under serious threat in January 1914 when the Austrian authorities finally caught up with him for avoiding military service. On Sunday afternoon, 18 January, an officer of the Munich criminal police visited Hitler at his Schleißheimer Straße room and presented him with an official summons to report for military service in Linz. Hitler appeared anxious and confused, and as a consequence the officer arrested him. On Monday morning Hitler was taken to the Austro-Hungarian general consulate in Munich. The general consulate viewed Hitler's situation with sympathy, and the consul sent a telegram to the Linz magistracy asking for a short delay until 5 February to enable Hitler to settle his affairs. This request was rejected and Hitler was ordered to report on 20 January. The unequivocal reply from Linz was passed on to Hitler, but not until Wednesday 21 January, a day after he was due to report. Now in a panic, Hitler wrote a long letter to the magistrate in Linz pleading his innocence. He claimed, somewhat disingenuously, that it had 'never occurred to him' to attempt to evade military service. He further pointed out that the immediate problems he had complying with the orders to report in Linz were due to bureaucratic slowness. The general consulate in Munich was convinced of Hitler's honesty. The consul not only agreed with Hitler's version of events, but he advised the authorities in Linz that 'the young man seemed extremely deserving of considerate treatment'. The consul also asked that Hitler be allowed to report to Salzburg for his examination because it was closer to Munich. This time the Linz authorities agreed. At the expense of the consulate, Hitler travelled to Salzburg on 5 February for his military examination. He was deemed 'unfit for combat and support duties', and described as being 'too weak and unable to bear arms'.[20] Disqualified from serving in the army, Hitler was allowed to return to Munich.

While Hitler was in Salzburg his friend Rudolf Häusler moved out of their shared room on Schleißheimer Straße. Apparently Hitler's nightly reading until the early hours had proved too off-putting, but a week or so later Häusler rented another room from the Popps, and despite the abrupt change the two men remained on friendly terms. Hitler, upon his return to Munich, effortlessly resumed his introverted Bohemian life style. He painted, sold his pictures as before, and read throughout the night. Frau Popp recalled that 'he just camped in his room like a hermit' and never accepted an invitation to share a meal with the family on the pretext that he had to work.[21] Hitler was comfortable with his solitary existence, but he did frequent a number of Schwabing's Volk cafés[22] as well as the Hofbräuhaus and the Löwenbräukeller where he often vented his scorn on the Austro-Hungarian Empire and the threat it posed to Germany. Hitler believed that 'Austria had long ceased to be a German state'. From his time in Vienna and his extensive reading of the newspapers he was convinced that the Slavic majority of the Habsburg Empire would sabotage any useful alliance with Germany, and that the Germans would pay dearly for their misguided loyalty and political naivety regarding such a capricious ally. Hitler reacted with incredulity when the Germans he spoke politics with in Munich asserted that Austria-Hungary was 'a serious power', which 'in the hour of need' would rise to the occasion and fight victoriously alongside their German ally. This divergence of views agitated Hitler even more as the storm clouds of war seemed to gather over Europe. The simmering crises in the Balkans filled Hitler and most Europeans with 'constant anxiety' and a 'sense of approaching catastrophe'. There was an uneasy sense of the inevitable, but also 'a longing to give free rein to the fate which could no longer be thwarted'.[23]

The countdown to war began on Sunday 28 June when the heir to the Austrian throne, Archduke Franz Ferdinand, and his wife, Sophie, were murdered in Sarajevo by Gavrilo Princip, a Bosnian-Serbian ultra-nationalist terrorist. In Munich, Hitler was reading in his third floor room on Schleißheimer Straße, when he suddenly became aware of a great commotion outside. As he descended the stairs to see what was happening he passed Frau Popp, breathless with excitement, who blurted out 'the Archduke has been assassinated!'[24] At first Hitler was worried that the assassin had been a German student, who in a fit of righteous anger had shot the heir apparent because of his Slavization policies. Once outside on the street Hitler saw hastily put up placards announcing the crime and that the perpetrators had been arrested, and they had been identified as Serbs. Hitler later recalled that 'a light shudder began to run through me', conscious of the irony that 'the greatest friend of the Slavs has fallen beneath the bullets of Slavic fanatics'. Munich, much like Vienna, seethed with indignation. Hitler was not alone in thinking that a war between Austria and Serbia, and most likely a major European conflict starting with Austria and Russia, was inevitable, that with the assassination 'a stone had been set rolling whose course could no longer be arrested.'[25]

War hysteria began to build up in Munich during July 1914. Students and their university lecturers roamed the streets in Schwabing singing patriotic songs and shouting for action. There was a growing feeling in the city that justice, no matter what the cost, had to be exacted for the heinous crime. Violence was in the air. On Saturday 25 July, Hitler observed a riot at the Café Fahrig, behind the Karlstor. A group of protesters destroyed the café because the band refused to play *Die Wacht am Rhein* over and over again.[26] Even the city's artists and intelligentsia got caught up in the call for vengeance and enthusiastically supported the call to arms. Ludwig Thoma, the editor of *Simplicissimus*, and Thomas Mann both saw the impending conflict as a battle to defend German culture against the aggressive expansionism of Russia and the revanchist French.[27]

Austria declared war on Serbia on 28 July. Russia mobilised, and in Berlin the Kaiser, Wilhelm II, gave a speech from the balcony of his palace proclaiming 'a state of imminent threat of war'.[28] Germany issued an ultimatum to the Russians to halt their mobilisation. The ultimatum was ignored, and on 1 August 1914 Germany mobilised and declared war on Russia. The next day in Munich, a large crowd of many thousands gathered on the Odeonsplatz in front of the Feldherrnhalle (the Field Marshals' Hall) to hear the announcement of Bavaria's general mobilisation. Close to the front of the crowd was 25-year-old Adolf Hitler. Ten years later Hitler described his feelings on that memorable day, 2 August 1914: 'Even today I am not ashamed to say that, overpowered by stormy enthusiasm, I fell down on my knees and thanked Heaven from an overflowing heart for granting me the good fortune of being permitted to live at this time.'[29] The atmosphere at the Odeonsplatz was euphoric: soldiers in their field grey uniforms, military bands playing martial tunes and the national anthems of Bavaria and Germany, and the jubilant masses intoxicated by the heady outpourings of national pride and resolve. The Austrian novelist, Stefan Zweig, said that 'there was something grand, captivating and even seductive about this eruption of the masses.'[30] Thomas Mann thought that the declaration of war was a 'liberation and an enormous sense of hope'.[31] Hitler was so elated by the whole experience that he decided to volunteer. Despite being declared unfit for military duty in the Austrian army six months earlier, on Monday 3 August, the same day that Germany declared war on France, Hitler submitted a personal petition to Ludwig III asking for the King's permission to serve as an Austrian in the Bavarian army.

The Artist Goes to War

Hitler claims that he received permission to join the Bavarian army by special cabinet order on 4 August. 'With trembling hands,' he recollected, 'I opened the document; my request had been approved and I was summoned to report to a Bavarian regiment.'[1] When Hitler tried to volunteer on 5 August however, he was sent home. The regular army regiments based at the Türkenkaserne and the Prinz-Leopold-Kaserne north-west of Schwabing were full. Less than two weeks later, on 16 August, Hitler was called up and inducted into Voluntary Recruit Depot VI of the 2nd Bavarian Infantry Regiment. This new replacement battalion was billeted at the Elisabethenschule (Elisabeth School) on Elisabethplatz 4, not far from the large military training ground, the Oberwiesenfeld, adjacent to the Prinz-Leopold-Kaserne. Hitler started basic military training on 17 August, and on 1 September he was transferred to the newly constituted 1st Company of the 1st Battalion of the Bavarian Reserve Infantry Regiment 16 (RIR 16), the 'List Regiment', named after its commanding officer Colonel Julius List. The regiment was a mixture of volunteers from all walks of life in Munich, including artists, students, farmers, labourers and professionals who had little if any military experience. On 7 September Hitler met a fellow painter and volunteer, Ernst Schmidt. Hitler and Schmidt became friends, would serve together throughout the war, and afterwards Schmidt became an early party member.[2] All of the volunteers in the List Regiment went through an intensive course of drill, bayonet practice, and route marching until the second week in October. On 8 October the regiment paraded before the König of Bavaria in the Türkenkaserne, and swore an oath of allegiance to Ludwig III as well as Kaiser Wilhelm II. Hitler and the other Austrian recruits were also required to swear their allegiance to Emperor Franz Josef. Afterwards the regiment was treated to a special luncheon where the men enjoyed double portions of roast pork and potato salad.[3]

The following day Hitler visited his former residence on Schleißheimer Straße to say goodbye to the Popp family as his regiment was about to leave Munich. Hitler shook hands with Joseph Popp and asked him to write to his sister if he should be killed in action. He also shook hands with Frau Popp, who was in tears because 'we were all that fond of him!' Hitler hugged Liesel and Peppi, the Popps' two young children, and then returned to his barracks.[4] Early the next morning, Saturday 10 October, the List Regiment marched out of Munich to begin its final combat training before deploying to the front. The regiment marched in full packs for four days, much of the time in the pouring rain, arriving on 13 October at Graben, on the outskirts of the Bavarian army's combat training area Lagerlechfeld, south of Augsburg and approximately 82 kilometres west of Munich. Hitler and his comrades spent a week at Lagerlechfeld rehearsing combat drills, practising brigade manoeuvres, and undertaking lengthy night time marches of up to 42 kilometres. On the last day of training, Hitler wrote to Frau Popp, telling her that 'the first five days at Lechfeld were the hardest of my life'.[5] The time for training was over. Very early (3 am) on Wednesday 21 October, the List Regiment was loaded onto trains destined for Belgium and the front lines near Ypres. They were much needed reinforcements for the 6th Bavarian Division, part of the army of Crown Prince Rupprecht.[6]

Spirits were high in the List Regiment. Private Ignaz Westenkirchner, one of Hitler's comrades, recalled how excited the men were at the prospect of joining 'the glorious fight'.[7] As the trains rumbled along, the morning sun rose and the mist cleared, the Bavarians could see – many, including Hitler, for the first time – the Rhine. When their train passed the *Niederwalddenkmal* (the gigantic Niederwald Monument of Germania overlooking the Rhine in commemoration of Germany's Unification in 1871), near Rüdesheim am Rhein in Hesse, they spontaneously erupted into a rousing rendition of *Die Wacht am Rhein*. Overcome by patriotic emotion, Hitler exclaimed: 'I felt as though my heart would burst.'[8] It took two days to reach Lille as the trains crawled through war-ravaged Belgium. The List Regiment had arrived in time for Crown Prince Rupprecht's great offensive at the end of October, marking the middle phase of the First Battle of Ypres.

In the early hours of 29 October, the List Regiment took part in an assault on the Flemish village of Gheluvelt north of the Menin Road. For four days and nights the Bavarians were engaged in fierce close-quarter fighting against British forces at Becelaere and Polygon Wood, and Gheluvelt, advancing, falling back, often fighting with bayonets in hand-to-hand combat, while throughout the artillery on both sides shelled the battlefield. On 31 October, Colonel List was killed leading an attack near Gheluvelt Castle. By the time the List Regiment was withdrawn from the line it had suffered more than seventy per cent casualties. Westenkirchner reckoned that only 500 of the 3,000 men in the regiment survived the battle, and all of them 'came out of it worn, scarred, and exhausted'.[9] Official figures record the List Regiment suffering 373 dead on its first day of battle, but when the number of wounded and missing along with the general chaos of inexperienced volunteers fighting a protracted battle is taken into account it is entirely understandable that Westenkirchner and his fellow survivors believed that their regiment had been destroyed. Hitler's 'baptism of fire' left deep scars. His initial idealism and 'the romance of battle', Hitler later wrote in *Mein Kampf*, 'had been replaced by horror'. A man's courage and resolve was severely tested by the industrialised slaughter that characterised war on the Western Front. In a letter to his friend and patron in Munich, Ernst Hepp, Hitler confessed that the unrelenting heavy artillery fire 'ruined even the strongest nerves in time'.[10] Traumatised by the inconceivable violence of his first battle Hitler openly acknowledged that 'every man had to struggle between the instinct of self-preservation and the admonitions of duty'. Hitler credits his reading of Schopenhauer during the winter of 1914/15 as the starting place from which he mastered his will and confronted cowardice 'until at last, after a long inner struggle', his 'consciousness of duty emerged victorious'. By the end of 1915, now no longer a young recruit but an old soldier calm and determined, Hitler was certain that 'Fate could bring on the ultimate tests without my nerves shattering or my reason failing.'[11]

Hitler was brave and committed rather than simply a conscientious and dutiful solider. At the start of November he was promoted to *Gefreiter* (corporal) and on 9 November he was selected to join a small group of eight to ten despatch messengers whose duty it was to keep up communications between the regimental headquarters and battalion and company commanders at the front line and in the trenches. Hitler remained a *Meldegänger* (messenger, trench runner) for the duration of the war. After the war, Hitler's detractors would claim that he lacked leadership qualities and this is the reason why he was not promoted. Max Amann, a staff sergeant in the List Regiment, and later the head of Eher Verlag, the official publishing house of the Nazi Party, points out that Hitler had rejected offers of promotion most likely because acceptance would have entailed leaving the regimental staff.[12]

Hitler's superiors held him in high regard, and his comrades respected him, especially the group of dispatch runners with whom he shared the dangers of delivering messages. Hitler had earned a reputation as a fearless and reliable soldier who never abandoned a wounded comrade. On 14 November 1914, Hitler and Anton Bachmann, another despatch runner, saved their regimental commander Lieutenant Colonel Philipp Engelhardt from being killed during an inspection visit to the front. For this act of bravery, Hitler was awarded the *Eiserne Kreuz, zweite Klasse* (Iron Cross, Second Class; EK II) on 2 December 1914. The next day Hitler wrote a letter to Joseph Popp, telling him about his promotion and what he did to be awarded the Iron Cross. 'It was the happiest day of my life,' Hitler wrote, but immediately tempered his joy with the stark recognition, 'Of course almost all of my comrades, who deserved one too, are dead.'[13] The high cost of war was a central theme in Hitler's long letter to Ernst Hepp on 5 February 1915. He starts the letter by telling his friend he has been awarded the Iron Cross, and then proceeds to describe in considerable detail what he and his regiment had experienced since they arrived at the front. The ferocity of the close combat combined with the nearly continuous shelling by the heavy artillery batteries conjures up instantly recognizable images of hell. Hitler ends the letter on a more philosophical note, expressing his hope 'that the sacrifice and agony we suffer' in our fight 'against an international world of enemies, will not merely destroy Germany's enemies abroad but also break our internationalism at home'.[14]

Between March 1915 and September 1916, the List Regiment fought first in the battle of Neuve-Chapelle, and afterwards in the trenches around Fromelles in the Ypres region of Flanders. In the autumn the Bavarians moved south down to the Somme where the List Regiment went into action against the British on 2 October 1916, in the sector between Bapaume and La Barque. It was all unfamiliar ground, and the casualties amongst the regimental runners were high. On the night of 5 October a shell hit the entrance tunnel to the regimental headquarters where Hitler and the other runners were waiting for their next assignments. Four men were killed outright, and seven others including Hitler were wounded. Hitler's friend Ernst Schmidt recalled how Hitler and Anton Bachmann were evacuated first to a field dressing station near the town of Hermies and then to a Red Cross hospital in Beelitz, south of Berlin. He, however, collapsed as the wounded men were being led away, and ended up at a different hospital, in Brandenburg.[15] Hitler was wounded in the thigh. It was less serious than originally feared, but Hitler convalesced in hospital from 9 October to 2 December, when he was discharged to join a replacement battalion of the Bavarian Reserve Infantry Regiment 16 in Munich.

Before Hitler arrived in Munich, he enjoyed a day's leave in Berlin on Saturday 4 November. It was his first visit to the German capital, and he spent much of it at the Alte Nationalgalerie admiring the Neoclassical and Romantic collections. He also saw first-hand the effects of war fatigue on the civilian population. 'Clearly there was dire misery everywhere,' Hitler wrote in Mein Kampf, 'The big city was suffering from hunger. Discontent was great.' He soon discovered that the conditions were even worse in Munich: 'I thought I could no longer recognise the city. Anger, discontent, cursing, wherever you went!' Food shortages, rampant inflation, war profiteering, a rise in anti-Semitism, and a strong sense that all the suffering as well as the protracted nature of the war was Prussia's fault, united Bavaria's soldiers and civilians in their desire for peace, almost at any price. War exhaustion was just as prevalent in the replacement battalion, particularly amongst the new recruits at the Elisabethenschule. Straight away Hitler noticed that no one honoured a frontline soldier. 'To be a slacker passed almost as a sign of higher wisdom.'[16] Disconsolate with what he experienced and saw during his first visit back to Munich since October 1914, Hitler longed to be back with his old comrades at the front. At the end of

December, Hitler sent postcards to Karl Lanzhammer, the regimental bicyclist, and Balthasar Brandmayer, a fellow despatch runner, telling them that his health was improving and that he wished he was back serving with them. Early in the New Year, Hitler wrote to the Regimental Adjutant, Lieutenant Fritz Wiedemann, stating that he was fit again, and implored him to arrange for his return to 'his old regiment and his old comrades'.[17] Wiedemann granted Hitler his wish, and on 5 March 1917 he rejoined his regiment at La Bassée, a village north of Vimy Ridge.[18]

Ignaz Westenkirchner recalled that he and the other despatch runners were glad to have Hitler back. 'He was one of the best comrades we ever had.' The company cook prepared a special meal of *Reiberdatschi* (potato pancakes), bread and jam, and tea to celebrate Hitler's return.[19] Adi, as they called him, was well liked by his immediate comrades, although his idiosyncrasies and quiet seriousness set him apart from the rest of the group of despatch runners and made him an easy target for their banter. His comrades nicknamed him 'the artist' and 'the monk'. Hitler was not a drinker, he did not smoke, he neither sought the company of local women nor visited the brothels, he spent his spare time either painting or reading, and after his return to the regiment in the spring of 1917 he received very few letters or parcels. Once he became a famous politician, his detractors claimed that he was utterly fanatical about his hatred of Marxism and the Jews, and that he often lectured his comrades on his political philosophy. Hitler is equally to blame for his portrayal as an outspoken anti-Semite with ultra-nationalist political views mainly because of his autobiographical account of the war in *Mein Kampf*.[20] His immediate comrades, however, did not recognise this political agitator in the trenches. Schmidt never heard Hitler discuss these subjects, and neither did Lieutenant Wiedemann, who later recalled: 'It really seems impossible for me to believe that Hitler's hatred for the Jews dated back to that time.' Max Amann was also adamant that Hitler did not harangue his comrades on politics during the war.[21]

Lieutenant Wiedemann regarded Hitler as being 'the paradigm of the unknown soldier carrying out his duty silently and calmly'. This praise was augmented by Lieutenant Colonel Friedrich Petz, who succeeded Engelhardt as the commander of the List Regiment. 'Hitler was an extremely hard-working, willing, conscientious and dutiful soldier, who was also completely reliable and obedient towards his superiors,' Petz wrote in February 1922. Further adding to his testimonial: 'His iron calm and cold-bloodedness never deserted him. When the situation was at its most dangerous, he always volunteered to make deliveries to the front and carried them out successfully.' After fighting in the Battle of Arras in the spring, and suffering heavy casualties in the Third Battle of Ypres during the summer of 1917, the List Regiment was withdrawn to Chemin des Dames, a quieter sector of the front in the département of Aisne. On 17 September Hitler was awarded the Bavarian Military Merit Cross, Third Class.[22] He then took a fortnight's leave in Berlin where he enjoyed this unaccustomed leisure time 'to get acquainted with the museums a little bit'.[23] The remainder of the autumn through to March 1918 was fairly quiet for the List Regiment until it took part in General Ludendorff's great spring offensives. Once again, Hitler distinguished himself, first receiving on 9 May the regimental diploma for bravery in attack, then on 18 May the black badge for being wounded twice, and on Sunday 4 August 1918 the Iron Cross, First Class (EK I).[24] Colonel Anton Freiherr von Tubeuf had personally witnessed Hitler's gallantry in action during the spring offensives, and Lieutenant Colonel Freiherr von Godin, deputy commander of the RIR 16, gladly signed the recommendation for the award. Writing after the Second World War about Hitler's bravery in the Great War, Wiedemann was unequivocal with his praise: 'On the field of battle, he proved his worth as a courageous and particularly reliable runner, who deserved his Iron Cross, First Class and who was put forward for that honour numerous times, before he actually received it.'[25]

The List Regiment fought in all of the major German offensives in the spring and early summer of 1918, on the Somme, the Aisne, and the Marne. It was withdrawn to La Cateau-Cambrésis for a period of recovery and regeneration just before the western allies began their counteroffensive on 8 August at Amiens, the first of a series of offensive battles all along the western front that ultimately ended the war in a 100 days' time. Hitler left the front on 23 August to attend a week-long signals course in Nürnberg. It was the first time he had visited the Imperial City of the Holy Roman Empire in the 'Heart of the German Reich', and where in the 1930s the National Socialists held their massive party rallies and passed the infamous Nürnberg Laws that stripped Jewish citizens of their property and legal rights. Hitler briefly rejoined his regiment on 31 August in the vicinity of Wytschaete and Messines, the same place where in 1914 he received his EK II, before going on eighteen days of leave in Berlin.[26] It is not clear if Hitler noticed the febrile atmosphere of revolution when he visited Berlin from 10 to 18 September. Berlin had been a centre of active protest against the war since the spring of 1916 when the Spartacus League, led by Rosa Luxemburg and Karl Liebknecht, staged a massive public demonstration. An increasing number of Berliners demanded a new democratic government and an end to the war. During the nationwide general strike at the end of January 1918, over 400,000 workers in Berlin downed tools for a week until they were forced back to work. Peace had been restored but it was only a question of time before a full-scale rebellion would break out. Hitler did not mention either the obvious defeatism or the hankering for political change. He appears to have spent most of his time on Berlin's Museum Island, looking at the various art and historical collections. What little is known of his visit comes from a brief remark he made at his field headquarters in October 1941, telling his special guest Heinrich Himmler, the Reichsführer-SS, that he used his two periods of leave during the Great War to become 'familiar with the museums of the capital'.[27]

Hitler rejoined his regiment at Comines just before the British launched a major gas attack to break through the Ypres–Comines Canal line. On the night of 13/14 October, Hitler and a number of his comrades were incapacitated by mustard gas. They were evacuated to the Bavarian 53rd Field Hospital at Oudenaarde. Hitler had been partially blinded. On 21 October he was transferred to the Prussian Reserve Hospital at Pasewalk in Pomerania where he remained until the end of the war. He was still receiving treatment when the revolution began in Kiel on 28 October. Hitler and his fellow patients from Bavaria confidently expected this 'sailors' revolt' to be crushed swiftly. Germany's military collapse in early November, the revolutions in Bavaria and Prussia, the abdication of Ludwig III on 7 November and Kaiser Wilhelm II on 9 November, and the announcement that Germany was a Republic with a left-wing government led by Friedrich Ebert and the Social Democratic Party (SPD), must have shaken them deeply. When the hospital chaplain relayed the news to the patients on 10 November, a stunned and disbelieving Hitler broke down in tears. He records his response in *Mein Kampf*: 'Again, everything went black before my eyes… Since the day when I had stood at my mother's grave, I had not wept.'[28] Hitler was discharged from hospital on 19 November 1918. Disconsolate and embittered, and facing an uncertain future, he returned to Munich.[29]

The Soldier Returns

Hitler spent most of the day of 19 November 1918 in Berlin. Before he took the overnight train to Munich, he witnessed at first-hand a large Marxist rally at the Lustgarten (Pleasure Garden) in front of the Altes (Old) Museum at Museum Island. Years later Hitler told Albert Speer how impressed he was by 'the sea of Red flags', a mesmerizingly powerful feature that Speer incorporated into the Nürnberg Party Rallies and other National Socialist spectacles in the 1930s.[1] When Hitler left the Munich Hauptbahnhof early in the morning on Wednesday 20 November, he emerged into a city that was unusually quiet considering the momentous events that had occurred over the previous fortnight. The Wittelsbach monarchy had been deposed. Munich was under the control of revolutionary soldiers' and workers' councils, or 'soviets' as they preferred to call themselves after the Russian example. Kurt Eisner, a Berlin-born Jew and a living caricature of the bomb-throwing Bolshevik, was the president of the newly proclaimed Free State of Bavaria. Eisner, who had only been released from Munich's Stadelheim prison in mid-October, was the chairman of the small moderate left-wing *Unabhängige Sozialdemokratische Partei Deutschlands* (USPD; Independent Social Democratic Party of Germany) in Munich, and he led a weak transitional government with Erhard Auer, the chairman of the *Mehrheitssozialdemokratische Partei Deutschlands* (MSPD; Majority Social Democratic Party of Germany). The Left were buoyant. Their political revolution in Munich had succeeded without any violence. 'Isn't it something wonderful?' Eisner proclaimed. 'We've achieved a revolution without shedding a drop of blood! It is a historical first!'[2]

The general mood amongst the people of Munich was more sullen. More than four years of war had taken its toll. Death and injury on the battlefields vied with deprivation, hunger, and psychological trauma on the home front that in many ways was as bad, or worse, than that suffered by the returning soldiers from the trenches. Anger competed with lethargy, and many Bavarians took a wait and see approach, at least in the short-term, a sort of quiet acceptance of an unwelcomed fate. Münchners also grumbled and waited. Their responses were not uniform. The war had divided the people in Munich on the lines of class, urban or rural, front or home front, and their individual experiences. What united them was their search for the culprits, those who were to blame both for the war and its ruinous result: the Prussians and the Jews. Traditionally

Bavarians disliked Prussia and all things Prussian, and there was a growing problem with anti-Semitism. Even before the war was lost, the various *völkisch* (folkish movement) and Pan-German organizations whipped up anti-Semitic hysteria. There was a proliferation of leaflets and pamphlets of a nationalist-racist origin, most if not all freely available in Munich's many beer halls and cafés, and it is highly likely that Hitler read some of them when he returned after the war. Heinrich Claβ, the leader of the Pan-German League, used his anti-Semitic publications, the *Alldeutsche Blätter* (Pan-German Pages) and the *Deutsche Zeitung* (German Newspaper) to emphasise the strong Jewish connection with the revolution in Russia, Bolshevism, and the defeatism that characterised the new socialist German government's capitulation to the western powers. The 'November Criminals' in Berlin were to blame for losing the war and all the suffering that came with defeat.

It was a comfortable thirty minute walk from the Hauptbahnhof to the army barracks at Lothstraβe 29 in northwest Schwabing, where Hitler would live for the better part of the next two years. He was assigned to the 7th Company of the 1st Replacement Battalion of the 2nd Bavarian Infantry Regiment Kronprinz (Crown Prince). Once Hitler arrived at the barracks, he soon discovered that most of the officers and soldiers were content to serve Eisner's government. He also found the indiscipline and the general indifference his new comrades had for the current political situation and those who served at the front 'so repellent' that he 'decided at once to leave again as soon as possible'.[3] His opportunity came two weeks later on 4 December. The regiment asked for volunteers to guard a prisoner of war camp in Traunstein, 110 km east of Munich on the road to Salzburg.

From the moment Hitler arrived at the Lothstraβe barracks he avoided contact with his 'new comrades', men who had never been anywhere near the trenches. As he did in the Men's Hostel in Vienna, Hitler read a lot, and he kept his political opinions to himself. His only friend was Ernst Schmidt, his old comrade and fellow despatch runner in the RIR 16, and who like Hitler had returned to Munich at the end of the war. Urged on by Schmidt, Hitler volunteered to guard PoWs, and along with a few additional 'men from the Front' they deployed to Traunstein on 6 December. Their commanding officer rejected all the 'new Revolution men' having judged them to be lazy and impudent. The camp was located in a large brewery and beer hall at Karl-Theodor-Platz, in the centre of the old town. Duties were light. Hitler and Schmidt provided security at the main entrance, monitoring the comings and goings at the camp. The prisoners were mainly Russian, but there were also a few English and French PoWs. Most of them had been returned to their home countries by the end of January 1919. The camp closed, and on 25 January 1919 Hitler and the rest of the guard company returned to Munich.[4]

Hitler was no longer the dreamy indolent artist of his pre-war years in Vienna and Munich. He had been hardened physically and psychologically by the war. The hardships he experienced as a youth in Vienna, and his meagre existence in Munich before he joined the army, provided him with a degree of experience to meet the challenges and harsh conditions of life on the western front. At the end of the war Hitler, like many Germans, soldiers and civilians, felt cheated, and questioned the point of all their sacrifice. Was Germany not worth fighting for? Hitler thought it was, but not the Germany he returned to in November 1918, a prostrate country run by pacifists and socialists and dependent on the mercy of its enemies. Defeat was betrayal. For the left-wing revolutionaries and many of the socialist politicians, men such as Ernst Toller, the expressionist playwright and leader of the very brief Bavarian soviet republic in April 1919, it was the war itself that was the betrayal. Eisner, Toller, and other socialist reformers in Munich and throughout Germany wanted to create a better world, and a new Germany that was a leading contributor to a fair, equal, democratic and non-violent international order. Hitler did not share their views. Hitler concludes his account of the World War in *Mein Kampf*, having just heard the news of Germany's defeat while recovering from his wounds in the hospital at Pasewalk, with the declaration: 'I, for my part, decided to go into politics.'[5] The evidence of his immediate life in Munich after the war does not support his claim. He returned to Munich to stay in the army; it was his home, and where his regiment was based. He did not have any other prospects. If Hitler's bank account details are to be believed, just before he returned to Munich he had slightly more than 15 Marks (Account No. 457896) at the Städtische Sparkasse München (Munich Municipal Savings Bank) on the Tal.[6] Volker Ullrich, in his unassailable biography of Hitler, regards the Pasewalk episode as a significant transition point in Hitler's ideological development, 'between the defining experience of war and the equally defining experience of revolution and counter-revolution in Munich'. It was in Munich in 1919 that 'politics', as the historian Ernst Deuerlein correctly recognized, 'came to Hitler'.[7]

II

Political Beginnings, 1919–23

Revolutionary Munich

Thursday, 7 November 1918, was a mild and pleasant autumn day in Munich, the day the main Socialist parties held a peace rally on the Theresienwiese, a large meadow south of the Hauptbahnhof where the annual Oktoberfest is held. Many of Munich's businesses and shops had closed at midday, and throughout the afternoon large groups of people congregated in front of the statue of Bavaria on the western edge of the meadow. The crowd comprised militant workers and trade unionists, soldiers and sailors who had abandoned their units, disgruntled farmers, quixotic university students, women and children, as well as a curious assortment of Schwabing bohemians and beer hall regulars eager not to miss out on all the excitement. They were entertained by traditional Bavarian folk dancers and musical bands, as men paraded with large political banners and colourful placards that demanded peace, democracy, and universal suffrage. Suitably stimulated, the crowd responded as the organizers of the demonstration had hoped, waving red flags to encourage the performers and enthusiastically showing their support for an immediate end to the war. The advertised speeches began just after three o'clock culminating with the two main party leaders, Erhard Auer of the moderate Majority Social Democratic Party (MSPD) and Kurt Eisner, the chairman of the idealistic and revolution-supporting Independent Social Democratic Party of Germany (USPD) addressing a crowd of between 100,000 and 150,000.[1] Auer spoke first, keeping to his agreement with Eisner to speak for about twenty minutes and then call for the adoption of a resolution against 'national defence' and for greater democracy in the running of the state. Auer and his party wanted to build a reformed constitutional monarchy, and avoid a revolution that risked introducing Bolshevism into Bavaria.

Eisner was not with the other political leaders in front of the Bavaria monument. He had taken up a strategic position on the north-west corner of the Theresienwiese, opposite the Hackerbräu-Keller and near a cluster of beer halls – Spatenbräu-Keller, Hacker-Brauerei, Pschorr-Brauerei, and Hirschbräu-Keller – all just off one of the main roads, the Schwanthalerstraße that led back into the centre of the city. Eisner spoke for more than an hour, condemning the war and criticising both the military dictatorship in Berlin and the monarchy in Bavaria. He implored his attentive and increasingly restless audience to seize the moment and throw off the shackles of oppression, announcing that the time had come for action.[2] At this point, Felix Fechenbach, a former soldier and one of Eisner's trusted aides, stepped forward, waved a red flag and shouted, 'Comrades, our leader Kurt Eisner has spoken. There is no reason to waste any more words. Follow us!'[3] Arm in arm with Fechenbach and the venerated peasant leader Ludwig Gandorfer, Eisner led his swelling band of followers not into the city, behind Auer and the great mass that followed him, but in the opposite direction west of the Theresienwiese along the Schwanthalerstraße towards the Guldein School, a temporary military barracks and munitions depot. Among the mob following Eisner was Oskar Maria Graf, the socialist-anarchist Bavarian novelist. He described the scene:

> All at once the howling mass started to move. Like an impatient black wave it rolled, thousands upon thousands strong... There was no opposition. All the police seemed to have disappeared. ... All along the route people joined our ranks, some of them armed. Most laughed and chatted as if on the way to a party. Occasionally I turned around and looked behind me. The whole city seemed to be marching.[4]

It was a twenty minute walk to the Guldein School. Fechenbach, wearing his army uniform, and another soldier who had defied orders to stay in barracks were the first inside. They were unopposed by the guards, who promptly joined the mob and assisted arming them. The revolution that Eisner had worked tirelessly to start since his release from Stadelheim prison in mid-October had begun. Leaving the school, the armed revolutionaries surged onto the Donnersberger Bridge, crossing over the city's main railway lines and into the military district of the city. They divided up into small groups, one occupying the Hauptbahnhof, the others proceeding on to the many barracks and military posts that stretched northwards up to the large army training ground on the Oberwiesenfeld. At each one a delegation entered the barracks and announced the revolution while the rest of the mob waited outside. Only the massive Prinz Arnulf Kaserne on Türkenstraße offered minor resistance, which ended quickly after a whiff of tear gas and a few warning shots. Most soldiers welcomed the proclamation of peace and happily endorsed the new Republic. By early evening the entire army in Munich had defected from royal authority.[5]

While Eisner's revolutionaries were co-opting the army in Munich to their cause, Auer's supporters marched into the centre of the city, parading past the Royal Residenz, through the Hofgarten and onto Prinzregentenstraße, before crossing over the Isar on the Luitpold Bridge and ending their demonstration at the Friedensengel, a column 38 metres high with a 6-metre-high statue of the Angel of Peace on the top. This impressive monument was built between 1896 and 1899 to mark twenty-five years of peace after the Franco-Prussian War of 1870–71. The crowd arrived at the monument in the Maximiliansanlagen (Maximilian Park and Garden) in the early evening, but quickly drifted off to the many beer halls south of the park in the brewery district of Au-Haidhausen. Eisner too, with a few close associates and bodyguards, had found his way to the sprawling Franziskaner-Keller on Hochstraße in the centre of Au-Haidhausen. It is not entirely clear why Eisner was at the Franziskaner-Keller. One rumour was that he was scheduled to speak there that evening, but another is that he left the city centre fearful of a counterstroke of some sort that would snuff out his audacious insurrection.[6] Whatever the reason, Eisner and many of those who attended the peace rally on the Theresienwiese were enjoying their beer while the King and his family hastily prepared to leave the city. Both Ludwig III and his wife, Queen Maria Therese, were relieved that the mob had not ransacked the Residenz and murdered them and their young daughters. The spectre of the Bolshevik revolution in Russia hung ominously over the royal household in Munich. At 8 pm two royal ministers, Otto von Dandl (Prime Minister) and Friedrich von Brettreich (Minister of the Interior), advised the King that it was too dangerous to stay in the city. The monarchy was all but finished without the support of the army. An hour later, Ludwig and his family were making their escape by car to Schloss Wildenwart, eighty kilometres south-east of Munich, and eventually to Schloss Anif across the Austrian border near Salzburg.

News of the revolution spread across Munich throughout the night. Eisner was informed that two large groups of soldiers and workers were organizing impromptu meetings at the Mathäserbräu, the largest and rowdiest beer hall in the centre of the city just off the 'Stachus' (Karlsplatz). Eisner left the Franziskaner-Keller to attend these meetings, and to offer them his political leadership. When he arrived the soldiers had already established a *Soldatenrat* (Council of Soldiers and Sailors) and were celebrating on the first floor. Beneath them on the ground floor, Eisner presided over the creation of an *Arbeiterrat* (Council of Workers), which selected him as their chairman, the first electoral office he had ever held. Later in the evening, Eisner and the executive members of the *Arbeiterrat* met with their counterparts in the *Soldatenrat* and together they agreed to merge their councils, or soviets as the Russians would call them, into one. The new *Arbeiter-und-Soldatenrat* immediately set out a plan of action: they despatched truckloads of armed men across the city to provide order; they occupied and stood guard in front of the main public buildings, centres of communication, and transportation; and they seized all the major newspapers and publishing houses and ordered them to print an announcement that the Council of Workers and Soldiers had seized power and deposed the Wittelsbach monarchy.[7]

The revolutionaries ended this momentous day with a late-night march to the Landtag building, the Bavarian Parliament in the Palais Preysing on

Prannerstraße 20 (now number 8). Eisner, the Council, a large band of admirers, and an armed guard of some sixty men, arrived at the Landtag just before 10 pm, finding it dark and vacant. They roused the custodian and made him open the doors and turn on the lights. About a half hour later, at 10.30 pm, Eisner stood at the presidential rostrum and declared on behalf of the Council of Workers and Soldiers that the Bavarian revolution was victorious. Speaking to a full house of supporters, who had taken up the deputies' seats in the Lower House, Eisner proclaimed the end of the Wittelsbach dynasty and the beginning of the Bavarian Republic. 'Now we must proceed to building a new regime,' he stated, and ended his speech by heralding himself as the provisional Prime Minister, an announcement that was greeted with enthusiastic applause.[8] Eisner spent the night in the Palais Preysing, sleeping on a plush red sofa. When he woke up the next morning bright red posters announcing the birth of the new Republic had already been distributed throughout Bavaria, and the red flag of the revolution was flying from the domed twin towers of the Frauenkirche, Munich's renowned central cathedral.[9]

Kurt Eisner and the Bavarian Republic

Eisner spent the morning of Friday 8 November establishing a government. He appealed to his socialist adversary Erhard Auer, who had been a member of the Chamber of Deputies in Bavaria's last Royal government, to help form a coalition government. Auer did not want a revolution but now that it had happened he seized the opportunity to pursue his own programme of moderate reforms to create a conservative yet democratic and socialist *Volkstaat* – people's state. Auer rejected Eisner's dreamy utopianism and political flirtation with anarchists and Bolsheviks, but he was also a pragmatist. Being a minister in the government of the new Free Republic of Bavarian would enable Auer and his MSPD to mitigate the radical ideas of Eisner's USPD and limit the role of the workers' and soldiers' soviets. The new coalition cabinet consisted of Eisner as both Prime Minister and Foreign Minister, Auer as Deputy Prime Minister and Interior Minister with control over the police, and Auer's MSPD colleagues holding most of the other important posts – Johannes Hoffmann (Culture and Education), Johannes Timm (Justice), and Albert Rosshaupter (Military Affairs).[1]

By late afternoon, with his cabinet established, Eisner opened the first plenary session of the Provisional National Council of the Bavarian People's State. He spoke about the need for a 'radical transformation of the constitution and the entire life of Bavaria' to create a 'new order' that was stable, democratic, and at peace with the rest of the world. He also promised, at an undefined date, but characterised as 'in times of more peaceful development', a democratically elected National Assembly that would decide the permanent form of the Republic. For the moment, however, he planned to rule through his appointed rather than elected cabinet and the 'elemental impulse' of the revolutionary councils. Eisner's first speech as the leader of the Bavarian Republic was moderate but full of ambiguity. His initial political problem was how to balance order and progress, how to appeal to the vast majority of Bavarians without thwarting the revolutionary spirit that had propelled him into power. It was always going to be a difficult task, and Eisner was not equipped with either the experience or the political acumen necessary to succeed. He was a coffeehouse philosopher, not a shrewd and wily political leader.[2] From the outset the coalition government was split over the fundamental problem caused by the revolution: was the new Republic going to be governed by a reformed and democratically elected parliament, or by revolutionary councils? While Eisner and Auer debated the structure of the political system, a rapid succession of domestic and foreign policy blunders undermined Eisner's position irretrievably.

Eisner assured landowners, financiers, and industrialists that he would not confiscate their holdings, and at the same time he introduced an eight-hour working day and improved working conditions for the proletariat. He placated the military by keeping returning soldiers and sailors on the state payroll, and by feeding and housing them at the state's expense. He also introduced female suffrage and committed to democratic elections where all men and women would determine the future of the new Republic and the shape of the National Assembly. More controversial was Eisner's plan to end the Catholic Church's authority in Bavarian schools. His most egregious error, however, was to say publicly that German militarism caused the World War.[3] Regarding himself an 'expert in the field of foreign affairs', Eisner sent a telegram on 10 November to the heads of the victorious powers – America, Britain, France and Italy – expressing his enthusiasm for President Woodrow Wilson's vision of a new international order and the League of Nations, and appealing to them and their peoples for a lenient peace.[4] His plea was ignored. The Allies preferred to deal with Berlin and the central German government rather than Munich and Bavaria. Eisner was not deterred by their silence. On 24 November, while attending a conference of the German states in Berlin hosted by Friedrich Ebert, the socialist leader of the new German republic, Eisner allowed the *Berliner Tageblatt* to publish secret documents held by the Bavarian Foreign Office on the origins of the war. His aim was to show Bavaria's innocence and Berlin's guilt for the outbreak of war in August 1914. The German government immediately issued formal denials that it had either wanted or caused the war, and Ebert publically berated Eisner for his diplomatic naivety and weakening Germany's bargaining position at the peace table. Eisner responded to Ebert's rebuke by breaking off relations with Berlin, though he fell short of declaring Bavaria an independent state. The Allies took little notice of this internal German spat. They did not need Eisner to tell them that Germany was responsible for the war. When the morning newspapers appeared across Germany on 25 November, it was also clear that Eisner had become the most controversial and reviled figure in Bavarian and German politics.[5]

Vorwärts, the left-wing SPD newspaper based in Berlin, ridiculed Eisner for living in a delusional world, and rejected his policies as having 'nothing to do with the gravity of our times'. The editorial went on to describe Eisner's government as little more than 'homemade theatre in the Munich-Schwabing style of Frank Wedekind, a Punch-and-Judy show in real life' that was destined to end quickly and in total failure.[6] Rosa Luxemburg added to Eisner's problems. She was bitingly scornful of his political stupidity, and even wrote to Eisner to express her hope that he would 'drown in the moral absolutes' of his beloved Immanuel Kant. Luxemburg further implored him to leave the revolution to the Marxists like herself and Karl Liebknecht.[7] In Munich, the *Münchener Neueste Nachrichten* accused Eisner of being 'simpleminded' to lay all the blame for the war on German militarists when everyone, even a half-wit, knew the French revanchists and Russian Pan-Slavists had long conspired to start the war. Eisner had, to be fair, approached the many challenges faced by his government as if they were little more than philosophical debates easily resolved by himself and his close literary friends at their *Stammtisch*, their reserved table at their favourite coffeehouse. His unorthodox notions of democracy owed little to either communism or socialism, but few believed or trusted Eisner that his new state could be built on ephemeral artistic notions of 'light, beauty, and reason'. The radical left felt betrayed and demanded a speedy escalation to the 'socialisation' of Bavaria along the lines of Lenin's achievements in Russia. Auer and the MSPD were fearful of the 'Bolshevisation of Bavaria', and the increasingly important role of the councils of workers, soldiers, and peasants in parliament as well as the economic and social life of the state. To counter the threat posed by the councils, Auer pressed Eisner to honour his promise and set the date for the Bavarian elections. Eisner hesitated because he knew that the majority of Bavarians were unlikely to vote for his party, and because the radical left viewed the elections as the 'death knell' for the revolution. By the end of November, Eisner had little choice but to call the elections. The Church and the liberal-but-with-monarchist-leanings *Bayerische Volkspartei* (Bavarian People's Party, BVP) were openly hostile, and Eisner could not run the government without the extensive organizational support provided by the MSPD which his tiny party the USPD lacked. At a cabinet meeting on 5 December, Eisner, under ever-increasing pressure but also following his conscience to fulfil his promise, set 12 January 1919 as the date for electing a new Landtag.[8]

These were not elections Eisner could win. On 30 November at a meeting of the Soldiers' Council, and later during the first week of February 1919 at the first post-war congress of the Second International in Bern, Eisner reiterated his claim that Germany was responsible for starting and prolonging the war.[9] Repeating these accusations not only alienated Eisner's cabinet colleague Erhard Auer and the MSPD, which had supported the war, it also united public opinion against him. Nationalists accused Eisner of treason, and in right-wing and radical *völkisch* circles he quickly became the target of vitriolic anti-Semitic attacks. Defamed as a 'Galician Jew', even Thomas Mann wondered how long Munich would 'put up with being governed by Eisner and his band of Jewish scribblers'.[10] It was common knowledge in Munich that no one in Eisner's clique of advisors and confidants was Bavarian. In fact, Eisner and his mob had become so offensive to former officers and servants in the Royal household, as well as many common citizens, that during the days leading up to the election hundreds of them paraded under Eisner's office window at the Ministry of Foreign Affairs on the Promenadeplatz shouting, 'We want a Bavarian! We want a Bavarian!'[11]

Ironically, it was another non-Bavarian, the Saxon-born Turkish national Rudolf von Sebottendorff, the founder and leader of the Munich chapter of the Thule Gesellschaft (Thule Society), who led Bavaria's counter-revolution. The Thule Society served as a focal point for ethnic-chauvinist and nationalist circles and established conservatives. Its headquarters was in the Hotel Vier Jahreszeiten (Four Seasons) on Maximilianstraße 17 (now 4), one of the most exclusive streets in Munich. At its height the Thule's membership exceeded 1,500 and included many of the most influential and wealthy members of Munich society, including the publishing magnate Julius Lehmann, the *völkisch* poet and playwright Dietrich Eckart, and future leaders in the *Nationalsozialistische Deutsche Arbeiterpartei* (NSDAP): Hans Frank, Rudolf Heβ, and Alfred Rosenberg. Membership was restricted to those who could prove they were of pure 'Aryan blood', and the society's twin mandate was to combat the Jewish-Bolshevik terror that had gripped Munich at the end of the war and encourage the rebirth of a pure *völkisch* utopia. To promote its objectives the Thule had its own newspaper, the *Münchener Beobachter*, and its own publishing house which printed and distributed leaflets urging the establishment of a right-wing dictatorship. Three days into the revolution, on 10 November, Lehmann convinced the Thule Society to establish the first Freikorps, the Kampfbund Thule (Combat League Thule), which obtained arms from the Bavarian Army Command and hid them in the Thule's rooms at the Four Seasons hotel and at Lehmann's publishing house at Paul-Heyse-Straße 26. A couple of amateurish attempts to abduct Eisner in December ended in failure and police raids on the Thule's headquarters. Lehmann and a number of others were arrested for counter-revolutionary activities and spent several weeks in Stadelheim prison, located in Giesing, a southern working class district of Munich.[12]

A week before the Bavarian elections, on Sunday 5 January, the Thule Society established the Deutsche Arbeiterpartei (German Workers' Party, DAP) the precursor to the NSDAP. Karl Harrer, a sports journalist and a Thulist, and Anton Drexler, a machinist and guest member of the Thule Society, had formed a small debating society called the Political Workers' Circle in October 1918. With Sebottendorff's encouragement and the Thule's financial support they turned their little group into a political party. The first meeting was held in the restaurant at the Fürstenfelder-Hof, a small hotel on Fürstenfelderstraße 14, a short five minute walk south-west of the Marienplatz, the main square in central Munich. The party was created to attract the working classes to the counter-revolution and to promote the establishment of a new *völkisch* state. The party held its second meeting on 18 January at the Thule's headquarters in the Four Seasons. Harrer was elected chairman and Drexler deputy chairman and leader of the party's chapter (its only local chapter) in Munich. Meetings were held regularly at the Thule's headquarters or the Sterneckerbräu, a small beer hall favoured by soldiers and nationalisits, on the Tal 54 (now Tal 38). The DAP's evening meetings usually featured a guest speaker who addressed small groups that very rarely numbered more than thirty on familiar topics denouncing capitalism and Jews. Fundamentally the DAP was still a small debating club and it did not play a role in the January elections.[13]

Election Day, Sunday 12 January 1919, was bright and sunny in Munich and throughout Bavaria. Turnout at the polls was high. Some 86 per cent of Bavaria's eligible voters cast their ballots, and many of them voted for the first time.[14] Among them were women, who accounted for 53.4 per cent of the total electorate. The minimum voting age for men had been reduced from 26 to 21 years of age, and 70 per cent of the men who voted did so for the first time. Despite the unprecedented number of ballots cast, more than three times the total recorded in the last election in 1912, the result was both predicted and followed traditional confessional (Catholic, Protestant, etc.) and regional lines. The Majority Socialists (MSPD) won 33 per cent of the vote and did particularly well in Munich taking ten of the twelve precincts. The Bavarian People's Party (BVP) took the remaining two, and did well in the rural areas, taking 35 per cent of the total vote, but even with Catholic support they could not form a majority in the Landtag. For Eisner and the USPD the election was a political disaster. They attained just 2.5 per cent of the popular vote. Despite the crushing defeat, Eisner still held out hope of leading a socialist coalition government. The election, according to Eisner, offered a stark choice between 'a socialistic or a bourgeois regime'. He also viewed himself as the best placed candidate to form a unity government that excluded the anarchists and far left, and the radical right. He also had not given up on finding a place for the councils in the government, and pursuing a substantive programme of socialisation. Three days after the Bavarian elections ultra-nationalist soldiers murdered Rosa Luxemburg and Karl Liebknecht in Berlin. Eisner saw in this atrocity an omen that Bavaria needed him to provide his unique version of conciliatory and socially responsible political leadership.[15]

Auer and the moderate socialists rejected Eisner's offer to stay on as Premier. Auer was confident that with support from the liberals and other moderate parties he could form a progressive majority in the Landtag. The BVP and the Catholic press restated the obvious: Eisner had lost. They demanded that 'this Jew, who is predisposed towards the Marxists, should no longer stand at the head of a *Volksstaat*'.[16] Until the new Landtag met, Eisner and his revolutionary Cabinet, the same one he had formed on 8 November, would remain in place and continue to run the government. No date had been set for the opening session of the new Landtag, when it would elect the next Prime Minister and he would appoint a new cabinet. Eisner's hopes of garnering support for his scheme of a united Socialist front during the transition period were also dashed by his friends and colleagues on the Left. Gustav Landauer, a humanist anarchist and a leading member of the Revolutionary Workers' Council, despised the Landtag and urged his friend Eisner to put his trust in the revolutionary councils to complete the socialisation of Bavaria. Playwright and prominent revolutionary Ernst Toller, the anarchist Erich Mühsam, and the two communist party (KPD) leaders in Munich, Max Levien and Eugen Leviné, went even further. They told Eisner to ignore the result of the election, seize power and complete the objectives of the revolution just as Lenin had done in Russia. Power politics not compromise was the only way forward if the revolution was to succeed. Mühsam summed up the way forward with one short sentence: '*den Räten gehört die Macht*' ('power belongs to the councils').[17] The more the left-wing radicals pressed Eisner to meet their demands the more Auer and his colleagues were determined to end Eisner's premiership and deny the councils any executive or legislative role. On 12 February, while Eisner was in Bern attending the Second International, his Cabinet met in Munich and set 21 February as the date for the opening session of the new Landtag.

Eisner's time was just about up. The right saw Eisner as a dangerous radical and the left no longer had confidence in him. Politically, he was both isolated and alone, and in no position to forestall his eventual resignation. On 20 February the Cabinet met at length, altered the constitution so that they and not the premier exercised 'supreme executive power' in the Landtag, and told Eisner that he must resign. Later that evening, Auer confided in a friend that Eisner had agreed to resign.[18]

Eisner's Assassination and the Second Revolution

E isner spent the early morning of 21 February in his office in the Foreign Ministry preparing his statement for the opening session of the new Landtag. Just before 10 am he placed the text of his speech in his briefcase. Accompanied by his two secretaries, Friedrich Fenchenbach and Benno Merkle, and a pair of armed guards, Eisner left his office to make the short walk to the Palais Preysing and announce his resignation. He never arrived. Lying in wait for him in a secluded doorway at Promenadestraße 1 (now Kardinal-Faulhaber-Straße 1) was Count Anton Arco auf Valley, a young Bavarian cavalry officer and Munich University law student, ultra-nationalist and anti-Semite, who hated the revolution and its 'non-German, Jewish-Bolshevik' leader.[1] Arco-Valley fired two shots at point blank range into Eisner's back and head; he was dead before he collapsed on the pavement. One of Eisner's guards shot Arco-Valley in the leg as he attempted to run away. He shot him a further four times in the chest, mouth, and neck as he lay on the ground, but somehow did not kill him. The other guard ran to the Landtag building to tell the assembly what had just happened outside. Frau Else Eisner, who was in the central chamber waiting to hear her husband's resignation speech, fainted. At the same time a member of the public in the visitors' gallery shouted: 'Revenge for Eisner! Down with Auer', instantly starting a rumour that Auer was responsible for Eisner's assassination. Before the Landtag descended into chaos the delegates adjourned the opening session for an hour.[2]

Outside, the police had arrived at the murder scene. Arco-Valley was rushed to hospital where his life was saved by the renowned Munich surgeon Ernst Ferdinand Sauerbruch. Eisner's body had also been carried away, and a large crowd of ex-soldiers and workers had gathered around the place where he had fallen. Sobbing women attempted to mop up his blood. The public mood was changing. The Prime Minister who had become universally loathed in Munich, now dead, quickly became the tragic hero of the proletariat. When the Landtag resumed, Erhard Auer delivered a short eulogy praising Eisner as 'a man of the most unsullied idealism'.[3] Auer had just returned to his seat when a man burst into the chamber and shot him, seriously wounding the prime minister elect in the chest. This second nascent assassin, Alois Lindner, was an unemployed butcher and a member of the workers' council. Before leaving the chamber

Lindner fired more shots at the BVP delegates, killing one of them, and killing a Landtag porter who had tried to disarm him. Adding to the madness, another armed man began shooting from the visitors' gallery, killing a second BVP delegate. The first session of the new Landtag ended in panic as the assembly fled in terror onto the streets.[4]

Auer was taken to the same hospital and treated by the same surgeon as Arco-Valley. Both Eisner's assassination and Auer's sudden exit from politics galvanised the left, but also exacerbated the tensions between the moderate and radical socialists, and polarised and radicalised politics in Bavaria.[5] Had Eisner been allowed to resign, as he had intended, Auer would have been the new prime minister leading a popularly elected parliamentary government. Instead a *Zentralrat* (Central Council), an ad hoc all-socialist executive committee drawn from the MSPD, USPD, and the KPD, was formed the day after Eisner's death to govern Munich and Bavaria. Ernst Niekisch, a MSPD delegate and chairman of the combined Bavarian workers' councils, was chosen as chairman. He suited all of the others in the *Zentralrat* because he was neither a foe of the council system nor an enemy of parliamentarianism. The *Zentralrat*'s first formal action was to establish a smaller internal committee to foster unity between all of the socialist parties and the councils. Their main problems – agreeing the date to recall and the role of the Landtag – remained unresolved. If the *Zentralrat* recognised the Landtag it was doubtful that the councils would recognise the *Zentralrat*.[6]

Addressing immediate practical matters was easier for the *Zentralrat* than resolving internal political disagreements. To safeguard the revolution from any reactionary response to Eisner's murder, the *Zentralrat* declared three days of mourning in the form of a general strike, imposed a curfew in Munich, established an armed Red Guard to patrol the city, closed the Ludwig-Maximilians-Universität (because students were already looking upon Count Arco as their hero), shut down all non-left-wing newspapers, and took fifty middle and upper class hostages to serve as a sort of 'human shield' for the Socialist state. The *Zentralrat* decreed that three hostages would be shot for every revolutionary harmed.[7] One of the hostages was Lieutenant Hermann Sedlmeier, a Thulist who had led one of the failed attempts to abduct Eisner in December 1918. The Red Guards forced him to make a public apology for harassing Eisner, and also because it was another member of the officer corps who had murdered him.[8] These were the sorts of radical gestures that Sebottendorff and other Thulists feared would happen in the wake of Count Arco's impulsive assassination of Eisner.[9] Count Arco was not even a Thulist. He had been refused membership of the Thule Society because his mother was Jewish. This did not stop Thulists from applauding his marksmanship. Melanie Lehmann, wife of the pan-German publisher Julius Lehmann, said that she and her friends 'breathed more easily' now that Eisner was dead because they believed he was 'an evil spirit'.[10] Other members of the society desecrated the shrine that had been erected around the place where Eisner had died, sprinkling it with a mixture of flour and the urine of a dog in season. Soon every stray male dog in Munich was urinating on the sacred site.[11]

Class warfare had been unleashed in Munich, and many feared that a violent Bolshevik revolution would soon follow. Niekisch was put under pressure by members of his own party (MSPD) along with officials from the BVP and Catholic parties to end the Draconian measures approved by the *Zentralrat*. Not everyone on the left agreed. At a massive meeting held in the Deutsches Theater on Saturday 22 February, the Munich councils demanded the revolution be intensified, and that Bavaria be proclaimed a *Räterepublik*. For the moderate socialists, Eisner's upcoming funeral on 26 February was seen as an opportunity to restore much-needed calm and order. Niekisch hoped it would encourage all of the socialist parties to work together to achieve the 'fulfilment of the legacy of the precious deceased'.[12]

Eisner's funeral was a state occasion.[13] The *Zentralrat* decreed a day of mourning for the whole of Bavaria. Public buildings flew black and red flags, and in Munich the Neues Rathaus (New Town Hall) was draped in black and church bells rang incessantly. More than 100,000 people attended the funeral, including Hitler, who having just returned to Munich from Traunstein was part of the army's large, official delegation.[14] At 9 am, to the muffled drums of twenty marching bands the funeral cortèges set off from the Theresienwiese for the Ostfriedhof, the old city cemetery east of the Isar in the district of Au-Haidhausen. Eisner's casket rested on an ornate royal carriage pulled by magnificent cart horses more regularly employed delivering beer to the city's beer halls. State officials in closed ranks walked directly behind, followed by thousands of peasants who marched in native dress. The funeral was an unprecedented public outpouring of grief but also a massive demonstration of united revolutionary force in the city. At the cemetery Eisner's friend Gustav Landauer delivered the eulogy. He compared Eisner to Jesus, lamenting that both misunderstood prophets had been killed by stupidity and greed.[15] Later, Heinrich Mann declared that 'Eisner, in just over one hundred days of rule, had more ideas, brought more joy, showed more plain common sense, and stimulated more intellectual energy than others had in the fifty years that went before.'[16] This hyperbole did not disguise the fact that socio-economic conditions in Munich had steadily worsened since the end of the war, and that Eisner's political revolution had been a failure.

The day before Eisner's funeral the *Zentralrat* convened a Congress of Bavarian Councils to debate whether the councils or parliament should govern Bavaria. Food shortages, rising unemployment (more than 40,000 by the end of February 1919), acute municipal debt approaching 100 million Marks, and rising inflation all required the government's urgent attention.[17] Walter Löwenfeld, representing the MSPD, thought there could be a role for the councils but he insisted on the restoration of the Landtag to rescue Bavaria from its current economic and political crisis. Max Levien, a Moscow-born Jew and Spartacist Leader, ridiculed Löwenfeld for his unimaginative return to the old parliamentary and bureaucratic structure. Levien demanded that the council system be reorganized to complete a Bolshevik revolution. Tempers ran high between the moderate socialists and the communists. They were at an impasse. Levien and the other communists vehemently rejected any political compromise. Nonetheless the Congress persisted with the debate, conducted over many nights at Munich's main beer halls: the Augustiner Großgaststätte, Hofbräuhaus, Löwenbräukeller, and Mathäserbräu in the centre of the city, and the Franziskaner-Keller, Hofbraü-Keller, Münchner-Kindl-Keller, and Wagnerbräu in the brewery district east of the Isar. At a meeting on Friday 28 February, the anarchist Erich Mühsam proposed a motion that 'Bavaria be declared a socialistic soviet republic'. It was defeated by a vote of 234 to 70. It was also clear that the majority of delegates still preferred a parliamentary government over the revolutionary councils. Sensing that a solution was possible, the Congress approved an alternative motion that advocated a recall of the Landtag as soon as possible. A number of the communists stormed out of the meeting, and over the subsequent nights there was violence on the streets and in some of the beer halls, mainly the Mathäserbräu and the Wagnerbräu.[18]

On 8 March 1919 the Congress met for the last time. It commanded the Landtag to select a new cabinet and draw up a constitution on parliamentary lines. Ten days later the incoming prime minister, the MSPD leader Johannes Hoffmann, a school teacher and former minister of culture and education in Eisner's cabinet, took charge of the new government. He opened the new Landtag with praise for his predecessor: 'the political act which Prime Minister Eisner wanted to undertake on 21 February is now accomplished.'[19] Hoffmann's declaration that parliamentary democracy was now safely established in Bavaria was premature. Levien and his communist colleagues continued to see Hoffmann's government as a betrayal of the true interests of the working class. Their ambition to create a *Räterepublik* in Bavaria still burned brightly. The spark that reignited the Bavarian soviet revolution came unexpectedly from a series of domestic and foreign events.

The Hoffmann Interregnum and the Bavarian Soviet Republics

From 2 to 6 March, Moscow hosted the first congress of the Third International. Communist and Socialist leaders from around the world came to hear Lenin reject the democratic reforms advocated by the now defunct and discredited Second International, and call for a worldwide Bolshevik revolution. To lead the way forward the Congress unanimously approved the establishment of the Communist International (Comintern). Communists in Berlin were the first to rally to Lenin's call to arms. Radical left-wing military groups besieged the police headquarters on the Alexanderplatz. They were joined by the Red Soldiers' League and soon the violence spread throughout the eastern part of the city. Gustav Noske, the Defence Minister in the Ebert-Scheidemann SPD government, had to call on 30,000 right-wing Freikorps troops to help the Reichswehr (the army) defend the German capital. By the time order was restored more than 1,500 revolutionaries were dead and another 10,000 wounded. News of the uprising spread throughout the country but it did not immediately trigger another revolution in Munich. It was news on 22 March of Béla Kun's popular front of communists and socialists establishing a Soviet Republic in Hungary that inspired Munich's radical left. Emboldened by the events in Budapest, and Lenin's call for others to follow the Hungarians' example, the ultra-leftists in the USPD decided to move against Hoffmann's government. First, Niekisch called an extraordinary meeting of the *Zentralrat* minus Hoffmann and the communists to discuss the 'Second Revolution'. Then on 1 April a newly formed council representing the unemployed met at the Münchner-Kindl-Keller to elect an executive, and petition the government to end inflation and create jobs. Across the city at the Löwenbräukeller, more than 3,000 revolutionary soldiers demanded a Communist government based on the soviet system and the immediate formation of a Red Army. Sensing the increase in public discontent and a sharp decline in his government's authority, Hoffmann notified his cabinet that the Landtag would return to work on Tuesday 8 April.[1]

Niekisch and the USPD rump of the *Zentralrat* immediately opposed the summons to reconvene the Landtag, citing Hoffmann's promise not to recall parliament before the summer and because the role of the councils still had to be resolved. The Munich barracks' council agreed with the *Zentralrat*, and declared that the army would not protect the Landtag. Further pressure against the Hoffmann government came from the Augsburg Council, which called for the establishment of a Bavarian Soviet Republic based on an alliance with the soviet governments of Russia and Hungary, and a radical programme of socialisation. Delegates from Augsburg travelled to Munich on 4 April to present their demands to Hoffmann, but he was in Berlin conferring with the Reich government on how to forestall a communist revolution in Munich. Later that evening at Munich's Löwenbraükeller a mass meeting chaired by Niekisch and Ernst Toller amplified the Augsburg resolutions, and the two socialist leaders restated their aim to establish a *Räterepublik* (literally, 'council republic'). Over the next three days leftist zealots ran around Munich shouting Bolshevik slogans – 'all power to the soviets' – singing the Internationale, and threatening ordinary citizens going about their daily business. Bands of 'red' soldiers were even more menacing loitering about at the Hauptbahnhof, the Marienplatz, and on street corners. Apprehension of a vengeful communist takeover was palpable throughout the city.[2]

The First Bavarian Soviet Republic

On Saturday 5 April, in a series of meetings held across Munich in the main beer halls, the councils voted in favour of turning Bavaria into a soviet republic. Hoffmann's cabinet resigned en masse. Ernst Schneppenhorst, Hoffmann's military minister, attempted to save the democratically elected Republic and prevent a violent revolution by proposing an executive-led Soviet. He chaired a meeting at the Bayerische Kriegsministerium (Bavarian War Ministry) on the Ludwigstraβe with the remaining members of Hoffmann's government and about 150 representatives from the socialist parties, the communists, and the councils, to obtain their support for his plan. The communists vehemently opposed this sham *Putsch*. Eugen Leviné, the communist leader, had seen through Schneppenhorst's stratagem, and reminded the assembled delegates that a genuine soviet could only be proclaimed by the councils, preferably communist-led councils. Angry and frustrated, Schneppenhorst's riposte was that the assembly did not need lessons from a 'Jewish goblin' from Russia about how to run the government. The meeting ended with an agreement to postpone the pronouncement of the Soviet Republic for forty-eight hours while the delegates gauged popular opinion for Schneppenhorst's plan in the provincial centres. On Sunday morning Schneppenhorst travelled to his native Nürnberg. He addressed an emergency SPD regional conference, which strongly rejected his 'radical experiment' and instructed him to return to Munich and withdraw his call for a soviet.[1]

It was too late. Back in Munich on Sunday 6 April, a group of idealistic anarchists, café intellectuals, soviet delegates, trade unionists, USPD members and a few SPD dissidents assembled in the queen's bedchamber in the Wittelsbach Palace. Niekisch in his capacity as chairman of the *Zentralrat* chaired the meeting, ably assisted by the anarchists Gustav Landauer and Erich Mühsam, and the USPD leader Ernst Toller. Through the night and into the early morning hours of 7 April these bohemian political dilettantes organized themselves as a government, and proclaimed the creation of a *Räterepublik*, that later became known as the First Bavarian Soviet Republic. Hoffmann and Schneppenhorst slipped out of Munich, and from Nürnberg issued a statement that the government of the Bavarian Free State had not resigned and remained the sole legitimate power in Bavaria. Leaflets stating Hoffmann's claim were dropped by government airplanes flying over Munich.[2] A few days later Hoffmann set up his government in exile in Bamberg in northern Bavaria, which became the centre for all anti-Soviet activists and the headquarters for counter-insurgency operations.

Conscious of the need to move quickly, the Bavarian Soviet Republic's newly appointed commissars issued a flurry of proclamations and regulations to usher in the new Socialist era. Banks were nationalized, sweeping agricultural reforms and plans for the collectivisation of Bavarian farms were announced, rents were frozen, and unused lofts were to be made freely available to artists for studio space. Landauer, the commissar for art, education, propaganda and a host of other things, opened Bavaria's universities to anyone over the age of 18, abolished fees, and stripped professors of their titles. He also ordered the newspapers to publish poetry rather than political commentary on their front pages. The commissar for military affairs, Wilhelm Reichart, an ex-waiter, formed a Red Army but waited until 11 April to order the bourgeoisie to surrender its arms. Despite the plethora of important matters to address, someone found time to legislate a change in the spelling of Bayern to Biern, the German name for Bavaria. Yet as odd as some of these measures were, they paled into the ordinary when compared with the actions of Dr Franz Lipp, the commissar for foreign affairs. Lipp declared war on Switzerland for refusing his request for foreign aid. He also wrote to the Pope to denounce Gustave Noske, claiming that 'the hairy gorilla hands' of the Reich's Defence Minister were 'dripping with blood' after his brutal suppression of the Spartacist uprising in Berlin. Yet most bizarrely he sent a telegram to Lenin to tell him that 'the fugitive Hoffmann … has taken with him the key to my ministry toilet'. Lenin was not impressed, and he advised Toller, who had replaced Niekisch as the head of state after only two days in office, to remove Lipp before he did some real harm.[3]

Many Münchners were horrified by the comic opera that was the new Soviet regime. They dubbed it the Schwabing Soviet because of the many crackpot schemes that emanated from the idealistic but politically inexperienced literati who were more at home running the world from Café Stefanie than they were serving as responsible government ministers. On Wednesday 9 April, at a huge rally in the Mathäserbräu to generate enthusiasm for the new Soviet Republic, Eugene Leviné attempted without success to convince Toller to turn over power to him and the communists, a genuine Soviet, to complete the revolution successfully and save it from the expected reactionary backlash. Support for Toller's regime was diminishing quickly. Outside Munich and a small triangle of outlying areas bounded by Augsburg, Garmisch, and Rosenheim, resistance was building. Schneppenhorst had 600 north-Bavarian soldiers, which he moved down to Ingolstadt, thirty miles north of Munich, in readiness to liberate the Bavarian capital. Inside Munich, Hoffmann had a semi-secret pro-Republican

Freikorps, the Schutzwehr, a force of a few hundred men commanded by Alfred Seyffertitz. The Thule Society was also busy recruiting anti-Soviet forces and infiltrating the Munich garrisons with informants and spies. Using its newspaper the *Beobachter*, the Thule stirred up support for a White reactionary counter-revolution to cleanse Munich and Bavaria of the degenerate and dangerous left-wing radicals and communists. It exposed Landauer's affair with Eisner's widow, and called Max Levien, the Bavarian communist leader, syphilitic. It also pointed out that virtually all of the communist leadership in Munich was Jewish. Jewish-Bolshevism, the *Beobachter* emphasised, had to be destroyed to halt the cultural, economic, and social decline in Bavaria. Lost in the considerable confusion was a statement made by the Jewish community in Munich decrying the popular belief that 'the Jews were the driving force of the revolution.'[4]

Initially Hoffmann was uneasy with the Thule's anti-Semitic and racist tactics, but he needed all the support he could get. Ebert wanted to send Reich troops from Berlin to Bavaria to crush the Soviet, but Hoffmann preferred an all-Bavarian solution. He toyed with starving the Reds out by blockading Munich, and also negotiating an end to the crisis through his former cabinet colleague Ernst Niekisch, but the quickest and most likely decisive solution was a military coup. Hoffmann planned his Putsch for 13 April, Palm Sunday. Days before aircraft from Bamberg dropped propaganda leaflets over Munich calling on the citizens of the city to 'Rise up!', 'take courage', and 'overthrow the tyranny of foreigners and fantasists'.[5]

On Sunday morning just before dawn, detachments of Seyffertitz's Schutzwehr secured the Hauptbahnhof and stormed the Royal Residenz where they captured Mühsam, Lipp, and other members of the Soviet leadership. By 9 am Seyffertitz announced he had control of the city and that the Munich garrisons were behind him. This was an overly optimistic assessment of the situation. Mühsam's wife had avoided capture and warned Toller about the attempted Putsch. Soldiers loyal to the Soviet began to form up on the Theresienwiese and prepared to retake the city. Seyffertitz's men waited in vain for reinforcement from Ingolstadt, unaware that their dispatch rider had been captured by Red Army soldiers and news of the city's capture had not reached Schneppenhorst. By mid-afternoon fighting had broken out on the Marienplatz. The Red Army aided by armed council members and soldiers from the First Bavarian Infantry Regiment drove Seyffertitz's men out of the city centre to their final redoubt at the Hauptbahnhof. Five hours of heavy fighting at the main train station left more than twenty men dead and over one hundred wounded. By 9 pm it was all over. Seyffertitz's remaining men escaped either on trains north to Bamberg and Nürnberg or they melted away into the beer hall searching crowds wandering about the city.[6]

The Palm Sunday Putsch signalled the end of the First Bavarian Soviet Republic, but not in the manner that Hoffmann had hoped. While the fighting still raged around the Hauptbahnhof, Eugen Leviné was presiding over a meeting in the cavernous ground floor beer hall at the Hofbräuhaus. The men he addressed were packed in shoulder to shoulder at the long wooden tables drinking litres of *Hofbräu-Helles* out of heavy stone *Bierkruge*. They were communists and council members of the newly formed *Betriebs- und Soldatenräte Münchens* (Factory and Soldiers' Councils of Munich). Leviné told them that the day's fighting confirmed the urgency with which they needed to act, set up a genuine Communist-led Soviet regime, and replace Toller and his band of poets with a Communist *Vollzugsrat* (Executive Committee). The council duly elected Leviné as their chairman, just as Eisner had been elected leader of the councils at the Mathäserbräu back on 7 November. Thunderous applause and cheering filled the Hofbräuhaus when Leviné, flanked by his Russian born, Jewish Bolshevik lieutenants, Max Levien and Towia Axelrod, proclaimed the new Soviet republic with the words: 'Today Bavaria has finally established the dictatorship of the proletariat … Long live the world revolution! Long live the Bavarian Soviet Republic! … Long live Communism!'[7] Toller's 'Schwabing Soviet' had lasted a mere six days.

The Second Bavarian Soviet Republic

The four-man *Vollzugsrat* immediately imposed a dusk-to-dawn curfew to be enforced by summary executions. An indefinite general strike was declared. Toller was arrested. The Munich police were disarmed, their weapons distributed amongst those who pledged loyalty to the new regime. Armed patrols fanned out across the city, to cow the bourgeoisie and enforce the *Vollzugsrat*'s revolutionary decrees. Private and business bank accounts were seized. Homes were searched and stripped of food, valuables, and guns. When Thomas Mann's house was searched, he gave the revolutionary looters 200 marks and asked them to leave his books and writing desk.[1] The new regime also rounded up hundreds of aristocratic and middle-class hostages, incarcerating them in Stadelheim Prison. Rudolf Egelhofer, a 26-year-old North German sailor who actively participated in the Kiel naval mutiny, was appointed commander of a new hastily assembled Red Guard of 10,000 men. His force eventually numbered as many as 20,000 men, all volunteers recruited from demobilised soldiers, unemployed workers, and even Italian and Russian former prisoners of war. Many of them 'signed up' to defend the revolution and the city because Egelhofer offered them generous amounts of food and money. When the real fighting started in May the vast majority of the Red Guards changed their minds. Preferring life over death they returned to their more mundane civilian lives.[2]

Leviné, Levien, Axelrod, and Egelhofer were cold, callous, and fanatical Bolsheviks, fully committed to seeing Lenin's project through in Munich and Bavaria. Their lack of empathy for anyone who did not fully embrace their extreme ideology led to untold brutality, hardship, and misery for the people of Munich, including the proletariat the Communist leaders purported to represent. When told that there was a shortage of food, especially milk, because the farmers refused to deliver it to the 'Red swine', Leviné laughed it off: 'What does it matter if for a few weeks less milk reaches Munich. Most of it goes to the children of the bourgeoisie anyway. We are not interested in keeping them alive. No harm if they die – they'd only grow into enemies of the proletariat.' By the end of Easter week opposition to 'the Russian Jews' was so widespread in Munich that even Toller and other more moderate socialists knew they had to challenge Leviné and his ardent disciples before the whole Soviet experiment ended in carnage.[3]

News of the atrocities committed by the Reds in Munich reached Hoffmann in Bamberg as well as Ebert and the Reich government in Berlin. After a detachment of the Thule's Combat League was chased out of Dachau on 16 April, Hoffmann reluctantly acknowledged that he needed outside assistance to retake Munich. He appealed to Bavarians and others to establish a true *Volkswehr* (people's army) to halt the 'rages of the Russian terror' and 'wipe out the alien elements responsible for the Munich disgrace'.[4] Württemberg offered Hoffmann a Freikorps of 3,750 men, and Noske authorised 20,000 Reichswehr troops (of which only 7,500 actually arrived, including the much feared 2nd Marine Brigade under the command of Hermann Ehrhardt) to move into Bavaria. The Thule Society, right under the noses of Leviné and Egelhofer in Munich, was also busy raising funds, procuring weapons, and recruiting university students and hundreds of Great War veterans for the Freikorps. The most important one being the Bavarian Freikorps, led by Franz Ritter von Epp, a former commander of the Bavarian Life Guards. Captain Ernst Röhm, one of von Epp's more able and committed officers, and later the head of Hitler's *Sturmabteilung* (Storm Troopers, SA), looked forward to giving Munich 'a thorough cleansing'.[5] Rudolf Heβ, soon another key figure in Hitler's inner circle and later deputy Führer, was the Thule Society's most successful organizer of aid for the Freikorps, getting money, men, and weapons out of Munich.

Berlin's support came with a price. Reich Defence Minister Gustav Noske placed Prussian General Burghard von Oven in supreme command of all the White counter-revolutionary forces with explicit orders to crush the Soviet republic. On 23 April, Noske issued his instructions for the campaign: 'The operational objective is Munich. In Munich the power of the legally constituted Bavarian regime [Hoffmann's government] is to be restored. ... As soon as Munich is occupied and the resistance in Munich is extinguished, the Bavarian General Arnold Ritter von Möhl is to assume command in Munich.'[6] Munich-born Möhl commanded a mixed Bavarian force numbering 22,000 men – the Bavarian Freikorps (Freikorps Epp, Friekorps Oberland, and other smaller formations) and the Volkswehr. The Bavarians, wearing a mixture of military field grey uniforms and Tracht (traditional attire, such as Lederhosen, that celebrate Bavaria's alpine and farming culture) were a colourful sight. By 28 April the combined White forces numbering approximately 35,000 men had surrounded Munich, and prepared for the decisive assault on the city.

Tensions were running high in Munich during the last week of April, especially when the Soviet authorities finally became aware of the extensive counter-revolutionary activity being coordinated by the Thule Society in the Hotel Vier Jahreszeiten. Tipped off by a hotel clerk and guided by a floor plan of the Thule's rooms, the Red Guards raided the hotel on 26 April. They found anti-Semitic materials, weapons, and membership lists. They also arrested a number of Thule members still in the hotel, including Gräfin Haila von Westarp, and Gustav Franz Maria, Prinz von Thurn und Taxis. Dietrich Eckart, soon to be Hitler's most influential mentor, and to whom the Führer would dedicate

Mein Kampf, arrived at the hotel shortly after the raid began, but acting on a 'sixth sense' he stayed in his car and drove away unnoticed and unharmed. The Thule's own extensive spy network responded to the raid quickly, warning members of the Society to avoid the Four Seasons and to lie low. Sebottendorff, the Thule leader, along with his mistress Kathe Bierbaumer, evaded arrest and slipped out of Munich using forged documents bearing the signature of Egelhofer, the commander of the Red Guards.[7]

Few if anyone in Munich expected the impending attack on the city to be anything other than a revenge filled blood-bath. In an effort to mitigate the mass slaughter, Toller called out the *Vollzugsrat* during a council meeting at the Hofbräuhaus on 26 April. He condemned the Communist leadership as 'a disaster for the working people of Bavaria', and further accused them of criminal incompetence: 'Unable to construct anything they simply destroy in the most senseless manner.'[8] Why, Toller asked, had they not negotiated an end to the siege with the Hoffmann government, and thereby saved the lives of the Munich proletariat from terrible carnage? Was it because they were Russian, blinded by their perverse doctrinaire Marxism, and their delusional sense of entitlement as Lenin's emissaries personally responsible for completing the Bolshevik revolution in Bavaria? Toller further denounced Leviné, Levien, and Axelrod for assisting a number of foreign Communists to escape from Munich before the battle began. To the cheers of many council members, Toller ended his tirade by declaring: 'We Bavarians are not Russians!' The Factory and Soldiers' Councils responded to Toller's speech with a vote of censure against the *Vollzugsrat* and proclaimed a new council-led government. The *Vollzugsrat*, for its part, refused to recognise either Toller's accusations or the Council's resolution, and immediately placed Munich under the direct control of the Red Guards. Leviné and his cronies eventually resigned before the end of April, but not before Egelhofer and the Red Army were the ones running the city. Orders were issued to man the barricades.[9]

The much anticipated assault by the White forces began on 29 April in the eastern suburbs of Munich, the villages of Dachau and Starnberg, and north of the city in the vicinity of Schloss Schleißheim. From the start it was clear that the battle would be characterised by butchery, class and racial hatred, and a thirst for vengeance. Eight Red Guards who had surrendered in Dachau were shot. Twenty medical orderlies attempting to treat wounded Red soldiers at Schloss Schleißheim were killed, and both workers and former Russian prisoners of war were summarily shot when they accidentally came into contact with White fighters. When news of these brutal acts reached the headquarters of the Red Guards in Munich, Egelhofer was put under pressure by his lieutenants to retaliate in kind, and execute hostages being held in the Luitpold-Gymnasium, a secondary school in the eastern part of the old city, Altstadt-Lehel. Members of the Thule Society, among many others, were being held at the gymnasium by soldiers of the 1st Red Infantry Division, the most loyal and fanatical supporters of the Second Soviet Republic. Fritz Seidel, their commander, viewed the Thulists as his 'most dangerous prisoners', and that 'all aristocrats in his custody deserved death'.[10] On the morning of 30 April, a courier arrived at the Luitpold with orders from Egelhofer to execute by firing squad two Prussian cavalrymen, both recently captured outside Munich and who were alleged to have taken part in the murders of the Spartacist leaders Karl Liebknecht and Rosa Luxemburg in Berlin. Their executions in the school's courtyard were followed by eight more, seven members of the Thule Society,[11] including Countess Westarp and Prince von Thurn und Taxis, and a Jewish art professor named Berger who had been apprehended while tearing down a Communist poster. Just before Countess Westarp was shot, the only woman executed, one of the soldiers who murdered her is purported to have said: 'a bullet is too good for you. A knife should be plunged into your body to exit on the other side. Too bad mine is too short.'[12] It was not entirely clear if he was referring to his penis or his knife. In the calamitous history of the Bavarian revolutions these killings proved to be the most senseless act of a regime characterised by its stupidity. They 'turned the civil war into a virtual slaughter'.[13]

News of the *Geiselmord* (hostage murder) shocked and revolted the citizens of Munich, unnerved the Reds, and enraged the White forces. Erich Wollenberg, a Red officer, noted that 'panic and revulsion spread through the ranks'. Many of the revolutionary fighters discarded their red armbands and threw their weapons into the Isar. 'Morale collapsed entirely'.[14] Fewer than 2,000 Red Guards opposed the White units when they entered the city on 1 May. General von Oven had planned his final assault for 2 May, in part to avoid creating Red martyrs for future May Day observances. His attack was preceded by another air drop of leaflets that warned the citizens of Munich to 'Avoid streets and squares. The government troops break all resistance pitilessly.' The Prussian commander's meticulous planning collapsed when the Bavarian Freikorps, after they learned of the Luitpold murders, broke ranks and stormed the city. The Ehrhardt Brigade marched into Munich with the *Hakenkreuz* (swastika) painted on their helmets, and von Epp's Freikorps had stencilled the Death's Head on the radiator grates of their lorries. Opposition to the White Guards was light but the lack of serious resistance did not prevent some of them from behaving like crazed vigilantes. Arbitrary killings were common. Anyone found carrying a weapon was shot on sight, and even innocent bystanders if they looked suspicious were liable to be either beaten up or shot. A hapless chimney sweep was shot and killed for carrying a small red flag, an age-old custom of his profession. The commander of Freikorps Lützow justified such killings by telling his men: 'It is a lot better to kill innocent people than to let one guilty person escape.'[15] The Thule Society's Combat League secretly hiding inside the city also sprang into action, occupying the Royal Residenz and the War

Ministry on the Ludwigstraße. Red flags disappeared from the public buildings in the city centre, replaced by the *Weiß und Blau* of Bavaria, thus heralding a friendly welcome for the liberating forces. The Ehrhardt Brigade marched down the Ludwigstraße as if on parade, cheered on by an appreciative audience that grew larger and louder as the troops passed under the Victory Arch near the university and down to the Feldherrnhalle. The triumphal procession ended on the Marienplatz where a priest dressed all in white celebrated an open-air mass.[16]

During the early afternoon of 1 May there was heavy fighting around the Karlsplatz. The Red Guards turned the Justizpalast (Palace of Justice) and the Mathäserbräu into strong defensive positions and put up a spirited battle. Eventually the Freikorps brought up some artillery and shelled the Justice Palace, driving the Red fighters out to the Mathäserbräu. By late afternoon, after bombarding the beer hall with heavy artillery and clearing the remaining defenders out of its numerous rooms with flamethrowers, the survivors retreated to the Hauptbahnhof where they made their last stand. The main railway station eventually fell to the White forces two days later, in the early hours of Saturday morning, 3 May. Amongst the very few prisoners taken was Egelhofer, who was physically abused and summarily executed. The official number of Red casualties was 519, but the actual number of dead is probably closer to 1,000 to 1,200. Some seventy soldiers in von Oven's combined forces were killed during the three days of fighting.[17]

The battle for Munich was over but random killings continued. Freikorps from northern Germany struggled to understand the Bavarian dialect and viewed Munich as an occupied enemy city. Irresponsible brutality reached its nadir on the night of 6 May when a group of drunken Freikorps slaughtered twenty-one members of the St Josef Society, a Catholic worker's club affiliated with the BVP, who had gathered for a theatrical performance. The victims were herded into a cellar, shot, trampled, and bayoneted. The officers responsible for this atrocity claimed they had eliminated a Spartacist conclave, and that their men had acted responsibly. Most people in Munich disagreed. They were horror-stricken by the sadistic incident, blamed 'the Prussians' and demanded an end to the wanton violence and revenge killings.[18]

An advance party from the exiled Bavarian government in Bamberg had arrived in Munich the previous day. They paved the way for Hoffman's return in August, and the departure of von Oven's Reichswehr troops and non-Bavarian Freikorps. Cardinal Faulhaber, the Archbishop of Munich, spoke for many of his fellow Münchners when he said there was little to choose between the atrocious conduct of the north German Freikorps and the Red Guards. Unlike most of the White units, Freikorps von Epp and its Bavarian commander were mythologised as the 'liberators of Munich'. Von Epp was appointed general commander of the newly constituted Reichswehr military district in Bavaria, and General von Möhl, as per the prearranged plan, was ensconced as the commandant of Munich.

Most of the leading figures in the two Bavarian Soviet Republics were arrested, as were thousands of their supporters. More than 1,700 were convicted of crimes ranging from treason to murder and theft. Of the Soviet leadership, only Max Levien escaped arrest. He fled to Austria, but later in Moscow he was, ironically, a victim of Stalin's purges in the mid-1930s, a gruesome fate also shared by Axelrod. Eugen Leviné was arrested at the end of May, and after a highly charged trial that depicted him as a stereotypical Bolshevik and the public face of the Soviet regime, he was convicted of high treason and executed by firing squad on 5 June as 'an alien infiltrator who had pursued his aims with total disregard for the welfare of the people'.[19] Fritz Seidel, the officer responsible for murdering the hostages at the Luitpold Gymnasium, and seven of his men were sentenced to death and executed in September 1919. Niekisch, Toller, and Landauer, the main leaders of the first Bavarian Soviet, were denounced and tracked down to their hiding places. Niekisch and Toller received prison sentences of two and five years respectively. Their colleague the anarchist Gustav Landauer was less fortunate. He was taken to Stadelheim Prison on May Day where he was brutally beaten by a group of soldiers before being shot dead by the officer responsible for his care.[20]

After six months of revolutionary chaos Munich began a period of tenuous calm. Hoffmann reshuffled his cabinet at the end of May and presided over a coalition in which the centre Deutsche Demokratische Partei (DDP) and the right-wing BVP outnumbered his socialist and left-wing SPD colleagues in the cabinet. Hoffmann's new cabinet colleagues, especially Gustav von Kahr, the BVP leader, were anxious to ensure the SPD did not slide down the road to Bolshevism again. Eisner's idealistic but ultimately divisive and violent political experiment to usher in socialist democracy and a new era of international peace had left the citizens of Munich battered, bitter and fearful of liberal ideas and socialist politicians. Military rule restored calm and a welcome return to conventional law and order. By the spring and summer of 1919 popular sentiment in Munich and throughout Bavarian society had shifted noticeably to the conservative right. Organizations such as the Pan German League and the Thule Society found sympathetic audiences for their message that foreigners and Jews were at the heart of all problems, and the strongest measures must be taken to stop them. The harsh terms of the Versailles Treaty that the Weimar government was forced to sign in June 1919 lent some credibility to a belief widely held by many Germans, but particularly by Bavarians, that the Entente Powers wanted to destroy Germany, and that the Reich's socialist government was either unable or unwilling to stop them. Support for Bavarian independence and succession from the Prussian-dominated Reich moved from the fringes of Bavarian political discussion to a credible alternative to extricate Bavaria from a growing number of unpalatable predicaments. The people of Munich and Bavaria, conceded historian John Lukacs, had become much more receptive of politics that were 'overwhelmingly radical, nationalist, populist, anti-cosmopolitan, anti-capitalist, anti-Marxist, and anti-Jewish'.[21]

Hitler Finds his Political Voice in Munich

Hitler returned to Munich from Traunstein on 25 January 1919, four weeks before Eisner was assassinated. There are photographs and film footage of Hitler, in an army great coat and cap, and wearing the red armlet of the Revolution, taking part in the funeral procession for the dead prime minster. Despite his public mark of respect for Eisner, Hitler did not participate in the revolutions. He was a spectator throughout. He looked out for his own safety, and left it to others to play an active role in the revolutionary and counter-revolutionary battles. Ernst Schmidt, Hitler's western front colleague and friend in the 2nd Infantry Regiment, recalled that Hitler spent most of his time in the Regiment's barracks on Lothstraße 29, doing odd jobs, such as testing old gas masks, and resuming his old habits, mainly reading during the day and attending the opera at night. 'Hitler was a regular Opera fan,' Schmidt declared with pride and enthusiasm, further noting that when the two of them were at the opera, 'Hitler was lost in the music to the very last note; blind and deaf to all else around him.'[1]

In mid-February the 2nd Infantry Regiment was reorganized and Hitler was assigned to the 2nd Demobilisation Company. All of his wartime colleagues, including Schmidt, were discharged, but Hitler was able to extend his army career because on 15 February he was elected as one of his company's *Vertrauensmänner* (trusted representatives) to represent his battalion on the *Soldatenrat*, an integral part of Eisner's revolutionary government in Munich. Hitler's main duty as a council representative was to 'educate and enlighten' the men in his company through pro-Republican propaganda. His first political job, therefore, was to defend the new regime, something that he would have been unable to do had he publicly opposed the Social Democratic government. Self-interest and opportunism aimed at avoiding demobilisation from the army rather than political convictions explain Hitler's apparent support for a political party that he had learned to loathe when he lived in Vienna.[2] It is also clear that the men in Hitler's barracks admired and respected him, as had his fellow residents back at the Männerheim during his Vienna days. When Ernst Toller and the moderate communists established the first Red Republic at the beginning of April 1919, Hitler's colleagues in the barracks re-confirmed his position as their representative on the *Soldatenrat*. Hitler did not support the *Räterepublik*, and he even instructed the men in his battalion not to join the Red

Army. Six days later, on Palm Sunday, 13 April, the day of Putsches and the start of the more extreme Second Bavarian Soviet Republic, Hitler persuaded most of the men in his barracks to remain neutral and stay out of the fighting, by reminding them that 'we're no pack of Revolutionary Guards for a gang of vagrant Jews!'[3] Despite his antipathy for the Jewish-Bolsheviks and the new Soviet government of Bavaria, on 16 April Hitler was re-elected as the second of two battalion spokesmen on the soldiers' soviet council.[4]

On 2 May, near the end of the battle for Munich, soldiers from von Epp's Freikorps arrested Hitler and his comrades billeted at the Lothstraße barracks and herded them into the cellars of the Maximiliansgymnasium in north Schwabing at Karl-Theodor-Straße 9. Hitler languished in the school's basement until he was spotted by an officer who knew him from the war. 'How is it that you are here,' the officer wondered out loud, then asserted emphatically, 'you're no communist.'[5] He had Hitler released immediately, and by 9 May Hitler was working as a Reichswehr informer in a three-person special commission set up to investigate revolutionary activity in the 2nd Infantry Regiment during the Räterepublik. The commission's task was to identify NCOs and men who had supported the communists. Hitler confirmed his counter-revolutionary credentials to his army superiors when he denounced two former colleagues on the battalion council, excoriating one in particular, Georg Dufter, whom Hitler labelled as 'the worst and most radical rabble-rouser in the regiment, … who had constantly spread propaganda for the soviet republic.'[6] Fearful of an infestation of Bolshevik sympathies in the Munich garrison, the new military command in Munich (Bayerische Reichswehr Gruppenkommando Nr. 4) discharged most of the soldiers, including all of Hitler's company, by the end of May. Hitler, however, was not demobilised with them. Rather he continued to serve in the army as an informant, and was posted to the Nachrichtenabteilung, Abt. Ib/P (Information Department), a new intelligence and propaganda unit established to monitor and extinguish any new revolutionary unrest in Munich, under the command of Captain Karl Mayr. Hitler's new unit was also charged with 'educating' the troops, demobilised soldiers, and returning prisoners of war about the dangers of Bolshevism, and rekindling the spirit of nationalism and militarism.

Mayr's authority extended well beyond his rank of captain, and he had considerable resources at his disposal to build up his team of informants and propaganda agents. Drawing on his personal acquaintances, Mayr enlisted academic help to run short 'speakers courses' to train his new cadres as patriotic agitators. Two of the main lecturers were Karl Alexander von Müller, the eminent nationalist historian at the Ludwig Maximilian Universität (LMU), and Gottfried Feder, the Pan-German economic expert and member of the Thule Society. The first course took place at LMU from 5 to 12 June, and

Hitler was one of the students on this first anti-Bolshevik instructors' course. Hitler had experience in propaganda work, albeit for the Socialist government, but he positively thrived on the counter-revolutionary course that spoke to his inner and long-held nationalist views. Writing in *Mein Kampf* about this experience, Hitler professed, 'the value of the whole affair was that I now obtained the opportunity of meeting a few likeminded comrades with whom I could thoroughly discuss the situation of the moment.'[7] After one lecture, Prof Müller noticed Hitler, surrounded by fellow students all spellbound by whatever it was Hitler was saying. Müller called Mayr over, pointed to 'a soldier with a pale face under an unsoldierly quiff of hair, a clipped moustache and light-blue, cold, glittering eyes,' and asked: 'do you know that one of your trainees is a natural-born speaker?' Mayr smiled, and replied to his academic friend, 'oh, that's Hitler of the List Regiment!'[8]

Hitler had distinguished himself as a talented speaker in front of Mayr and some of the other course organizers who soon would influence his political career. The short course had also given Hitler plenty of ideas that bolstered his ethnic chauvinist and pan-German nationalist *Weltanschauung*. It was to Feder that Hitler attributed his first real understanding of political economy. Financial problems that Hitler had previously suspected or sensed now appeared to him to be 'scientifically unexceptionable'.[9] 'For the first time,' Hitler effused, 'I really achieved an understanding of the contents of the Jew Karl Marx's life effort.'[10] Feder's lecture to the course on the 'breaking of interest slavery' made a huge impression on Hitler as well as the other three to four hundred people in attendance who regularly interrupted with sustained applause. Feder appealed to his right-wing audience by contrasting 'productive' capital, in the service of the state, with 'rapacious' capital, which he blamed on Mammonism (a fixation on money) and the evil lending practices of the Jewish-dominated financial markets. Hitler quickly recognised the propaganda potential of Feder's theories, combining anti-capitalist and anti-Semitic resentments, and embraced them as an integral part of his political ideology.[11]

Upon completion of the counter-revolutionary course at LMU, Mayr assigned Hitler to a special education group of twenty-six army instructors whose main task was to 're-educate' returning German prisoners of war with Spartacist leanings and turn them into anti-Bolshevik patriots.[12] Before Hitler started his new assignment with the Education Kommando at the army transit camp Lager-Lechfeld, he attended another short propaganda course from 10 to 19 July held in the rooms of the Museum Society in the Palais Porcia on Promenadestraße 12 (today Kardinal-Faulhaber-Straße 12). This course focused on the content of the indoctrination lectures that Hitler and his colleagues would give to the demobilised troops on anti-revolutionary, pro-national, and anti-Semitic themes. Again, Hitler received affirmation that the pan-German and anti-Semitic ideas he had read and learnt in Linz, Vienna, and Munich, and inwardly digested during the war, were an essential prerequisite in Munich's counter-revolutionary politics for the rebirth of the German people and the restoration of Germany as a great nation after the twin humiliations of defeat in 1918 and the communist revolutions in 1919.[13]

Hitler was an instant success as a political instructor and orator on the anti-Bolshevik course held at Lechfeld from 20 to 25 August. He spoke eloquently and passionately on the disgrace of the Versailles Peace Treaty, the 'November criminals', and the Jewish-Bolshevik menace, quickly winning over angry and disillusioned men who were bitter about their experiences at the front and resentful of the chaos and hunger they found on their return home.[14] Many participants on the course singled out Hitler as the 'star performer', contrasting his compelling lectures very favourably with those given by the much less charismatic Rudolf Beyschlag, the commander of the education detachment. Hans Knoden, an artilleryman, thought Hitler was 'an outstanding and fiery speaker, able to grip the attention of his listeners'. Another participant, Eward Bolle, who had served on a Zeppelin, noted Hitler's ability to 'carry away his audience by his dialectical skill'. But the most effusive praise came from Lorenz Frank, a medical orderly, who wrote on 23 August 1919: 'Herr Hittler [sic] is a born popular orator, whose fanaticism combined with the common touch … unfailingly compels his audience's attention and commands their sympathy.' Even the commander of the Lechfeld guard unit, Oberleutnant (First Lieutenant) Walther Bendt, was impressed with Hitler. Bendt, in his daily reports to 4 Group Headquarters, informed his superiors that Hitler 'knew how to arouse real enthusiasm among the men', and that he had succeeded where others had failed 'to instil fresh hope, hatred for Germany's enemies, and a thirst for revenge'.[15] Bendt also noted Hitler's zealous opinions on the 'Jewish question', and that he had instructed Hitler to moderate his anti-Semitic speeches to avoid creating the impression of Jew-baiting.

Captain Mayr was well aware of Hitler's anti-Semitic views, which he also shared. When Hitler returned to Munich, Mayr did not waste any time redeploying the demagogic talents of his star propaganda man. Hitler was ordered to repeat his Lechfeld lectures in the army barracks on Lothstraβe and Türkenstraβe, and at the Marsfeldkaserne (Mars Field barracks). Mayr also delegated to Hitler the task of replying to a letter from Adolf Gemlich, a former participant on one of the 'instruction courses', inquiring about the 'Jewish question' in relation to the policies of the Social Democrats in Munich. Most conservative groups in Munich believed that Kurt Eisner was a tool of Jewish Bolshevism. They also pointed to the 'Jewish tyranny' that characterised the executive leadership and policies of the two soviet republics. Even the Munich police were worried that an anti-Jewish pogrom was 'entirely possible'.[16] Hitler deliberated on his new task as an 'expert' on the Jewish Question for twelve days before he wrote a long reply to Gemlich. The letter, dated 16 September 1919, is Hitler's first written declaration of anti-Semitism. He explained to Gemlich why Jews were a menace to Germany. Drawing on Feder's economic explanation that portrayed Jews as deceitful and greedy in their pursuit of money and power through usury, and Houston Stewart Chamberlain's depiction of Jews as 'cultural destroyers', Hitler classified Jews as an alien race (not a religious community) whose activities were a form of 'racial tuberculosis' that had to be eradicated before it consumed the host nation. Only a 'government of national strength', which Germany did not have in the Social Democrats, would be able to remove the threat posed by the Jews. To achieve this end, Hitler wanted the Jews to be classified as illegal foreigners, a policy first advocated by the Pan-German League. This was the 'anti-Semitism of reason' rather than emotion that Hitler feared would lead to ineffective pogroms. There must be, Hitler argued, a rational and systematic removal of the legal rights of Jews in Germany, and ideally their removal from German society altogether.[17] Mayr was pleased with Hitler's letter, although he did not agree with Hitler's reliance on Feder's economics. Nonetheless, Mayr, the Reichswehr leadership in Munich, the Freikorps, and even the mainstream conservative parties and organizations in Bavaria were in complete agreement that 'the ruling social democrats were chained to Jewry' and that 'all harmful elements, especially the Jews, should be cast out'.[18]

Hitler Joins the *Deutsche Arbeiterpartei* (DAP)

The small and outside-of-Munich unknown *Deutsche Arbeiterpartei* (German Workers' Party) was fundamentally an anti-Semitic party that shared Hitler's racial interpretation of the Jewish problem and aimed to combat it through a unifying nationalism based on the pan-German ideas of *Heimat* and *Volksgemeinschaft* (homeland and a national community).[1] Hitler attended his first meeting of the DAP on Friday 12 September 1919 at the Sterneckerbräu on the Tal 54 (today Tal 38). He wrote in *Mein Kampf* that he was 'told to go and take a look at the organization and then make a report'.[2] Hitler implied that he was ordered to spy on the DAP, but there was no need for such information. Mayr already knew all about the party. Both the Reichswehr and the Thule Society provided the DAP with financial and organizational support. Rather than go as an undercover agent, Hitler and several of his colleagues from the Lechfeld propaganda unit went to hear the *völkish* poet, Thulist, and anti-Semitic journalist and publisher of the newspaper *Auf gut deutsch* (In Plain German), Dietrich Eckart.[3]

The meeting began at 8 pm in a small private function room, later renamed the *Leiberzimmer* (bodyguards' room or veterans hall), off to the side of the main beer hall. Forty-one people attended. Hitler signed the guest book as Lance Corporal Adolf Hitler, 2nd Infantry Division. Gottfried Feder was the evening's speaker because Eckart was ill. Feder spoke on his favourite topic, the evils of capitalism and interest slavery. It was after the formal lecture that the meeting got interesting. During the free discussion period Hitler clashed with the first speaker, Professor Baumann, who had suggested Bavaria separate from Prussia, join Austria, and form a Danubian State. Hitler's fierce opposition to this idea rumbled the professor and startled the audience, but also impressed Anton Drexler, the chairman of the party and the evening's talk. Reflecting on these events, Drexler said: 'He [Hitler] spoke uncommonly well, and used his arguments with force ... He seemed to know his ground too, better than most.' Drexler had not met Hitler before, but he was keen to recruit him into the DAP. 'Herr Gott! here's a chap worth getting hold of!' When the meeting concluded, Drexler introduced himself, gave Hitler a copy of his recently published pamphlet *Mein Politisches Erwachen* (*My Political Awakening*), and asked him to come again.[4]

Very early the next morning, Saturday 13 September, Hitler still in bed in his barracks read with interest Drexler's pamphlet. 'It reflected a process similar to the one which I myself had gone through twelve years before.' Hitler wrote in *Mein Kampf*: 'Involuntarily I saw my own development come to life before my eyes.'[5] Events moved quickly from this point onwards as Hitler's political career took shape. Later the same morning Hitler received a postcard from Drexler inviting him to attend a DAP committee meeting on Wednesday evening at the Altes Rosenbad, a scruffy little restaurant and tavern at Herrnstraße 48, just around the corner from the Sterneckerbräu on the Tal, and the Isartor. Hitler acknowledged in *Mein Kampf* his initial reluctance to get involved with this group, but his curiosity got the better of him and he attended the meeting. He was greeted warmly by Drexler, the Munich District chairman, and met for the first time Karl Harrer, the chairman of the 'national organization'. The minutes of the last meeting were read, and the accounts declared. The party had a paltry seven marks and fifty pfennings. Hitler was not impressed. 'This was club life of the worst manner,' Hitler later recorded in *Mein Kampf*, further noting that other than good faith and good intentions 'there was nothing, no programme, no leaflet, no printed matter at all, no membership cards, not even a miserable rubber stamp.'[6] Hitler must have reported what he learned about the DAP to Mayr, who despite Hitler's reservations encouraged his propaganda man to join the party. Hitler applied for membership on 24 September and was accepted into the party on 26 September as member number 555.[7]

Hitler was the 54th member of the party. The DAP began its membership list with the number 501 to give the impression that it had more members than it actually did. Keen to emphasise the importance of his decision, Hitler claimed in *Mein Kampf* that joining the DAP was the most decisive resolution of his life.[8] Hitler did not acknowledge Mayr's role in helping him join the DAP, nor the introduction Mayr gave him to Dietrich Eckhart – soon to become his closest friend and political mentor – in late September or early October 1919.[9]

Once Hitler became a member of the DAP he immediately set out to turn what was an insignificant debating society and drinking club into a proper political party. He convinced the DAP's executive committee to hold a large public meeting in the Hofbräukeller, one of Munich's impressive beer halls on the east side of the River Isar at Inner-Wiener-Straße 19, in the brewery district of Au-Haidhausen. The DAP purchased an advert in the *Münchener Beobachter* announcing their political event for Thursday evening, 16 October 1919. More than a hundred people turned up. Hitler was the second speaker and he talked for approximately thirty minutes, much to the delight of his audience. This was the 30-year-old Adolf Hitler's first public speech, and he proved that he was a charismatic political speaker. His former sergeant, Max Amann, barely recognised him: 'there was an unfamiliar fire burning in him.'[10] Joseph Popp, who was there, joined the party, becoming member number 609.[11] Captain Ernst Röhm, the future leader of the *Sturmabteilung* (Storm Battalion, SA) was also at the meeting. Two days later, as a direct result of the positive reception Hitler's speech had received, Hitler was introduced to Kronprinz Rupprecht, the last heir to the Bavarian throne. Even the *Münchener Beobachter*, in its write up of the DAP's successful night at the Hofbräukeller, singled out Hitler for specific praise as a 'talented speaker'.[12]

The DAP raised over 300 marks at the Hofbräukeller and Hitler strongly advocated that the party repeat the event. On 13 November the DAP held its second, and larger, public meeting at another big beer hall, the Eberlbräukeller, at Rosenheimerstraße 15–17, a ten minute walk away from the first venue. Hitler was the main speaker and he spoke for over an hour on the shameful peace of Versailles, the November criminals and the politicians in Berlin who had signed the treaty in June 1919, and the *Dolchstoßlegende* (stab-in-the-back legend). There were a few scuffles in the audience after someone yelled out 'the work of Jews' in support of Hitler's condemnation of those who had 'sold out' Germany both during and after the war. More than 130 people had come to the beer hall to hear Hitler speak, and the local police report on the meeting acknowledged Hitler's 'extraordinary talent as an orator'.[13] The *Münchener Beobachter* eulogised Hitler again, reporting that 'repeated and frenetic applause' followed his masterful speech.[14]

Hitler's influence in the DAP was growing quickly. Immediately after his successful performance at the Eberlbräukeller, Harrer invited him to join the party's inner circle. Harrer organized a dinner for himself, Drexler, Feder, Dr Tafel, and Hitler in the Adelmann restaurant at Herrnstraße 36 on Sunday evening, 16 November. The men agreed that they would form a 'Programme Committee of Five' with Hitler being responsible for the party's propaganda. Ten days later, Hitler was back at the Eberlbräukeller speaking to another receptive audience, this time numbering 300 men and women, on the theme of creating a Greater Germany through the union of Austria and Germany. It was also around the end of November that Hitler met up with Dietrich Eckart and the two men began their close friendship.[15]

Eckart missed most of the DAP's autumn meetings due to illness, but he had followed Hitler's rapid rise from obscurity to the leading spokesman in the party. He saw in Hitler the type of leader that Germany needed, and he had written about often in *Auf gut deutsch* during the summer of 1919: 'A guy who can stand the rattle of a machine gun, who won't fill his pants in fear. I can't use an officer; the people don't respect them any longer. Best of all would be a worker who's got his mouth in the right place.'[16]

Having decided to take Hitler under his wing, Eckart introduced his political protégé to Munich society, his network of *völkisch* colleagues in the Thule Society and the Reichswehr, and his 'intellectual' editorial assistant Alfred Rosenberg, a Baltic German and virulent anti-Semite who had fled

Bolshevik Russia for Munich in December 1918 to meet Eckart and write for his newspaper. Rosenberg translated into German *The Protocols of the Elders of Zion*, a scurrilous forgery concocted by the tsar's secret police and published in Russia in 1905 that purported to 'prove' the existence of a Jewish conspiracy to dominate the world. Rosenberg also alleged that Russia was Germany's most dangerous enemy and that it must be conquered for essential living space just as it had been by the Teutonic Knights when they expanded eastwards in the thirteenth century to civilise and colonise the pagan Slavs. Hitler was already an aggressive anti-Semite when he met Rosenberg, but it was Rosenberg more than anyone else who convinced Hitler that the threat posed by communism came from its Jewish origins. By the start of 1920, Jewish Bolshevism joined the Versailles Treaty and the November criminals as the main targets of Hitler's hate.[17]

Together Eckart and Rosenberg helped Hitler shape the pan-German *völkisch* nationalist and anti-Semitic ideas he had acquired since his days in Vienna into a coherent National Socialist ideology. Hitler also used his new friends as a sounding board, to test his ideas for future speeches, especially when they all met up at Eckart's favourite cafés. From November 1919 to November 1923 Hitler was a regular member of Eckart's Monday evening *Stammtisch* at the Café Neumayr at Petersplatz 8, just across the road from the Viktualienmarkt and south of the Tal. When they were together Hitler and Eckart often spoke for hours, discussing art, literature, music, opera, and politics. Eckart was the father Hitler longed to have had when he was a boy back in Austria. In Munich, with Eckart's support and under his watchful eyes, Hitler's confidence and political acumen matured. Hitler's *Weltanschauung* and the conviction with which he expressed it made him a political figure of extraordinary dynamism in the ethnic chauvinist milieu of post-revolutionary Munich.[18]

Based on his recent successes Hitler was certain that the best way to build up the DAP was through mass public meetings that attracted new members and raised funds for the party through donations. Harrer and others on the executive committee were less convinced. Hitler ignored their reservations, and acting on his own instincts found a new and larger meeting room at the Zum Deutschen Reich, at Dachauerstraße 143, in north-west Munich, not far from his barracks on Lothstraße. A meeting was planned for 10 December, and was advertised in the *Münchener Beobachter*. Hitler was the main speaker, and the title of his talk was 'Germany as it faces its worst humiliation'.[19] Various sources claim the attendance was between 140 and 300 people. Hitler writes in *Mein Kampf* about his disappointment that 'the meeting in the new hall was not so well attended ... barely one hundred and forty persons.' He also states that 'the bad attendance' reopened the debate in the executive committee on the 'excessive repetition of our demonstrations' and led to a struggle between himself and Harrer over the control and future direction of the party. Hitler rejected Harrer's concept of the DAP as a conspiratorial secret society, and eventually with Drexler's help succeeded in pushing for a complete reform of the party's organization from a small *völkisch* club to a genuine political party. Harrer resigned on 5 January 1920 and Drexler became the party chairman. Once again, Hitler had prevailed.[20]

On Hitler's insistence, the DAP rented an office in the Sterneckerbräu (the party's second headquarters) and hired Rudolf Schüßler, one of Hitler's former army colleagues, to be the party's first *Geschäftsführer* (business manager). Hitler also engaged Drexler, Eckart, and Feder to work with him on drafting the party's manifesto. The mass public meetings, with Hitler as the star performer, also continued to be a significant feature in the DAP's efforts to raise its profile and increase its membership. Hitler understood the power of 'the spoken word', and stressed the value of propaganda to prepare the German people for the political struggles ahead. From mid-December until late January 1920 Hitler held six more public meetings at the Zum Deutschen Reich, each one bigger and more successful than the last. He spoke on his favourite topics: the sham treaty of Versailles; those responsible for military defeat and revolution; the threat posed by foreigners, especially Jews; the rekindling of the German spirit as the precursor to national rebirth; and the restoration of Germany as a great power after the disasters of 1918 and 1919. The seventh meeting at the Zum Deutschen Reich, on 23 January 1920, attracted over 400 people, too many to squeeze into the banquet hall, but they all cheered Hitler's call for the creation of a 'Germany for Germans'.[21]

The Birth of the *Nationalsozialistische Deutsche Arbeiterpartei* (National Socialist German Workers' Party, NSDAP)

D rexler and Hitler chose the Hofbräuhaus as the location for announcing the party programme, and booked the Festsaal, the largest room on the first floor of the famous beer hall, for Tuesday evening, 24 February 1920. The event was heavily advertised on big red posters and leaflets that were distributed all around the city. During the preceding weeks Hitler spent many evenings at Drexler's apartment on Burghausener-Strasse 6 in Nymphenburg, the leafy north-west district of Munich, revising drafts of the DAP's programme. Often the two men were so deeply involved in their work that Frau Drexler had to call them to supper several times before they stopped and ate the meal she had prepared for them. As the day of the meeting drew closer, doubts began to grow: would they complete the manifesto in time and would they fill the beer hall, a much bigger venue than the DAP had used for a meeting so far. The risk of embarrassment was made all the more acute on 21 February when the Hofbräuhaus was filled to overflowing with socialists and communists marking the first anniversary of Kurt Eisner's assassination. On 22 February, Hitler and Drexler worked long into the night in Drexler's office at Sonnenstraße 6/II Wiegand Ferdinand to complete a 25-point party programme. Later Drexler recalled that when they had finished, Hitler sprang to his feet, banged his fist on the table, and proclaimed that 'these points of ours are going to rival [Martin] Luther's placard on the doors of Wittenberg!'[1] The two men had also agreed to rename the party the *Nationalsozialistische Deutsche Arbeiterpartei* (National Socialist German Workers' Party, NSDAP), a name change that more accurately reflected the party's aim to unite the right and the left in the battle against Germany's internal and external enemies, particularly Jews, and regenerate a strong and racially pure German nation.[2]

Drexler was more hopeful than confident that the first public meeting of the NSDAP would be a success. To 'shore up' attendance for the still little-known Hitler, Drexler invited Dr Johannes Dingfelder, a well-known Munich physician and Thule Society member, to be the main speaker. Dingfelder had also recently published an article in the *Münchener Zeitung* entitled '*Was uns not tut*' (what we need) condemning usury and profiteering, which was well received by the newspaper's readers.[3] Drexler and Hitler need not have worried.

The Festsaal was packed with more than 2,000 people when the meeting began at 7.30 pm although not all of them had come to cheer Hitler and support his right-wing party. Some 600 were leftists, Communists and Independents, and many had come just to disrupt the meeting.[4] Even before the meeting began, the long rows of tables were laden with heavy stone beer mugs while the waitresses fetched even more foaming litres of beer for their thirsty patrons. Dingfelder began the night's proceedings as advertised. He did not say anything that upset the Communists, and the Festsaal was relatively quiet when Hitler got up to speak. Hitler began with a simple history of Germany before the war, the war years, and then the revolutions. This is when the Communists woke up. They heckled Hitler's interpretation of the Bavarian revolutions, beer steins began to fly, and clashes broke out between the rival groups of supporters. Hitler paused briefly but continued to speak through all the commotion while a handful of his most faithful war comrades and supporters, led by Emil Maurice, bundled the dissenters out of the hall and restored order. Maurice was an early member of the DAP, party number 594, and later became Hitler's first chauffeur. This fracas also marked the beginning of the *Saalschutzabteilung* (meeting hall protection squad) the forerunner of the *Sturmabteilung* (Storm Battalion, SA). Hitler continued his speech with attacks on the Treaty of Versailles, the socialist government in Berlin, and finally the Jews, to enthusiastic applause. He then announced the twenty-five points of the NSDAP's programme and asked his audience to 'pronounce judgement' on each one of them.[5]

The twenty-five points showed many similarities to programmes previously proclaimed by both the German Socialist Party and the Thule Society, and offered something for almost everyone but Jews. The programme started with a demand that all Germans be united in a greater Germany, the revocation of the peace treaties of Versailles and St. Germain, and the return of Germany's colonies. There were points aimed at raising health standards, protecting women and children, encouraging a vibrant middle class, land reforms to benefit farmers, respect both physical and mental labour, nationalize big businesses and heavy industry, abolish usury and land speculation, criminalise war profiteering, and harsher penalties for common criminals to enhance public order and safety. Finally there were points on citizenship, the creation of a peoples' army, ending foreign immigration, and deporting all non-Germans, especially Jews who were to be registered as 'aliens' and denied the right to hold any public office. The programme ended with a demand for 'the creation of a strong central state power for the Reich'.[6] There were a few cries of derision from left-wing protesters but they were increasingly drowned out by shouts of approval and tumultuous applause. In the audience was Hans Frank, at the time a 20-year-old law student, and later Hitler's lawyer, a Minister in the Nazi government, and during the war the governor of the occupied territories in Poland, who was struck by Hitler's sincerity. 'Here was a man who spoke honestly about how he felt and was not trying to put something across that he did not strongly believe.' At the end of the four-hour meeting, Frank was utterly convinced that 'if anyone could master the fate of Germany, Hitler was that man.'[7]

There was a noticeable sense of relief and joy in the audience that shuffled out of the Hofbräuhaus into the cold winter's night, awakened by the prospect that Hitler and the NSDAP offered the German people a way out of their despair.[8] Hitler sensed the same phenomenon at the end of his speech, noting: 'There stood before me a hall full of people united by a new conviction, a new faith, and a new will.' He was convinced that the movement was underway, and eventually it would be embraced wholeheartedly by the German people. 'A fire was kindled from whose flame one day the sword must come which would regain freedom for the German Siegfried and life for the German nation.'[9] Hitler's mythologizing of the Hofbräuhaus meeting in *Mein Kampf*, as a heroic and foundational act in the birth of the party, was not how the Munich newspapers viewed the event at the time. Even the supportive *Völkischer Beobachter* (formerly the *Münchener Beobachter* until late 1919) restricted its comment on the meeting to a short and unembellished account.[10] Nonetheless, Hitler was right. The NSDAP's first public meeting at the Hofbräuhaus on 24 February 1920 was the first significant step forward for the movement.

Munich was not the only city in Germany where the radical right flexed their muscles. On the night of 12 March 1920, the Ehrhardt Brigade, wearing their iconic swastika helmets, marched into Berlin and through the *Brandenburger Tor* (Brandenburg Gate) providing military support for General Walther von Lüttwitz, commander of the Berlin military district, and Wolfgang Kapp, a Pan-German and one of the founders of the *Deutsche Vaterlandspartei* (German Fatherland Party). They aimed to overthrow the Republic. News of the Kapp-Lüttwitz Putsch travelled quickly. Hitler, Dietrich Eckart and Captain Mayr were surprised yet supportive, and hastily sought to extend the putsch to Bavaria. On 15 March, at an evening meeting of the NSDAP in Munich, Hitler demanded that Hoffmann resign, and further called for a general strike against the Socialist-dominated Bavarian government. The next morning at Mayr's request Robert Ritter von Greim (the Luftwaffe's last commander in April 1945) flew Hitler and Eckart to Berlin to make contact with the Kapp-putschists. Mayr paid for the trip using Reichswehr funds. The army command in Munich forced Hoffmann to resign, ostensibly to avoid another bloody civil war, and thereby enabled the Landtag on 16 March to appoint Gustav Ritter von Kahr, the ultra-right-wing leader of the *Bayerische Volkspartei* (Bavarian People's Party, BVP) as the new Bavarian premier.[11]

Kahr's Bavaria immediately lurched to the right, and Munich became the centre of counter-revolutionary and anti-Prussian radicalism. Kahr turned

Bavaria into an *Ordnungszelle* (Cell of Order) that promoted and protected conservative tastes and values, like his own and those held by many conservative Bavarians. His efforts were supported by Ernst Pöhner (the Munich Police President), Wilhelm Frick (the Director of the Police's Political Division), the local Reichswehr command, the justice system, and even Michael von Faulhaber, Munich's monarchist Catholic Archbishop (promoted to Cardinal in October 1921). Munich became the cultural and political antipode to 'red Berlin', and beginning in the spring of 1920 the Bavarian capital city was a rallying point for right-wing radicals from all over Germany, attracting monarchists, Bavarian separatists, Pan-Germans and conservative nationalists, ethnic-chauvinists and anti-Semites, all loosely united by a general anti-liberal and anti-socialist outlook.[12]

By the time Hitler and Eckart checked into their rooms at Berlin's legendary luxury hotel, the Hotel Adlon, on the south-west corner of Unter den Linden and Wilhelmstraße, just east of the Brandenburg Gate, the Kapp Putsch was over. The putsch was nothing short of a fiasco. Having boldly seized power three days earlier, Kapp and his followers were completely unprepared to govern. They did not even have a copy of their manifesto, and had to cajole Kapp's daughter into typing it up. The government bureaucracy remained loyal to President Ebert, and on 17 March Kapp and many of the other leaders of the Putsch fled Berlin. While the putsch was both chaotic and comical, it did open the way for another wave of leftist agitation in Berlin and other parts of northern Germany. Workers in Berlin staged the most effective and largest strike in German history, and in both Saxony and the Ruhr workers set up Soviet governments. The Reichswehr, which had neither mobilised troops against the coup d'état nor supported it, was forced to defend the Ebert government against short-lived but bloody Red revolts.[13] Hitler and Eckart returned to Munich on 18 March, but not before Eckart had introduced his protégé to the salon of Helene Bechstein, wife of the piano manufacturer Edwin Bechstein, General Ludendorff, and Heinrich Claß, leader of the Pan-German League and editor of the ethnic-chauvinist *Alldeutsche Blätter* (Pan-German Journal).[14]

Retired general Erich von Ludendorff also left Berlin because he had supported the Kapp Putsch. He found refuge in Munich, in the form of a luxury villa in the south of the city, in the suburb of Solln-Ludwigshöhe, at Heilmann-Straße 5.[15] His new residence quickly became a meeting point for ultra conservatives, and a headquarters of sorts for counter-revolutionary activities throughout Germany. Captain Hermann Ehrhardt, his staff, and the men of the Ehrhardt Brigade also obtained sanctuary in Bavaria. They were invited to Munich by Pöhner, the new police chief. Ehrhardt set up his headquarters on Trautenwolfstraße 8, from where he ran a new secret society, the 'Organization Consul' (OC), which undertook political assassinations all across Germany.[16] The publisher Julius Lehmann and the Thule Society helped Ehrhardt's men find seasonal employment and settle in the farming communities surrounding Munich.[17] The men of the Ehrhardt Brigade brought practised military experience to the *Einwohnerwehr* (Citizens' Defence Force), a massive volunteer militia of 400,000 men established immediately after the fall of the Räterepublik committed to defending 'white and blue' Bavaria from Bolshevism. Captain Ernst Röhm, who joined the NSDAP in December 1919 after hearing Hitler speak at Zum Deutschen Reich, used his position in the local Reichswehr command to provide weapons for the *Einwohnerwehr* and funds for Hitler and the NSDAP.[18]

Hitler Leaves the Army and
Returns to Civilian Life

Hitler left the army on 31 March 1920. Free from military duty he threw himself full-time into expanding the party, and establishing himself as its indisputable leader. He planned to hold one major NSDAP event each week and to introduce the party to a wider audience. Four such events were held in April. Hitler drew audiences well over 1,000 people when he spoke at the Hofbräuhaus on 9, 17, and 27 April. On 20 April, Hitler celebrated his 31st birthday by giving a speech on 'The Preservation of the German Nation' at a meeting of the *Arbeitsgemeinschaft deutsch-völkischer Verbände* (Working Association of German Nationalist Groups) in the Löwenbräukeller on Nymphenburger Straße 4 and Stiglmaierplatz. Initially financial support for Hitler's speaking engagements came from secret local Reichswehr funds, as the NSDAP could not afford to pay Hitler a salary. Later on Hitler was able to command a substantial fee when he spoke at political events or for another party association. Hitler's early efforts to expand the party were working. On 18 April the first *NSDAP-Ortsgruppe* (NSDAP local branch) was established by Theodor Lauböck in Rosenheim, a significant regional town 65 km south-east of Munich. Lauböck was a Government Counsel, and both he and his wife Dora became close friends of Hitler. He spent Christmas with the Lauböcks in 1922, befriended and later employed their son Fritz as his private secretary in 1923, regularly sent postcards to them when he travelled, and visited often when passing through Rosenheim. On 1 May 1920, the first local branch of the NSDAP outside Bavaria was established by Wilhelm Ohnesorge in Dortmund.[1]

Some time between the end of March and 1 May 1920, Hitler moved out of the barracks on Lothstraße and sublet a small room in his second private residence in Munich at Thierschstraße 41/I. He would live here for the next nine years (1 May 1920 to 5 October 1929), until then his longest stay in one place. By preference Hitler would have liked to return to his old lodgings with the Popp family, but they did not have a room to rent. His new landlord was Marie Reichert, who shared the first floor flat with her mother Frau Dachs. Hitler's room was slightly larger than his one in Schleißheimerstraße, but it was unheated and very modestly furnished. There were a couple of well-worn rugs on the floor, a single bed, a small table and chair, and an unfinished bookshelf, which Hitler filled with his own books on art, military history, heroic German mythology, and Houston Stewart Chamberlain's biography of Wagner.[2] The building was in a middle-class residential district, a ten minute walk east of the Isartor, near the Isar River, and just up the street from the Eher Publishing House (Thierschstraße 11–17), the main publisher for the NSDAP, including the *Völkischer Beobachter*, the official party newspaper. It was typical of the five-storey brick buildings in the area, with offices and shops on the ground floor and small apartments above, but distinctive owing to its statue of the Madonna in an alcove centrally located on the first floor.[3]

Across the street from Hitler's new residence was Magdalena Schweyer's small fruit and vegetable shop, where Hitler often bought apples and *Radi* (large white radishes). At first, Frau Schweyer did not take much notice of Hitler, but she was struck by how well-spoken and polite he was. It was her neighbour who told her that Hitler was the leading speaker in the NSDAP, and that they should go and hear him next time there was a meeting. On Monday 9 June 1920 the two women went to hear Hitler at the Sterneckerbräu. Recalling the event, Frau Schweyer confessed, 'I got all worked up'. Hitler, for his part, was succeeding at getting his message across to the people he needed to build his party, especially working women. 'It was wonderful, what he said and all,' recounted Frau Schweyer, 'I could understand every word.' Both Frau Schweyer and her neighbour firmly believed that Hitler had found 'a way out of all our troubles and miseries'. Eager to help, the two women joined the party.[4]

Hitler aimed to create a Völkisch nationalist party without equal. On 29 May 1920, the NSDAP published its first membership list. There were 676 registered members, of which 73 (11 per cent) were women.[5] Hitler still had a lot of work to do to build a popular movement that influenced Bavarian politics, never mind dominate the national political agenda. His strategy was to win over the middle class first, by appealing to their prejudices and resentments, and repeating popular dogmas. He also maintained his faith in the power of the spoken word, and the effectiveness of mass meetings in building up the party, where the prospective new member is drawn into a larger community of people who share the same hopes and fears as he or she does. This sense of community, no longer being alone but part of a great comprehensive body, was exactly what Hitler had experienced as a soldier with his regiment in the Great War. The mass meetings were Hitler's way of recreating this transformational experience to politics: 'through the mighty effect of suggestive intoxication and enthusiasm, visibly successful in the agreement of thousands, the correctness of the new political doctrine is confirmed.' The 'seeker', Hitler stressed, succumbs to the magic influence of 'mass suggestion'. 'The will, the longing, and also the power of thousands are accumulated in every individual.' Hitler was certain that 'the man who enters such a meeting leaves it inwardly reinforced: he has become a link in the community.' This, Hitler exhorted, was something the National Socialist movement 'must never forget'.[6]

The NSDAP held roughly three large-scale events every two weeks from May through December 1920. Hitler always was the main speaker, and as his audiences increased in size from 2,000 to over 3,500, the party added the larger Bürgerbräukeller (Rosenheimer Straße 29) and the Münchner-Kindl-Keller (Rosenheimer Straße 18–22) to its list of preferred venues.[7] Both beer halls were located on the east side of the river Isar, and they became important sites in the history of the NSDAP in Munich. By the summer of 1920, Hitler's increasing public popularity had attracted the attention of Munich's more established right-wing political leaders. On 16 June, General Ludendorff invited Hitler to join him for lunch at the Osteria Bavaria, a small artists' restaurant at Schellingstraße 62 in Schwabing. The restaurant would become Hitler's favourite place to eat lunch when he lived in Munich and on visits back to Munich after he came to power in 1933.[8] Ludendorff was in the audience at the Sterneckerbräu later that evening when Hitler spoke to the party faithful in the Leiberzimmer, a room permanently reserved for NSDAP events. Hitler's special talent as a public speaker was his ability to merge his political narrative with the events of the day to inspire an emotional response in his audience merely by tapping into their worries and resentments. Having gained their trust, it was relatively easy for him to attain their support. One of the most striking examples of this process was Hitler's fundamental anti-Semitic speech '*Warum sind wir Antisemiten?*' (Why are we Anti-Semites?) on Friday evening, 13 August 1920, in the Festsaal at the Hofbräuhaus.

Hitler sensed correctly the growing anti-Semitism in Munich and further afield in Bavaria and wider Germany. After the war more and more respectable middle-class and middle-aged Germans heeded the words of Heinrich Claß, the Pan-German leader, that 'the Jewish race is the source of all dangers' but 'a Führer will arise to lead them in the fight against Jewry.' Hitler told his receptive audience in the Hofbräuhaus that only the NSDAP, and by implication he himself, will 'free them from the power of the Jew!' Hitler spoke exclusively on this subject for over two hours, often interrupted by shouts of approval and applause. The historian and Hitler biographer John Toland suggests that Hitler's anti-Semitism was personal rather than historical, but Hitler invoked history when he called for 'the removal of Jews from the midst of our people', paraphrasing a demand made by Martin Luther in the sixteenth century, and more recently in 1915 by Houston Stewart Chamberlain, who warned of the need to protect the German Volk and the German nation from the destructive influences of Jews. Hitler had successfully put into practice the politics of resentment and hate that he had witnessed during his time in Vienna, used by the Christian Social leader Dr Karl Lueger and Pan German Georg von Schönerer to win over the broad masses of German-speaking Austrians.[9]

Hitler continued to draw large crowds when he spoke at Munich's main beer halls. His recurrent themes were the Treaty of Versailles, the threat of Bolshevism, and Jews. By the end of 1920, the party had staged forty-six big events and Hitler had spoken to more than 60,000 people. Membership in the NSDAP in the last half of the year had increased to 2,138 registered members. Hitler also undertook a long speaking tour in Austria from 29 September to 14 October, raising funds for the party and spreading the National Socialist message outside Bavaria. To reach an even wider audience, Hitler convinced the party's leadership that the party needed its own newspaper. Consequently they purchased the *Völkischer Beobachter*.[10]

The *Völkischer Beobachter* or *VB* as it was known locally had been on the verge of bankruptcy since the summer of 1920 because of numerous libel actions. In December its eight shareholders, all members of the Thule Society, including Kathe Bierbaumer, the wealthy 32-year-old mistress of Rudolf von Sebottendorff, seriously considered selling the paper to a rival nationalist organization that advocated Bavarian separatism. Fearful of this prospect, Hitler, along with his young friend and fellow NSDAP speaker Hermann Esser and the deputy party-chairman Oskar Körner, woke up Anton Drexler at two o'clock in the morning on 17 December at his apartment in the Nymphenburg district to discuss buying the debt-ridden paper for the NSDAP. Huddled together in Drexler's kitchen, and drinking many cups of coffee, the men agreed a strategy. Hitler took an early train to Augsburg to secure funds from Dr Gottfried Grandel, who also financed Dietrich Eckart's *völkisch* newspaper *Auf gut deutsch*. Drexler arrived at Eckart's house at eight o'clock and was reproached for getting him out of bed at such 'an unspeakable hour'. By midday, however, Eckart had secured 60,000 Marks from secret Reichswehr funds arranged by General von Epp and Captain Röhm. Eckart also remortgaged his house and borrowed money from his cousin Simon Eckart. Even Drexler, who only earned 35 Marks a week, signed a guarantor's note for the paper's debts of more than 100,000 Marks. Having raised the 120,000 Marks asking price, Drexler and Eckart completed the purchase at 4 pm that afternoon. The *VB* was registered in Hitler's name. The NSDAP now had its own newspaper to promote its *Völkisch* propaganda, advertise the activities of the party, and provide practical information at local and regional levels to help party members further the movement's political objectives. The *VB* was published twice a week, with a circulation that rose gradually from around 8,000 to 17,000 copies by the end of 1922. Eckart was the editor and Alfred Rosenberg his associate editor. Rosenberg took over as chief editor in March 1923 due to Eckart's declining health.[11]

Hitler celebrated the party's recent successes with a special end-of-the-year evening talk at the Sterneckerbräu on 20 December. He publicly thanked Drexler and Eckart for their considerable efforts promoting the party and securing the purchase of the *VB*. The next day he travelled with Hermann Esser to Berlin on a three-day fund-raising trip. Hitler spent Christmas 1920 with his friend and party colleague Oskar Körner at his home on the Tegernsee, an exquisitely beautiful lake an hour's journey by train, south of Munich.[12]

Hitler began 1921 with a flurry of activity. On 1 January he wrote the first of many leading articles in the *VB*. Entitled 'The Nationalist Idea and the Party', Hitler expounded on the reasons behind Germany's current miseries and how the NSDAP, a strong and united *völkisch* party, would remedy them. His second article on 3 January, 'Stupidity or Crime', was a vitriolic attack on the socialist government in Berlin for accepting the humiliating terms of the Versailles peace treaty. Over the first two weeks of January he spoke at the Högerbräu at Tal 6, the Kindl-Keller and the Sterneckerbräu. He also spoke at small venues including a bakery on Gabelsberger Straße in Munich and the Café Maximilian in Augsburg. The big event in January was the first NSDAP conference of the Munich branch of the party held on the 21st at the Hofbräuhaus. Anton Drexler was confirmed as the party's first chairman, and the 411 delegates were told that the party had grown to 3,000 registered members.[13] Two weeks later, the party held its first public meeting at the Zirkus Krone (Circus Crown), an enormous 6,000 seat venue on Marsstraße 43 in west Munich.

News at the end of January that the Supreme Allied Council had imposed the punitive sum of 226 billion Gold Marks[14] to be paid in reparations outraged the German people. Despondency quickly turned to anger throughout the country, and in Munich it led to deeper antipathy between von Kahr's Bavarian conservatives and the 'November criminals' in Berlin who signed the peace treaty and 'ran but did not represent' the nation. Capitalising on this new surge of resentment, Hitler and the NSDAP hastily organized their biggest meeting to date in the Zirkus Krone. Having only two days to organize an event of this size was risky, but the manager was a party member and reportedly charged little or nothing for the use of his arena. Posters were printed late in the afternoon and distributed the next morning, Thursday 3 February, the day of Hitler's talk. Conscious that failure could severely damage the party, Hitler hired two trucks to drive around the city all afternoon distributing leaflets advertising the mass demonstration. Each vehicle was 'swathed in as much red as possible' and flew 'swastika flags'. An hour before Hitler's speech the arena was only half full. A short time later, Hitler received more favourable reports, and by the time he arrived in front of the Circus there was a large crowd outside, some in the queues to buy tickets, and others, including Marxist opponents, who were there either to protest or just curious to see what was happening.[15]

When Hitler approached the podium he was overjoyed by what he saw: 'Like a giant shell this hall lies before me filled with thousands and thousands of people.' He spoke for almost three hours on the theme 'Future or Ruin' contrasting the fortunes of Germany ruled by the National Socialists or the chaotic continuation of a country drifting in decline and despair because of the traitors in Berlin. His talk was interrupted often by thunderous applause. The evening ended with the mass audience spontaneously singing the *Deutschland* song, sung, Hitler recalled, 'with the highest fervour'.[16]

One of the over 6,000 people in the audience was Elsa Bruckmann, the wife of Hugo Bruckmann the publisher. Elsa later recalled that she 'felt reawakened by his voice'. A few years later the Bruckmanns became Hitler's good friends and vital patrons, introducing him to the cultural and wealthy elites in Munich and raising money for the NSDAP.[17] Photographs taken at the Zirkus Krone on the night show that the hall was full to bursting with people who were in a state of euphoria over what they had heard. Hitler was becoming the darling of the *völkisch* nationalist right. Munich's newspapers either praised or pilloried Hitler's speech depending on their political affiliation. Hitler was pleased with both. He thrived on the publicity, particularly from his critics, because when his enemies took the time to censure him they confirmed that he had arrived as a political force.[18] Party chairman Anton Drexler wrote to Gottfried Feder to tell him that Hitler was 'the most suitable leader for our movement'.[19] Hitler received a tumultuous reception from his supporters when he spoke in the *Festsaal* at the Hofbräuhaus on 24 February, to commemorate the first year anniversary of the NSDAP. The event was given extensive coverage in the *VB*, which also printed for the first time the party's 25-point programme. The *VB* praised Hitler's 'fabulous speaking talent' further, noting that he 'aroused enthusiasm and forced thousands to a state of admiration' both for himself and the Movement.[20] Further events at the Zirkus Krone throughout the spring drew capacity crowds.

Hitler was in a buoyant mood in early June when he travelled to Berlin with Dietrich Eckart to raise money for the party and the *Völkischer Beobachter*. The Movement was doing well in Munich. Paid memberships ran into the several thousands, and the number of 'friends' and 'supporters' into several tens of thousands on the evidence of the mass audiences at NSDAP public meetings.

Despite this the party's finances were very weak after buying the *VB*, and this held up expanding the Movement outside Bavaria. Hitler and Eckart planned to spend most of the summer in Berlin to raise money and increase awareness of the party on the national stage. These plans ended abruptly on Saturday 9 July when Hitler rushed back to Munich to confront Drexler and the Working Committee (the 'old guard' in the party leadership) over the provisional merger of the NSDAP with the Nürnberg association of the *Deutsche Sozialistische Partei* (German Socialist Party, DSP), a small far-right workers party run by Julius Streicher[21] and backed by the Thule Society, and the German Works Association, established in Augsburg in March 1921 by university lecturer Otto Dickel.[22]

Hitler Takes Control of the NSDAP

Drexler and a few others in the party leadership had long harboured the notion of expanding the NSDAP into a national party by joining with other like-minded ethnic-chauvinist parties and setting up a new headquarters in Berlin. Hitler was furious that he had not been consulted on the advanced state of the amalgamation plans and felt deeply betrayed by Drexler. The unification meeting took place in Augsburg on Sunday 10 July 1921. Hitler made a surprise appearance, and over the course of the three-hour meeting he raised numerous objections and interrupted the proceedings often. After making an emotional speech in defence of National Socialism and the terrible consequences for the Movement if the merger proceeded, Hitler stormed out of the meeting hall and took a train back to Munich.[1]

On Monday 11 July, Hitler resigned from the party. Later in the week he issued an ultimatum to the party leadership, stating he would rejoin the party only if he was made party chairman with dictatorial powers, the headquarters of the party permanently remained in Munich, and all talk of mergers with other parties ended. Other groups and parties, Hitler insisted, were welcome to join the NSDAP providing they relinquished their leadership role and dropped their programmes. They must submit themselves completely to the Movement. A week passed, yet Drexler and the Working Committee refused to act. Hitler responded by giving a speech entitled '*Diktatur des Genies*' ('Dictatorship of Genius') to a capacity audience in the Zirkus Krone on Thursday night, 20 July. Hitler told his ardent supporters that without 'iron leadership' the NSDAP would cease to be a party fighting for National Socialism. The applause that followed was loud and prolonged. Fully satisfied that he had increased the temperature in the row between himself and the 'old guard' of party leaders, Hitler left Munich to spend the next two days with his friends the Lauböcks in Rosenheim. At roughly the same time, an anonymous pamphlet entitled 'Adolf Hitler – Is He a Traitor' was distributed to party members and reprinted in several Munich newspapers, including the Social Democratic *Münchener Post*, a daily paper that relished every opportunity to lampoon Hitler and the NSDAP. Hitler was portrayed as an interloping megalomaniac who lusted for power and called himself 'The King of Munich'. He was also accused of wasting large sums of party money cavorting 'with smoking ladies' and 'chorus girls'. The most ludicrous accusation of all was that Hitler was 'in the pay of the Jews'.

Most of the allegations were so fanciful that even the pamphlet's authors must have struggled to believe that their libellous concoctions contained even a hint of truth.[2]

On Monday evening, 25 July, Drexler and his fellow members in the Working Committee met at the Sterneckerbräu to discuss how to resolve the crisis. Most of them were so incensed with Hitler and his recent behaviour that they refused to compromise. Drexler, however, also knew that the party could not succeed without him. While the meeting continued, and much to Drexler's annoyance, Hitler spoke to 350 party members in another room at the Sterneckerbräu. He told them that the party was at a precarious stage in its development and that it must adopt the most radical methods to achieve its aims, including the use of violence. The evening ended without anything being resolved. The next day, Dietrich Eckart had a long private conversation with Drexler. Later that night, both Hitler and Drexler somewhat surprisingly appeared together at a NSDAP meeting hastily organized at the Hofbräuhaus. Hitler reaffirmed his friendship for Drexler. The two men, along with the party members present, celebrated their own and the party's 'newly achieved unity'. Eckart had succeeded in reconciling Hitler with Drexler, but it was Hitler who had triumphed.[3]

Hitler rejoined the party as member number 3,680, and on Friday 27 July, at an extraordinary meeting held at the Hofbräuhaus, the 554 Munich-NSDAP members in attendance unanimously endorsed him as their new First Chairman, 'responsible for the leadership of the whole movement'.[4] All of Hitler's demands were met, and the party's charter was amended to incorporate his concept of leadership based on the *Führerprinzip* (a strong leader obeyed unconditionally).[5] The leader's personal authority replaced majority voting in the party. Hitler's friendship with Drexler was reconfirmed, and Drexler was made honorary chairman. In a short acceptance speech, Hitler thanked the membership, and pledged that the Movement, which began in Munich, will always have its headquarters in Munich. Later the same evening, Hitler spoke to a much larger audience at the Zirkus Krone. Hermann Esser introduced him as *unser Führer* (our leader) to rapturous applause. Hitler spoke on issues that mattered to the party, and the aims and principles of National Socialism. He concluded his speech with personal reflections on the strength that comes from unity and the enormous power of one's own will.[6]

Despite his new unrestricted authority, Hitler refrained from purging the 'old guard' in the Working Committee, and spent the rest of the summer healing the divisions and consolidating inner-party support in Munich. Weekly, large crowds assembled at the Zirkus Krone and the Hofbräuhaus to hear Hitler speak, or just to get a glimpse of the NSDAP's charismatic leader. The *VB* did not mention there had even been an internal party squabble until the end of July, by which time it was over, and the paper focused on praising Hitler's leadership and the new bright future of the party.[7] It was Rudolf Heβ[8] who best summed up what had happened and what it meant to the party: 'Do you really think that the masses would pack the Zirkus Krone without him?' Heβ was in no doubt that 'Hitler is the leader personality who alone is able to carry through the struggle.'[9]

Hitler Builds the Party

Violence had been an integral part of Bavarian politics since the end of the war. All of the political parties had a *Saalschutz* (hall protection squad) to safeguard their leaders and meetings from physical attacks. What distinguished the National Socialists from the others in their use of violence was that it became a core element in their political and social ideology. Hitler firmly believed that a radical approach was required to solve Germany's many post-war problems. Violence was justified as being a necessary means to build up the National Socialist *Volksgemeinschaft* (people's community) and further the aims of the party in the service of the nation.

On 3 August 1921, the NSDAP set up a *Turn- und Sportabteilung* (Gymnastic and Sports Section) under the command of Hans-Ulrich Klintzsch, a 23-year-old former marine lieutenant. It was especially designed to bring together (and recruit) young party members who would serve as 'a battering ram for the whole Movement'. The *VB* advertised the party's new sports section on 14 August, outlining its dual purpose as a protection squad and an agent for ideological education. 'It will above all inculcate an unbending will to action in the hearts of our young supporters,' the advert stated, 'loyalty to one another will be cultivated, as well a cheerful obedience to the leader.'[1] All young supporters, irrespective of class or circumstances, were urged to visit the party office at Tal 54, in the Sterneckerbräu, to enrol. Above all, the party had set out to create a cult of youth and violence.

The first iniquitous action of the young protection squad was on 14 September when a small group accompanied Hitler to the Löwenbräukeller to break up an evening meeting of the separatist Bavarian League. Boldly they marched up to the platform where the leader, Otto Ballerstedt, was speaking. The hall went dark when someone switched off the lights. When the lights came back on Ballerstedt lay on the floor battered and bruised, bleeding profusely from a head wound. Soon afterwards the police arrived and closed the meeting. Hitler's young thugs had achieved their objective. Ballerstedt insisted on pressing charges, but on this occasion the police merely warned Hitler not to do it again. Hitler took little notice of the warning. Two nights later, he gave an intemperate speech against Bavarian separatism at the Kindl-Keller, and praised his young followers for their courage and resolve in battle at the Löwenbräukeller. The matter was not over. Premier von Kahr and Police President Pöhner had been forced out of office in September. The new and more liberal Bavarian government, and Munich police, were less inclined to ignore the shenanigans of the NSDAP. An inquest into the brawl at the Löwenbräukeller was held on 25 October, but an unrepentant Hitler shamelessly 'justified' his men's actions: 'We got what we wanted. Ballerstedt did not speak.'[2]

Hitler changed the name of the Gymnastic and Sports Section to the *Sturmabteilung* (Storm Division, SA) on 5 October 1921. The same night he spoke to forty SA leaders at the Gasthaus Högerbräu on the Tal. The Högerbräu soon became the unofficial headquarters of the SA in Munich, and the storm troopers quickly gained a reputation for drinking and carousing, as well as for their aggressive tactics and involvement in brawls with left-wing opponents.[3] The first real test of the SA came on a Friday night, 4 November 1921, when Hitler spoke at a party rally in the Hofbräuhaus. His opponents planned to disrupt the event, and they came early. Over 800 Social Democrats, 'Red' factory workers, and supposedly fighters from a 'Judeo-Marxist hit-squad' had taken up positions close to the speaker's platform. Their tables were covered with heavy beer steins, and many more empty mugs were piled high on the floor beneath, ominously ready to be used as missiles when the fracas began. Hitler recognised the danger when he entered the Festsaal and warned his forty-six SA men. 'I made it clear to the lads that today probably for the first time they would have to show themselves loyal to the movement through thick and thin,' Hitler wrote later in *Mein Kampf*, 'and that not a man of us must leave the hall unless we were carried out dead.' Hermann Esser introduced Hitler, and there were a few angry shouts that pierced the applause. He spoke for about an hour and a half, then suddenly a 'Red' jumped onto a chair and roared '*Freiheit!* (freedom), the greeting of the Social Democrats and the Marxist battle cry, and on this occasion the signal for the fight to begin.[4]

'Three, four, five heavy stone pots flew within an inch of the speaker's [Hitler's] head,' recalled Magdalena Schweyer. The next instant she witnessed the SA surge forward. For twenty minutes the battle raged. 'An idiotic spectacle,' Hitler called it, 'the cracking of chair-legs, the crashing of the mugs, bawling, howling, and screaming.'[5] Bloodied but unbowed the storm troopers drove their enemies down the stairs and out of the beer hall. Hitler had remained at his place on the speaker's rostrum throughout, and with order restored Esser calmly announced that the meeting would continue. 'That's famous now,' Frau Schweyer exclaimed. 'Everyone in Germany remembers those words: '*Die Versammlung geht weiter*' (The meeting will proceed). The Festsaal was a wreck. Hundreds of smashed beer mugs lying everywhere and piles of broken tables and chairs.[6]

The Battle of the Hofbräuhaus instantly became a party legend. Five days after the event, with many of the SA men including Emil Maurice and Rudolf Heß still in bandages, Hitler hosted a celebratory dinner at the Restaurant Adelmann. He praised his SA men on their successful 'baptism of fire', telling them, 'Comrades! We have won a battle.' Public approval of the NSDAP soared, showing the extent to which nationalist and *völkisch* resentment was rising in Munich. The SA's victory over vastly superior opposition, especially Marxists and Jews, was portrayed in National Socialist newspapers and pamphlets as proof of the superiority of party's ideas, ideas that awakened courage and superhuman strength, and in turn legitimised both the ideas and the methods used to defend them.[7]

On 5 and 9 November, the *Völkischer Beobachter* reprinted its mid-August recruitment advert directed at young followers, but this time it encouraged new members to join the SA and to sign up at the new party offices at Corneliusstraße 12.[8] The party needed larger premises than the single room it occupied in the Sterneckerbräu. Through the efforts of one member, the party secured the funds needed to move its headquarters to the Gasthaus Cornelius, just west of the Gärtnerplatz and a short walk from its former location on the Tal. This was the NSDAP's second headquarters until mid-November 1923. It was another tavern, but the party now had four rooms for its use, including a large meeting room. The *VB* 'urgently requested' members to donate money to help repay the 'generous loan', and to assist in furnishing the new offices 'by providing pictures, cabinets, shelves, books, etc.'[9]

By the end of 1921 the party had 4,100 registered members, almost doubling its membership in a year.[10] The party attracted its new members from all age groups and segments of society. Hitler was the main reason they joined. His speeches were printed in the *VB* and he regularly contributed articles addressing both current events and matters of importance to the party. Twice a week the NSDAP held mass meetings in Munich's major beer halls, and small events took place in the restaurants and taverns in the city centre, on the Tal, and around both the Marienplatz and the Viktualienmarkt, the city's oldest and grandest food market. The SA, one of the party's most important instruments of power, had been established; it was attracting new recruits, and revitalizing idle and frustrated young men in the service of the Movement. The party was also slowly developing its emblems and regalia, along with its distinctive tribal character. Hitler fashioned the party insignia and the flag using colours that 'honoured the German people and attested to the party's veneration of the past'. Both the flag and the insignia were designed along the same lines with a red background, a white disk in the centre, and a black swastika in the middle. The same model was used for the armbands and lapel pins. Hitler summarized his concept in *Mein Kampf*: 'In *red* we see the social idea of the movement, in *white* the nationalistic idea, in the *swastika* the mission of the struggle.'[11] By the time Hitler was the undisputed leader of the party, members greeted each other with a vibrant *Heil* and a rigid straight arm salute. Dietrich Eckart provided the party with its first original marching song, the *Sturm-Lied* (Storm Song), based on a poem he had written. He also gave the movement its slogan and rallying cry '*Deutschland Erwache*' (Germany Awake), which appeared at the top of all SA Standards, first given to SA units by Hitler in 1922. Hitler possessed an extraordinary sense of political symbolism, and the National Socialists excelled at using imagery, insignia, parades, and sound to create a powerful aesthetic. Party events increasingly became colourful and uplifting ceremonies, overflowing with emotion, and with established rituals that created a feverish atmosphere in anticipation of the Führer's appearance. For many, especially the disheartened, the fearful, and those filled with hatred against Germany's real and imaginary enemies, Hitler was a symbol of hope for a brighter future.[12]

Hitler celebrated New Year's Day 1922 with his SA at the Högerbräu on the Tal. At the start of the second week of the year he spoke to 4,000 supporters in the Hofbräuhaus, but the week did not end well. On Thursday 12 January, Hitler, along with Hermann Esser and Oskar Körner, appeared before the People's Court of Munich, where they were convicted of affray for their part in the attack on Otto Ballerstedt in the Löwenbräukeller back in September. The court pronounced a suspended sentence of three months' imprisonment, and further warned the men against any further violent disturbances. Despite the guilty verdict, the month ended on a high note for Hitler and the NSDAP. Over two days, 29 and 30 January, the party held its first *Parteitag* (party congress) in Munich. About 1,000 delegates attended, including delegations from Austria and Czechoslovakia. The main events took place at the Hofbräuhaus and the new party offices on Corneliusstraße. Hitler's position as first chairman was strengthened, and the party's statutes were amended to give him complete authority over the membership, both individuals and local associations.[13]

The party continued to grow, numbering 44 local groups in Bavaria and another 56 outside Bavaria by the end of 1922. They all recognised Hitler and the Munich group as the party leadership. The party also wanted to enlist 'all the young supporters of our cause, who due to their age cannot belong to the SA or a political organization'. To get them involved, and prepare them for future service to the Movement, Hitler founded on 8 March the *Jugendbund der NSDAP* (the Youth League of the National Socialist German Workers' Party), the forerunner of the *Hitlerjugend* (Hitler Youth, HJ). The first leader of the Youth League was Gustav Adolf Lenk. He joined the DAP when he was 15 years old and had already attempted to create a youth movement in 1920. The main purpose of the *Jugendbund* was to provide recruits for the SA. In its first appeal for members, the *VB* called on boys of German blood aged between 14 and 18 'who have the distress and misery of our Fatherland at heart, and who sometime later will wish to combat the Jewish enemy'. The organization, as stated in its statutes, combined exciting outdoors and physical activities with education in the *völkisch* idea to prepare its young fighters for the difficult tasks of the future. Hitler spoke at the official foundation of the Youth League on 13 May 1922 in Munich, where it concentrated its activities and flourished. A lack of resources hindered its progress in other parts of Bavaria and other regions of Germany.[14]

In a deliberate effort to extend the NSDAP's appeal and influence, Hitler increased his speaking engagements outside Munich, broadcasting his message and soliciting support in the cities and larger towns around Bavaria, in Vienna, and on two occasions during the spring in Berlin. Hitler spent 23 days in Berlin in March and another 30 days between May and June. His travelling speaking tours ended abruptly on 24 June when he was arrested and incarcerated in Munich-Stadelheim prison.[15] Earlier that day, Walther Rathenau, the German Foreign Minister, had been assassinated. Rathenau was Jewish, and regarded by many extreme nationalists as a traitor because he advocated meeting Germany's obligations as set out in the Versailles Treaty. Hermann Ehrhardt's 'Organization Consul' (OC) was suspected of committing the murder. Ten months earlier, the OC killed Matthias Erzberger, a Centre Party politician who had signed the armistice agreement in 1918. Munich was widely regarded as a breeding-ground for right-wing terrorism. As a direct consequence of Rathenau's murder, the Reichstag in Berlin hastily passed a Law for the Protection of the Republic, an emergency decree designed to halt radical right-wing violence. A day later the Bavarian government passed an amendment suspending the 'Prussian' law, and declared Bavarian criminals would be dealt with in Bavaria, in accordance with Bavarian laws. Relations between Munich and Berlin deteriorated even further, but Hitler remained in Stadelheim for five weeks. He was released on 27 July and the very next night he gave one of his most formative speeches on anti-Semitism in the Bürgerbräukeller.[16]

Entitled 'Free State or Slavery', Hitler's speech was in part a denunciation of the weak politicians in Berlin and their contemptible 'self-protection' law, but more importantly it was a warning against the mortal danger of the Jews to the German people. He talked about 'a vast battle in progress between *national-völkisch* ideas and international Jewry, linking together both Jewish-Bolshevism and Social Democratic capitalism. He called upon the German youth to join the Storm Divisions, and praised those already fighting for the protection of the Movement and through it the nation. The battle, Hitler claimed, would be long and hard, but it was a necessary fight 'to remodel Germany in a revolutionary fashion ... to the Germany of the German people!'[17] The capacity audience was in a frenzied state of ecstasy by the time Hitler stepped down from the platform. He was mobbed by well-wishers, and those eager to join the party and the SA. Throughout the summer and into the autumn Hitler continued to speak out against the socialist politicians in Berlin, the international exploitation of Germany, and the Jews.

All of Bavaria's conservative and far-right associations opposed the compliance policies of the Reich's 'fulfilment politicians' and rejected their attempt to 'subject Bavaria to Berlin's course'. Led by the largest patriotic society, the *Bund Bayern und Reich* (League Bavaria and Reich), they staged a mass demonstration on Munich's Königsplatz on Wednesday 16 August. Hitler and the NSDAP were invited. The crowd numbered about 50,000, but before Hitler's arrival there was little excitement. Then the SA made a dramatic entrance to the rousing sound of two brass bands. Wearing their distinctive armbands, the SA marched onto the Königsplatz in six columns, with large swastika flags flying. Kurt Lüdecke, an ardent nationalist and wealthy businessman, witnessed the event and saw Hitler speak for the first time. He recalled the crowd swelling to well over 100,000, 'filling the beautiful square to the last inch and overflowing into the surrounding streets.' Lüdecke was overawed by the way Hitler held the attention of his mass audience, himself included, 'under a hypnotic spell by the sheer force of his conviction'. 'Bavaria is now the most German land in Germany,' Hitler told his like-minded listeners. Hitler assailed the 'Novemberlings', pledged his own undying love for the Fatherland, and urged his followers to set the country free, ending his speech with the NSDAP's defiant slogan: '*Deutschland Erwache!*' 'Then there was thunderous applause,' Lüdecke recalled, and 'the masses took a solemn oath 'to save Germany in Bavaria from Bolshevism.'[18]

Hitler's influence and the party's popularity were in the ascendancy. In October he was invited as a principal speaker at 'German Day' a *völkisch* festival organized by the *Vaterländische Verbände* (the Union of Fatherland Associations) in the northern Bavarian city of Coburg.[19] This was a big test for Hitler and the NSDAP. The guests of honour were the Grand Duke and Duchess of Coburg. Both supported the nationalists' cause, but politically Coburg was decidedly left-wing. Hitler brought a 'large escort' of 800 SA men with him for the two-day event over the weekend of 14–15 October. When they arrived at the Coburg train station, local politicians asked Hitler to avoid clashes with leftist groups by not marching through the city. Hitler refused. The SA, on Hitler's orders, 'immediately lined up in companies and marched into the city with resounding music and flags flying'. The march, as the city officials had feared, provoked a series of pitched street battles. To Hitler's delight, the storm troops thrashed their Red opponents. On Sunday the SA marched through the city again, this time unmolested and to 'spontaneous cheering in many places'. Coburg would become a National Socialist stronghold, and when Hitler became Reich Chancellor he had a commemorative medal struck for the SA who had rid the city of its 'Marxist madness'.[20]

The victory at Coburg enhanced the brutal reputation of the SA, but, as Hitler noted in *Mein Kampf*, 'the outside world also began to follow our doings more closely.'[21] A number of the party's future senior leaders made their way to the

Corneliusstraße headquarters and joined up in late 1922 and early 1923. Julius Streicher, the Nürnberg political leader, joined just before accompanying Hitler to Coburg.[22] Ernst (Putzi) Hanfstaengl joined immediately after hearing Hitler speak, on 21 November, in Munich's *Salvatorkeller*, at Hochstraße 40 (now 77) in Nockherberg on the east side of the Isar. 'Putzi', which means 'little fellow', was the six-foot-four Hanfstaengl's nickname. He was a respected Munich art publisher and an early associate of Hitler's, opening doors to Munich's cultural elite and providing funds for the chronically 'short of money' party.[23] Hermann Göring, fighter ace, the last commander of the Richthofen squadron in 1918 and a future Reich Marshall who became the second most powerful man in the Third Reich, joined on 30 November after hearing Hitler give a speech at a party event in Munich.[24] The last in this list of early members who became high-ranking Nazi officials was Heinrich Himmler, an agricultural student at the Munich Technical College and future *Reichsführer-SS* who joined in early 1923.[25]

The term 'Nazi' is a contraction of the first word in the name of the *Nationalsozialistische Deutsche Arbeiter Partei*, and, according to Lüdecke, 'a sound of a sort that is common in Bavarian speech'.[26] It was also a word that in the autumn of 1922 was increasingly heard on Munich's streets, in the beer halls and cafés, and at the university. Both Göring and Rudolf Heß, Hitler's private secretary and subsequently Deputy Leader of the Party, were students at the Ludwig-Maximilians-Universität (LMU). Heß studied geopolitics under Professor Karl Haushofer, the leading exponent of *Lebensraum* (living space – a Prussian imperialist concept and Pan-German ideology that justified territorial conquest at Russia's expense to end Germany's strategic isolation and unite ethnic Germans scattered throughout eastern Europe).[27] Julius Streicher also took the occasional short course at the university. On the occasions when Streicher came to Munich from Nürnberg, he would invite Hitler, Heß, and Göring to join him at the Nürnberger Bratwurst Glöckl am Dom at Frauenplatz 9, in the shadow of the Frauenkirche on the south-east corner of the square. This old-fashioned candlelit restaurant, with its dark wood panelled walls, heavy tables and sturdy benches, was a cosy venue for informal meetings. Hitler and his close associates discussed party matters, *völkisch* philosophy, and *Lebensraum*, over plates of *Nürnberger Rostbratwürst*, small pork sausages roasted over an open beechwood fire, and mugs of beer. Serious conversation in convivial surroundings made for the type of evening that Hitler now enjoyed.[28]

On Monday evening, 13 November, Hitler along with his entourage of bodyguards and regular companions, Max Amann, Hermann Esser, Ulrich Graf, Christian Weber, and Lieutenant Klintzsch, joined Dietrich Eckart and Gottfried Feder for Eckart's *Stammtisch* at the Café Neumayr on the edge of the Viktualienmarkt. Café Neumayr was another traditional Munich hostelry with rows of benches and long tables that facilitated camaraderie while the patrons drank litres of beer or cups of coffee. Hitler was in a reflective mood. He explained to his companions the essence of the *völkisch* Nazi party. Jews were excluded. 'Only a person of German blood can become a member of the party.'[29] Hitler's views reflected the opinions held in ethnic-chauvinist and nationalist circles in Munich and Bavaria. LMU appointed Fritz Lenz as its first-ever professor for Racial Hygiene in 1923, and Munich's publishers, especially Hugo Bruckmann, Julius Lehmann, and the Eher-Verlag run by Max Amann, spread and popularised racist and *völkisch* nationalist ideas. The radical ideas and the increase in violence attributed to the Nazis over the recent months frightened other states in Germany. Prussia, citing the Republic Protection Act, banned the NSDAP on 15 November.[30] Hitler responded by holding the two largest mass rallies in the party's history up to that time. The first 'Night of Speeches' took place on Thursday 30 November. Hitler spoke in quick succession at five major Munich beer halls spread widely across the city. At the second, on Wednesday night, 13 December, between 8.30 pm and midnight, he spoke at ten of Munich's most prominent beer halls. He delivered the same speech each time, warning his eager listeners about the danger Jews and Marxists posed to the German people and the Reich. The two *NSDAP-Großkundgebungen* (NSDAP-Large Rallies) combined with Prussia's ban on the party had the desired effect: membership soared from roughly 8,000 in early November to over 18,000 by the end of the year.[31]

1923 – the Beer Hall Putsch

The year 1923 started badly for Germany. Disagreements over reparations payments were used as a pretext by Raymond Poincaré, France's vindictive premier, to justify sending troops into Germany. On 11 January, the first contingent of French and Belgian troops occupied the Ruhr valley. The Reich government in Berlin responded with a policy of 'passive resistance'. France and Belgium reacted harshly. The French put the Ruhr under military rule, dismissing German government officials who disobeyed them, arresting striking workers, and taking direct control of the coal mines and the railways. Economic life pretty much came to a standstill. German currency values plummeted and there followed a year-long period of hyperinflation. The German mark had been in a steady decline against the US dollar since the end of the war but it suffered an apocalyptic devaluation following the military occupation.[1] The mark was at a rate of 7,000 to one US dollar at the start of January. Two weeks into the occupation it had slumped to 50,000 and by 9 November it took 628,500,000,000 Reichsmarks to buy one dollar. Nationalist organizations across Germany were outraged and called for a 'united front' against both the occupying forces and the Reich government. Elements of the Reichswehr, especially in Bavaria, wanted to resist the invaders with force.[2]

On the evening of the foreign occupation crisis, Hitler gave an impromptu speech in the Zirkus Krone. He criticised the French and the Belgians for their greed and inhumanity, but he seethed with anger against the feckless government in Berlin for allowing the humiliation to happen, and further excoriated the 'November criminals' for leaving Germany defenceless and exposed to 'total enslavement'. Hitler concluded his speech by calling on his audience to run the 'treacherous Jewish-Marxist regime out of Berlin'. Three days later he gave a similar speech at the Bürgerbräukeller. He was back at the Zirkus Krone on Thursday 18 January speaking to another packed audience of 7,000 supporters, where again he called for the elimination of the criminal and incompetent government in Berlin, and announced that the NSDAP's annual party conference would take place in Munich over three days at the end of January.[3]

Rumours had been circulating since November 1922 that Hitler and his National Socialists were planning to overthrow the Berlin government in a manner somewhat similar to Benito Mussolini and the Italian Fascists who had come to power in October after their successful march on Rome. These rumours plus the occupation crisis in January alarmed Eugen von Knilling, the moderate conservative BVP president of Bavaria. Initially he thought Hitler was little more than a populist slogan merchant, but with rising public resentment against both the Berlin and Bavarian governments Knilling imposed restrictions on Nazi public events, including the planned party conference, to safeguard against anything audacious Hitler might try. Hitler threatened violence if his marches and mass meetings were curtailed. Knilling responded by declaring a state of emergency throughout Bavaria on 26 January, the day before the NSDAP's *Reichsparteitag* was to begin. A series of hastily organized meetings ensued. First, Röhm and von Epp spoke on behalf of Hitler with General Otto von Lossow, the commander of the Reichswehr in Bavaria. The general then met with Hitler, who gave his 'word of honour as a former soldier' that he would not attempt a putsch. Hitler repeated his promise to von Kahr, who afterwards spoke with Knilling. Later that evening, Hitler met with Eduard Nortz, the police president, and after Hitler agreed to some minor restrictions (which he later ignored) he received permission to hold his conference.[4]

The NSDAP's rally began on Saturday 27 January and went on for three days and three nights, during which time the Nazis virtually controlled the city. Delegations came from all over Bavaria, as well as the rest of Germany, Austria, and Czechoslovakia. Hitler opened the conference with another *NSDAP-Großkundgebungen*, speaking in quick succession at twelve party meetings, all held simultaneously across Munich. His popularity had never been greater. Historian Karl Alexander von Müller, one of Hitler's 'propaganda course' instructors, recalled the 'hypnotic mass-excitement' at the meeting he attended in the Löwenbräukeller. 'The audience rose as one man, with shouts of "Heil!" as Hitler strode down the aisle.' The teacher was awestruck by his former pupil's charisma and power: 'Fanatically hysteric romanticism with a brutal will'.[5] The next day, in violation of the police agreement, 6,000 SA men paraded before Hitler on the *Marsfeld* (Field of Mars) in west Munich, a couple of blocks west of the Zirkus Krone. Despite the cold and the snow, the brass bands played and the swastika flags waved as Hitler consecrated banners and standards for new SA formations. Some units wore a prototype of the later SA uniform, consisting of grey riding breeches, a canvas jacket, the swastika armband, and the distinctive ski cap. The brown shirts were introduced nationwide in 1926.[6]

The party congress ended with a general meeting held at the Zirkus Krone. Hitler outlined the three essential elements of National Socialism: the social principle (based on a duty to serve), the national idea (the *völkisch* community and concept of struggle for the national good), and the idea of anti-Semitism (racial purity to protect the German people and the German state). Hitler's ideas were simplistic and imprecise, but the sustained applause showed that his audience were in complete agreement. Hitler's popular support, especially in Munich, was the main reason why neither Knilling nor Nortz took action against the NSDAP for its many brazen challenges. Time and again the Bavarian government and police had been humiliated, but they feared they would lose public support if they moved against the Nazis. The Reichswehr in Bavaria took a more pragmatic view, and set out to profit from the Nazis' popularity.[7]

The Reichswehr leadership regarded the nationalist paramilitary groups as a potential reserve army that they could deploy in case of an armed confrontation with the French in the Ruhr. In early February, Captain Ernst Röhm established the *Arbeitsgemeinschaft der vaterländischen Kampfverbände* (Working Association of Patriotic Combat Groups); the SA was one of its core organizations, along with the Bund Oberland and the Reichskriegsflagge. Under the command of retired *Oberstleutnant* (First Lieutenant) Hermann Kriebel, the combined combat groups received arms and military training from the Reichswehr and were reorganized into an auxiliary army. Göring was appointed the new commander of the SA, and it became a force designed for national service rather than a party meeting protection squad.[8] As a result, Hitler established the *Stabswache*, a small bodyguard of twelve men to provide his personal security. At the end of April this group was enlarged to twenty-two men and renamed *Stoßtrupp Hitler* (Shock Troop Hitler). Their founding meeting took place in the Torbräu, another small Munich beer hall at Tal 41, directly across the street from the Sterneckerbräu. During a solemn evening ceremony on 30 April the men swore allegiance to their leader, Adolf Hitler, '*Treue bis in den Tod*' (loyalty to the death). By the end of May the assault squad numbered over 100 men. They wore the old field grey army uniform, swastika armband, black revolver strap and belt, high black boots, and a black ski caps with a silver death's head insignia. These shock troops were the forerunner of the *Schutzstaffel-SS* (protection squad) that under Heinrich Himmler, Reichsführer-SS from January 1929, became an elite arm of the Nazi party.[9]

In mid-April Hitler discussed his preferred tactics for dealing with Germany's internal and external enemies with Röhm. He agreed with his former SA leader that the army could be a significant factor in unifying 'all Germans in a common Fatherland' and that the combat league played its part, but he insisted that ridding Berlin of the 'November criminals and Marxist traitors' took precedence before armed resistance to France, or any other potential external adversary, could succeed. Celebrating his 34th birthday in front of 9,000 followers at the Zirkus Krone, Hitler expanded on his fears that the most severe and present danger to Germany was the internal threat of Jewish Bolshevism and the 'scoundrels, swindlers, and windbags' that masqueraded as a national government in Berlin. He told his supporters that 'the first requirement was always the elimination of the Marxist poison from our national body.' National Socialists, he vowed, 'were resolved to declare a war of annihilation on Marxism'. Hitler repeated his message on two consecutive nights, 26 and 27 April, again to large crowds at the Zirkus Krone. Exhausted and in need of a rest, he spent the weekend in the mountains surrounding Berchtesgaden visiting his old friend Dietrich Eckart.[10]

It was Hitler's first trip to the Obersalzberg and the beginning of his lifelong love for the lakes and mountains in the Berchtesgadener-Land. On Saturday morning, 28 April, Emile Maurice drove Hitler, his sister Paula, and Christian Weber from Munich to the Pension Moritz (later the Platterhof hotel) on the Obersalzberg. They spent their days walking in the mountains and evenings talking with Eckart. Hitler was introduced to the Schuster family, who owned the Gasthaus Türken. Later on Saturday evening he spoke to a small group of guests and residents who had gathered at the Türken especially to meet him. On Monday Hitler and his party returned to Munich to make final preparations for May Day celebrations.[11]

May Day in Munich was the German Labour Day celebrated by leftists and the working class, and also the anniversary of the city's liberation from soviet control by Freikorps and Reichswehr units in 1919. Hitler petitioned the Bavarian government to ban the socialists and communists from holding festivities on the Theresienwiese, where Oktoberfest is held. His request was refused, but Hitler expected as much. Undeterred, he pressed on with his desire to prevent the Marxists and Reds from marching through Munich's streets. He ordered the SA to assemble on the Oberwiesenfeld, the old Bavarian army training ground in north-west Munich, and prepare for a major clash with the Reds. Some 2,000 men armed with rifles, machine guns, hand grenades, and a few cannon turned up in the early hours of 1 May. Hitler was standing at the head of his forces, wearing a steel helmet and his Iron Cross, First Class, when they were encircled by the Bavarian police who were determined not to let the Nazis turn the day into a bloody civil war. Later in the morning a detachment of local Reichswehr troops marched onto the Oberwiesenfeld and demanded the storm troopers hand over their weapons and retire from the field. A few hotheads, including Hermann Kriebel, urged Hitler to fight, but he knew better than to lose a pitched battle with the Reichswehr and the police. The standoff ended peacefully, although Hitler gave a violent speech later that evening to a full house in the Zirkus Krone, heaping scorn 'on the Marxists and their feeble accomplices in the Bavarian government'.[12]

Through the spring and early summer Hitler stepped up his attacks on both the Bavarian and Berlin governments, speaking to large crowds in Munich's beer halls but also taking his message to the cities and towns around Munich. In May he gave speeches in Murnau am Staffelsee, Erlangen, and Augsburg; in June he spoke at NSDAP meetings in Passau and Regensburg; and in July he visited Augsburg again and Ingolstadt. On weekends Hitler returned to the Obersalzberg. He embraced mountain life completely, trekking on mountain paths, wearing lederhosen, and becoming a regular at the small picturesque inns such as the Hochlenzer and the Alpengastwirtschaft Vorderbrand. He was also a regular visitor at Eckart's house, the Göllhäusl on Scharitzkehlstraβe 40 at the top of the Vorderbrand. Years later, during the war, Hitler told his friend and photographer Heinrich Hoffmann that his visits to the mountains were both restorative and useful. 'All of my great decisions were taken at Obersalzberg.' The beautiful landscape distracted him 'from petty things' and he was able 'to think clearly'. On the Obersalzberg, Hitler claimed, 'my imagination is stimulated.'[13]

After the humiliating retreat from the Oberwiesenfeld on May Day, Hitler realized that all his plans were doomed to failure if he did not have the army's support. On 1 and 2 September, the Fatherland Associations held a 'German Day' in Nürnberg to celebrate the German victory over the French at Sedan in 1870. Hitler joined Ludendorff in a public demonstration of political and military solidarity in front of some 100,000 uniformed men. Ludendorff's status as a war hero was invaluable in winning over the Reichswehr. The meeting in Nürnberg also produced a new patriotic association called the *Deutscher Kampfbund* (German Fighting Union). This was a more formal coming together of the SA, the Reichskriegsflagge and the Bund Oberland than the earlier combat league. Hermann Kriebel continued in his role as the military commander, and Hitler's friend, the former diplomat and Baltic German, Max Erwin von Scheubner-Richter ran the day-to-day operations. Later, on 25 September, Hitler was confirmed as the association's political leader. The fighting union's manifesto called for an immediate overthrow of the Berlin government. Once again, Hitler emphasised the primary importance of 'putting down Marxism'. His plan of action called for taking political control of Bavaria first and then marching on Berlin to complete the national revolution.[14]

Constant chatter about an imminent revolution, combined with economic chaos and social deprivation that affected all segments of society, produced a febrile and malevolent atmosphere in Munich. There was rampant inflation; in August the exchange rate with the dollar surpassed one million Reichsmarks. Unemployment rose dramatically, people were starving, and over 100,000 Munich residents were dependent on poverty aid. Widespread despair and destitution provoked mass demonstrations, food riots, and strikes all across the country. By 23 August, the Reich government of Wilhelm Cuno had collapsed and was replaced by a socialist coalition led by Gustav Stresemann. Throughout the rest of August and September the NSDAP headquarters on Corneliusstraβe was inundated by visitors off the street, letters, and telephone calls, all urging Hitler to take action, save Bavaria, and rescue the country from catastrophe.

The NSDAP announced a day of mass protest for Thursday 27 September, with fourteen events spread across the city. Rumours intensified that Hitler's putsch was about to begin.[15]

The Nazis' big day of rallies did not happen. On 26 September Reich Chancellor Stresemann ended 'passive resistance' to the French in the Ruhr and instituted a policy whereby Germany paid reparations and fulfilled the terms of the peace agreement. Nationalist organizations and the Bavarian government were appalled. They believed it was a national betrayal, capitulation and compliance at their worst, and feared that it was the first act in establishing a Communist regime. Thuringia and Saxony already had state governments that were coalitions of Communists and left-wing extremists. The Bavarian government reacted immediately, declared a state of emergency, and banned all Nazi party events in an effort to lessen Hitler's appeal and prevent him from staging a coup d'état. Premier Knilling appointed Gustav von Kahr as general state commissar, with near-dictatorial powers. Reich President Friedrich Ebert responded to Kahr's appointment by declaring a national state of emergency. The next day, Berlin ordered General von Lossow to shut down the *Völkischer Beobachter*. The general refused. He was sacked by Reich Defence Minister Otto Gessler for disobeying a direct order. Kahr, in an act of further defiance of Berlin's authority, reinstated Lossow as commander of the Reichswehr in Bavaria. Historian Volker Ullrich summed up the fiery exchange between Kahr and Ebert succinctly: 'the break between Munich and Berlin was complete.'[16] A triumvirate of Kahr, Lossow, and Colonel Hans von Seisser, the chief of police, became the de facto rulers of Bavaria, and quietly they began their own plans to overthrow the government in Berlin and possibly re-establish the Wittelsbach dynasty.[17]

While the battle of wills between Kahr and Ebert continued, Hitler left Munich to speak at another 'German Day' on Sunday 30 September, organized by nationalists and paramilitary groups in Bayreuth. Hitler was the main speaker at a protest march against the French occupation of the Ruhr. Albert Preu, the ultra-nationalist mayor of Bayreuth, welcomed some 6,000 uniformed men to his 'old town with a world reputation as a centre of art and the home of Wagner'. He told the parade, 'it is the spirit of Siegfried that we need, so that, like our Master, Richard Wagner, who triumphed over all hostile forces, we can once more achieve respect in the world.'[18] The main event was Hitler's evening speech to a full house crammed into the *Reithalle* (riding hall). His patrons, the Bechsteins, had travelled down from Berlin to hear him and see their 'adopted daughter' Winifred Wagner and her young family. Hitler began his speech by lamenting the current crisis in Germany. In sonorous voice he told his attentive listeners that only a strong leader could restore Germany's strength and greatness. 'What we need,' he said, is not diplomats, experts or politicians but

'10 million soldiers' to fight for the German people and defend the country. The comparison between himself and Wagner's hero Siegfried was obvious to his audience, as was their wholehearted approval. Thunderous applause brought the evening to a close. Hitler was delighted by the enthusiastic reception he had received, but even more so by his knowledge that the next day he was going to visit, for the first time, Villa Wahnfried, the Wagners' family home.

The Bechsteins hosted a reception for Hitler after his speech, and introduced him, 'a Wagner enthusiast and connoisseur', to Winifred, who in her youthful enthusiasm invited the 'saviour of Germany' to breakfast the next day at Wahnfried, at Richard-Wagner-Straβe 48. Hitler met Siegfried, the son of the *Meister*, and the children: Wieland six, Friedelind five, Wolfgang four, and Verena three years old. The Chamberlains were also present. Houston Stewart Chamberlain was married to Wagner's youngest daughter Eva. Winifred recalled that Hitler was modest, had good manners, and took a genuine interest in the Wagner family's problems. After a tour of the house and breakfast, the Wagners escorted Hitler to the grave of the Master at the bottom of the large garden behind the villa. Hitler remained there alone in contemplation for some time. When he returned to the house he promised to do all he could to support the family and the revival of the Wagner Festival. Siegfried spoke for the entire family when he said, 'he [Hitler] won all our hearts.'[19] Later the same day, Hitler had an audience with Chamberlain. He made an extraordinarily good impression on the *völkisch* writer and guardian of Wagner's life work. In fact, Chamberlain was so moved by the experience of meeting Hitler that he wrote to him a week later, praising him as the key figure of the German counter-revolution from the right, who 'warms people's hearts' and has given 'new hope for "Germanness"'.[20] Hitler had made his pilgrimage to Wahnfried and come away with the Wagners' blessings. The *VB* report on German Day in Bayreuth gave prominence to Hitler's visit to Wahnfried, noting the coming together of the Movement and the Bayreuth ideal of culture: 'the practical fulfilment of the renewal of the German people in the spirit of Richard Wagner'.[21]

Brimming with confidence, Hitler returned to Munich determined to seize control in Bavaria and then complete the national revolution by marching on Berlin. He believed the time to act had arrived. Wilhelm Brückner, commander of the Munich SA, confirmed Hitler's intuition, warning that his men were restless, and the critical time for action was at hand. Similar advice came from Scheubner-Richter, who proffered, 'one must finally undertake something.'[22] Hitler had approximately 4,000 men in the Kampfbund that he could call upon to start his putsch. They were enough to overwhelm the 2,600 government forces in Munich (the Bavarian Reichswehr and Landespolizei) should they resist rather than join the Putschists. But without support from the Reichswehr and the police Hitler knew that his counter-revolution was doomed to failure.

Hitler spent much of October trying to win over General von Lossow and the chief of police Colonel Seisser, promising them both high offices in the new national dictatorship that he planned to establish. Lossow was the most sympathetic to Hitler's plot, nonetheless he was unwilling to pledge his own and the Bavarian Reichswehr's support. The 'time wasn't right,' he said, plus he feared that General von Seeckt and the Reichswehr in Berlin would march against them. Lossow, like Kahr, preferred to wait for 'nationalistic and patriotically minded forces in the North' in concert with von Seeckt and the Reichswehr leadership in Berlin, to topple the 'hated Reich government of Ebert and Stresemann'. The triumvirate in Munich chose to collaborate with the northern conspirators rather than lead a national revolution from Bavaria. Hitler and Ludendorff needed it to be the other way around. They planned to change the course of German politics from Munich. After establishing their new national dictatorship, together they would lead an army of liberation under the swastika flag against Red Berlin.[23]

On 6 November, Kahr convened a meeting with the leaders of the Fatherland Associations and Oberstleutnant Kriebel, the military leader of the *Kampfbund*. Kahr told them that the triumvirate was ready to establish a right-wing dictatorship in Bavaria, but it would exclude Hitler and Ludendorff. The triumvirate was also eager to see the creation of a new patriotic regime in Berlin that would restore Germany's 'honour and glory'. Bavaria's contribution to the counter-revolution, Kahr claimed, would be the support provided by Bavaria's patriotic fighting associations concentrated under a strong Bavarian state authority, cooperating with the Reichswehr leadership in Berlin, and if necessary fighting alongside their north German nationalist allies. It was essential, Kahr rather disingenuously stated, that Bavaria complied with 'the legal path to creating a national dictatorship'. This was a requirement that von Seeckt had insisted 'must be followed'. A march on Berlin from Bavaria, an idea Hitler and Ludendorff were flirting with, was out of the question. Kahr ended his meeting with a warning: unilateral action by any group would be 'countered by all means at the Bavarian government's disposal, including, if necessary, the force of arms'.[24]

Hitler got word of the meeting, as Kahr had intended. His reaction was not what Kahr had expected. Later that evening Hitler met with a few of his close advisers at Scheubner-Richter's apartment. They agreed with Hitler to stage a putsch on Sunday 11 November. Sunday was Hitler's preferred day to start his revolution. 'All the people in the administration will be away from their offices and the police will only be at half-strength,' he told Putzi Hanfstaengl. 'That is the time to strike.'[25] It also had symbolic importance, marking the fifth anniversary of the armistice, the *Dolchstoßlegende* (stab-in-the-back legend), and therefore was an appropriate day to take the first steps in reversing the humiliation inflicted on Germany by the November criminals. The men agreed that detailed planning for the putsch would start the following morning, beginning with a meeting of party and Kampfbund leaders at the editorial and production offices of the *Völkischer Beobachter* on Schellingstraβe 39–41.

All of the key Putschists were present. Joining Hitler, Esser, Hanfstaengl, Heβ, and Scheubner-Richter were Kriebel (the military commander of the Kampfbund), Göring (chief of the SA), Röhm (head of the Reichskriegsflagge (RKF) and one of General von Lossow's staff officers), Dr Friedrich Weber (political leader of the Oberland League), Rosenberg (managing editor of the *VB*), and Max Amann (the party's business manager). Over the course of the morning they established the final arrangements for seizing control of Munich: occupying the key public offices – the town hall in the Marienplatz, the Reichswehr headquarters in the old Bavarian War Ministry on the corner of Ludwigstraβe and Schönfeldstraβe, the main military barracks in west Munich, the police headquarters on Ettstraβe, telegraph and telephone exchanges, radio stations, and the central train station. A list of the leading Communists, socialist leaders, and unsupportive government and police officials to be arrested was hastily drawn up. Measures for assembling the SA and the other Kampfbund fighters discreetly so as not to draw police attention were agreed. Hitler confirmed with Rosenberg that on the day the *VB* would publish a special edition announcing the establishment of the new national directorate of Hitler and Ludendorff, and finally Max Amann was to ensure that posters and proclamations were printed in time for wide distribution in Munich and the major cities and towns in Bavaria.[26]

A follow-up meeting at the *VB* offices was scheduled for later that evening. Hitler invited two new participants, the former police president Ernst Pöhner, and his assistant Wilhelm Frick, who was still with the police as the chief of political surveillance. During the course of the day, news had circulated that von Kahr was going to outline his political agenda for Bavaria's immediate future in a major speech at the Bürgerbräukeller the next evening. Lossow and Seisser, the other two members of the triumvirate, would be there, as would Knilling and his cabinet. Leading figures in the Reichswehr, the police, industry and Munich society had also been invited, including Count Josef Soden, Crown Prince Rupprecht's chef-du-cabinet. Even Hitler received an invitation. Hitler and his fellow putschists feared that Kahr would declare Bavarian independence, and proclaim the restoration of the Wittelsbach monarch. To stop these possibilities from happening, Hitler proposed moving the putsch forward to 8 November. The putschists would march into the Bürgerbräukeller, interrupt Kahr's speech, and declare a new government under a Hitler-Ludendorff dictatorship. Hitler's co-conspirators were less optimistic about the plan. The putsch, they felt, could only succeed with the cooperation of the triumvirate and through it the army and the police. They debated the audacious plan long into the night.

'*Wir müssen die Leute hineinkompromittieren*' ('we have to compromise these people into it'), Hitler asserted.[27] Eventually at around 3 am an agreement was reached. The putsch would begin tomorrow evening, five years on from the day Kurt Eisner launched the Bavarian Republic, another infamous anniversary of a humiliation Hitler aimed to quash.[28]

Thursday 8 November started out as a quiet day in Munich. The people went about their ordinary lives and the SA and other putschists made their final arrangements without causing any alarm. Kahr had no inkling of Hitler's plans. He even ordered the police to reduce their numbers in and around the Bürgerbräukeller to minimise public concerns. Around midday Hitler met with Göring at the *VB* offices to confirm their movements later that evening. Despite the hasty and improvised preparations Hitler was reasonably calm. When Hanfstaengl asked him what would happen if they failed, Hitler replied, 'If that should be the case or if I should die it would only be a sign that my star has run its course and my mission is fulfilled.'[29] Hitler spent much of the afternoon with his friend and photographer Heinrich Hoffmann. They had tea at a favourite café on Gärtner Platz near the party offices, and afterwards visited Hermann Esser at his flat on Bergmannstraße. Hitler asked Esser to take his place speaking at a large rally in the Löwenbräukeller that Röhm had organized. Keep the crowd happy, Hitler insisted. You will receive a call shortly after eight-thirty, Hitler continued, and then you can announce the revolution. Röhm knows what to do after that. Hitler returned to the *VB* offices shortly after 7 pm. After another quick conversation with Göring, Hitler and his small entourage including his bodyguard Ulrich Graf, Amann, Rosenberg, and Scheubner-Richter drove to the Bürgerbräukeller.[30]

More than 3,000 invited guests packed the Festsaal in the Bürgerbräukeller. Professor von Müller had a seat near the speaker's rostrum and noted the 'ominously electric atmosphere'. Kahr began his speech at 8 pm, reading from his prepared script in his monotonous voice. Bumbling on about the evils of Marxism, he almost put the audience to sleep. Unbeknown to those inside, Göring and 600 heavily armed SA men had surrounded the beer hall and blocked all of the access roads. A cannon was deployed on the Ludwigsbrücke (Ludwig bridge over the Isar) to ward off any army or police units coming from the city centre, and heavy machine gun units cut off Rosenheimerstraße east of the beer hall. At the designated time of 8.30 pm, Göring accompanied by a squad of SA men burst into the beer hall. A machine gun unit set up in front of the main entrance and other SA men quickly blocked all of the other exits. Rising pandemonium woke the audience from their stupor. Kahr thought the meeting was being attacked by Communists. Others noticed the swastika armbands, and some began to shout: Hitler! Heil! Flanked by two *Stoßtrupp* members Hitler slowly pushed through the crowd to the rostrum. He called for quiet, climbed onto a table, and a storm trooper fired his revolver at the ceiling. The auditorium fell silent. Hitler declared both the Bavarian and Reich governments deposed, and told the audience that he was forming the new government. He invited Kahr, Lossow, and Seisser to join him in a small side room that Heβ had booked earlier in the day. As Heβ, Graf, and a few others brandishing revolvers ushered the triumvirate out of the hall, Hitler told the stunned audience that all of the details would be worked out in ten minutes.[31]

Angry and dumbfounded, the triumvirate listened to Hitler's excuses for staging the putsch and his plan for the make-up of the Bavarian and Reich governments: Kahr was to be the Regent of Bavaria; Pöhner Bavarian prime minister; Lossow the Reichswehr Minister; Seisser the police minister; and Ludendorff the commander-in-chief of the Reichswehr. Hitler was the Reich government.[32] Hitler's hostages were unmoved. Negotiations stalled and the crowd waiting in the beer hall became restless. Göring sensed the danger. He stepped up on the speaker's rostrum and beseeched the audience to be patient while a new Germany was being born. Lightening the mood, he reminded them that all was well, adding 'you've got your beer!'[33] Eventually Hitler returned to the Festsaal to face an increasingly hostile crowd. His speech, claimed Professor von Müller, was a rhetorical masterclass on how to win over an audience. 'With just a few sentences,' von Müller noted, Hitler had turned the crowd in his favour, and 'loud approval roared forth.'[34] Hitler announced the positions that Kahr, Lossow, and Seisser would hold in the new government, and asked the assembled audience if they stood behind them. Almost as one, 3,000 voices shouted '*Jawohl!*' (Yes!), then Heil! Hitler!, followed by a lusty rendition of '*Deutschland, Deutschland über alles.*'[35] Hitler returned to the side room but still none of the triumvirate were willing to join his regime. More influential persuasion was required.

General Ludendorff and Ernst Pöhner entered the side room, and the atmosphere changed immediately. Lossow especially held Ludendorff in high regard. After another fifteen minutes of discussion, Ludendorff appealed to the three gentlemen to 'stand up for the Fatherland and join our great national cause'. Turning to Lossow, he said, 'what do you say?' Lossow paused, then snapped to attention clicked his heels and exclaimed: 'Your Excellency's wish is my command.' The two generals shook hands, and almost immediately Seisser joined them, pledging his commitment to the new regime. While this little ceremony was taking place, Hitler and Pöhner still struggled to convince Kahr. Appealing to his monarchist leanings, Pöhner reminded Kahr that 'it is our obligation to stand in front of our king and shield him, not trot along behind him'. Kahr agreed. He would cooperate, but as a royal governor, representing the crown, not as regent. A sense of elation filled the room. Everyone shook hands warmly, and Hitler with a triumphant smile ushered them back into the

Festsaal to publicly proclaim their agreement. Slightly more than an hour had passed since the whole commotion began. All six men spoke and received loud and heartfelt approval from the crowd. When they shook hands a thunderous ovation swelled up from the floor. More shouts of Heil! Heil Hitler! were followed by the jubilant mass crowd singing the national anthem.[36]

Elsewhere in Munich the putsch was proceeding with mixed results. At the Löwenbräukeller, 2,000 members of the Oberland, RKF and SA were enjoying a night of revelry when Esser's expected telephone message was received from the Bürgerbräukeller. Röhm motioned to the brass bands to put their instruments down and announced that the long-desired national revolution had begun. Hats and beer mugs were thrown into the air and tumultuous applause greeted the news. Spontaneously the bands played the national anthem. When calm was restored, the fighting units were ordered to form up in column and march to Hitler at the Bürgerbräukeller. Röhm, Esser, and a young Heinrich Himmler carrying the battle-flag led the way. While en route, Röhm received new orders to occupy Lossow's headquarters in the old War Ministry. The storm troopers were accompanied by many jubilant followers as they marched along Brennerstraße onto Ludwigstraße and the War Ministry. Röhm's men quickly occupied the building and surrounded it with barbed wire. This was the only successful occupation carried out by the Kampfbund. The police headquarters on Ettstraße, the telephone and telegraph exchanges, and the central train station were left unoccupied. Attempts to win over the Reichswehr were mostly unsuccessful, particularly at the 19th Infantry Regiment barracks where the SA were turned away, and at the engineer barracks where Captain Cantzler locked up 400 Oberland troopers in the drill hall. News of these failures reached Hitler at the Bürgerbräukeller, and he decided to intervene personally. Hitler and Friedrich Weber, the head of the Oberland, accompanied by three squads of armed SA, drove to the engineer barracks. Ludendorff was left in charge.[37]

The SA checked the identity of everyone as they left the Bürgerbräukeller. SA squads under Heß and Scheubner-Richter detained those whose names were on the list of 'potential enemies of the new regime'. Bavarian premier Knilling and members of his cabinet were placed under 'house arrest' and moved to Julius Lehmann's villa. Kahr, Lossow, and Seisser were allowed to leave after promising Ludendorff that they would abide by their earlier agreement. When Hitler returned to the Bürgerbräukeller at around 11 pm, having been turned away at the engineer barracks, he was aghast to learn that the triumvirate had been allowed to leave. Ludendorff huffed and reproached Hitler: 'a German officer would never break an oath.' Hitler did not share the general's confidence in 'military honour'.[38]

The night went from bad to worse for the putschists. Lossow and Seisser started to work against Hitler almost from the moment they left the

Bürgerbräukeller. General Lossow issued orders to loyal Reichswehr battalions in Augsburg, Ingolstadt, Regensburg, and Landshut to come to Munich to put down the putsch. Lossow set up a makeshift headquarters in the 19th Infantry Regiment barracks where he was joined by Seisser and von Kahr. At 2.55 am they issued a joint statement repudiating the putsch, and Seisser had Pöhner and Frick arrested in the police headquarters on Ettstraße. By 5 am Röhm knew the triumvirate had renounced Hitler. All three were claiming they had only agreed to the putsch at gunpoint. Reichswehr forces surrounded Röhm and his men at the War Ministry. The Reichswehr and the police were prepared to end the putsch, by force if necessary. Morale amongst the SA at the Bürgerbräukeller was low. Kriebel suggested they retreat to Rosenheim. Well aware that he had been betrayed by the triumvirate, Hitler pondered his options. His last hope was to appeal to the people, to mobilise Münchners loyal to the Movement. The party now had almost 56,000 members. The way forward came from Ludendorff: *Wir marschieren!* (We will march!).[39]

From the Bürgerbräukeller
to the Feldherrnhalle

There were roughly 2,000 SA and other Kampfbund members at the Bürgerbräukeller. Most camped out in the gardens overnight. At first light on the morning of 9 November, Joseph Berchtold, one of Hitler's most trusted storm troopers, conducted a reconnaissance of the city centre. He reported back that enormous crowds were gathering in the Marienplatz. The people were angry and confused. Had the national revolution and Germany's revival begun? Contradictory placards were everywhere and local radio stations broadcast news that Kahr and Lossow opposed the putsch. Hitler decided to put it all to the test of popular feeling. Later he described his decision: 'We would go into the city to win the people to our side, to see how public opinion would react, and then to see how Kahr, Lossow, and Seisser would react to public opinion.'[1] The putschists planned to march to the Marienplatz, hold a mass protest rally, and then move on to the War Ministry to rescue Röhm and his men. Hitler instructed his followers that no arms were to be used.[2]

At 12 noon the procession got underway from the Bürgerbräukeller. Two standard-bearers led, followed by a long column of rows of eight. Hitler, Ludendorff, Scheubner-Richter, Göring, Kriebel, Weber, Graf, and Wilhelm Brückner were in the first row. Directly behind them marched the Stoßtrupp-Hitler, followed closely by row after row of SA and Kampfbund members, and then Nazi sympathisers from all segments of Munich society. Swastika flags waved, the marching band played patriotic songs, and the column sang in full voice. 'Deep joyful enthusiasm' is the way one participant, Hans Hinkel, described it as they marched along Rosenheimerstraße onto the Ludwigsbrücke.[3] A small police cordon attempted to halt the march, but it was swept aside quickly and no shots were fired. The putschists proceeded along Zweibrückenstraße through the Isartor, the medieval city gate, up the Tal and into the Marienplatz where they were greeted by a great roar and shouts of Heil! and Heil Hitler! Berchtold, Julius Schaub, and a dozen storm troopers had already deposed and detained the socialist city council and hung a large swastika banner from the balcony on the neo-gothic Rathaus (town hall). Standing in an open-top car Julius Streicher whipped up the Marienplatz crowd with a rousing speech, praising Hitler and inviting all patriots to join the march marking the beginning of a glorious German future. Winifred and Siegfried Wagner watched on from the edge of the crowd. Hitler was in an ebullient mood. He started to feel more certain that with the public's support the Putsch would succeed after all. Ludendorff gave the orders to the column to reassemble and march on to the War Ministry.[4]

The putschists, followed by the multitude in the Marienplatz, marched up Theatinerstraße, but when Hitler and Ludendorff saw another police roadblock they directed the column to the right along Perusastraße then left up the Residenzstraße to the Feldherrnhalle on the south face of the Odeonsplatz. A line of heavily armed police backed up by machine-gun squads and an armoured car barred their way onto the square. Someone at the front of the column, it may have been Ulrich Graf, shouted, 'Don't fire, Ludendorff and Hitler are with us!' A shot rang out, fired most likely by a nervous policeman. It was immediately followed by a murderous volley from the steps of the Feldherrnhalle. One of the standard-bearers fell. Scheubner-Richter was shot dead, and in falling dragged Hitler to the ground, dislocating his shoulder. Göring and Graf both fell badly wounded. Ludendorff somehow escaped uninjured but fourteen putschists and four policemen were dead when the shooting stopped.[5]

One eyewitness to the massacre was Suzanne St. Barbe Baker, an English tourist and travel writer. She was on the Odeonsplatz when 'within half a minute the square was surrounded by troops and police and transformed into a battlefield.' She remembered, 'machine-gun bullets whizzed by my head, so that I had to creep on all fours to cover,' which she found 'in a café that could no longer boast of a single window-pane.'[6] Scores of wounded groaning in agony lay on the ground, while many others struggled to get away. Someone managed to rescue the Nazi flag, soaked in blood. During the mayhem Hitler limped into a side street behind the Feldherrnhalle. He was found by Dr Walter Schultze, the 'staff physician' of the Munich SA. Hitler was helped into the doctor's car and driven to Putzi Hanfstaengl's holiday home seventy kilometres south of Munich in Uffing am Staffelsee. Helene Hanfstaengl recalled how shocked she was when she opened the door and saw Hitler, 'pale as a ghost' and needing support from two medical orderlies.[7] Helene's husband along with Hermann Esser escaped to Salzburg. Carin Göring collected her wounded husband from Dr von Ach's private clinic in Munich and took him to safety in Innsbrück. Other leading putschists were less fortunate. Röhm surrendered and was taken to Stadelheim Prison. Both Heß and Kriebel avoided immediate capture, but later surrendered to the Bavarian authorities and were imprisoned in Festung Landsberg. Dr Weber was also incarcerated in Landsberg. The police eventually caught up with Hitler on 11 November. He was arrested at the Hanfstaengls' Uffing home and driven to Landsberg am Lech, 65 km west of Munich, where he joined other putschists already in prison.[8]

General von Lossow and von Kahr were quick to crow about their 'victory'. Lossow sent a short telegram to General von Seeckt, telling him, 'No more troops needed. The Putsch was liquidated.'[9] Kahr issued an ordinance on 9 November, dissolving the NSDAP and confiscating its property. This included the headquarters on Corneliusstraβe, the *Völkischer Beobachter*, and over 170,000 gold marks.[10] The left-wing writer Stefan Zweig summed up the day's events: 'The famous putsch that was supposed to conquer Germany began in the morning and, as we all know, had been put down by midday. Hitler fled, and was quickly arrested. No one thought of him as a potential political force anymore.'[11] A leading article in the *New York Times* on 10 November came to the same conclusion. The satirical magazine *Simplicissimus* was more circumspect. On 3 December 1923 it printed on the front cover an artist's drawing of 'Munich man' with a warning verse below: '*Der Münchner* was under the spell of the swastika. He was resolute in his fanatical belief in the Führer and the dictator's plans to make Germany great again.'[12]

III

Der Kampfzeit – The Long Struggle, 1924–33

Hitler in Prison

Landsberg-am-Lech suffered through a torrential rainstorm on Sunday night, 11 November 1923. Earlier that wet and windy evening Otto Leybold, the prison's warden, was warned to expect Hitler's imminent arrival, along with a strong detachment of the local Reichswehr for extra security. Franz Hemmrich, the chief warder, was roused from his quarters and told to prepare a cell in the *Festung* (fortress wing) where political prisoners and convicted duellists were housed. Ironically, the only cell large enough to accommodate Hitler and his military guards was already occupied by Anton Graf von Arco auf Valley, Kurt Eisner's assassin. Arco-Valley was hastily moved, and all of the arrangements were in place when Hitler arrived at around 10.30 pm. Hitler was registered as prisoner number forty-five, and examined by Dr Josef Brinsteiner, the prison physician, who diagnosed him to have a fracture dislocation of the left shoulder. Hitler was clearly still in pain, but he declined both food and drink, and on reaching his cell went straight to bed. His first night in prison undoubtedly was uncomfortable. In addition to his dislocated shoulder, soldiers from the Bavarian 7th Division had arrived, and very noisily turned the Festung and the whole area around it into a heavily armed camp. Armed guards were posted outside Hitler's cell, the cell beside it was turned into a makeshift headquarters, and machine-gun positions were set up inside and outside the fortress wing.[1]

A few days later Hitler had to be taken to the infirmary for treatment on his shoulder. He was thoroughly demoralised. He had been betrayed by Kahr, Lossow, and Seisser, and many of his colleagues and friends who had marched with him to the Feldherrnhalle, singing *Deutschland über Alles*, had been shot down by the Bavarian state police. Hitler even feared that the small group of soldiers outside his cell were a firing squad just waiting for orders to execute him.[2] When he learned that the state prosecutor would be coming to question him, he went on a hunger strike. The guards tried to get him to eat, as did the prison psychologist Alois Maria Ott. Anton Drexler was shocked by Hitler's marked deterioration from one visit to the next. 'He'd got thinner and thinner, and weaker and whiter, every time.'[3] Dr Brinsteiner told Drexler that Hitler had lost five kilos in a week, down from 73 to 68 kg, and that he would die if he could not be persuaded to end his hunger strike.[4] Drexler was determined to save Hitler. He went to Hitler's cell and spoke to him for almost two hours, first attempting to reason with him, and then talking at him, telling him that 'he'd no right to give up' and that 'without him and his Movement Germany was doomed.'[5] Helene Bechstein also visited Hitler and encouraged him to stop this starvation nonsense because if he died he would just be doing what his enemies most wanted. Dr Lorenz Roder, Hitler's lawyer, and Hans Knirsch, the founder of the Sudetenland Nazi Party in Czechoslovakia, also visited Hitler. They both reproached him for abandoning his followers and encouraged him to continue the fight. Knirsch eventually convinced Hitler that the Putsch was actually a victory. 'It had raised everyone's enthusiasm' and, Knirsch continued, 'the great leaders succeed over their failures because failure is a necessary component of the long struggle to ultimate triumph.'[6]

After another bolstering visit from his lawyer, and numerous letters of encouragement and support from Winifred Wagner, Helene Hanfstaengl, and Helene Bechstein, Hitler ended his hunger strike on Saturday 24 November. Drexler was delighted how quickly Hitler's 'old spirit' had reasserted itself once he started eating again.[7] Even the unwelcome visit by Hans Ehard, the deputy state prosecutor, on 13 December did not diminish Hitler's new resolve. He refused to cooperate with the Bavarian authorities and their pre-trial inquiries, but he gave a lengthy 'off-the-record' interview on his politics and future strategy to Ehard, which the prosecutor typed up from memory later that night. Numbering some fifteen pages, Ehard believed he had all the information he needed to convict Hitler and have him deported back to Austria.[8] While the jurist was undoubtedly an expert in the law, he was much less astute at reading the public mood and the current political climate in Munich and Bavaria. Throughout December Hitler's cell filled up with precious books, expensive gifts, and Christmas hampers of fine foods, sweets, brandy and wines.[9] Some of his high-society benefactors even petitioned the Bavarian government to grant Hitler a pardon.[10] Hitler's popularity was in the ascendancy, especially in right-wing and nationalist circles. When his half-sister Angela visited him in Landsberg in mid-December, she noticed that his previous visitor was a count, who had brought Christmas gifts from Villa Wahnfried and other influential supporters in Bayreuth. Angela was struck by the loyalty her brother was accorded by the prison staff and his many friends and followers. She wrote a letter about her visit to her brother Alois Hitler, telling him that physically their half-brother Adolf was 'quite well', and that 'his spirit and soul were again at a high level'. She was certain that his political accomplishments were 'as solid as a rock', and concluded the letter with her conviction that 'the goal of victory is only a question of time. God grant it be soon.'[11]

Christmas 1923 was bitter-sweet for Hitler. Although he was in prison he had been rejuvenated by the encouragement and generosity bestowed upon him by his many friends and followers, but on 26 December his close friend and mentor Dietrich Eckart died of heart failure, age 55, on the Obersalzberg. Eckart was buried in Berchtesgaden's *Altfriedhof* (old cemetery). Hitler was not allowed out of Landsberg to attend the funeral.[12]

The Trial

Hitler and the other leaders of the Putsch were charged with *Hochverrat* (high treason), and their trial was held in the *Bayerischen Völksgericht München* (Bavarian People's Court in Munich). The penalty if convicted was life in prison (or fortress confinement), and for a non-German citizen, such as the Austrian-born Hitler, deportation. Trials for high treason were supposed to take place at the *Staatsgerichtshof*, a special national court in Leipzig established in July 1922, but Franz Gürtner, the Bavarian Justice Minister, and most of prime minister Knilling's cabinet, refused to recognise the Reich government's authority in this case. Officially they were asserting Bavaria's independent right to conduct the trial, but the real reason for keeping the court case in Munich was to hide how entwined the triumvirate was in collaborating with Hitler and Ludendorff, and the plans for the putsch. Kahr, Lossow, and Seisser attempted to distance themselves from the fiasco of 8/9 November 1923, and in their official statements always referred to those events as the 'Hitler putsch'. Despite their many protestations of innocence, they could not dispel the evidence of their complicity in the plot. On 18 February 1924, the day the trial was meant to start, both Kahr and Lossow resigned from office.[1]

The venue chosen for the trial was the *Kriegsschule* (War School) the former Bavarian military academy on Blutenburgstraβe 3 in the Neuhausen district of central west Munich. It was a relatively secure location and easily surrounded by the large detachment of Reichswehr and police assigned to keep order and ensure that Hitler and his fellow conspirators were not 'liberated' by any of their zealous supporters. Gürtner appointed Georg Neithardt, a Superior Court director, as the presiding judge to lead a tribunal of seven justices: two professional judges (and one alternate), and three jurors called lay judges (and one alternate). The Bavarian authorities wanted a short trial and a swift verdict with as little publicity as possible. They really should have known better. During the weeks leading up to the trial, speculation over its course and outcome was the predominant topic of conversation in Munich's cafés and beer halls.[2]

On Tuesday morning, 26 February, the trial began. A long queue of men and women shuffled forward in the cold and snow to have their entry passes checked and undergo an invasive security search before gaining access to the spectators' gallery. One journalist working for the *New York Times* reported how annoyed the women were when 'their hair, hats, purses, muffs and even stockings were inspected for daggers, hand grenades and bombs.'[3] Journalists as well as the judges, lawyers, and court officials arrived to find a scene more reminiscent of a military fortress preparing for battle rather than a court house. They navigated their way inside, passing through cordons of barbed wire, tank obstacles, and multiple checkpoints manned by armed guards. The reporter for the right-wing newspaper *Das Bayerische Vaterland* complained that 'there are too many women in the gallery'.[4] More than three hundred reporters representing Bavarian and German newspapers, and some fifty foreign papers including the *New York Times*, the London *Times*, and the Paris newspapers *Le Temps* and *Le Petit Parisien*, came to Munich for the trial. Only sixty correspondents, columnists, and cartoonists were admitted into the makeshift courtroom set up in the former mess hall each day. They vied with the elegantly dressed women and other influential Münchners for the best seats, often losing out and being crammed together at the back of the public gallery.[5]

Hitler had been brought back to Munich from Landsberg five days earlier, and was held in Stadelheim prison until Monday 25 February, when he was moved to 'secure accommodation' in a two-story building adjacent to the War School. He would remain in custody there until the end of the trial.[6] Ten defendants made up the main trial, and they were lead into the court by General Ludendorff, wearing a dark blue suit rather than his military uniform, which he vowed never to wear again after General Lossow's shameless betrayal of military honour, and as a result of having been shot at by the police at the Feldherrnhalle. Hitler entered next, wearing a frock coat with his Iron Cross, First Class, pinned on, and carrying a thick leather briefcase under his arm. The *Völkischer Kurier* reported that Hitler looked well rested and ready for the fight.[7] The other defendants were Oberstleutnant Hermann Kriebel, Dr Friedrich Weber, Ernst Pöhner, Wilhelm Frick, and Captain Ernst Röhm, the SA leaders Wilhelm Brückner and Robert Wagner, and Ludendorff's stepson Heinz Pernet. Each was charged with high treason, except Pernet who was charged with being 'an accessory to the crime of high treason'. Hans Ehard, the deputy prosecutor, then read out the indictment against the ten men.[8]

For more than an hour Ehard outlined the evidence of guilt against each defendant. He began by chiding Ludendorff for lending his name as a 'decorated general' to the Nazis, and for encouraging disgruntled patriots to support the putsch. He then named Hitler 'the soul of the whole undertaking', a charge that, no matter how much it inflated Hitler's role, he gladly accepted. In fact it served as a key component in Hitler's defence. When Ehard finished his statement, Ludwig Stenglein, the chief prosecutor, interrupted proceedings and asked Neithardt to dismiss the public audience and conduct the remainder of the trial in closed session because the case was 'a threat to national security and public order'. Roder, Hitler's lawyer, objected, as did the lawyers of the other defendants. There were gasps of disbelief and shouts of anger from the public gallery, and later the newspapers speculated on why the state prosecutor really wanted to shroud the trial in secrecy. The judges had little choice but to empty the courtroom so that the prosecution's motion could be discussed in private.[9]

Once the courtroom had been cleared, the prosecution and the defence counsels waged an increasingly acrimonious debate on the proper procedure for the trial. Stenglein was worried about the trial leading to further violence in Munich and even an international incident, possibly war with France over a perceived violation of the Versailles Treaty. The defence counsels dismissed Stenglein's concerns as preposterous. Collectively they demanded that their clients had the right to defend themselves and explain the reasons for their actions in public. The defendants too joined the debate. Ludendorff claimed the charges made against him were themselves an act of high treason. He further added, 'If I were a prosecutor, I would take action against the prosecutor!' Neithardt was compelled to act and defend the court against Ludendorff's 'intolerable slur'. He cautioned the general. Hitler also spoke for the first time at the trial, acting as a sort of peace-maker. He promised that he and his fellow defendants would show discretion. All they wanted was the opportunity to defend themselves in public. Hitler concluded his appeal with a pledge: 'We will not hurt Germany!' Stenglein accused Hitler of being disingenuous, and warned that the courtroom would become a circus. Immediately, both sides began shouting at each other, prompting Neithardt to end the debate. He further demanded no disclosures of these 'private' discussions.[10]

After a short deliberation with the other members of the tribunal, Neithardt announced that the trial would be held in public. He qualified his ruling with the proviso that 'the court will decide whether the exclusion of the public is necessary on an issue by issue basis.' This compromise ultimately led to serious questions over the fairness of the trial and the motives of the judges for allowing secret sessions. The defendants were given a lot of leeway in presenting their cases, and the frequency and timing of the secret sessions gave the impression that the court was protecting Kahr, Lossow, and Seisser, and by extension the reputations of the Reichswehr and the Bavarian police for their complicity in the putsch. Neithardt had also set the conditions for a long trial that would be susceptible to public opinion.[11]

The afternoon session began in an unorthodox manner. Judge Neithardt discussed Hitler's war record 'fighting for Germany' with the defendant, listing his awards and war injuries, and sharing with everyone in the courtroom his observation that Hitler was 'a good German patriot'. Neithardt was an ardent nationalist, and he strongly believed that the putsch had been a 'national deed'. He sympathised with the defendants, and openly praised their 'unsullied patriotic spirit' and 'noble will'. Before the trial even began, Neithardt is reputed to have said that Ludendorff was 'still the only champion which we in Germany possessed', and that he would be acquitted.[12] Franz Gürtner, the justice minister, appointed Neithardt specifically because he had shown an unmistakable bias in favour of right-wing defendants. Neithardt had been the presiding judge in Count Arco auf Valley's murder trial and Hitler's first trial in January 1922 for the assault on Otto Ballerstedt, and both defendants received the lightest of sentences.[13]

Hitler began his defence with a four-hour speech, meandering through his personal biography, emphasising his early years of struggle in Austria and Vienna, his anti-Marxist and anti-Jewish beliefs, his war record, and his passion for Germany. He told the court that he had founded 'the Movement' to save Germany, and that he intended to lead Germany back to a position of glory in the world. He also accepted full responsibility for the putsch, but rejected the state's charges and confidently stated that he and his co-defendants were not guilty because there was no such thing as 'high treason against the national traitors of 1918'.[14] Drawing on his considerable rhetorical skills, Hitler portrayed the Weimar Republic as a treasonous enterprise, and blamed the Bavarian leaders who had abandoned him on 9 November for the tragedy at the Feldherrnhalle and the failure of the national revolution. Hitler then asked the court, politely, why 'the gentlemen who wanted the same things as we did and held talks to prepare them' were not also on trial. Hitler honoured his promise to the court not to hurt Bavaria or Germany with his testimony, and saved his accusations against Kahr, Lossow, and Seisser for the closed segments of the trial. He ended his opening defence by restating his service to Germany as a soldier and as a nationalist, before appealing to the judges to allow him to remain in the country. 'I have never felt myself to be an Austrian,' Hitler told the court, before closing with, 'I do not consider myself a traitor, but rather a German who only wanted the best for his people.'[15]

The chief prosecutor called Hitler's testimony 'exhaustive evidence of his guilt'. Neithardt was less quick to judge. He ended the first day's proceedings announcing that 'examination of the witnesses will reveal more'.[16] Hitler and his co-defendants were popular in Munich, and the right-wing press published glowing reviews of Hitler's first day in court. *Das Bayerische Vaterland* said that Hitler was on top form and the *Markt Grafinger Wochenblatt* waxed lyrical about Hitler's 'dazzling performance'.[17] Even the *Vossische Zeitung*, a socialist paper in Berlin, called Hitler 'a genius' for the way he appealed to the people, and that 'his strong performance in the courtroom showed unquestionable skill'.[18] Not all of the press were enthralled with Hitler or the trial. Judge Neithardt was criticised for allowing Hitler too much freedom to interpret the case against him. The headline in the *Vancouver Sun* read: 'Putsch Trial Called Joke', a sentiment shared by the *Daily Express* in London, which regarded the trial as 'a farce'.[19] Closer to home in Munich, the Social Democratic *Münchener Post* lamented that the proceedings were 'increasingly taking on comedic qualities' thus echoing chief prosecutor Ludwig Stenglein's warning against a public trial.[20]

The extensive newspaper coverage of the trial gave Hitler and the Nazi movement much greater exposure than they had ever had before. Popular opinion, especially in Munich, was with the putschists. The *Münchener Neueste Nachrichten*, the city's leading nationalist paper, was unequivocal in its support, stating that 'our sympathies lie on the side of the defendants and not with the November criminals of 1918.'[21] In the courtroom there were more women in the spectators' gallery each day than would normally be the case and most of them brought flowers and gifts for the defendants. Judge Neithardt was forced to rebuff his critics that he favoured right-wing supporters, especially the women who seemed to worship Hitler, when he distributed the coveted day passes. Conversations in the beer halls and even new acts at the comedy theatres confirmed the city's obsession with the trial. At the Augustiner-Keller on Arnulfstraße 52, slightly north-west of the Hauptbahnhof, students sang cheeky songs mocking Kahr and other Bavarian politicians who did not support the putsch. The comedian and Nazi supporter Weiß Ferdl celebrated the defendants as 'the German men who only want to save their German Fatherland' in a new act for his popular show at the Platzl, his theatre just across from the Hofbräuhaus.[22] The Bavarian authorities were so alarmed by the outpouring of public support for Hitler and his co-defendants that they banned political rallies at the Löwenbräukeller and other Bierkellers in the vicinity of the War School.[23]

The trial continued with each of the defendants addressing the court in turn, answering the charges against them and explaining how they came to be involved in the putsch. Starting on 11 March, day twelve of the trial, the key witnesses for the prosecution – Kahr, Lossow, and Seisser – began their testimony. Kahr had to be told repeatedly by Neithardt to stop reading his notes.[24] By the time all three men had made their statements it was clear that the triumvirate had colluded in their testimony. Neithardt was unimpressed and the newspapers did not hold anything back in their condemnation of the three former Bavarian leaders. The *Völkischer Kurier*, an ethnic-chauvinist newspaper filling the void left by the banned *Völkischer Beobachter*, declared that the state could no longer be trusted, and demanded that this important case 'must be decided by the people'.[25] When the three men that made up the triumvirate all 'skipped town' before the trial had ended, the Munich papers slated them as 'small men who confirmed their cowardice and guilt'.[26]

Collectively the ten defendants shared three common beliefs and objectives: they hated the Versailles Treaty and wanted it revoked; this would only happen, they stressed, after the country rid itself of Marxism, Jews, and the Weimar parliamentary system; and to successfully deal with the internal threat, they asserted, required national rebirth, which must begin with moral and spiritual renewal. Only then would Germany be great again.

The defendants had portrayed themselves as German heroes launching a crusade to save the Fatherland. Their defence played well to the gallery, but for much of the press outside the nationalist camp it was 'measureless hubris'.[27]

After the prosecution and the defence counsels made their closing statements, Neithardt invited the defendants, as was conventional in German law, to make a final statement before the judges went into deliberation. Thursday 27 March, one month and one day after it began, was the last day of the trial. Judge Neithardt would read the verdict on Tuesday 1 April.

Kriebel was the first to address the court on the final day of testimonies, then Pöhner, followed by Frick, Weber, and Ludendorff. All five men stood by their respective records as patriots serving their country. They strongly rejected the notion that they had committed high treason. Ludendorff also issued a warning. Should the movement not succeed, 'we will be lost, lost forever.' He then urged the court to acquit all of the defendants, and reminded the judges that men who serve the Fatherland have no place in prison but ultimately will be honoured in Valhalla, by the Gods. Tumultuous applause filled the courtroom.[28]

Röhm, Brückner, Wagner, and Pernet all waived their right to make a final statement. Hitler had the last word, and he spoke for over an hour. He covered old ground, restating that the Weimar Republic was founded on 'a crime of high treason' and that the international system of the Allied powers and the League of Nations had cheated the German people and condemned the German nation to an ignominious future of servitude. The national revolution, he declared, was a patriotic duty, not treason. He criticised the triumvirate for 'losing their nerve' and reaffirmed his determination to fight for Germany's future. Hitler told the court that he alone was responsible for the putsch, and after restating his war record and eagerness to serve Germany in the future, he appealed to the court not to deport him if they found him guilty. History, he predicted, would commend him and his men as 'those who wanted the best for our country'. Looking directly at Neithardt, Hitler calmly said, 'you may find us guilty but the eternal goddess of the eternal court [history] will tear up the prosecution's petition and the court's verdict with a smile, for she will acquit us.' Hitler sat down, and Neithardt announced, 'the trial is concluded.' The gallery applauded and honoured the defendants with a standing ovation as they were escorted out of the courtroom.[29]

Hitler was driven to Stadelheim Prison, where he remained until the day of the verdict. The atmosphere in Munich over the weekend was tense. The trial had polarised opinions in the city, and the Bavarian authorities feared an outbreak of violent demonstrations and even riots. Newspapers on the extreme left and right, such as the socialist *Münchener Post* and the nationalist *Grossdeutsche Zeitung*, were banned from publishing. Both the Reichswehr and the state police were put on high alert, and reinforcements from neighbouring cities and towns were called into Munich. Trains arriving at the Hauptbahnhof were monitored to prevent large bands of Nazis from gathering in the city. Armed guards were also posted in front of government buildings, the residences of senior government officials, and the homes of Judge Neithardt and the prosecutors.[30]

The Verdict

The courtroom in the War School on Blutenburgstraße was full to overflowing on Tuesday morning, 1 April 1924. Flower bouquets and other gifts for the defendants piled up on a table in the guard room. In the interior courtyard, Hitler and the other defendants (except Pöhner who was absent because of illness) posed for a photograph taken by Heinrich Hoffmann. Hitler wore his familiar trench coat, Frick a suit, and all the others were in full military uniform including medals. When the defendants entered the courtroom at 10 am there were cheers from the gallery, and several women waved their handkerchiefs. Five minutes later Judge Neithardt and the tribunal took their seats. Without any fanfare Neithardt read the verdict and passed sentence on the accused. Hitler was guilty of high treason and sentenced to five years of 'fortress confinement' plus a fine of 200 gold marks. Kriebel, Pöhner, and Weber all received the same verdict and punishment. Frick, Röhm, Brückner, Wagner, and Pernet were convicted of the lesser crime of aiding and abetting treason, and immediately paroled. Ludendorff was acquitted. Neithardt then surprised the courtroom by announcing that Hitler and the others given custodial sentences would be eligible for parole in six months. The last matter Neithardt dealt with was Article 9, paragraph 2, of the Law for the Protection of the Republic, which stipulated that 'foreigners who commit high treason are to be deported', stating that Hitler, being 'so German in his thinking and feeling', was exempt from this law of mandatory expulsion. The gallery shouted their approval of Neithardt's ruling.[1]

Newspaper reports on the verdict reflected the political bias of the respective papers. Conservative and nationalist papers, such as the *Völkischer Kurier* and Berlin's *Deutsche Zeitung*, generally welcomed the verdict, especially Ludendorff's acquittal, whereas the *Kreuz-Zeitung* called the verdict 'harsh'. Berlin's liberal and socialist papers including *Die Zeit* and *Vorwärts*, called the outcome a disgraceful joke. International coverage was also mainly negative. The London *Times* thought the verdict was an 'excellent joke for All Fools Day' and questioned the leniency of a six-month sentence for high treason.[2] Neithardt received most of the blame for the light sentences, but the lay judges were only prepared to accept guilty verdicts on condition that minimum sentences were applied, and that they included early parole.[3]

While Hitler was waiting for his transport back to Landsberg, a large crowd of people had gathered outside the War School hoping to get a glimpse of the defendants. Hitler spotted them from a window on the first floor. He smiled and waved. His elated admirers cheered and shouted Heil! in reply.[4] Both the putsch, despite its abysmal failure, and the trial turned out to be spectacular triumphs for Hitler and the movement. Hans Knirsch, who had been instrumental in getting Hitler to break his hunger strike back in November, was right when he told Hitler that the putsch would be a successful step forward on his path to power. Hitler acknowledged its importance when he became chancellor: 'Before the march to the Feldherrnhalle I had seventy or eighty thousand followers. After this march I had two million.'[5] In the Bavarian Landtag elections held on 6 April 1924, five days after the verdict, the Völkisch Bloc (a cover organization for the banned NSDAP) won a surprising 17.1 per cent share of the state-wide vote; and over 25.7 in Munich, the highest percentage of any party.[6] *Simplicissimus* had predicted Nazi fortunes would soar. 'The swastika,' it proclaimed, 'had become a shooting star.'[7]

One new star-struck follower of Hitler and the trial was Joseph Goebbels, a young nationalist who had recently completed his doctorate in German Literature at Heidelberg University. Goebbels was living in Rheydt, a regional town in the Ruhr, some four hundred miles north of Munich. He followed the trial through the daily newspaper reports, writing in his diary that Hitler's speeches 'carried him to the stars'. Goebbels saw Hitler as 'an idealist' who, through 'his wonderful *élan*, his verve, his enthusiasm, and his German feeling is bringing new belief to the German people.' Goebbels wrote to Hitler when he was in Landsberg, initiating a close friendship and political collaboration that would last until the end of their lives in Berlin, in April 1945.[8]

Back in Landsberg Prison

itler arrived back at Festung Landsberg at 5 pm on 1 April. Franz Hemmrich, the chief warder, recalled that Hitler 'looked more wretched than ever' even though he was warmly welcomed back by prison staff and other inmates as a national hero. Hitler was applauded for his efforts to take power and restore order in the country, somewhat similar to Rienzi, Richard Wagner's Roman Tribune in the opera of the same name, rather than looked upon as a criminal just convicted of treason. Hitler was re-registered as prisoner number 21 and assigned cell 7, the same cell he had occupied before the trial and the largest in the Festung. Lt Kriebel and Dr Weber joined Hitler on the first floor, in cells 8 and 9, which soon after was called the 'commanders' wing'. They were joined by Rudolf Heß and Emil Maurice, Hitler's chauffeur, who along with more than forty storm troopers had been convicted as accessories to treason in subsequent trials in May.[1]

The Festung had been refurbished during the trial in anticipation of the arrival of a number of political prisoners. Hitler's cell was clean and bright with freshly whitewashed walls. It had simple furnishings, a bed, a night stand and reading lamp, a writing table, and two chairs. It also had a spectacular view of the garden, and on a clear day he could see the Bavarian Alps in the distance. Hitler complained about the bars on the windows, but the cell doors were never locked, and life in the Festung was more akin to a spa or a sanatorium than a prison. The 'Politicals', as Hemmrich called them, shared a spacious common room where they read, socialised, took tea and ate their meals. The room contained comfortable wicker chairs surrounded by flowerpots, and a large dining table covered with a white tablecloth. A swastika banner hung behind Hitler's seat at the head of the table, and on the wall just above his favourite reading chair was a laurel wreath sent to 'the Chief' by a loyal admirer. There were also two pictures of Frederick the Great hung on the wall.[2] Hitler and his followers did not have any prison duties or obligations. They were allowed to use the garden after breakfast and again before and after dinner in the evening. They dressed as they pleased, and Hitler normally wore traditional Bavarian lederhosen and a white linen shirt, and a tie when he took his daily walk in the garden.[3]

The prison authorities were highly accommodating to their celebrity detainees. Sympathetic warders greeted Hitler with a 'Heil!', the customary Nazi salutation. Visitors were allowed on a daily basis, and Hitler's friends and followers alike took full advantage, keeping up a constant pilgrimage to Landsberg. On quite a few days in April and May, Hitler saw one visitor after another without pause until visiting hours ended. Alfred Rosenberg and Max Amann, whom Hitler had appointed as chairman and deputy-chairman of the party while he was in prison, were among the first to visit him.[4] Lorenz Roder, his lawyer, Ulrich Graf, his bodyguard who was severely wounded at the Feldherrnhalle, Julius Streicher from Nürnberg, Anton Drexler, Putzi Hanfstaengl and his son Egon, and Heinrich Hoffmann all visited Hitler during his first week back inside Landsberg.[5] Female visitors also made their way to Landsberg. Hitler's half-sister Angela and her 16-year-old daughter Angelika (Geli) visited him in July. His landlady Marie Reichert and his neighbours Marie Bechtold and Magdalena Schweyer came out from Munich to see him, as did many of the wives of the party's senior leaders, and his most influential patrons Helene Bechstein and Elsa Bruckmann. On one of her visits Helene Bechstein brought Hitler a gramophone for the common room, and a generous collection of records of military marches, waltzes, symphonies, and Wagner. She visited Hitler twelve times while he was in Landsberg, each visit lasting over an hour, and she brought along her 16-year-old daughter Lotte on two occasions, sparking rumours that Hitler could be her future son-in-law.[6]

Elsa Bruckmann was made to wait two hours before her visit with Hitler. She had seen him speak at the Zirkus Krone in February 1921, but it was in Landsberg on 22 May 1924 that she actually met Hitler for the first time. The visit lasted a mere eight minutes, but it made a lasting impression. Years later she described how overwhelmed she was by his 'chivalry and simple greatness', and how this brief encounter had confirmed her belief that he was Germany's future. Her visit was, in part, she said, to bring greetings from Houston Stewart Chamberlain, 'their mutual friend' who likewise 'had foreseen Hitler's destiny as Führer the first time he met him' in Bayreuth in October 1923.[7]

On Easter Sunday, 20 April, also Hitler's 35th birthday, over twenty admirers ventured out to Landsberg laden with flowers and birthday presents, eager to celebrate the day with him. The warders remembered the large quantities of food, ranging from breads, hams, and sausages to cakes, chocolates, and pastries. Bottles of wine, brandy, and liqueurs, along with huge bouquets of flowers covered the large dining table. Otto Lurker said, 'the common room looked like a forest of flowers' and 'smelled like a greenhouse.' Well-wishers from around the country deluged the prison with cards, letters, telegrams, and packages all for Hitler. Franz Hemmrich claimed that 'laundry baskets were needed just to bring in the letters.' Putzi Hanfstaengl said 'the place looked like a delicatessen.'[8] Hitler shared his exquisite bounty with his fellow prisoners and the warders, an act of generosity that further enhanced his already high reputation in Landsberg.[9]

Not all days were as pleasant or visitors as welcome as on Hitler's birthday. General Ludendorff was a frequent visitor, eager to obtain Hitler's endorsement for his plan to bring together all the ethnic-chauvinist and nationalist groups into one unified völkisch party to contest the national elections on 4 May. Hitler did not like the idea. He consistently rejected an alliance between the NSDAP and any another political group or party. He also was reluctant to participate in the Reichstag elections, 'at least on this occasion', a judgement he had already shared with Siegfried Wagner and his supporters in Bayreuth. Ludendorff was not put off and went ahead with his plans. The ethnic-chauvinist parties won 6.5 per cent of the vote and 32 seats in the Reichstag, 10 of which were taken up by National Socialists including Röhm, Feder, Frick and Otto Strasser's brother Gregor from Landshut. Both Strasser brothers would play leading roles in the party's rise to power, especially in northern Germany. Ludendorff took credit for the election success and under his leadership brought the ultra right wing deputies together in the newly formed National Socialist Liberation Party.[10]

Rosenberg had assisted Ludendorff in pursuing a new policy of parliamentary participation much to the distaste of the old party faithful who still wanted to achieve power through an armed coup. Drexler favoured the more conciliatory and legal approach. Both he and Feder put pressure on Hans Frank to work with them to restrict Hitler's 'adverse influence' as they rebuilt the party. Drexler was still incensed by the way Hitler 'pushed me out' and he feared that 'once Hitler was released from prison the rowdy storm troopers would take to the streets again.'[11] Renewing the revolution is exactly what Ernst Röhm wanted. Hitler appointed Röhm as the military leader of the Kampfbund immediately after Kriebel had been convicted and imprisoned for high treason. Röhm worked industriously to recruit the old members of the banned fighting leagues and Storm Troop Hitler, and soon had a force of 30,000 men serving under him in the newly formed *Frontbann* (Front League). Julius Streicher and Hermann Esser fully supported Röhm's efforts, which brought them into direct conflict with Rosenberg over the party's future direction. Hitler was undecided and, despite telling Röhm in mid-June to stop his work immediately, he was unable to soothe the tensions and reconcile the squabbling factions in the party. Röhm was deeply disappointed. He believed that both the military and the political organizations had to be consolidated, and with Hitler 'unable to see things clearly' from inside Landsberg, Röhm turned to Ludendorff. Together the two military officers presupposed that they were the new leaders of the movement and acted accordingly in pursuit of their respective plans. Almost all of the *völkisch* deputies in the Reichstag and the Bavarian parliament did not endorse their leadership. Nor, as it turned out, did Hitler's many adherents.[12]

By mid-June Hitler was writing to supporters that he could not control the party while he was in prison, and that he intended to withdraw from politics until his release. On 7 July he made his decision official, publically declaring in the *Völkischer Kurier* that he had 'stepped down from the leadership of the National Socialist movement'. Hitler also announced that he would 'refrain from all political activity during the duration of his imprisonment'. He said he needed time and freedom to think and work. He was writing a substantial book and he needed privacy. He therefore beseeched his admirers to stay away from Landsberg. It was a request Hitler had to repeat a little more strongly in the *Völkischer Kurier* on 29 July.[13]

Mein Kampf

Writing a book was neither a new idea nor a sudden shift in direction for Hitler. As early as 1922 the *Völkischer Beobachter* had reported that Hitler was going to outline his politics in a comprehensive book, but building up the party and giving speeches in 1922 and 1923 left Hitler with little energy and time for the 'hard graft of writing'. His unexpected sojourn in Landsberg gave him ample opportunity to set the record straight on his political aims and objectives, and to substantiate his recent claim to be the one and only true leader of the *völkisch* movement. The trial had also helped him consolidate his ideas and outline a coherent narrative. For his defence he had written over sixty pages of notes, which formed the basis of his courtroom speeches. Julius Lehmann had also asked Hitler to write an article for his pan-German journal *Deutschlands Erneuerung* (Germany's Renewal) explaining the politics behind the putsch. Hitler began writing his piece for Lehmann almost as soon as he returned to Landsberg.[1]

Otto Leybold, the Warden, endorsed Hitler's writing projects and even gave him permission to procure a typewriter. Franz Hemmrich, the chief warder in the Festung, found a writing table and provided paper. Winifred Wagner also sent Hitler a large package containing bonded paper, pens, ink, and typewriter ribbon. Hitler's article '*Deutschlands Erwachen*' ('Germany's Awakening') was published in the April edition of *Deutschlands Erneuerung*, and much of it is repeated verbatim in *Mein Kampf*. In addition to justifying the putsch with the same arguments that he and the other defendants made during the trial, Hitler outlined his view of German foreign policy. France was an implacable enemy, therefore expansion, Hitler believed, was essential for Germany's rebirth as a great nation and for its longer term survival in a hostile world. This meant making a choice between either sea power and international trade or land power and agrarian space. The former required an alliance with Russia against Britain and the latter an alliance with England against the Soviet Union. In a 5,000 word article, Hitler introduced his concepts of power politics, race and culture, and the need for 'living space' both inside the German nation for the protection of the *Volk* and external to the Reich through continental expansion. In both cases, the mortal enemy was Marxism, a creation of the Jew. The existential threat of Jewish-Bolshevism would receive significant prominence in *Mein Kampf*, but in his article Hitler left the choice open on what alliance would be best for Germany.[2]

Eher-Verlag, the National Socialist publishing house in Munich, announced Hitler's book in early June. Initially it was entitled 'Four-and-a-half years of

Struggle against Lies, Stupidity and Cowardice'. As the title suggests it was a book designed to 'settle accounts', and Hitler's colleague and publisher, Max Amann, expected a book full of political revelations. It was not, as historian Richard Evans points out, a blueprint for either Hitler's policies or later the actions of the Third Reich.[3] Hitler's account of the political problems in Germany, the rise of the Movement, and the failed putsch, all reflected the political climate in Munich, Bavaria, and Germany at the time the book was written. After Hitler decided to withdraw from politics in July he expanded his concept of the book and added autobiographical sections. The final product, as summarised by Joachim Fest, was 'a mixture of autobiography, ideological tract, and theory and tactics'.[4] Hitler recognised the unique opportunity he had to connect his biography to his political programme, and to portray his early life and the recent setbacks as a prelude to his historical mission. Volker Ullrich contends that 'the book underscored his claim to party leadership in an intellectual sense.'[5] Most of all, Hitler's mythologised self-portrait was meant to indulge his fanatical supporters and attract new adherents to the Movement.

Hitler's *Mein Kampf* (My Struggle), both in its format and style, was strikingly similar to Richard Wagner's *Mein Leben* (My Life) written for his devoted follower and patron Ludwig II. 'It would give me inexpressible joy to receive from you a detailed description of your intellectual development and also of the external events of your life,' Ludwig wrote to Wagner on 28 May 1865.[6] Wagner obliged and began work in July. He dictated a selective and flattering account of his life to his mistress and from 1870 his wife Cosima von Bülow, covering the period from his birth to when he was summoned to Munich by Ludwig in 1864. The book is factually unreliable, but it is nevertheless a masterfully romanticised account of Wagner's perception of himself as an artist and a natural genius.[7] *Mein Kampf* was always intended for a mass audience, but in writing his early life story the way he did, Hitler followed in the footsteps of his cultural idol and created a past to buttress the Führer legend.

Helene Bechstein gave Hitler a brand new Remington portable typewriter in early June. Typing his manuscript himself on the American-manufactured machine made the work go much quicker.[8] Hitler aimed to have a completed draft by October, when he was due to leave Landsberg on parole. Even Leybold, the Warden, witnessed how hard Hitler worked, noting in his mid-September report that Hitler spent 'several hours each day' writing.[9] On Saturday evenings, Hitler read aloud draft chapters to his colleagues assembled in the common room. The warders, especially Franz Hemmrich and Otto Lurker, also used to listen. The myth that Hitler dictated *Mein Kampf* to Rudolf Heß comes from the memoirs of both Hemmrich and Lurker, and has been repeated uncritically by many historians. When Hitler completed a section he often rushed over to Cell 5 to discuss it with Heß. These were exhilarating moments for Heß. He wrote to his fiancée Ilse Pröhl, telling her that when 'the Tribune' read, he 'felt enraptured and breathless' and that 'the language was exquisite.' Heß often called Hitler 'the Tribune', a conscious and deliberate comparison with the hero in Wagner's opera *Rienzi*. He told Ilse in another letter that Hitler was Germany's 'coming man' and that she should bring her mother to Landsberg to meet him.[10]

Ilse Pröhl brought her mother to Landsberg. Hitler kissed Frau Pröhl's hand in his gallant Viennese manner before leading the two women and Heß into the common room for lunch. Frau Pröhl had little interest in politics, and was unsure about her daughter's impending marriage to Heß, particularly as he was a convicted criminal serving a prison sentence. The afternoon with Hitler changed all that. When Frau Pröhl returned to Munich she went directly to the NSDAP's clandestine headquarters in the Eher-Verlag offices on Thierschstraße 15, not far from Hitler's apartment at Thierschstraße 41, and joined the party. Ilse Heß described these events to historian John Toland during an interview in 1971, still convinced that her mother's approval of her marriage to Heß was 'all because of that hand-kiss'.[11]

Hitler had completed large sections of his book by the time he left Landsberg, but the expanding text needed editing and the book had to be restructured. In February 1925 Eher-Verlag announced the official title, *Mein Kampf*, and that it would be a two-volume work. Hitler spent most of the spring and summer of 1925 on the Obersalzberg working on the manuscript. He stayed at the Pension Moritz, and during the day had access to a small cottage a little higher up the mountain, appropriately named the *Kampfhäusl*, where he worked. By the end of April he had made the final changes to volume one, ending this part of his story with the announcement of the NSDAP and its twenty-five point programme at the Hofbräuhaus on 24 February 1920. Ilse Pröhl and Josef Stolzing-Cerny (the music critic for the *Völkischer Beobachter*) quickly completed the final editorial work, and volume one was published on 18 July 1925. The first print run was 10,000 copies. Initially sales were sluggish, in part because of the high price of 12 marks, but by the end of the year the book had sold out. Hitler returned to the Obersalzberg in 1926, and over the summer and early autumn wrote the philosophical and programmatic chapters for volume two, which was published in December. In the early 1930s the two volumes were combined into one book, a cheaper 'people's edition' edited by Rudolf and Ilse Heß. Hitler dedicated *Mein Kampf* to his sixteen party comrades who died at the Feldherrnhalle and in the courtyard of the former War Ministry on 9 November 1923.[12] By the end of 1932 some 228,000 copies had been sold, and at the end of 1944 sales numbered almost twelve and half million copies in eighteen languages. *Mein Kampf* made both Hitler and Max Amann very rich men. The book also played a significant role in Hitler's political career.[13] It established his political credentials and confirmed his leadership of the *völkisch* movement.[14]

Parole Postponed

On 15 and 18 September 1924, Warden Leybold submitted reports to the State Prosecutor in Munich and the Bavarian Ministry of Justice recommending Hitler's release from Landsberg on 1 October, the first day he was eligible for parole. Leybold told the Bavarian authorities that Hitler had been a model prisoner, that he had become a 'more mature and thoughtful individual during his imprisonment than he was before and does not contemplate acting illegally or using violent methods against the government'.[1] This was not a view shared by either the police or the two prosecutors, Stenglein and Ehard, who acted against Hitler at the trial. In a letter to the Minister of the Interior on 22 September, the police opposed Hitler's release, and further argued that he should be deported immediately as a security measure. The next day, Stenglein filed a nine-page motion with the court arguing against Hitler's release on the grounds that he and his co-defendants were still dangerous and unrepentant, and would resume their criminal intentions at the first opportunity.[2] Despite these objections, on 25 September the criminal division of Munich's Superior Court ruled in favour of parole. Hitler, Kriebel and Weber would be released. Four days later the prosecutors submitted another appeal, this time to the Bavarian Supreme Court, effectively blocking the prisoners release, at least temporarily.[3]

Hitler received some good news on 6 October when the Supreme Court rejected the Munich prosecutors' petition, although a new date for his release was not set, leaving him in an uncomfortable state of limbo. Warden Leybold wrote further reports to the court attesting to Hitler's 'strong character, self-control, and unimpeachable conduct' throughout the thirteen months he had been in Landsberg. He acknowledged that Hitler was a 'political idealist' but in Leybold's opinion he was not politically dangerous anymore and he should be released. Still, Hitler waited. The court was in no hurry to conclude its deliberations.[4]

More worrying, for Hitler, was the Bavarian government's attempt to deport him. The new Bavarian premier and Bavarian People's Party (BVP) leader, Heinrich Held, sent a representative to Vienna in early October to see if Austria would take Hitler once he was released from prison. The answer was no. Austrian Chancellor Ignaz Seipel and his cabinet were determined not to let such a 'dangerous political agitator' into the country, especially one who had served in the Bavarian army and by doing so 'had forfeited his Austrian citizenship'. Hitler was delighted to learn that Vienna no longer recognised him as an Austrian, although in April 1925 he had to submit a formal application to be released from his citizenship, which the Austrian government granted immediately. Hitler was stateless until 1932 when he became a German citizen.[5]

Suddenly, less than a week before Christmas, the Bavarian Supreme Court ruled that Hitler was to be released on parole immediately. Leybold rushed over to the Festung to convey the long-awaited news. 'Herr Hitler, you are free,' exclaimed the Warden, breathless but obviously delighted.[6] 'Word flew round the cells,' recalled chief warder Hemmrich, 'enormous jubilation broke out,' and Hitler was 'most loyally and cordially congratulated'. Hitler shook Hemmrich's hand and thanked him for all he had done. He collected his belongings, said his farewells and gave all his money and other parting gifts to his comrades and the prison staff. 'We all held him in the utmost esteem,' proclaimed Hemmrich, 'everyone here, from the Governor to the furnace man, had become a convinced believer in his ideas.'[7]

The timing of Hitler's release coincided with the Reichstag elections held on 7 December. Ludendorff's National Socialist bloc had suffered a humiliating defeat. They received only three per cent of the popular vote, down from 1,918,300 to 970,300 votes, less than half of what they had attained in May, and were reduced from 33 to 14 deputies in the Reichstag. The results were even worse in Bavaria.[8] The ultra-nationalist right appeared to be in terminal decline and the established political parties in Bavaria, such as the conservative BVP and the socialist SPD, no longer saw it as a threat, especially since the NSDAP was still banned and therefore not a legal party. An improving economy with the rescheduling of reparation payments under the Dawes Plan and currency reform fostered a return to moderation in Bavarian politics.[9] Hitler was regarded by many as 'yesterday's man', but it was far too early to write his political obituary, as *Simplicissimus* regularly pointed out. As Hitler walked out of Landsberg, a free man again, Warden Leybold turned to Hemmrich and said: 'Well, if it's any way possible to uplift this country again and set her on her feet, that's the man to do it!'[10]

Hitler left Landsberg shortly after midday on Saturday 20 December. He was collected by Heinrich Hoffmann and Adolf Müller, owner of the printing company used by Eher-Verlag and the future printer of *Mein Kampf*. Hoffmann was eager to capture the moment when Hitler left prison, but Leybold told him photographs were forbidden. There had already been too much publicity surrounding Hitler's time at Landsberg and the Bavarian state authorities did not want any fanfare to mark the occasion of his release. The three men got into Müller's car, a brand new shiny black Mercedes/Daimler-Benz, and drove away. When they reached Landsberg's old city gate, a massive archway that looked like the entrance to a fortress, Müller stopped the car. Hitler got out and briefly posed for Hoffmann's photographs, and then they drove back to Munich, directly to Hitler's apartment on Thierschstraße. Hermann Esser, Julius Streicher, and Julius Schaub were waiting for them. Hitler's German Shepherd, Wolf, was so excited he almost knocked Hitler down the stairs. The apartment was decorated with flowers and laurel wreaths, and the table was covered with fine foods and a bottle of wine.[11] Hoffmann was curious to know what Hitler planned to do next. 'I shall start again, from the beginning,' Hitler answered decisively, but first he needed to rest.[12]

Serious thought was required before Hitler could recommence his political career. First he needed to re-establish his connections with the Bavarian authorities, and get them to lift the ban on the NSDAP. On 21 December Hitler was received by Heinrich Held, the Bavarian president. Hitler promised that in the future he would only act legally.[13] Two days later Hitler was the honoured guest at the Bruckmanns' salon, held in their Munich villa on Karolinenplatz 5. After months of aesthetic austerity in prison, Hitler was slightly in awe at the splendour of the house. Over the next few years Elsa and Hugo Bruckmann would introduce Hitler to Munich's cultural elites as well as financiers and leading industrialists.[14] Ernst and Helene Hanfstaengl invited Hitler to spend Christmas with them and their children, 4-year-old Egon and infant daughter Hertha, at their new house in Munich at Pienzenauerstraße 52 on the east side of the Isar River in the elegant district of Bogenhausen. The Hanfstaengls combined American and Austrian traditions, serving a roast turkey dinner with all the trimmings on Christmas Eve followed by Viennese pastries. Hitler had a good appetite and thoroughly enjoyed himself. He cooed appropriately over Hertha much to Helene's delight, and entertained Egon by imitating the sounds of artillery barrages and machine-gun fire as he remembered them from his time on the Western Front. After dinner they exchanged gifts. The Hanfstaengls gave Hitler an autographed document signed by Frederick the Great, and Putzi played excerpts from Wagner's operas on his grand piano. Hitler especially enjoyed the 'Leibestod' from *Tristan und Isolde*, 'hammered out with Lisztian embellishments'.[15]

Rebuilding the Party

In early January 1925, Hitler met with Dr Heinrich Held, the Bavarian Prime Minister, to appeal for the early release of his fellow-prisoners in Landsberg and to discuss the terms under which Bavaria's bans on the NSDAP and its newspaper the *Völkischer Beobachter* might be lifted. Initially Held was cool to Hitler's requests. Both he and Karl Scharnagl, the lord mayor of Munich, worried about future violence and even a second putsch, but most of all they were enraged by Ludendorff and his attacks against the Catholic Church. Hitler saw Held twice more in January. He dissociated himself from Ludendorff's anti-clericalism (which was deeply offensive in catholic Bavaria) and gave additional assurances that he would pursue his political objectives legally and would 'never again attempt another putsch'.[1] He even offered to work with the Bavarian government in its struggle against the Communists. Held warmed to Hitler's willingness to submit to the state's authority, and his apparent humility. Eventually Held agreed to remove all restrictions. He told Hitler that he would not oppose 'orderly action and agitation' because there was 'a great need for the patriotic development of our people, especially the youth'.[2] On 16 February, the Bavarian government repealed its ban on the NSDAP and the *Völkischer Beobachter*, leading nearly all of the other German states to do the same by the end of the month.[3]

Ten days after the ban was lifted, the *VB* published its first new issue. The front page announced that 'The Movement is free again!' and called on former members of the National Socialist Party to join in the renewal of the movement. A large advertisement announced a mass meeting at the Bürgerbräukeller the following evening at 8 pm, Friday 27 February 1925, when Hitler would re-establish the party.[4] The rest of the page was dominated by an article Hitler had written, outlining his ideas and plans for the reconstituted party. He emphasised the need for unity in the struggle against their enemies, Marxism, and its creator the Jews. He called for an end to internal divisions, religious quarrels, and the damage being done by eccentric *völkisch* interpretations, and he reiterated his demand for unconditional obedience in all matters concerning the party and its political direction. The NSDAP needed and wanted talented people, Hitler asserted, and it was his task as leader to direct 'the diverse temperaments, abilities and also qualities of character in the Movement into those channels in which, by supplementing one another, they benefit everybody.'[5] Further guidance in these matters was provided in the 'Fundamental Guidelines for the Reorganization of the National Socialist German Workers' Party' printed on the next page. The aims, the programme, and the regulations of the old party were still extant, as were the tactical rules for achieving the political objectives. Primacy of the leader was the fundamental principle. Anyone not prepared to submit to the leader and control by the party headquarters (permanently based in Munich) was not welcome in the new NSDAP. Discipline and unity were identified as key prerequisites for the party's growth as a political force, and in time 'the salvation of the Fatherland', and future success depended on all individual party members and organizations, including the reformed SA, subordinating themselves to the programme of the Movement as it was determined by the leadership.[6]

There was an electric atmosphere in the bursting-full Bürgerbräukeller, and the excitement intensified as Hitler walked up to the podium to begin his speech. His expectant followers raised their beer steins, cheered, and even hugged each other.[7] Hitler spoke for more than an hour, restating the aims of the Movement and the key points he had made in the *VB* the previous day. Riotous shouts of approval and loud applause greeted his declaration that the party was reborn, and there was unanimous consent from the audience when he told them that the future of the Movement depended on his absolute control. He reasserted his intention to take up the battle 'with all means necessary' warning 'either we walk over the dead bodies of our enemies, or they will walk over ours.'[8] Hitler concluded his speech with an impassioned appeal for unity and loyalty. Max Amann jumped up and called out: 'The quarrelling must stop. Everyone for Hitler!'[9] Hitler's squabbling lieutenants, the anti-parliamentarians Esser, Streicher, and Artur Dinter from the *Großdeutsche Volksgemeinschaft* (Greater German People's Community) and their opponents Rudolf Buttmann co-founder of the *Deutschnationale Volkspartei* (the German National People's Party DNVP), Feder, and Frick from the parliamentary *Völkischer Block*, rose from their seats, advanced to the speaker's rostrum, and embraced each other. Spontaneous shouts of 'Heil Hitler' rang out, and many in the crowd, men and women, wept tears of joy. 'There had been strains and rifts and strife among us in [Hitler's] absence,' recalled Hermann Esser, 'that he could heal them all at one stroke, and weld the warring and embittered elements together again, merely shows what a leader he is.'[10] The evening ended with everyone present swearing their undying loyalty to 'the *Führer*'.[11]

Hitler left the Bürgerbräukeller with Winifred Wagner. They drove to Bayreuth and Hitler spent the night alone with her at Wahnfried.[12] Hitler was pleased by the enthusiastic reception of his speech and the unqualified support he had received from the over 3,000 devotees at the meeting, but not everyone in the party was willing to accept his leadership or his new political programme. For many, Ludendorff not Hitler was seen as the leader of the *völkische* movement, and for the general's protestant ultra-nationalist supporters Munich was too soft on Catholicism. Ludendorff and other prominent Nazi leaders such as Drexler, Röhm, Gregor Strasser, and Rosenberg did not attend the meeting. Röhm openly denounced Hitler's plan to turn the reconstituted SA into a political organization subordinate to the party. He also accused Hitler of abandoning violence as a means to power. Strasser, Goebbels, and many nationalists in north and west Germany thought that the NSDAP programme was too vague, and that more concrete proposals in a 'Socialist' direction were needed to win over the industrial working class. They also questioned the decision to keep the party headquarters in Munich, and despised its 'dictatorial clique' under Esser and Amann. Both Drexler and Rosenberg were disconsolate, preferring to skip the meeting and sulk because of their diminished importance in the party and within Hitler's inner circle.[13] Hitler had a difficult mission ahead to soothe the internal disagreements and to unite the party, and at the same time avoid further sanctions from the Bavarian and other German state authorities. Simultaneously he had to present himself as a revolutionary and as a regular politician conforming to the rules, 'a radical and a moderate at once'.[14]

Without warning, Hitler's task suddenly looked impossible. On 28 February 1925, the day after the refounding of the NSDAP, Reich President Friedrich Ebert died aged 54 from complications following a ruptured appendix. Less than two weeks later, on 9 March, the Bavarian Interior Minister Karl Stützel banned Hitler from public speaking. Acting on a combination of fears of public violence during the upcoming presidential elections and the uncompromising language Hitler used in his Bürgerbräukeller speech, especially on destroying his enemies and seizing power by any means, the Bavarian government decided Hitler was too dangerous to leave unchecked. Other German states quickly followed suit. Hitler's preferred method of attracting new members and building up the party had been cut off.[15] Both internal NSDAP detractors and political opponents may have comforted themselves with the belief that Hitler had reached the end, that he had been relegated to the margins of regional politics. Despite all the setbacks, Hitler's political fate and the future of the Movement enjoyed two significant advantages: Hitler's personal charisma and the party's strong organizational base in Munich.

The Charismatic Führer

Hitler had already demonstrated a genius for crowd psychology. His ability to express in simple terms what his audience wanted to hear and to fuse their deepest desires with his own sense of personal mission had won him many adherents in Munich's largest beer halls. Hitler drew on the same skills with even greater success when he met small groups of influential people at the Bruckmanns' renowned salon in Munich, Helene Bechstein's salons in Munich, Bayreuth, and Berlin, and the innumerable intimate conversations he had with prospective patrons in his favourite Munich cafés and restaurants. The combination of his old world charm, his excessive politeness and Viennese manners, with his vision and the strength of his conviction that he alone could rescue Germany and the German people from their current malaise, won over many powerful and wealthy members of high society and drew them inexorably into the National Socialist orbit. This would not have happened without the public speaking ban that altered Hitler's approach to rebuilding the party. By the time the ban was lifted in March 1927, Hitler had come into direct contact with the entire Munich membership of the party, winning them over individually through his magnetic attraction, and solidifying his position as the indispensable leader of the Movement.[1]

Hitler was a regular guest at Hugo and Elsa Bruckmann's villa on Karolinenplatz 5. The Bruckmanns ensured that Hitler met leading business figures, architects and artists, and luminaries from the academic and literary communities who would help him and the party. On 4 July 1927, Elsa Bruckmann hosted a meeting between Hitler and Emil Kirdorf, the patriarch of Rhineland and Westphalian industry. The two men spoke for over four hours. Kirdorf was so impressed with Hitler's ideas on the relationship between private industry and the state that he asked Hitler to write a pamphlet. Entitled 'The Road to Resurgence', Hugo Bruckmann published it, and Kirdorf distributed it to his many business colleagues.[2] Hitler also met a number of ethnic-chauvinist and nationalist-inclined professors from the Ludwig-Maximilians-Universität, namely the racial hygienists Fritz Lenz and Max von Gruber, the theologian Bernhard Stempfle, and the zoologist Karl Escherich. He was also reacquainted on more equal terms with the historian Karl Alexander von Müller, whom Hitler first met while taking the propaganda instructor's course in June 1919. These professors and their likeminded colleagues at the university were instrumental in converting many of their bright young students into fanatical National Socialists.[3]

Of all the people Hitler met at the Bruckmanns' salon, the two who became his closest friends and artistic collaborators in Munich were Paul Ludwig Troost and his young wife Gerhardine (Gerdy). Troost had established his reputation as an interior designer fitting luxury ocean liners for North German Lloyd. Gerdy, twenty-five years younger than her husband, was an accomplished artist and pianist, and she collaborated with him on architectural commissions. The Troosts and Hitler, who became their most important patron, revered the classical tradition and conceived of the arts, especially architecture, as 'a sacred duty and mission'. Paul and Gerdy Troost regarded Hitler as 'an immensely sympathetic and knowledgeable lover of art and music' and enjoyed working with him because he had 'so much feeling and sensitivity for architecture'.[4] Immediately after Hitler came to power in 1933 he commissioned Troost to build a monumental new art gallery, the *Haus der Deutschen Kunst* (the House of German Art) on Prinzregentenstraße at the southern end of the Englischer Garten. Troost also transformed the Königsplatz into a centre of Nazi power, with *Ehrentempel* (two temples of honour) for the 'martyrs' killed in the 1923 putsch, flanked by two identical major party structures, the *Führerbau* (the Führer Building) and the *Verwaltungsbau der NSDAP* (the Administration Building of the NSDAP) on the east face of the square. Troost's designs established a distinctive National Socialist style of architecture, devoid of ornamental embellishments, combining Greco-Roman classicism with modernity.[5]

In July 1925 Hitler attended the Bayreuth Festival for the first time. The Bechsteins had invited him to stay with them and they used this opportunity to introduce 'their friend' to the cultural elite. Hitler attended the full cycle of operas – the four-part *Der Ring des Nibelungen*,[6] *Parsifal*, and *Die Meistersinger von Nürnberg*. 'It was a sunny time,' Hitler recalled fondly, 'there was a luminous beauty about Bayreuth!'[7] The Bechsteins spoilt him. During the day they took him on outings in the surrounding countryside. After the performances he often sat with the artists in the Festival Theatre or mingled with other festival-goers in the Anker, one of Bayreuth's luxury hotels next to the Margraves' Opera House in the baroque-styled city centre. 'I had reached that pleasant level of popularity where everybody was nice to me without expecting anything from me,' Hitler enthused, 'I was left in peace. By day I wore Bavarian Lederhosen, and I went to the festival in a dinner-jacket or tails. Those were marvellous days.'[8] Hitler spent nearly two luxurious weeks in Bayreuth, from 21 July through 3 August, returning to Munich briefly, and then on to the Obersalzberg where he continued writing the second volume of *Mein Kampf*.[9]

Between 1925 and 1928, Hitler became the outright leader, and the NSDAP was transformed into a 'leader party' that was unique in the German political milieu. The main focus was always on Hitler, not the party, and not the NSDAP programme. Hitler's ideological vision and scheme for national redemption and rebirth attracted many adherents, especially when the economy collapsed at the end of the decade, but it was to Hitler the 'mythical redeemer' that they were drawn. Paving the way for Hitler's rise to power were loyal activists in Munich. It was they who created the 'cult of the *Führer*' through a multifaceted and sophisticated public relations campaign. Starting within the Munich membership, formal oaths of allegiance were sworn to Hitler, a practice that quickly spread to newly formed branches and regional NSDAP organizations. The ritual of celebrating 'the Führer's birthday' was revived on 20 April 1925, and it promptly became a 'most important day' in the Nazi calendar of events thereafter. Sometime during the spring of 1925, '*Heil Hitler*' became an official greeting. The *VB* first used it in April 1925, and in 1926 it was enshrined as the compulsory form of address. Even the party headquarters in Munich confirmed Hitler's central role, issuing 'official postcards' that bore an etching of the head of the Führer and the *Heil* greeting.[10]

Inside the party, Hitler either won over or pushed away his most serious leadership rivals to the outer edge of politics. Putting General Ludendorff forward as the NSDAP's candidate in the 29 March 1925 election for Reich President was a master stroke. The party lacked the financial and organizational means to support Ludendorff's campaign. These shortcomings combined with the general's bizarre conspiracy theories, offending northern nationalists and Bavarian Catholics alike, virtually guaranteed a crushing defeat. Hitler was not surprised that Ludendorff received a derisory 1.1 per cent, a mere 285,793 votes out of 27,000,000. The once-united nationalist and *völkisch* movement under Ludendorff disintegrated. Hitler transferred his support to former Field Marshal Paul von Hindenburg, another war hero, who with the NSDAP's support on 26 April won a narrow victory over the centre-left candidate Wilhelm Marx in the second ballot for the presidency. Ludendorff disappeared into the political wilderness with Mathilde von Kemnitz, whom he married in 1926, and founded the Tannenberg League. He remained on the fringe of the radical right until he died in 1937.[11]

Röhm was the next to go. He had already and in public rejected Hitler's new plans for the SA. On 16 April 1925, Röhm went to Hitler's apartment on Thierschstraβe and hand-delivered a memorandum outlining his demands for the Frontbann and the SA. Röhm regarded both organizations as part of an auxiliary army under his command for the protection of the Fatherland. He categorically rejected their involvement in party politics, and forbade SA leaders from 'accepting instructions from party political leaders'. Hitler read the short memorandum in silence. Röhm outlined his plans for the expansion of the SA and the incorporation of the Frontbann into it, and told Hitler that he would resign immediately if he was not allowed to lead the SA as set out in his memorandum. It was a high risk strategy giving Hitler an ultimatum. Writing about his conversation with Hitler in his memoirs Röhm noted that it was unsatisfactory. 'He did not look upon this advice as friendly service but as a deliberate disparagement of his work, which of course was not my intention.'[12] Hitler reiterated his intention to merge the SA into the party where it would have a political rather than a military role. Despite their disagreements he also asked Röhm to be the SA's new leader. Unable to persuade Hitler that the SA should be a conventional paramilitary organization, Röhm wrote to Hitler the following day to decline his offer and resign as leader of the Frontbann. On 30 April, having not had a reply, Röhm again wrote to Hitler. He included a draft resignation announcement to be published in the National Socialist press, thanked Hitler for his comradeship, and asked him 'not to withdraw from me your personal friendship'.[13] This too went unanswered. The *Völkischer Beobachter* eventually made a short announcement that Röhm had resigned. Röhm left the party and found work as a salesman and a factory hand before accepting an invitation to train the Bolivian army in European warfare.[14]

Goebbels and Gregor Strasser established an *Arbeitsgemeinschaft* (working group) of *Gauleiters* (regional party leaders) in north and west Germany to revise the NSDAP programme and contest the authority of the party headquarters in Munich. These efforts floundered from the start. Other than agreeing to cooperate on matters that were similar among their regions and which the Munich headquarters appeared incapable of understanding, there were deep disagreements on almost all aspects of policy. At two meetings held in Hanover on 22 November 1925 and 24 January 1926, they dithered over whether or not they should support a referendum proposed by the Left to confiscate the property of the former royal princes. Goebbels and Strasser were in favour. Endorsing the referendum would demonstrate that the party was serious about winning working class support. Gottfried Feder, the party's leading ideologue and Hitler's representative at the working group, disagreed with the principle of expropriation. It sent out the wrong message, especially as it would undermine the Führer's attempts to win the approval of businessmen. Members of the working group failed to find common ground on the party's structure, the future National Socialist state, and foreign policy. Some members, including Goebbels, favoured an alliance with Russia against the 'Jewish-capitalist' west. Others viewed the Soviet Union as the cradle of Jewish-Bolshevism, which had to be destroyed and in doing so would open up Russia for German expansion.[15]

Despite the working group's problems, Hitler was mindful that it just might challenge the authority of the Munich headquarters. He summoned party leaders to a conference on 14 February at Bamberg. The north Bavarian town was famous for its artistic heritage, particularly its Baroque architecture and also its excellent beer. Goebbels and Strasser attended the meeting full of confidence and joy. 'The socialist spirit is on the march in all towns,' Goebbels wrote in his diary, 'Not a soul has faith in Munich.' A few short hours later, when the meeting had ended, he was crestfallen. 'I feel devastated. What kind of Hitler? A reactionary?' Hitler had rejected all of the working group's policies. 'A horrible night! … Grey dawn appears,' Goebbels wrote in his diary. 'I can no longer wholly believe in Hitler.'[16] On 22 May, at the party's general meeting held in the Bürgerbräukeller, the original NSDAP programme of 24 February 1920 was declared immutable. Goebbels, however, quickly reconciled with Hitler. In November he was appointed Gauleiter in Berlin. It was Goebbels more than anyone else who turned the German capital into a National Socialist stronghold.[17]

At the second *Reichsparteitag* (NSDAP national rally), a two-day festival held over 3–4 July 1926 in Weimar, it was clear that Hitler had succeeded in uniting the party under his complete control. Some 8,000 party members, including 3,600 SA and 116 *Schutzstaffel* (Protection Squad, SS),[18] attended. Weimar was chosen because of its location in Thuringia, one of the few German states where Hitler was permitted to speak. The rally consisted of speeches, the swearing of personal oaths to Hitler, and parades. In his main address to the congress on 4 July, Hitler outlined his vision for the party and the National Socialist state, announced the formation of the *Hitler-Jugend* (Hitler Youth, HJ) and that Munich was the permanent location of the party headquarters, forbade working groups, and declared his own veto authority over all party resolutions. Hitler received 'a rapturous reception' from the delegates after his speech. 'Deep and mystical – almost like a Gospel,' wrote Goebbels. 'I thank destiny for giving us this man!'[19] Hitler left Weimar as the exclusive exponent of the 'idea' of National Socialism and the sole leader of the NSDAP. During the march past marking the end of the congress, Hitler stood in an open-top car greeting each of the SA and SS units with a raised right arm salute. This was the first time that the SS under the command of Julius Schreck had paraded in public, carrying the Blood Flag that had been retrieved from the carnage in front of the Feldherrnhalle on 9 November 1923. The rituals first performed in Weimar would become the basis of the mass party rallies held in Nürnberg after Hitler and the NSDAP gained power in 1933.[20]

Thomas Theodor Heine's iconic red bulldog cover illustration, *Simplicissimus* 1910.

Inside Alter-Simpl, famous meeting place for the bohemians of Schwabing, Türkenstraße 57.

Café Stefanie – Munich's most famous Großenwahn Café, Amalienstraße/Theresienstraße.

'Der Alter Hof' –
Hitler's watercolour
of the Old Residence,
Burgstraβe 8.

Main Gate – all
that remains of the
Türkenkaserne,
Türkenstraβe.

Statue of Bavaria,
Theresienwiese.

Friedensengel (Angel of Peace),
Maximilian Park.

Kurt Eisner Memorial, Ostfriedhof.

Thule-Gesellschaft (Thule Society) logo, 1919.

Haus Neumayr,
Petersplatz 8.

Hofbräukeller, Innere Wiener
Straße 19.

Hofbräuhaus, Am Platzl 9.

Hofbräuhaus-Festsaal.

Feldherrnhalle – Odeonsplatz.

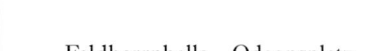

Hitler's second private residence
(1920–1929), Thierschstraβe 41.

Hitler and his co-defendants, Putsch Trial, 1924.

Karl Arnold's 'Munich Man', *Simplicissimus*, 3 December 1923.

Hoffmann Photo Studio and fourth NSDAP Party HQ, Schellingstraße 50.

Newspaper Wagon, *Völkischer Beobachter*.

Neues Rathaus (New Town Hall), Marienplatz 8.

Braunes Haus (Brown House), fifth NSDAP HQ, Brienner Straße 45.

Hitler in his office, Braunes Haus.

Postcard of SS honour guard and memorial at the Feldherrnhalle to the dead putschists of 1923.

North Temple of the Ehrentempeln containing the coffins of the first 'blood witnesses' of the Movement, the 'martyrs' of the failed putsch of 1923.

Polizeipräsidium (Police Headquarters) and Himmler's Munich HQ, Ettstraße 2.

Paul Ludwig Troost's Haus der Deutschen Kunst, Prinzregentenstraße 1.

Poster for the 'Bolshevism' exhibition, 1936.

Hitler opens the first Große Deutsche Kunstausstellung (Great German Art Exhibition), Haus der Deutschen Kunst, Sunday, 18 July 1937.

Poster for 'The Eternal Jew' exhibition, 1937.

Catalogue covers for the 'Great German Art' and the 'Degenerate Art' exhibitions, 1937.

Front row from left to right: Hitler, Gerdy Troost, Adolf Ziegler, and Joseph Goebbels, Haus der Deutschen Kunst.

The Axis leaders arrive for the Munich Conference. From left to right: Hermann Göring, Count Ciano, Hitler, and Mussolini.

The Führerbau decorated for the Munich Conference, 29 September 1938.

Altes Rathaus (Old Town Hall), Marienplatz 15.

Hitler's third private residence (1929–1945), Prinzregentenplatz 16.

Prinzregenten Theater, Prinzregentenplatz.

New housing estate and air raid bunker, Prinzregentenstraβe.

Hitler and Eva Braun at the Berghof, Obersalzberg.

Air raid bunker, Blumenstraβe.

Inspection of the
Bürgerbräukeller,
9 November 1939.

Hitler at the state funeral for
the Bürgerbräukeller bombing
victims, Feldherrnhalle,
11 November 1939.

Siegestor (Victory Gate) with
the Feldherrnhalle in the
background, Ludwigstraße.

Justizpalast (Palace of Justice), Elisenstraße 1a/Prielmayrstraße 7.

Permanent memorial to the Weiße-Rose, historic courtroom 216 (now 253), Justizpalast. From left to right: Willi Graf, Kurt Huber, Alexander Schmorell, Hans Scholl, Sophie Scholl, and Christoph Probst.

Löwenbräukeller, Stiglmaierplatz.

City centre in 1945 with
the Neues Rathaus and
the Frauenkirche in the
background.

Art installation in memory
of Georg Elser, Georg–Elser–
Platz

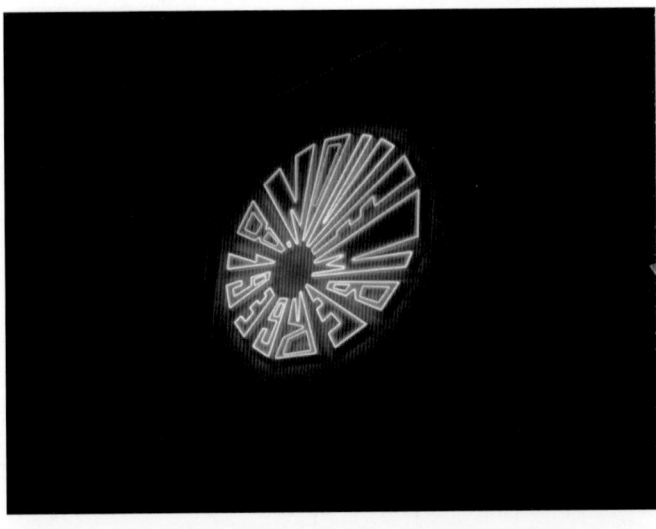

Memorial to Elser illuminated
9.20 pm, Georg-Elser-Platz.

Creation of the Party Cadre and National Organization

etween 1925 and 1929 the NSDAP became a formidable organization. On 4 June 1925 the party opened its new headquarters at Schellingstraβe 50. The building was owned by Heinrich Hoffmann; it was where he ran his photographic agency until October 1929, when he moved to larger premises at Amalienstraβe 25, on the corner of Theresienstraβe. Hoffmann offered Hitler thirteen rooms in his studio, of which Hitler, being 'very superstitious', took twelve.[1] The new party headquarters was a major improvement. It was spacious and more befitting of a major political party than the offices it previously occupied in Eher-Verlag, the party's publishing house on Thierschstraβe. In addition to having appropriate facilities and modern office equipment, the new party headquarters had an impressive reception area, which was set up as a Hall of Honour for the SA and where the Blood Flag was put on public display.[2] Hitler also made two key appointments to the central office in 1925: Philipp Bouhler as party secretary and business manager, and Franz Xaver Schwarz as the national treasurer. In the capable hands of these efficient bureaucrats, the day-to-day running of the party became highly professional, and financial, organizational, and propaganda matters were centralised under the control of the Munich headquarters. Max Amann continued in his role as head of publishing, and Alfred Rosenberg happily returned as editor of the *Völkischer Beobachter* after Hitler praised him for his integrity and called him 'a most valuable collaborator'.[3] After a number of discussions with Gregor Strasser, Hitler replaced Hermann Esser as the party's propaganda chief, first with Otto May and later, on 2 January 1928, with Strasser himself, popular moves that placated many north German supporters. Calm and efficiency characterised the new central office as it set about turning the party into a national political force.[4]

Indispensable to the party's growth and future success was the creation of new regional organizations called *Gaue* that all conformed to a similar structure right across the country. Each regional leader, or *Gauleiter*, was appointed by Hitler, and reported to the party headquarters in Munich. Below the *Gaue* were districts (*Kreise*) and local levels that varied in size depending on the area of the country. Local branches provided real opportunities for a new generation of younger Nazi activists to engage in prominent roles, such as canvassing support, distributing pamphlets, fund raising, and generally promoting the party.

Developing leadership skills at the local level was also encouraged, and rewarded with promotions up to district and regional organizations. In 1928 the *Gaue* were realigned to correspond with the thirty-five Reichstag electoral districts, signalling their importance in building up the party's electoral machinery.[5]

Another increasingly important factor in the development of the Nazi movement was the establishment of occupational associations and specialist organizations that reflected the bourgeois fabric of German society, such as doctors, lawyers, students, teachers, and women from 1925 onwards. Most sprung up out of the private initiatives of enthusiastic Nazi activists, and started as local or regional associations. Hitler recognised the usefulness of these groups, and with his support many of them became national organizations approved by the party headquarters in Munich. The first of these was the *Nationalsozialistischer Deutscher Studentenbund* (National Socialist German Students' League, NSDStB) founded by Wilhelm Tempel, a law student, in February 1926. Baldur von Schirach, also a university student at the time, joined the branch at LMU in Munich. He succeeded Tempel as the League's national leader in 1928, and was appointed leader of the Hitler Youth by Hitler on 3 October 1931, before marrying Hoffmann's daughter Henriette in 1933.[6] In September 1928, Hans Frank set up the *Bund Nationalsozialistischer Deutscher Juristen* (the League of National Socialist German Lawyers, BNSDJ). Frank regarded the BNSDJ as a sort of 'combat society designed to protect the party from "new-German law" aimed against Hitler and the NSDAP'.[7] Rosenberg copied his colleague and in January 1929 he created the *Kampfbund für deutsche Kultur* (the Combat League for German Culture, KfdK). The *Völkischer Beobachter* heralded the timely arrival of this 'vital organization for the defence of German cultural values amidst the contemporary culture decay'. The KfdK aimed to 'enlighten the German race about the connections existing between race, art, and knowledge, and moral and responsible values.' Protecting 'cultural Germandom', proclaimed the *VB*, was of 'primary importance in the life-and-death struggle for German freedom.'[8] In Munich avant-garde art was harshly criticised and sometimes even removed from exhibitions. Plays by Bertolt Brecht, Karl Kraus, and Alfred Döblin were cancelled, and a performance of the 'Danse Sauvage' by the American-born entertainer Josephine Baker was banned by the city's authorities 'in the interest of public morals'.[9] Other less controversial specialist organizations that attached themselves to the NSDAP in 1929 were the *Nationalsozialistischer Lehrerbund* (the National Socialist Teachers' League, NSLB), and the *Nationalsozialistischer Deutscher Ärztebund* (the National Socialist German Doctors' League, NSDÄB).[10]

Elspeth Zander had established a *Deutscher Frauenorden* (German Women's Order, DFO) in Berlin in 1923. She was an outspoken anti-feminist and had strong views on what women should and should not do. Zander addressed party members on traditional values and the role of women at the Weimar Party Rally in July 1926. It took another two years before the DFO attained official party affiliation, and shortly after that it was the centre of embarrassing public attention due to a number of financial and sexual scandals. Zander herself was accused of having an extramarital affair with her chauffeur. Gregor Strasser gently eased Zander out of the picture and replaced her discredited women's order with the new *Nationalsozialistische Frauenschaft* (National Socialist Women's Organization, NSF) in July 1931.[11]

Many other sectors of German society were represented in official Nazi organizations by the early 1930s. Civil servants, farmers, war veterans and those still suffering from war-wounds, all had their own associations. The party also catered to the lower-middle and working classes, forming associations for artisans, factory workers, shopkeepers, and both the self-employed and the unemployed. Winter aid programmes and other charitable activities, including the distribution of clothing and shoes, and even a free meals-on-wheels service for the disabled and the elderly who belonged to the party were established in all of the *Gaue* by the end of 1931. Cultural and leisure activities, organized holidays, and sport also brought many non-political people, and most noticeably young people, into the 'greater Nazi family'. By the end of the 1920s membership in the NSDAP started to soar. In 1927 the official paid-up membership was less than it was in November 1923, but by October 1928 it had exceeded 100,000. A year later it was over 150,000, and in December 1931 it surpassed 800,000.[12]

Diversity and dynamism distinguished the NSDAP very favourably from any of the other political parties. Richard Evans also notes that the development of the Nazi movement after 1927 'was dependent on the energy and fanaticism of its active members'.[13] Twenty-nine-year-old Magda Quandt joined the party during the summer of 1930, more than a year before she married Joseph Goebbels. She was attractive, intelligent and urbane, and moved in Berlin's high-society circles even after she divorced Günther Quandt, her first husband who was a wealthy industrialist. Despite her privileged lifestyle, she like many of her generation believed that democracy had failed in Germany and that the future would be determined by either the left or the right. Both the cult of Hitler and the 'idea' of a new society, a *Volksgemeinschaft* (national community) led her into the burgeoning ranks of the NSDAP. The Movement embodied youthful, revolutionary dynamism – populist nationalism – which Magda Quandt found reassuring when so much in Germany was in a state of chaos and decay. Hitler and the NSDAP offered simple answers to complicated questions and made it possible to 'flee the grey everyday'.[14]

Hitler's popularity, and by the mid-1930s his near legendary status as the Messianic leader who would restore Germany's national greatness, was a key factor in the development and success of the Nazi party. National Socialism came to be known as 'the Hitler Movement'.[15] Not to be overlooked however, is the dynamism of Nazi ideology, specifically because of its diffuseness. The twelve central 'tenets', comprising popular dogmas, resentments, and prejudices, were combined to give the impression of an irrefutable *Weltanschauung*.[16] They could also be linked in a variety of directions, making them more or less radical depending on the political sensibilities of the individual supporter, specialist organizations, town, city or region of the country. Hitler too, despite his many protestations on the party's immutable programme, proved adept at being flexible and pragmatic, and even indifferent towards ideological issues that fixated some of his followers. What mattered most to Hitler, and what the reconstituted party worked tirelessly to achieve, was power.

Erholung (Rest and Recovery)

Hitler enjoyed Munich. He often strolled around the old city centre admiring the architecture and ending up in an art gallery or a museum. He revelled in the bohemian lifestyle, visiting artists' studios, cafés and restaurants. 'I'm at home here,' he told Kurt Ludecke, 'I mean something here; there are many here who are devoted to me, to me alone and nobody else. That's important.'[1] Hitler had a *Stammtisch* (reserved table for regulars) in the Café Heck at Odeonsplatz 6, on the corner of Ludwigstraße and Galeriestraße, which he used as an unofficial office. During the summer his table was outside on the terrace in the Hofgarten, where Putzi Hanfstaengl regularly joined him to read the daily newspapers. In the early 1930s, after Hitler became a prominent national politician, he entertained companions in the Café Luitpold at Brienner Straße 11 or found a secluded corner at the Carlton Tea Room on Brienner Straße 8, where his conversations remained private. Hitler's favourite restaurant was the Osteria Bavaria, specialising in Austrian cuisine, at Schellingstraße 62 on the same street and a very short walk from both the party's fourth headquarters and the printing workshops of the *VB*. Hoffmann's new photographic shop was nearby and he often joined Hitler, who always came with a small entourage, his chauffeur and bodyguard, and one or two of his inner circle, namely Heß, Hanfstaengl, Julius Schaub, Christian Weber, Max Amann and Hermann Esser, for lunch.[2]

One of Hitler's great passions was films, which he avidly pursued in Munich. He regularly went to the cinema at the Sendlinger Torplatz. His taste in films was fairly diverse, ranging from the silent historical film *Fridericus Rex* to the epic *Ben Hur*, which he saw with Heß,[3] and the controversial and erotically charged *Girls in Uniform* that he watched with Goebbels. 'Charming girls,' Goebbels wrote in his diary, 'I'm completely taken in and dumbfounded. Hitler too.'[4] Hitler remained a film enthusiast till the end of his life, but after he became Chancellor he had films screened privately at the Berghof, on the Obersalzberg, the Reich Chancellery in Berlin, and even his field headquarters during the war.

Hitler spent many evenings in Munich at either the opera or the theatre. Wagner's operas were his favourites, but he also liked the ballet and symphony concerts. Hitler saw many of Germany's most distinguished dancers, orchestras, and singers perform at the National Theatre on Max-Joseph-Platz. He also enjoyed operettas, and saw Franz Lehár's *Die lustige Witwe* (*The Merry Widow*) and Johann Strauss II's *Die Fledermaus* multiple times at the Gärtnerplatz-theater not far from the party's second headquarters on Corneliusstraβe.[5] By the end of the 1920s, royalties from the sales of *Mein Kampf* substantially increased Hitler's personal wealth, enabling him to afford the best opera and theatre tickets, and also to upgrade his accommodation and living arrangements.

In October 1928, Hitler rented Haus Wachenfeld on an annual lease of 1,200 Reichsmarks from Frau Margarete Winter, a party member and the widow of a north German businessman. The two-storey cottage was constructed in traditional Bavarian alpine style. It was located on the shaded edge of a meadow on the northern slope of the Obersalzberg just below the Platterhof, formerly the Pension Moritz, which had been renamed after Hitler's friends and former owners the Büchners had sold it and left. The scenery was breathtaking overlooking Berchtesgaden and on into Austria. From the front balcony Hitler looked directly at the Untersberg, where according to local legend Emperor Frederick Barbarossa and his army lay sleeping deep inside the mountain awaiting the moment when they had to rise again and defend the Holy German Empire. On a clear day Hitler could trace the River Ache running out of Berchtesgaden towards Austria, and see the Festung Hohensalzburg, the fortress castle in Salzburg.[6]

Once Hitler acquired Haus Wachenfeld he asked his widowed half-sister Angela Raubal to come and be his housekeeper. She happily agreed, and immediately moved from Vienna to the Obersalzberg with her two daughters, Angelika (Geli) and Friedl. Hitler recalled their first Christmas together on the mountain as being a 'marvellous time'. He also made sure that he was back on the Obersalzberg at Haus Wachenfeld to celebrate Geli's 21st birthday on 4 June 1929. Geli was an attractive, tallish, and vivacious girl who had 'the famous Viennese charm' according to Ilse Heβ,[7] and whom Hitler 'loved very much', recalled Goebbels, even though he thought 'she distracted [Hitler] from serious business.'[8] Later in August Geli was by her uncle's side at the Nürnberg Rally, and in October she moved into his new apartment in Munich.[9] Sometime after that she became his mistress.[10]

Shortly after Hitler became Chancellor he persuaded Frau Winter to sell Haus Wachenfeld to him. He purchased the house with all its contents on 26 June 1933, for 40,000 Goldmarks, and later that summer started an extensive renovation programme that would last until 1936. Working from designs Hitler had drawn, the architect Roderich Fick converted the modest alpine retreat into an elegant formal residence renamed the Berghof.[11]

Hitler's third, and last, private residence in Munich was an opulent apartment in a stylish building designed in 1907–8 by Franz Popp, on Prinzregentenplatz 16. Measuring some 317 square metres of living space, there was a large entry hall, nine rooms divided into two wings that followed the contours of the corner building facing the square, two bathrooms, a kitchen, and chambers for two servants. Hitler's apartment occupied the entire second floor and was accessible by either an elegant staircase or an elevator, which was quite a luxury for an apartment building in Munich in the 1920s. Helene Bechstein and Elsa Bruckmann decorated the apartment, filling its generous spaces with expensive furniture, ornaments, and works of art. Moving into sumptuous rooms in the affluent district of Bogenhausen instantly conferred a higher social respectability on Hitler, but it also could have damaged his image with the working classes and reduced his appeal as 'the people's leader'. To mitigate this potential problem, Hugo Bruckmann acted as Hitler's legal representative, both to secure the lease and pay the yearly rent of 4,176 Reichsmarks.[12]

One significant attraction of Hitler's new apartment was its connection to Richard Wagner. Before the Great War, Isolde Wagner and her husband Franz Wilhelm Beidler moved into the same second floor apartment that Hitler rented in 1929. Isolde, or Loldi as her parents called her, was the first born child of Wagner and Cosima Bülow, five years before they were married in 1870. Loldi suffered from a number of illnesses when the Beidlers lived in Munich, and she died in 1919. Hitler never met her, but Loldi was not the only link between the great composer and the area. Looking out of the apartment's windows facing up Prinzregentenstraße, Hitler could see the Prinzregententheater. It opened in 1901 as the Richard Wagner Festival Hall and its architectural style was strikingly similar to the festival theatre in Bayreuth. Years before Hitler became the Prinzregententheater's most famous neighbour he regularly attended the annual Wagner festival. The theatre was forced to close in 1932, a victim of the Great Depression, but with Hitler's help it reopened in 1933 for performances of *Parsifal*. It secured its finances the following year when it joined the *Kraft durch Freude* (Strength through Joy, KdF) organization in Munich, and provided state-subsidised leisure activities for party members and workers. Wagner's operas continued to feature in the programme, especially when the theatre director knew that 'Hitler was in residence', but overall the theatre's offerings became much more eclectic and included 'propagandistic works' that struggled to fill half the seats even for a single performance. Next to the theatre in a small shaded park is a massive Wagner memorial that was created by the sculptor Heinrich Waderé in 1913, using stone from the Untersberg.[13]

Hitler moved into his Prinzregentenplatz apartment on 1 October 1929. He brought his former landlady Maria Reichert together with her husband Ernst and mother Frau Dachs with him from Thierschstraße. Anni and Georg Winter were hired as domestic staff and also lived in the apartment. Anni did the cooking and Georg became the house manager. Hitler also hired Anna Kirmair as his cleaning lady. Later in October Geli arrived. She had a large corner room to herself, which Hitler let her decorate as she pleased. Geli quickly unsettled the household staff with her casual manner and moodiness. They were unaware of the intimacy developing between her and Hitler, and thought that she was exploiting her uncle's generosity. It was also around the same time that Hitler met Eva Braun in Hoffmann's photographic studio.[14]

Eva Braun was 17 and had just started to work for Hoffmann when he introduced her to Hitler. It was a Friday afternoon, either 4 or 11 October 1929. Hitler came into Hoffmann's studio and noticed high up on a ladder a pretty young girl with darkish blonde hair wearing a short skirt, re-shelving some documents. Hoffmann later recalled that Hitler clearly admired his young assistant's legs. After she climbed down, Hoffmann introduced them: 'Herr Wolf – our good little girl Eva.' Hitler made a habit of visiting Hoffmann's studio more often, sometimes asking his friend in advance if Eva 'was working' on the day he planned to visit. Hitler beamed in her presence, and exhibited all of his Viennese charm. He paid her compliments, gave her flowers and small gifts, took her out for afternoon tea, and even dinner, a film, or the opera every once in a while.[15] Geli learned about their flirtatious trysts on 17 September 1931 when by chance she found a note from Eva peeking out of a pocket in Hitler's jacket thanking him for 'a memorable evening'. Two days late Geli was found dead in her room, she had bled to death after shooting herself with Hitler's Walther 6.35-calibre pistol.[16]

Geli's death was treated as a suicide, although Winifred Wagner thought it was more likely to have been an accident or an unintentionally lethal attempt to get Hitler's attention.[17] There was no suicide note, and neither the Reicherts nor the Winters could offer any motive. When they were interviewed by the police they all said that Geli seemed agitated after Hitler had left the previous day for a campaign trip in northern Germany. She locked herself in her room, but nothing pointed to suicidal intentions. She had been 'very emotional of late', added Maria Reichert.[18] Perhaps she was still angry after finding Eva's note?

Hitler had just left Nürnberg on the morning of 19 September when he received the news. He was devastated. He and his entourage turned around and raced back to Munich. When Hitler spoke to the police later that afternoon, he told them that Geli was the only relative that he was close to, and that her death 'had shaken him badly'.[19] In addition to Geli's tragic death, Hitler faced a scandal that threatened to destroy his and his Movement's political future. Left-wing newspapers asked embarrassing questions and gave slanderous answers. Why was Hitler living with his niece? What was the nature of the relationship between the 23-year-old girl and her 42-year-old uncle? The socialist *Münchener Post* claimed that in a jealous fit of rage Hitler had physically assaulted Geli, and may have even killed her. The story was untrue and the paper was forced to retract its allegations,[20] but the rumours persisted. Newspapers across Germany published the most vile and potentially damaging accounts of Hitler's supposedly depraved private life.[21] Hitler's political adversaries salivated over the prospect of destroying their rival. They sought to expose an unconventional domesticity and questionable private morality that would disqualify Hitler from holding high public office. Hans Frank recalled that Hitler 'agonised over the sordid stories spread about him and Geli, and swore that one day he would take his revenge'.[22] This was no idle threat. Hitler unleashed the full fury of his SA and the SS on his tormentors once he came to power.[23]

Hitler's private life has always attracted an inordinate amount of attention and been the subject of much conjecture. In part this is because there is very little authentic evidence about it, especially when it comes to Hitler's relationships with women. After 1929 Heinrich Himmler's SS confiscated and destroyed anything that was regarded as 'compromising' in Hitler's past, and any documents or letters that Hitler and Eva had kept safely in their possession were destroyed by Julius Schaub at the end of the war. Both Hitler's contemporary enemies and many of his biographers either have relied on (and embellished) myths, or spread rumours and concocted salacious lies to fit their preconceptions and specific agendas. Hitler's own excessive discretion and his reluctance to discuss his private life, even with those closest to him, was borne out of fear that it may be used by his political opponents against him. These fears have in fact come to pass, albeit after his life and mostly by historians. A number of these historians, which sadly includes some highly acclaimed and respectable ones, have deceived themselves and their readers with a comforting but unproven conclusion that a man who was responsible for so many horrifying crimes must have been sexually perverse.[24]

After Geli's death Eva Braun's relationship with Hitler intensified and she became his lover at the beginning of 1932.[25] This was an affair that Hitler was determined to keep secret. Few knew about the relationship, even at the very end when they were married in the Führer bunker, in the garden behind the Reich Chancellery, on 29 April 1945, the day before they committed suicide together. Braun, unlike Geli, did not appear in public with Hitler. She was kept in the background. When she went out with Hitler, to the opera, an art exhibition, or a party function, she was always escorted by a member of Hitler's entourage, such as Hanfstaengl, Hoffmann, Rudolf Heß or his wife Ilse. Eva attended the 1936 Olympic Games in Garmisch-Partenkirchen and Berlin, and she went to the Nürnberg Rallies, as 'the guest' of other party officials, either Karl and Anni Brandt, or Theodor and Hanni Morell, Hitler's personal physicians and their wives, and sat a row or two behind Hitler. Most of the time she spent with Hitler was in private, and it was kept a closely guarded secret.[26]

Not surprisingly, Eva felt neglected. Depressed and prompted by jealousy she attempted suicide on two occasions: shooting herself on 31 October 1932, and taking an overdose of sleeping pills on the night of 28/29 May 1935.[27]

Neither episode caused the scandal that Geli's death created, but Hoffmann was very worried that one day Eva might succeed in killing herself. Christa Schroeder, one of Hitler's secretaries, was much less charitable and accused Eva of attempting to blackmail Hitler.[28] Both incidents upset Hitler terribly and led him to spend more time with Eva (which is what she wanted) in Munich and on the Obersalzberg. He took her to Italy, and bought her expensive gifts, including a small villa with a garden in Bogenhausen where Eva and her younger sister Gretl could live 'more independently'. He got her two Scottish Terriers, Negus and Stasi, to keep her company. He also provided her with a room of her own at the Berghof and in his apartment on Prinzregentenstraße.[29] What he was unwilling to do was merge his private and public life. After Geli's suicide he regularly declared that he had sacrificed his personal life to serve the German nation and its people.[30]

In the summer of 1943, at the *Führerhauptquartier Wolfsschanze*, at Rastenburg East Prussia (Hitler's main field headquarters, the Wolf's Lair), he often talked about Eva with his secretaries over lunch. On this occasion, he had just spoken with Eva on the telephone about the air raids on Munich, and he was visibly relieved that she was safe and well. The conversation with his secretaries turned to marriage and weddings. Traudl Junge, who had just returned to the Wolf's Lair after her honeymoon, having married Hans Junge, an SS man who had been Hitler's valet, innocently asked: 'My Führer, why haven't you married [Eva]?' Hitler's answer surprised Junge and the other secretaries. He said he would be a poor husband because he could not devote enough time to his wife.[31] Hitler had said something similar back in January 1942 after dinner with Martin Bormann and other members of his inner circle. His main concern was leaving a wife behind if he had been killed or sent back to prison.[32] Those who were closest to Hitler over the years of his political ascendancy knew that the only woman he ardently desired to marry was his niece Geli, but he could not marry her.[33] The scandal which would have followed the inevitable accusations of an incestuous marriage between a much older man and his young niece might well have killed Hitler's political career and destroyed the Movement. After Geli's death he took solace in a comparison he did little to discourage between himself and Wagner's operatic hero, the Roman Tribune Rienzi, who had given himself completely to his exalted bride, 'Rome'.[34]

The Path to Power

itler and the party approached the Reichstag elections on 20 May 1928 with much optimism. In terms of its finances, structure, and propaganda, the party was confident and ready to make a breakthrough in its bid for power. The results proved otherwise. The NSDAP won 10.7 per cent of the vote in Munich, but slumped to a miserable 2.6 per cent nationally and secured only 12 of 491 seats in the Reichstag. The results in the big cities where the party had concentrated its propaganda were worse. The NSDAP attained only 1.4 per cent of the vote in Berlin, 1.5 per cent in Düsseldorf, and a derisory 1.1 per cent share of the vote in Cologne-Aachen.[1] The tactic of trying to win over industrial workers had failed. Stung by the poor results, Hitler altered the party's strategy. He ordered an immediate shift in the party's propaganda, away from factory workers and targeted instead the middle classes and the farming community. To increase the party's share of the national vote, Hitler believed it must shake off any comparison with the Communists and demonstrate that the NSDAP would protect private property and support small business. Hitler also reconfirmed his intention, as set out in February 1925 when he refounded the party, to follow the path to power legally through electoral success.

Not everyone in the party agreed. Opposition to Hitler's plan, according to Hermann Esser, was both 'fierce and obstinate'.[2] Many in the SA still hankered for another putsch. A number of the north-German party members, led by Otto Strasser, wanted an even more intensive 'socialist commitment' that included the expropriation of land and property for communal purposes. Hitler strongly rejected both of these approaches. There was a nucleus of fanatical supporters working hard to promote the party, but there were fewer than 75,000 members in the whole of Germany. To build a strong national party Hitler knew that he needed to woo the moderate middle class and the farmers otherwise the NSDAP would remain a small demagogic protest group without influence on the fringe of German politics.

What Hitler wanted in terms of the party's revised propaganda and structure was decreed by the Munich headquarters, and implemented throughout the party countrywide by late 1929. Hitler further strengthened his position as the undisputed leader of the party and the arbiter of its programme with his appointment of the fiercely loyal and highly capable Heinrich Himmler as *Reichsführer-SS* on 7 January 1929. Joseph Goebbels and Hermann Göring also actively supported Hitler and his plans for taking the party forward. In contrast, Otto Strasser was expelled from the party in June 1930. Hitler also dismissed Franz Pfeffer von Salomon, briefly taking over the role of *Oberste SA Führer* (SA Commander-in-Chief) himself until he officially reinstated Ernst Röhm as the head of the SA on 5 January 1931.[3] Later, in June 1931, Himmler recruited Reinhard Heydrich, 26 years old, athletic, cultured, highly intelligent and well educated, and appointed him as SS Chief of Intelligence, responsible for internal security. Heydrich ran this menacing organization, which was renamed the *Sicherheitsdienst* (Security Service, SD) in March 1933, from a small office at Türkenstraβe 23. The party's reconstituted senior leadership was adroit, dynamic, and increasingly fanatical in its support of the Führer and his chosen path to power.

In addition to the party's major reforms, the onset of economic crises and the concomitant social tensions throughout Germany created a political climate conducive to the growth of National Socialism. By the end of 1927, farmers and agricultural communities across Germany were suffering from the worldwide agricultural depression. Cheap imported food, while welcomed by organized labour and urban industrial workers, had destroyed the rural economy. Artisans and small traders were put out of business, farms were repossessed, and many peasants and tenant farmers were evicted from their homes. Bankruptcy and foreclosure ravaged rural Germany as the crisis deepened. Two years later the Wall Street crash ushered in the Great Depression. Panic selling on the New York stock exchange began on 24 October 1929, 'Black Thursday', as frantic traders scrambled to sell shares that plummeted in value. The following week, on 29 October, 'Black Tuesday', the financial disaster intensified. Over 16.4 million shares were sold and ten billion dollars were wiped off the value of the major American companies, twice the amount of money in circulation in the United States at the time. American banks called in their loans and the import market in the US dried up. This hit Germany the hardest of all the European economies.[4] German industry had financed itself on American short-term loans and exports. Forced to rely on its own resources and internal market, the German economy collapsed in the summer of 1931. Unemployment in Berlin rose from 133,000 in 1928 to over 600,000 in 1932, and more than 4½ million, over 20 per cent of the working-age population, were out of work nationwide.[5]

The German government responded by cutting spending and raising taxes, making a dire situation for many Germans even worse. Masses of people slipped into poverty, and a foreboding sense of doom prevailed. Hordes of homeless men congregated in the main cities and towns, while others wandered aimlessly in the countryside. Official estimates at the time, always notoriously low, numbered some half-a-million men as homeless. Gangs and informal 'hiking clubs' of callow unemployed youths lived in abandoned factories and farmsteads, scavenged food, and stole to make a living. Arrests for theft increased by 24 per cent between 1929 and 1932. Prostitution became more widespread and noticeable, as was begging in the streets and depravity in many guises and forms. 'German society,' notes the historian Richard Evans, 'seemed to be descending into a morass of misery and criminality.'[6] Bitterness, loss of self-esteem, the sense of betrayal and exploitation, were powerful emotions felt by many Germans from a wide variety of backgrounds in most cities, towns, and regions, not just young unemployed urban men. There was a common visceral hatred for the Weimar 'system', what the failing post-war democratic government was disparagingly called. There was also a desperate desire for change, and an acceptance by the German electorate that a new type of government was urgently needed. Hitler and the NSDAP benefitted from the shift in public attitudes towards more radical politics. The traditional ruling parties were blamed for the economic and social catastrophes at the end of the 1920s and early 1930s, and discredited by their political ineptitude in dealing with them. Increasingly the German people turned to an authoritarian leader and believed in his promises of salvation.

The NSDAP was much better prepared than it was in 1928 for the near continuous election campaigns fought between 1930 and 1932. First and foremost, the party's propaganda machine was larger and more sophisticated than any of the other parties. Preceding the national election on 14 September 1930, the Nazis launched a propaganda campaign the likes of which had not been seen anywhere before, either in Germany or elsewhere. 'Hitler flooded the land with speakers,' recalled Hermann Esser, 'and organized meetings to be held high and low, near and far, in the most negligible little village as well as the most important places.' Esser further claimed that the NSDAP were conducting up to thirty thousand meetings a day for a month or two before the election. In addition to speaking engagements and mass rallies, the Nazis introduced and used modern electioneering methods for the first time, including door-to-door canvassing, radio broadcasts, films, and flights over Germany to advance their message. These techniques evolved and were further refined from election to election, building on earlier successes and devising new techniques that captured their target audience and stunned their opponents. During the Presidential elections of March–April 1932, the Reich Propaganda Department in Munich issued a distinctive white on black poster of Hitler to all the *Gaue* 'to be put up only during the final days [of the campaign]'. This was sheer genius according to Joseph Goebbels, who admired the instructions issued by the Munich headquarters: 'during the final days there are a variety of coloured posters, this poster of Hitler's head on a completely black background will contrast with all the others and will produce a tremendous effect on the masses.'[7] The propaganda campaigns were crafted in accordance with Hitler's wishes, and coordinated centrally through the party's headquarters in Munich. On 1 January 1931 the party moved its headquarters from Schellingstraße 50 to a large elegant building on Brienner Straße 45, the Palais Barlow. Nicknamed the '*Braunes Haus*' (Brown House) by the people of Munich, after the colours of the party uniform, it was the fifth and last party headquarters in Munich, in a building befitting that of a major political party.[8]

Built in 1824, the neo-classical mansion had been the home of the chargé-d'affaires of the kingdom of Sardinia at the Bavarian Court before it was purchased in 1876 by the English merchant Richard Barlow. His widow, Elizabeth Barlow, sold the building for 805,864 Reichmarks on 26 May 1930 to the National Socialist Worker Association, which acted as the purchasing agent for the NSDAP.[9] The steel magnate Fritz Thyssen, who had generously supported the party financially since meeting Hitler in 1923, raised a bank loan of 300,000 marks to help the party buy the building. The remaining funds were obtained from party members, each paying an additional two Reichsmarks on their annual membership fee. Hitler drew up the plans to convert the building into the 'party home' – the seat of the party leadership and an outward sign of the power and strength of the Nazi Party. He commissioned his friend Paul Troost to refurbish the interior and carry out the reconstruction. Work began immediately, and on Saturday 5 July 1930 the party planned a public ceremonial raising of the swastika flag, but the Munich police banned the demonstration. On 9 October, Hitler brought Goebbels with him on his first official visit to the redeveloped Brown House. Over the entrance was the party motto: '*Deutschland Erwache*' (Germany, Awaken). Inside, Hitler was pleased with the modern administrative rooms and offices, especially the new Index Card File Hall, where the details of all party members were held and meticulously kept up to date. The 'Senators' Hall for formal meetings and receptions was impressive, as was the Hall of Flags where the Blood Flag and party standards were proudly displayed.[10]

Not everyone in the party approved of the luxury villa as the new party headquarters. Some objected because the building's splendour seemed at odds with the party's 'socialist' credentials. Disgruntled SA fighters condescendingly referred to it as the 'Munich Palace of the Nazi Big Shots', a not-so-subtle axiom that all politicians regardless of party are the same, corrupt, self-indulgent elites. Left-wing Münchners called it the 'Palace of Megalomania', a humorous putdown that dismissed it as one more *Größenwahn* café similar to Café Stefanie, nicknamed Café Megalomania, a short walk away on Amalienstraße. For Hitler's masses of followers it was a 'temple devoted to the cult of the Führer' and 'a site of almost sacred significance'.[11] Most importantly, the new fully-functioning headquarters on Brienner Straße had the staff and the resources to control the party and coordinate its propaganda, thus enabling Hitler and his close advisors to spend more time in Berlin and northern Germany fighting election campaigns.

The Breakthrough

In the national elections held on 14 September 1930, the NSDAP received over 6½ million votes (18.3%) and won 107 out of 577 seats, making it the second largest party in the Reichstag after the SPD. Even Hitler was surprised by the magnitude of the party's success. He had hoped to win between 50 and 60 seats. The hard work preparing for the election had paid off, but the deepening hardships caused by the Great Depression also accounted for the massive surge in support for the Nazis. Party membership in Munich nearly doubled from 2,700 in 1929 to over 5,000. The NSDAP won 21.7% of the vote in Munich, its highest percentage in any German city.[1] National Socialist supporting newspapers declared that the party's march on Berlin had begun, and in London both *The Times* and the *Daily Mail* hailed Hitler as 'a bulwark against Bolshevism'.[2]

Otto Dietrich, Hitler's press chief, identified the reasons behind the stunning increase in support for Hitler and the party since the disastrous 1928 elections. He recognised that many Germans who voted for Hitler did not approve of all of his ideas or all of the points in the NSDAP programme. Many rejected anti-Semitism, but they did agree with Hitler's other national and social policies, especially the repeal of reparations payments and reducing unemployment. 'The great majority of them,' Dietrich noted, 'favoured the national community and the socialist "folk state" that Hitler proposed.'[3] The combination of idealism and a growing public belief that Hitler could solve the country's problems made him and the NSDAP an attractive alternative to the other traditional parties.

The four nationwide elections in 1932 proved decisive for the NSDAP and its successful ascent to power. First were the two Reich presidential elections in March and April. Hindenburg's initial seven-year term was up and new elections were required. Goebbels convinced a reluctant Hitler that he should stand. Hitler campaigned hard, even though he preferred a bohemian life in Munich, visiting galleries or the studios of his architect friends, spending time at the Café Heck, or being with Eva Braun. There was 'fantastic belief' throughout the party that Hitler would become the new President. On the morning of the election, 13 March, Goebbels wrote in his diary that he was confident of victory.[4] The election did not go as he and Hitler, and their party comrades, had planned. Hindenburg received more than 18½ million votes (49.6%) to Hitler's 11½ million (30.25%). 'We set our sights too high,' Hitler told Goebbels during a telephone call later that evening. The good news was that Hindenburg did not win an outright majority, so the leaders had to contest a run-off election on 10 April. Again, Hitler and the party machinery campaigned hard. Between 3 and 9 April, Hitler undertook his first 'Flights over Germany' campaign. He flew to twenty cities, giving three or four speeches each day. Despite these efforts Hitler still lost. Hindenburg received 53 per cent of the vote. Hitler won 2 million more votes than he did in the first election.[5] He also captured the public's imagination and increased his and his party's profile as a serious political force in Germany.

The national elections on 31 July were a great triumph for Hitler and the NSDAP. The party's campaign had been one long mass spectacle that ended with Hitler's third and most ambitious 'Flights over Germany' taking in fifty cities between 15 and 30 July. Hitler, wearing the SA uniform for the first time, gave hundreds of speeches, and was the one political leader that the public most wanted to see. They also voted for him. The NSDAP received almost 14 million votes (37.3%) and won 230 seats, more than twice as many as in 1930. Though not an outright majority, Hitler's party was the largest in the Reichstag. The SPD, the second largest party, saw its share of the vote drop from 24.5 to 21.6 per cent. The conservative BVP increased its share slightly from 11.8 to 12.5 per cent, and, more worryingly, the Communists increased their share from 13.1 to 14.5 per cent. The moderate centre parties had been destroyed. It was obvious to almost everyone that the choice was between the left and the National Socialists. Hindenburg and his political cronies, former Reich Chancellors Dr Heinrich Brüning and Franz von Papen, and General Kurt von Schleicher, hated the Communists, but they were unwilling to trust Hitler and his Nazi colleagues to run the government. On 13 August, Hindenburg asked von Papen to form a cabinet and offered Hitler the vice-chancellorship. Hitler refused. Unable to form a working government during the summer von Papen was forced to dissolve the Reichstag in mid-September and call new elections for 6 November.[6]

Ideological strife and violent political confrontations preceded the new Reichstag elections just as they had before the previous elections in 1932. Bloody fights between the SA and the paramilitary forces of the Communists and Socialists occurred in most major cities across the country. In Munich there was fighting in the streets. 'Bolshevism waged open war on the middle classes,' lamented Hermann Esser, 'and the Government merely looked on.'[7] The SA became increasingly rebellious and Hitler struggled to contain their yearning for another putsch. At the Zirkus Krone on 15 September, Hitler urged a fractious audience of 5,000 SA and SS men to be patient. The party had made significant strides in its bid for power legally for seven years, 'it would not hurt to wait a little longer.'[8] Hitler's appeal to the revolutionary wing of his party looked hollow when the results of the election were announced. The NSDAP lost 2 million votes. Their share of the national vote had declined to 33.1 per cent. They were reduced to 196 seats in the Reichstag, down 34 seats from July. In Munich, the party also experienced a sharp decline, down from 28.9 in July to 24.8 per cent in November. The big winners in the election were the Communists. They took 100 seats in the Reichstag and saw their share of the vote increase from 14.5 to 16.9 per cent.[9] Hitler and other angry conservatives blamed von Papen for enabling the Bolsheviks to take over the Reichstag.[10]

Election fatigue and a lower turnout (roughly 80 down from 85 per cent voter participation) were cited by the NSDAP as the main reasons behind their poor showing compared with July. The left-wing press crowed that Hitler had failed, and the liberal press in Berlin smugly asserted that 'the National Socialist idea has lost its power to win people over.'[11] Much of this criticism was hubris and wrong. The National Socialists remained the largest party in the Reichstag by a considerable margin, and the circumstances that had led to von Papen's failure to form a government in the summer were unchanged. Hitler reiterated his refusal to work with von Papen. Desperate to appoint a conservative and compliant chancellor, Hindenburg turned to General Schleicher and asked him to 'try his luck' forming a government.[12] Schleicher was a bad choice. His reputation for disloyalty, political intrigue and as a shameless self-promoting schemer virtually guaranteed he would fail.[13] Hitler returned to Munich before heading to the Obersalzberg for Christmas. He spent a full week relaxing at his mountain home before returning to Munich to celebrate New Year.[14]

Hitler spent New Year's Day with Eva Braun. They went to the Stadtmuseum (Munich City Museum) at St. Jakobs-Platz, and later in the evening attended a performance of *Die Meistersinger* at the Hof Theater (National Theatre) with Rudolf and Ilse Heß, Hoffmann and several other members of Hitler's entourage. Braun sat with Heß and his wife, a discreet distance away from Hitler. Afterwards they all went to the Hanfstaengls for coffee and cake. Before leaving for home, Hitler wrote his name and the date in the Hanfstaengls' guest book. As he put the pen down and looked up and saw Putzi, Hitler smiled, and in a muted tone of excitement said to his friend: 'This year belongs to us. I will guarantee it in writing.'[15]

On 4 January, Hitler travelled with Heß, Himmler, and Wilhelm Keppler (Hitler's economic adviser) to Cologne to speak with von Papen. The meeting was organized by the banker and party member Kurt von Schröder, and it was held in his home. Hitler and von Papen spoke alone for two hours. They agreed that Schleicher must not be allowed to form a government. Papen suggested a new conservative and nationalist government that included the Nazis, jointly led by Hitler and himself. Hitler insisted on being chancellor, but said he was willing to have non-Nazi party members in his cabinet. This concession paved the way for von Papen and Hindenburg to create on 30 January 1933 the 'Government of National Concentration' with Hitler as Reich Chancellor.[16]

National Socialists celebrated Hitler's ascendancy to power throughout the night in Berlin. A huge torchlight parade numbering more than 20,000 SA men marched through the Brandenburger Tor and down the Wilhelmstraße, past the Kaiserhof Hotel, where Hitler was staying, and the Reich Chancellery.[17] In Munich a jubilant Gauleiter Wagner celebrated with local Nazis and 2,000 SA men on the Königsplatz. Two days later, on 1 February, Hitler addressed the nation over the radio, outlining his political aims and objectives. Under his leadership, Germany would pursue a policy of peace with her neighbours and the wider community of nations. He would reorganize the economy to save the farmer from penury and rescue the worker from unemployment. He also pledged to rid Germany of the scourge of Communism. Hitler concluded his speech with an appeal to the German people to give him four years to end the crisis of the previous fourteen years and lead Germany to a new and glorious future.[18] He was eager to build up his mass support and legitimise his position. This would increase his leverage, not only with von Papen, Hindenburg, and their right-wing allies but also against his opponents in the Reichstag. One of Hitler's conditions for accepting the chancellorship was an immediate dissolution of the Reichstag. Hindenburg granted Hitler's request and called for new elections on 5 March 1933. With the combined resources of the state and the propaganda machine of the party behind him, Hitler was confident he would increase his popular mandate and strengthen his hold on power.[19] Hitler was on the threshold of achieving his totalitarian regime through legal means.

The NSDAP gained over 17 million votes and took 288 seats out of 647 in the Reichstag, compared with the 196 seats the party won in November 1932. In Munich, support for the Nazis reached a record high of 37.8 per cent. Country wide, the party increased its share of the vote from 33.1 to 43.9 per cent.[20] Still, it was not an outright majority, and Hitler needed a two-thirds majority in the Reichstag to pass the Enabling Act that would give him absolute power. This looked highly unlikely, unless something extraordinary happened that permitted Hitler and his Nazi colleagues to change the Weimar constitution. Help came unexpectedly a week before the elections when Marinus van der Lubbe, a Dutch Communist, set fire to the Reichstag. The building was still smoking when the first piece of legislation was passed, the Decree of the Reich President for the Protection of People and State, on 28 February 1933.[21] It gave the Reich government extensive powers to suppress enemies of the state. Göring, Hitler's cabinet minister responsible for Prussia's interior, immediately ordered the arrest of 4,000 communists and banned the entire communist and socialist press. Throughout the country the SA went on the rampage, attacking known communists and other enemies of the party. After the elections further draconian measures in the form of decrees and laws, ostensibly to protect the state against a 'German Bolshevik Revolution', and other acts of violence and terrorism, were passed. The Nazis used the law and legal means to eliminate their enemies and cajole support from their reluctant conservative allies while they systematically dismantled the constitution and parliamentary democracy. The Enabling Law of 24 March 1933 was passed the previous day by 444 votes to 94, all the dissenting votes came from the Social Democrats. The SPD was banned on 22 June, followed shortly thereafter by the demise of other organizations, political parties, and trade unions.[22] The Nazis moved swiftly against all their enemies. Goebbels was jubilant: 'The Führer's authority is now complete,' he wrote in his diary on 22 April, 'There will be no more voting. The Führer's personality decides. All this has been achieved much more quickly than we had dared to hope.'[23]

IV

Munich, 1933–39

Consolidation of Power

Measures to impose National Socialist control over the cities and regional states began in Hamburg the week before the national elections on 5 March 1933. Typically, the local Gau leadership started the process, urging councillors and regional politicians to take more rigorous action against Communists and other 'enemies of the state'. They also demanded a Nazi be put in charge of the police to lead the defence against the threat of Red terror. The SA intensified the pressure for political change by staging public rallies, beating up Jews and leftists, occupying government offices and raising the swastika flag on public buildings. Under the pretext of restoring public order Wilhelm Frick, the Reich Interior Minister, appointed a pro-Nazi Reich commissioner who in turn presided over a pseudo-legal transfer of power to the National Socialists. The Nazis took control of city councils, regional administrations, and the police all across the country, acting on an opportune interpretation of the emergency legislation for public safety passed by the Reich government immediately after the Reichstag fire. Between 6 and 8 March the same pattern of procedures forced Bremen, Lübeck, the Free Cities, and Hesse, Baden-Württemberg, and Saxony to accept Nazi control.[1] On 9 March it was Bavaria's turn to fall into line with the new order.

Adolf Wagner, the Gauleiter of Bavaria, accompanied by Röhm and Himmler, dressed in their full SA and SS regalia, made an unannounced visit to Bavarian Premier Held's office to inform him that Hitler had installed General Franz Ritter von Epp, the former Freikorps commander and the liberator of Munich from Soviet control in 1919, as the Reich Commissioner for Bavaria. They warned Held to step aside immediately. Held resisted and sent a telegram to Hindenburg remonstrating against Epp's appointment. Hindenburg, in his reply, confirmed the change of government and told Held to address any further complaints directly to Adolf Hitler. Held resigned. At 7 pm, Max Amann appeared on the balcony of the Neues Rathaus to announce the change of government. He also announced that Himmler was taking over the Bavarian police. As Amann addressed the crowd gathered below in the Marienplatz a long swastika flag cascaded down from the clock tower above. For twelve years, from 9 March 1933 until American forces occupied Munich on 30 April 1945, the iconic Nazi symbol flew permanently above Munich's new town hall.[2]

Throughout the night of 9/10 March 1933, Munich's Nazis celebrated. Wild scenes of rejoicing occurred in the Marienplatz, on the Königsplatz and in front of the Braunes Haus, and von Epp addressed a large crowd in front of the Feldherrnhalle. He reminded them that Munich was 'the cradle of the National Socialist movement', and to loud cheering he vowed that Bavaria would now shape the future of the entire Reich. Three days later Hitler flew to Munich to join in the celebrations. Hitler, dressed in a SA uniform, stepped off his plane at Munich's Oberwiesenfeld airport where he was greeted by General von Epp, an honour guard, and a boisterous crowd of fanatical followers. Hitler was overjoyed that Bavaria was at the forefront of 'the awakening of the German nation', and he stopped to deliver an impromptu speech in the *Flugplatz*. 'Munich is the city of Germany closest to my heart,' he told his attentive audience. 'It was in this city that years ago I began the struggle the first part of which can now be regarded as finally closed.'[3] Hitler and his National Socialists had accomplished something that no German leader or government had achieved before: the coordination of the political will of the German states and free cities with the will of the nation. Through *Gleichschaltung* (forcible coordination) the Nazi political revolution aimed to harness both the levers of state power and the popular support of the *Volksgemeinschaft* (community of our people) to create a single mighty German Reich. Hitler assured his supporters that 'we shall do everything in our power to secure that this coordination shall never be lost'.[4] Immediately after his speech Hitler and his motorcade left the airport. They drove to the city centre, a slow triumphal procession along a circuitous route through the streets of Munich to the Feldherrnhalle where Hitler laid a giant wreath to commemorate the martyrs of the putsch of 9 November 1923. The banner attached to the Führer's wreath read: 'You have triumphed in the end!'[5]

The Nazis completed their consolidation of power in Munich on 20 March when Karl Fiehler, a city councilman, party member, and veteran of the November putsch, replaced the long-serving Karl Scharnagl (BVP) as Lord Mayor. Fiehler's first act in office was to ban communists from serving on the city council. He also expelled socialist councilmen, thereby reducing the council's size and ensuring a majority for the NSDAP. Many of the deposed communist and socialist councillors were taken into 'protective custody' and sent to Dachau. Fiehler also introduced a number of idiosyncratic anti–Semitic measures. He decreed that Jewish firms be excluded from municipal contracts, and that city offices not use Jewish consultants and lawyers. He also instructed municipal employees not to shop in Jewish stores. Jews were banned from participating in public auctions and trade fares, as well as public swimming areas and municipal pools. He further declared that Jewish doctors treat only Jewish patients and that Jews must be buried in Jewish-only cemeteries. As a consequence, both Kurt Eisner and Gustav Landauer were exhumed from their graves in the

Ostfriedhof.[6] Fiehler justified his Draconian reforms by stating: 'we have the responsibility to see to it that the will of our Führer is implemented.' Fiehler was determined that Munich, the birthplace of the Movement, would play a leading role in Germany's cultural and political renaissance. 'We must make Munich once again a truly German city,' he implored his fellow Nazi councillors, 'a city in which German art and German ideals, German customs and German style, German sensibilities and German joyousness reign supreme.'[7]

By the end of April 1933, Hitler had control of the entire executive branch of government, the states, the judicial system, the regional police, and the country's entire security apparatus. On 10 April, Hermann Göring had been appointed Prussian state president, which gave him *de facto* control over more than half of Germany's police. At the beginning of April, Heinrich Himmler, the new police chief in Bavaria and Munich, appointed his executive deputy, Reinhard Heydrich, chief of Bavaria's political police. Both Himmler and Heydrich were ably assisted by Heinrich Müller, a native Münchner and Munich police veteran who ran the anti-communist division.[8] Earlier, on 20 March, Himmler had announced the establishment of a mass detention centre on the outskirts of Dachau, a small town twenty kilometres north-west of Munich. The *Völkischer Beobachter* provided more details on the Third Reich's first concentration camp, loosely based on what the British had pioneered in South Africa during the Boer War, and described as an experimental detention and rehabilitation centre capable of holding up to 5,000 political opponents of the regime.[9] Additional camps opened across Germany and by mid-1933 more than 30,000 people were interned for crimes allegedly committed against the state. Dachau's first sixty prisoners arrived on 22 March. Claus Bastian, a left-wing lawyer from Munich, had the dubious honour of being designated 'prisoner number one'. Communists and social democrats were the first prisoners sent to Dachau, but Jews and anyone the Nazis did not like were soon detained in the camps, which quickly gained a reputation for arbitrary persecution, torture, and even murder. By the end of April, Heydrich's political police had arrested more than 5,000 political opponents in Bavaria. Some 2,033 were incarcerated in Dachau where eighteen were murdered or driven to suicide.[10] Hitler's election promise in February 1933, that 'the hour for smashing the communists is coming!' had come.[11]

Linked to the control of state and local government and the persecution of political opponents was an ambitious campaign to coordinate and neutralise all private and public agencies, institutions, and organizations that might challenge the regime's claim to total power. All political parties other than the NSDAP were banned. Censorship, state interference and supervision transformed Germany's cultural and media landscape. The trade unions were eradicated in stages and occupational and special interest associations were either shut down or turned into Nazi organizations. Remodelling private corporations and professional organizations into instruments that served the Reich, essentially the National Socialist dictatorship, was also part of Hitler's planned *Gleichschaltung* (forced coordination).[12]

At Hitler's request, Hindenburg appointed Joseph Goebbels as Germany's first propaganda minister, in charge of the newly created Reich Ministry of Public Enlightenment and Propaganda, which was to preside over the press, radio, and film.[13] The media was subjected to rigorous supervision in terms of its content and its employees. Max Amann, the director of Eher Verlag, the main Nazi publishing house in Munich, was appointed President of the Reich Press Chamber and the chairman of the Association of German Newspaper Publishers. He exercised total control over the German press, and many publishing houses and printing presses were taken over by the Nazis. The circulation of the *Völkischer Beobachter*, now both the official paper of the party and the regime, doubled from 160,000 to 314,000 per issue, and its sister paper, the less serious *Illustrierter Beobachter* (*IB*), almost trebled its circulation from 302,000 to 840,000 in 1933.[14] Munich's satirical magazine, *Simplicissimus*, underwent an extraordinary editorial transformation in the spring of 1933. Instead of its customary biting criticism, as was *Simpl*'s penchant when commenting on the establishment and the ruling regime, it supported the Nazis wholeheartedly: 'Our patriotic duty,' announced the editors, 'is to defend in our way the great domestic and foreign policy goals of the new Germany.'[15]

Bringing German Society into Line

nti-Semitic agitation had risen noticeably throughout Germany since the Nazis had taken power at the end of January 1933. The discrimination, exclusion from society, and violent persecution of the Jews was not only Nazi ideology but increasingly government policy that became more radical over the years, beginning with a nationwide boycott of Jewish businesses and the dismissal of Jews from the civil service and professions on 1 April 1933. Goebbels, with Hitler's support, had called for the boycott in response to foreign criticism in Britain and the United States after a spate of highly publicised attacks on Jews by the SA in many German cities and towns.[1] The boycott was not as successful as the Nazi leadership had hoped, but neither was there broad or sustained public opposition. In Munich, Cardinal Faulhaber cautioned against 'hatred for another people', which prompted local Nazis to defame him as the 'Jewish cardinal' and quickly stifled any further debate. Faulhaber did not want to start a war between the Catholic Church and the Nazis. Moreover, the swift collapse of the boycott allowed the Cardinal to convince himself that 'the Jews could take care of themselves'.[2] The Nazi leadership confidently pressed on with its efforts to create a racial and political *Volksgemeinschaft*.

On 7 April 1933, a new law for the Restoration of the Professional Civil Service allowed for non-Aryans and undesirables to be fired. Jews and leftists lost their jobs. By July 1934, the city of Munich had dismissed 83 civil servants and 250 municipal workers either because they were Jewish or for taking part in 'Communist activity'. Both of Munich's universities, the Ludwig-Maximilians-Universität (LMU) and the Technical University (TUM) sacked professors and lecturers because of their Jewish heritage, political views, or artistic attitudes. By 1937, seven academics at TUM and forty-five at LMU had been fired. LMU also revoked 183 doctorates, held by 'undesirable' graduates, many of whom had already fled Germany. Between 1933 and 1939, LMU replaced roughly half of its core academic staff. National Socialist associations for lecturers and students, with their central offices located near Karolinenplatz, on Max-Joseph-Straße 4 and Karlstraße 16 respectively, exerted significant influence on academic appointments, course curriculum, and research. On 10 May 1933 university students in Munich joined fellow students across Germany in mass book-burning ceremonies organized by the SA and called 'German Students against the un-German Spirit', a slogan coined by Joseph Goebbels. Consigned to the flames were works by writers deemed *Reichsfeinde* (enemies of the state). Among the more notable authors whose books were burned in Munich on the Königsplatz and in front of LMU were Bertolt Brecht, Albert Einstein, Lion Feuchtwanger, Sigmund Freud, Oskar Maria Graf, Heinrich Heine, Franz Kafka, Karl Marx, Heinrich Mann, Erich Mühsam, Erich Maria Remarque, and Ernst Toller. Afterwards Goebbels regularly published a list of authors whose works were regarded as 'un-German' and therefore had to be removed from bookshops, libraries, and students' reading lists. Thomas Mann, whose works avoided immolation on the initial book pyres, was an early addition to Goebbels' rising number of banned authors.[3]

Art, culture, and sport were also subject to Nazi reforms and *Gleichschaltung*. Bayern Munich (FCB) had just won its first German Fußball Championship in 1932, defeating Eintracht Frankfurt 2–0 in the final played in Nürnberg's exquisite (though detested by the Nazis) Bauhaus-style stadium, located in the centre of the Nazi Party Rally Grounds.[4] It was a fitting reward for Kurt Landauer, club president since the end of the First World War and the man credited with inventing the modern professional football club. He had built up FCB from an amateur team of part-time enthusiasts to a squad of German and international star players who had succeeded in becoming first regional (Bavaria) and ultimately national champions. FCB's success was short-lived once the Nazis came to power. Both Landauer and Richard Kohn, the head coach, were Jewish. They were forced to resign and leave the club on 22 March 1933. A number of the 'professional players' were also hounded out of the club. FCB was labelled a *Juden-Klub* (Jew club) in the press and by supporters of other football clubs, and regarded by the Nazi authorities in Munich as being 'politically unreliable'. In spite of the pressure exerted on FCB by the Nazi regime, the club, its players and fans, continued to support Landauer and the many other Jewish members who had been expelled. Landauer spent many uncomfortable weeks in Dachau before he was allowed to emigrate. Eventually, on 15 May 1939, he fled to Switzerland. After the war Landauer returned to Munich and served another short term as club president, making him the longest serving President in Bayern Munich's illustrious history. Many of Munich's smaller sports clubs, fencing fraternities, amateur musical and theatre groups, and art societies, disbanded rather than submit to the regime's zealous reforms and regulations. 1860 Munich (the city's other football club) developed close ties with the Nazi party. Its board consisted of a number of Hitler's 'Old Fighters', elite early party members, SA leaders, and veterans of the Putsch. Wilhelm Brückner, who had marched in the front row with Hitler on 9 November 1923, was a member of 1860 München football club.[5] Most of the city's main cultural institutions, the art galleries, museums, opera, orchestras, and theatres, complied with the Nazis. Institutions, just like many ordinary German citizens, voluntarily accepted and adapted to the new system, regarding even the most brazen behaviour and discriminatory policies of the Nazis as unfortunate but inevitable growing pains of 'national awakening'. Through the use of creative language, such as 'Rebirth', and 'National Rising', and relentless propaganda campaigns and slogans, the Nazis effectively paralysed most of German society, stifled criticism and legitimised their ruthless consolidation of power.[6]

The Nazi regime systematically stripped German citizens of their rights and freedoms, curtailed associations and clubs, and dissolved all other political organizations and parties. One area of society that Hitler was initially hesitant about dealing with was the trade unions. Collectively they had over four million members, were well organized, and had a formidable reputation for 'putting up a fight'. Hitler need not have worried. The SA ransacked Munich's Trade Union House on 9 March, and throughout the rest of March and April the SA targeted union buildings and attacked union leaders around the country. Rather than fight back, the unions attempted to ingratiate themselves to the Nazis as working-class partners rather than opponents in the great 'national revolution'. On 9 April, Theodor Leipart, the chairman of the Confederation of German Trade Unions (ADGB) wrote to Hitler offering to put the unions 'at the service of the state' and asked the Führer to appoint a 'Reich commissioner for unions'.[7] Hitler did not reply to Leipart's letter. He knew that the unions were no longer a threat, and he acted quickly to eliminate them. On 2 May, the unions were dissolved, their assets confiscated, and many union leaders were arrested and put into 'protective custody'. Hitler replaced the unions with the *Deutsche Arbeitsfront* (German Labour Front, DAF), a massive organization established on 10 May under the direction of Robert Ley, whose goal was to unite all 'working Germans' regardless of their occupation and social status and integrate them into the Nazi state.[8]

The DAF immediately set out to improve working conditions and to create a sense of 'dignity of labour' where every German worker was valued as a full member of the ethnic-popular community, the *Volksgemeinschaft*. Businesses and factories established subsidised canteens and undertook wide-ranging measures to improve safety, including air quality, noise reduction, and general hygiene. Green spaces were created around places of work, and sports facilities and swimming pools were built especially for workers and their families. In a further effort to improve morale and boost productivity in the labour force, Ley founded *Kraft durch Freude* (Strength through Joy, KdF) a subsidiary leisure programme within the DAF in November 1933. Obliging and reliable workers received free tickets to concerts, the opera, sporting events, and theatre performances. Other KdF-sponsored activities included museum visits, riding and sailing lessons, and adult education courses. Days out to visit exhibitions and historic sites, travel and tickets to festivals such as the Oktoberfest in

Munich and the Richard Wagner festival in Bayreuth, weekend excursions, and even all-inclusive holidays on KdF's own fleet of cruise ships were the coveted rewards for loyalty and service. Overseas travel and consumer goods, *Volksprodukte* (people's products), including luxury items such as state-of-the-art radios, televisions, and cars (the *Volkswagen*), were enormously popular. All of these initiatives increased public participation in Hitler's political and societal revolution, and support for the National Socialist state.[9]

On 30 January 1933 there were 850,000 members in the NSDAP. Less than three months later the membership had tripled to 2.5 million. Hitler publicly celebrated the party's extraordinary success on 8 April, during a major speech to the SA in the Berlin Sportspalast, a speech that was also broadcast on the radio throughout the country. Hitler began by stating: 'The great age for which we have hoped fourteen years long has now dawned. Germany has now awakened.' The Führer's speech was interrupted by the SA men who had suddenly become a mass chorus singing '*Deutschland, erwache!*'[10] In Munich, party membership rose from 10,000 in 1933 to over 63,000 in early 1939. By 1939 slightly more than two thirds of all Germans were members of one Nazi organization or another.[11] Berlin was the centre of government but Munich remained the party's centre of power – its documentation, finance, and party apparatus for the control of all aspects of life in Germany. A vast network of Nazi organizations competed for office space in the Maxvorstadt district, along Brienner Straße and around Karolinenplatz, and just off the south face of Königsplatz. The party eventually acquired 68 buildings and employed some 6,000 people to run its administrative headquarters. Rudolf Heß, the Deputy Führer, and his staff played a leading role in coordinating and managing the expanding party bureaucracy. The DAF obtained offices at 46–47 (now 26–28) Brienner Straße, and 'Strength through Joy' moved in next door after the forced purchase of the house and business premises of the Jewish antiquarian bookseller Jacques Rosenthal.[12] Other influential branches of the party including the SA, the Gestapo, the Hitler Youth, the National Socialist Women's League and all the professional associations set up offices in what quickly became known as the NSDAP Quarter. Hitler's rapidly established 'new order' in Munich also demanded a new aesthetic to showcase its dynamism and power. Art and architecture were called upon to honour the Movement.

Hauptstadt der Deutschen Kunst
(Capital of German Art)

Hitler shared Richard Wagner's belief that the destinies of societies and of the arts were inextricably linked, and that the only way to effect a profound and long-lasting change in society was to bring one about in the arts. By rejuvenating German art, Hitler believed that he was simultaneously rejuvenating the German people and thereby securing the victory of the National Socialist revolution for the greater glory of both *Volk und Vaterland* (the people and the fatherland). In a major speech Hitler gave at a convention of NSDAP leaders in Munich on 21 April 1933, he set out his aims for reshaping the German world, both externally and internally, through the transformation of the arts and architecture:

> The Movement has taken on two thousand years of German history and culture. It will become the bearer of German history and culture of the future. It will ensure that new, unforgettable documents are created which will continue to award the Volk its place among the circle of great civilised peoples in world history. We are not working for the moment, but for the judgement of millennia.[1]

The first monumental building commissioned by Hitler and thereby the starting point of his major construction projects to represent Nazi cultural politics through stone was the *Haus der Deutschen Kunst* (House of German Art). Hitler had already pledged several times since 1928 that he would create a home for German art in Munich, 'the most German of all German cities'. The requirement to act on this promise became all the more urgent after the night of 5/6 June 1931, when fire destroyed Munich's Glass Palace, the largest and most important art gallery in Bavaria. Once the National Socialists had secured power, Adolf Wagner, the Gauleiter and newly appointed Deputy Bavarian Minister-President and Minister of Culture, established a museum fund, eventually raising 9.5 million Reichmarks, and turned Hitler's vision into reality.[2] Hitler commissioned his friend the architect Paul Troost to design and build an art gallery, 'exuding great dignity … as appropriate to the German character' at the southern end of the Englischer Garten on Prinzregentenstraße. Troost understood the dimensions required to promote

National Socialist ideology and to impress Germans and foreigners alike. His new temple for German art would be 155 metres long and 55 metres wide. Its gigantic columned colonnade made for an imposing classical façade. Other than the massive *Reichsadler* (national eagle), designed by Kurt Schmid-Ehmen,[3] above the main entrance, the outside of the building was intentionally left without decorative elements. Inside, the centre point was an enormous sky-lit *Ehrenhalle* (Hall of Honour) flanked on both sides by two identical sets of twenty-four classically-designed gallery rooms. Blood red Tegernsee marble was the dominant interior colour, a not-so-subtle nod to the main colour of the NSDAP's swastika flag and a clear indication of the aesthetics being politicised in the Third Reich.[4]

Hitler's concept of art and his cultural perspective were well known to anyone who read the *Völkischer Beobachter* in the spring of 1933. Troost shared Hitler's aesthetic perspective and he was adept at translating Hitler's ideas into architecture. He had already been tasked by Hitler to transform the Königsplatz into a 'Forum of the Movement', and to design a memorial for the east side of the Feldherrnhalle on the Odeonsplatz to commemorate the sixteen Nazis killed there during the Putsch on 9 November 1923. Troost was eulogised for creating a style of architecture that 'never lost touch with national soil'.[5] His angular, imposing, strong yet simplified form of neo-classicism became the architectural model for almost all of the Nazis' later buildings and monuments. When the 55-year-old Troost died prematurely of pneumonia on 21 January 1934, Hitler ordered a state funeral. Troost was Hitler's favourite architect and he was revered by many as a genius, a neo-Ludwig I, and the greatest German architect since Karl Friedrich Schinkel.[6] In the canon of National Socialist cultural history Troost was 'the Führer's First Builder'.[7]

Construction of the *Führerbau* (Führer Building) at Arcisstraße 12 and the *Verwaltungsbau der NSDAP* (Administration Building of the Nazi Party) at Arcisstraße 10 (now Katharina-von-Bora-Straße 10) began in September 1933. Pringsheim Palace, the family home of Thomas Mann's wife Katia, and two other adjoining houses were demolished to make way for the redevelopment of the Königsplatz.[8] An elaborate programme of cultural events took place across Munich on the weekend of 14 and 15 October to celebrate the laying of the foundation stone for the House of German Art. The ceremonies began with a reception co-hosted by Munich's Lord Mayor Karl Fiehler and Gauleiter Adolf Wagner at the *Künstlerhaus* (House of Artists) in the city centre on Lenbachplatz 8, approximately a hundred metres north of Karlsplatz (Stachus). Munich's opera houses and leading theatres, including the Residenz-Theater and Theater am Gärtnerplatz, held gala performances for specially invited guests. The National Socialist Reich Symphony Orchestra under the baton of Germany's leading conductor, Wilhelm Furtwängler, and the choir of the Munich Bürgersängerzunft guild of singers performed several concerts at various places throughout the city enabling 'the poorest fellow Germans to participate'.[9] On Sunday morning at 8 am processions of artists, students, and members of the Hitler Youth, as well as ceremonial contingents of the SS, SA, and Bavarian state police, converged on Prinzregentenstrasse and the location of the future art museum. At 10.30 the bells from what seemed like every church in Munich rang, heralding the arrival of the Führer and the beginning of the laying of the foundation stone ceremony. Preceding Hitler's speech, the Reich Orchestra played the prelude to Richard Wagner's *Die Meistersinger*.[10]

Hitler stepped onto the podium and began his short speech: 'It is wonderful to live in an age which assigns great tasks to its people.' The 'challenge of the age,' he continued, was the restoration of the German people, asserting that 'the German Volk will rise anew if German culture and above all German art emerge once more.' The symbolic deed of laying the foundation stone was the first step. 'A *Haus der Deutschen Kunst* shall rise up,' he said, 'a monument to our age. Young Germany is constructing a special building to house its art.' In bestowing this task on Munich, Hitler reaffirmed the city's long cultural history, and Ludwig I's vision to make his capital 'one of the shrines to German art'. He also announced Munich's new prestigious role in the National Socialist mission to restore the greatness of the Reich and the greatness of the German nation: 'Since Berlin is the capital of the Reich; Hamburg and Bremen are the German shipping capitals; Leipzig and Cologne the capitals of German trade; and Essen and Chemnitz the capitals of German industry, so should Munich once more become the capital of German art.'[11]

Hitler completed his ceremonial duties with these final words: 'It is in this spirit that we wish to lay this cornerstone for the first fair building of the new Reich, in thanks to a German architect, in trust to the city of Munich, and dedicated to German art.'[12] He then struck the cornerstone with a silver hammer that Troost had designed especially for the occasion. The hammer broke in two. Goebbels made light of the awkward situation, joking: 'When the Führer strikes he strikes mightily.' Hitler was less sanguine and saw it as a bad omen. Not long afterwards Troost was hospitalised with angina pectoris. Three months later he was dead.[13]

The *Völkischer Beobachter* did not report on the broken hammer. Rather it celebrated the renewal of Munich's 'proper mission' as the home of the sublime and of the beautiful. It paraphrased Hitler's contention that Munich was the 'metropolis of German art' and 'if one would know Germany one must have seen this city', a claim he had originally made in *Mein Kampf*.[14] It also described the ostentatious grandeur of the *Tag der Deutschen Kunst* (Day of German Art) taking place around the city throughout the afternoon. Munich's artists and craftsmen had decorated the city in accordance with the Gauleiter's instructions. Garlands of pine branches and floral arrangements adorned every doorway and windowsill. The city centre was immersed in a sea of swastika flags, and the Feldherrnhalle had been turned into a shrine, with the addition of an altar, a massive golden laurel wreath, and a burning flame in memory of the National Socialists who fell during the ill-fated putsch. The highlight of the afternoon was a parade celebrating 'The Golden Ages of German Culture'. Floats designed by Munich's artistic societies depicting German fairy tales, German history, and German mythology were escorted by people dressed in pseudo-mediaeval and historical costumes. Groups representing Bavarian life – farming, forestry, fishing and hunting – wearing traditional Bavarian Tracht, marching bands, and local units of the Hitler Youth carrying eagle standards and flags – the emblems of the new state – marched through the main streets in the city centre to the Königsplatz. The chief attraction was the huge model of the House of German Art, 'shimmering with gold' and carried by eighteen men dressed in green, further surrounded by a larger entourage wearing multi-coloured costumes. There was even an English language souvenir book published to commemorate the occasion for non-German-speaking tourists.[15]

Hitler was serious about repositioning Munich at the centre of the artistic universe and turning his favourite city into a showcase of German genius. Consequently the NSDAP invested heavily in Munich's artistic and entertainment infrastructure. Munich's reputation as the city of *Gemütlichkeit* (easy going, love-of-life atmosphere) was also emphasised, to highlight its unique Bavarian character but more importantly to underline the historic continuity of its cultural pedigree. The artistic community in Munich accepted their new National Socialist patrons with the same gratitude and veneration as their predecessors had the Wittelsbachs throughout the century leading up to the Great War. There was widespread ideological consensus between artists and the regime. They, like most Germans, were enthusiastic about what they saw as national renewal. They welcomed the antidotes the Nazis offered for the chaos of the Weimar years, reclaimed dignity, economic safeguards, and political stability, and they enthusiastically embraced the new opportunities open to them as valued members of the *Volksgemeinschaft*.[16] The world famous composer Richard Strauß publicly declared how impressed he was with the changes Hitler had made. He first met Hitler during the intermission of a new performance of his opera *Der Rosenkavalier* in Berlin and instantly became an outspoken fan of the Führer. Strauß and Furtwängler were two of many leading artists in Germany who when asked placed themselves at the regime's disposal.[17] Despite Hitler's charisma and popularity not all artists or influential public figures were enamoured with the Nazis, nor did they yield to the mighty neo-nationalistic wave. Two distinguished dissidents in Munich were Thomas Mann and Father Rupert Mayer.

Dissent and Resistance to the New Nazi Regime in Munich

T homas Mann had won the Nobel Prize for Literature in 1929. He had lived in Munich most of his life, and by 1933 he had written many of his great literary works in the city. He had also come to the attention of the Reichsführer-SS because of his criticisms of the NSDAP, the movement, and its new ranks of sycophantic supporters. Both in Berlin and in Munich, Mann had delivered public speeches arguing for a more conciliatory politics between the middle classes and labour to avoid the Nazi calamity. In an article Mann published in the *Berliner Tageblatt* on 8 August 1932, he condemned the street fighting that characterised Nazi politics. He also criticised the party's 'half-clownish drooling so-called leaders' for promoting violence and the 'babbling pastors, professors, lecturers and literati who follow them' thereby reducing 'everything German to the level of the mob'.[1]

In the eyes of the regime, and the cultural dignitaries that supported it, Mann's greatest sin was an essay he wrote to commemorate the 50th anniversary of Richard Wagner's death. Entitled '*Leiden und Größe Richard Wagners*' ('The Sorrows and the Grandeur of Richard Wagner'), Mann warned against uncritical attitudes to Wagner's ideology which the Nazis had appropriated and twisted in an unholy alliance with their own ethnic-chauvinist nationalism. The essay had been commissioned by the Goethe Society in Munich and was first given as a lecture on 10 February 1933 in the Great Hall of the Ludwig-Maximilians-Universität. Shortly afterwards, Mann left Munich on an international tour, repeating his lecture to great acclaim in Brussels, The Hague, Amsterdam, and Paris. The *Völkischer Beobachter* branded it as 'disgraceful' and condemned Mann 'the half-Bolshevik' for disparaging the name of *Der Meister*, and heaping scorn on the Führer's favourite composer. One of Himmler's first undertakings as head of the Bavarian police was to issue a 'protective custody' warrant for Thomas Mann.[2]

Erika and Klaus Mann were at the family home in Munich at Poschingerstraβe 1, in the fashionable district of Bogenhausen, when they heard news of their father's impending arrest. It seemed that they were also in trouble. Hans, the family chauffeur and a Gestapo informant, warned them: 'The Nazis are after you. Don't go out! Don't tell anyone you're here!' Several of the Manns' friends were already under arrest, others had left the city, and some had even fled the county. Klaus and Erika made a long-distance telephone call to Arosa, Switzerland, where their parents were enjoying a short holiday. The family agreed that Munich was no longer safe. Erika left immediately and joined her parents in Switzerland. The following day, 13 March 1933, Klaus was driven by Hans to the *Hauptbahnhof* where he caught a train to Paris. His luggage consisted of two suitcases, a typewriter, a topcoat, and a bunch of magazines and books. He never lived in Munich again.[3]

Thomas and Katia Mann resigned themselves to a life in exile. Their intuition that they were in real danger if they returned to Munich was reinforced in mid-April when a manifesto against Mann's contentious Wagner essay was published. Many of Munich's academic and cultural elites attacked him in an open letter entitled '*Protest der Richard-Wagner-Stadt München*' ('Protest by the Wagner City of Munich') that appeared in the Easter edition of the *Münchner Neueste Nachrichten*. The defamation campaign was initiated by Hans Knappertsbusch, the Director of the Bavarian State Opera, and endorsed by forty-eight signatories including the Nazi mayor of Munich, Karl Fiehler, party leaders Max Amann and Adolf Wagner, Reich Music Director Richard Strauβ, the Director of the Bavarian State Theatre Clemens von Franckenstein, the painter Olaf Gulbransson, and musical director Hans Pfitzner, one of Mann's close friends. They accused him of engaging in the worst kind of 'aestheticizing snobbery' and for 'ignorantly and pretentiously characterising Wagner as a modern dilettante'. They also refused to forgive him for failing to appreciate the great German Master as the 'musical-dramatic embodiment of the deepest German sensibilities'. Mann was horrified. He wrote in his diary, 'dastardly document. … It strongly confirmed our decision not to return to Munich but rather to devote all our energies to the plan of settling in Basel.'[4] Five years later, the Manns immigrated to California. Their villa in Munich was confiscated by the SS. The contents were sold and from 1936 the house was used as offices for the SS-run *Lebensborn* (Well of Life) programme, a bizarre breeding scheme for racially approved unmarried Aryan women made pregnant by SS officers.[5]

Pater Rupert Mayer was not one of Munich's sycophantic clerics that Mann regularly vilified. He, like Hitler, was a Catholic, a veteran of the Great War, and a proud holder of the Iron Cross First Class. This is where the similarities ended. Mayer was a Jesuit priest. He was sent to Munich to work as a preacher and confessor in January 1912. On 22 August 1914 he volunteered to work as an army chaplain in a military field hospital. He served in Alsace, Galicia, and Romania, where in December 1916, in the Sulta Valley, he was severely wounded. His left leg had to be amputated in January 1917, and he was repatriated to the Heiliggeistspital (hospital for the war-wounded) in Landsberg-am-Lech. After the war he resumed his pastoral work in Munich at Michaelskirche (Saint Michael's Church) and the Bürgersaal church, the headquarters of the Marian

Men's Congregation (from 28 November 1921, Mayer was the President of the congregation). The two churches are approximately 200 metres apart from each other on the north side of Neuhauser Straße, between Ettstraße and Karlstor (Karlsplatz-Stachus). Father Mayer's first confrontation with the Nazis came early in the autumn of 1923, when all of Munich was preoccupied with rumours of an imminent putsch. Mayer, the charismatic priest and decorated war hero, was an invited speaker at an NSDAP meeting in the Bürgerbräukeller. His talk was entitled 'Can a Catholic be a National Socialist?' He received a rousing ovation as he limped up to the podium. The applause quickly turned to jeering after he warned his listeners that they could not be both a German Catholic and a National Socialist.[6]

Mayer's work with the poor, the disabled, and Munich's many victims of the devastating inflation of the 1920s, had led him to find out more about Hitler, the anti-communist, and his new nationalist party. A staunch nationalist himself, Mayer attended several of Hitler's beer hall speeches, but was not impressed. Hitler, he concluded, was a dangerous 'rabble-rouser'. Hitler's anti-Semitism and political extremism were diametrically opposite to his own humanity and spiritual convictions. When Mayer spoke at the Bürgerbräukeller he stunned his initially receptive audience with harsh criticism of Hitler and the party's reckless enthusiasm for violent revolution. He was shouted down before he completed his speech, and he required protection as he was escorted from the hall by the SA men monitoring the meeting. On the day of the putsch, after hearing gun fire at the Feldherrnhalle, Mayer rushed to the scene to help the wounded and comfort the dying. Later many of the 'old fighters' blamed Mayer's outspoken opposition as a key reason for the failure of the putsch on 9 November 1923.[7]

After the Nazis came to power in 1933, Mayer continued to speak out against them. He used his sermons at St. Michael's and speaking engagements elsewhere to renounce prejudice and hatred and to encourage compassion for all people with their diverse needs. 'Someone who hasn't sometime been fooled has never done anything good,'[8] was one of his favourite sayings, a subtle reminder that the will of God was better served by praising Jesus Christ and helping others rather than shouting 'Heil Hitler!' and subordination to an unscrupulous political system.[9] Mayer was always careful to craft his comments and criticisms of the regime in religious terms: 'The more uncompromisingly we give ourselves to God, the better for us. Believe me: God is unspeakably kind.'[10] Mayer refrained from making overtly political statements, but unlike most of the Catholic and Protestant church leaders he constantly challenged Nazi ideology and condemned the regime's campaigns of violence and murder. He was a serious threat to the regime because he inspired his listeners through his use of simple language and by making clear distinctions between right and wrong. His enemies soon loathed him because 'Father Mayer preached the truth – there was no gap between his words and life.'[11] On 7 April 1937, Gestapo Headquarters in Berlin banned Mayer from speaking in public. Two months later he was arrested for violating the ban and taken to Munich's Stadelheim prison. Mayer was released in early July after Cardinal Faulhaber agreed to order him to stop preaching, but fearing that his silence would be misconstrued as support for the Nazis, Mayer convinced his religious superiors to allow him to preach again. The Nazi authorities in Munich moved swiftly against him. Mayer was subjected to a short two-day trial on 22/23 July, before Munich's special court in Room 211 (now Room 248) at the Justizpalast (Palace of Justice) on Prielmayerstraβe 7, south of the Alter Botanischer Garten (old botanical garden). The court rejected Mayer's claim that his 'sermons are religious self-defence' and found him guilty of making 'malicious attacks on the Party and the State' and of 'abusing the pulpit'. He was sentenced to six months in prison, but this was commuted to house arrest at Rottmannshöhe, an exclusive sanatorium on Starnberger See (Lake Starnberg).[12]

Mayer was arrested again in January 1938 for violating his ban on speaking in public, and he spent three months in Landsberg prison. When he was released he left his Iron Cross behind in his cell, a symbolic continuation of his protest against the oppressive Nazi state. He was arrested a third time on 3 November 1939 and held for two months in the Cornelius jail inside Munich's Gestapo Headquarters in the Wittelsbacher Palais on the corner of Türkenstraβe and Brienner Straβe, before being transferred to Sachsenhausen concentration camp outside Berlin. The combination of Mayer's deteriorating health and fears that his death would give the regime's opponents a martyr to rally around, prompted the Gestapo to move him to the Benedictine abbey at Ettal, set in an idyllic Alpine valley between Garmisch-Partenkirchen and Oberammergau in Upper Bavaria (South). Forced to live in solitary confinement, Mayer remained at Ettal until 6 May 1945, when he was liberated by the US Army. He returned to Munich and resumed his post at St Michael's church, taking a leading role in rebuilding his shattered city. While celebrating Mass amid the bombed-out ruins of St Michael's on 1 November 1945, All Saints Day, Pater Mayer suffered a stroke and died shortly afterwards in the Josefinum hospital aged 69. He was buried on 4 November in the Jesuit cemetery in Pullach, a suburb of Munich. Less than three years later, on 23 May 1948, Mayer's mortal remains were transferred to a special crypt in the Bürgersaal. More than 300,000 people lined the route of the procession. In 1950, Cardinal Faulhaber began the diocesan process for collecting information for Mayer's beatification, which was celebrated on 3 May 1987 by Pope John Paul II in Munich's Olympic Stadium.[13]

Ernst Röhm and 'The Night of the Long Knives'

Resistance to the Nazi regime was not limited to leftists, a few conscientious authors and artists, and some courageous priests and lay people from the grass roots of the Church. It also came from within the regime. Ernst Röhm, the Chief of Staff of the SA, and a number of other SA leaders were alarmed by what they increasingly saw as a betrayal of the national uprising. Hitler, they fretted, had been co-opted by the capitalists and conservative elites, and had made too many concessions to 'the gentlemen with uniforms and monocles'.[1] Many SA men were also disappointed that they had not shared in the 'spoils of victory' with jobs and positions of influence in the new regime. As early as April 1933, Röhm made the first of his many calls for a 'second revolution', not against the Left, but against the Right,[2] and on 30 May 1933 he reminded 80,000 of his Brownshirts assembled on the Tempelhofer Feld (Tempelhof airfield) in Berlin, that they were the true guardians of the National Socialist ideal and it was their task to complete the German Revolution.[3] All over the country the SA responded to Röhm's rallying call by unleashing a torrent of violence. In Munich, SA units extorted protection money from businesses; blocked the entrances to banks, large department stores, and the stock exchange; roughed up Jews; and coerced ordinary citizens into making 'donations' to SA charities. Mass formations of Brownshirts regularly paraded through Munich shouting revolutionary slogans and singing SA fighting songs until they eventually arrived at a beer hall where they demanded free beer in exchange for not destroying the place.[4] Many in the SA were ex-soldiers, the unemployed, and those who had experienced persistent hardship. Most of them had enrolled in the SA in part to improve their economic and social prospects. In January 1933 the SA had fewer than 500,000 members, but by the end of the year its active membership had increased to nearly three million.[5] This mass influx of new and increasingly radical members emboldened Röhm to complete one of his long cherished ambitions, that of transforming the SA into a citizens' militia, independent from and possibly even replacing the Reichswehr. By early 1934, Röhm was openly demanding a position of power for himself and his organization in the Third Reich. Through violent activism and an insatiable sense of entitlement the SA had raised the spectre of civil war. Röhm had also become a dangerous rival to Hitler, both as leader of the party and the government.[6]

Hitler addressed the challenges to his authority and the country in his New Year's message, which was published in the *Völkischer Beobachter*.[7] It contained a detailed recapitulation of the progress made during the first year of his National Socialist government, and the Führer's forecast for the future. 'The year of the German Revolution,' Hitler declared, 'was over, and the year of German Restoration had begun.' Hitler attributed much of his success to the National Socialist principle of leadership, which had enabled him to conquer parliamentary incompetence and pave the way to restoring honour to the German Volk. In a firm warning to Röhm and his supporters, Hitler rejected the purely theoretical notion of a working class revolution and emphasised the higher value that the German people placed on practical improvements to the way they lived their lives. He also pleased the army by reaffirming its role as the nation's guarantor against external threats, and his commitment to an aggressive foreign policy aimed at recovering German territories lost by the Versailles Treaty and *Lebensraum* (expansion and settlement) in the east. Ultimately this meant rearmament and the reinstitution of general conscription to equip the army properly in order that it may 'serve our German Volk for the benefit of its peace and good fortune.'[8]

The *VB* also published, among Hitler's several other New Year's greetings, a personal letter to Röhm. The letter stands out for its extraordinary friendliness and warmth. Hitler employed the intimate form of the second person singular 'du' throughout in thanking his 'friend and fellow-combatant' for the 'imperishable services' he had rendered to the Movement and the German people by building the SA into a domestic political instrument that had vanquished their Marxist opponents.[9] Röhm either missed or chose to ignore Hitler's subtle suggestion to leave the defence of the country to the military. A few weeks later, Röhm wrote to General Werner von Blomberg, the Minister of Defence, informing him that the SA was responsible for national security and that the Reichswehr should assume the role of a subordinate training army.[10] The generals were outraged. Blomberg, who had spent much of 1933 manoeuvring the Reichswehr leadership away from its traditional political neutrality to a position of open support for the regime, appealed to Hitler to bring the SA under control and confine it to internal political matters.[11]

In a highly symbolic demonstration of loyalty to Hitler and the Nazi leadership at a meeting of Reichswehr commanders on 2 and 3 February, Blomberg announced that the army would implement the regime's new race laws.[12] Jews were banned from serving in the army and all officers were required to prove their Aryan heritage. On 19 February, at Hitler's prompting, Hindenburg ordered the armed forces to adopt the Nazi insignia as its official military emblem. Henceforth the eagle clutching the swastika was to be worn on the uniform cap and above the right breast pocket of the tunic. German warships also began to fly the swastika from their bows.[13] Back in March 1933, Hindenburg had already decreed that the old black–white–red and the swastika flags were to be flown jointly. 'These two flags,' announced the Reich President, 'unite the glorious past of the German Empire with the powerful renaissance of the German nation.'[14] In February 1934, the Reich war ensign was redesigned to incorporate the swastika.

Hitler was ready to curb the SA's power. On Wednesday 21 February, he visited the British Embassy, at Wilhelmstraße 70, for an informal luncheon with Anthony Eden, who later became Foreign Secretary. They discussed disarmament, Hitler's proposals for an Anglo-German Naval Treaty, and the SA. Hitler told Eden that he planned to reduce the SA by two thirds and to disarm the remainder. Germany did not need two armies, he assured his British host.[15] Hitler hoped to achieve an amicable compromise between Blomberg and Röhm, and he invited the senior Reichswehr commanders and the leaders of the SA and SS to a meeting on the last day of February at the Reich War Ministry, the Bendlerblock, south of the eastern end of the Tiergarten, at Stauffenbergstraße 13–14.[16] Before the meeting took place, Hitler made a flying visit to Munich on 24 February to address his *Alten Kämpfer* (old fighters) at the Hofbräuhaus, marking the 14th anniversary of the founding of the NSDAP. The next day, he was in Berlin taking part in *Heldengedenktag* (Heroes' Memorial Day) a new official holiday to honour German soldiers who died in the Great War. Back in Munich on 25 February, Rudolf Heß supervised the 'greatest swearing-in in history'. Slightly less than one million party leaders, including Hitler Youth and Labour Service leaders, from cities and villages across the country, simultaneously swore their allegiance to Hitler by means of a joint radio broadcast. The Führer was visibly confident when he addressed Röhm, the other SA and SS leaders, and the generals on 28 February. He rejected Röhm's plans for a civilian militia in which army grey was absorbed into SA brown. Germany required a professional army, Hitler asserted, well-trained and equipped with the most modern weapons for swift and decisive military operations. The SA was not suitable for this role and therefore it would remain a domestic political organization controlled by the party. Hitler encouraged close collaboration between the Reichswehr and the SA, particularly in border protection and pre-military training, but he left no doubt that the SA was to abstain from acting as a military force. Hitler had not changed his views on the SA since its reorganization in 1925, which had led to Röhm's resignation as leader of the *Frontbann*. In 1934, however, their differences were played out on the centre stage of national politics, and for very high stakes.[17]

At the end of his speech, Hitler compelled both Blomberg and Röhm to sign in his presence the pre-prepared agreement that set out the respective roles of the Reichswehr and the SA. Röhm pretended to acquiesce in Hitler's ruling, but inwardly he was seething. After Hitler, Blomberg, and the other generals left the reception, Röhm exploded: 'I have not the slightest intention of keeping this agreement. Hitler is a traitor and at the very least must go on leave.' Röhm's insubordination escalated to sedition when he raised the possibility of staging a coup d'état with his fellow SA leaders. 'If we can't get there with him, we'll get there without him.'[18] Throughout March there were persistent rumours that Röhm wanted to create an SA-state, and that the SA were planning a 'night of the long knives' against Hitler and the Nazi leadership. SA Obergruppenführer Viktor Lutze was one senior SA leader who strongly disapproved of Röhm's treachery. On Sunday 1 April, Lutze travelled alone to the Obersalzberg to see Hitler and report Röhm's insults and vile threats. He also warned Hitler of the dangerous intrigues being discussed in the highest ranks of the SA. Hitler spent several hours talking with Lutze, a clear sign of his gratitude to the commander of the Hannover SA. Hitler probably did not tell Lutze that he had been concerned about Röhm's attitude for some time, or that in early January he had asked Rudolf Diels, the first head of the Gestapo, to monitor the senior SA leaders. In late April, Himmler and Heydrich moved from Munich to Berlin and began to cooperate more closely with both Göring and the Reichswehr collecting incriminating material against Röhm and the SA.[19]

The dispute between the SA and the Reichswehr intensified in April when Max Heydebreck, the SA leader in Rummelsburg, publicly referred to the general staff as swine. 'We want to wait until Papa Hindenburg is dead, and then the SA will march against the army. What can 100,000 soldiers do against such a greatly superior force of SA-men?'[20] The Reichswehr was restricted to 100,000 men by the terms of the Versailles Treaty, and it was very vulnerable to being overrun by the SA's four-and-a-half million men in the event of a civil war. Hindenburg was 86 years old and in declining health. His death and the succession of a new Reich President had been topics of conversation Goebbels regularly raised with Hitler. The prospect of addressing both of these problems simultaneously and to the regime's satisfaction was just too good to pass up. From 11 to 14 April, Hitler observed the German Navy's spring manoeuvres in the Baltic on board the pocket battleship *Deutschland*. He was accompanied by General Blomberg, Admiral Erich Raeder (commander-in-chief of the navy), and several other high-ranking Reichswehr officers. Historian and Hitler biographer Alan Bullock hypothesised that during this four-day cruise the heads of the Reichswehr agreed to support Hitler's plan to combine the offices of Reich Chancellor and Reich President after Hindenburg's death in exchange for suppressing Röhm and the SA. The Reichswehr's virtually unconditional support for Hitler throughout the tumultuous summer and autumn of 1934 strongly endorses Bullock's deduction.[21] On 17 April, Hitler attended the SS

Spring Concert at the Berlin Sportpalast, sitting between Blomberg and Röhm. It was the last time Röhm and Hitler were seen together in public.[22]

Röhm's enemies in the party busied themselves building a case against the SA supreme leader. Heydrich, head of the SS Security Service, reported that he had irrefutable evidence that Röhm and other SA leaders were intent on launching a Putsch. He also warned about 'scandalous homosexuality' in the highest ranks of the SA. Himmler, Göring, and Goebbels all urged Hitler to take immediate action against Röhm and the SA. The truth was that Röhm was not plotting a coup d'état against Hitler, and his homosexuality, and that of others in the upper ranks of the SA such as Edmund Heines the powerful head of the Silesian SA, was an open secret within Germany.[23] Hitler still held slim hopes of reaching a compromise with his old comrade. On Monday 4 June, Hitler invited Röhm to the Chancellery where they talked for almost five hours. As was the case back in April 1925, when they spoke in Hitler's flat on Thierschstraβe, the two men could not agree on the SA's role. Röhm was never going to agree with Hitler's proposal to turn the SA into a military sports association, but he was loyal to the Führer. Acting on Hitler's suggestion, he agreed to go on leave immediately. He would take a cure for exhaustion at a spa in Bad Wiessee on the Tegernsee, an attractive lake close to Munich, popular with the upper class. Röhm also promised to send the entire SA on leave for the whole month of July.[24] Both 'holidays' were publicised by the *Deutsches Nachrichtenbüro* (German News Bureau, DNB). The announcements pleased Blomberg and the generals, who felt that this was the end of Röhm and the SA. They were even more elated on 6 June when Hitler declared that the Reichswehr would increase to twenty-one divisions numbering 300,000 men.[25]

Hitler's dilemma over the fracas between the Reichswehr and the SA was under control. He had good reason therefore to be satisfied when he departed for Venice on 14 June. His first state visit and meeting with Mussolini was in Richard Wagner's favourite Italian city and where he died on 13 Feb 1883, in his apartment in the Palazzo Vendramin-Calergi on the Canal Grande. Hitler's mood slumped when he disembarked from his plane at the San Niccolò airfield wearing civilian clothes and a rumpled trench-coat to greet Il Duce, who was dressed immaculately in the black and grey uniform of the Italian Fascists.[26] When Hitler returned to Germany, his mood crashed completely. On Sunday 17 June, while the Führer was addressing 70,000 party members from Thuringia who had come to Gera for their summer festival, Franz von Papen, the vice-chancellor, was speaking at the University of Marburg.[27] Papen attacked the cult of personality around Hitler and excoriated the regime for its unchecked radicalism and use of violence. 'No nation can afford an eternal revolt from below,' Papen asserted to a surprised audience of professors, students, and a few party members. 'The government,' he continued, 'is well informed concerning the elements of selfishness, lack of character, mendacity, beastliness and arrogance that are spreading under the guise of the German Revolution.'[28] Papen received thunderous applause from most of his listeners, who generously overlooked his personal responsibility for the conditions he criticised. Goebbels attempted to stop all radio broadcasts of the speech scheduled for later that evening, and he banned its publication in the press, but it was read on the radio in Frankfurt and Papen's supporters distributed an abridged version that appeared in several papers. Hitler was furious. The Nazi leadership – Göring, Heß, Himmler, and Goebbels – feared that Papen yearned to be President and that a cabal of conservative reactionaries around the vice-chancellor were also conspiring with the army and Hindenburg to depose Hitler and restore the monarchy. Papen offered Hitler his resignation, but then agreed to withhold it until the two of them went to Schloß Neudeck together to see Hindenburg.[29]

On Thursday 21 June, Hitler travelled to the Reich President's estate alone. Hindenburg reassured him that he need not concern himself with Papen, but as Hitler was leaving to return to Berlin, Blomberg, who was also at Neudeck, curtly told him that he needed to ensure internal stability otherwise the President would declare martial law and hand over control of the country to the army.[30] Was this a veiled threat to Hitler to move against the SA? On Monday 25 June, General Freiherr Werner von Fritsch, the commander-in-chief of the army, put his troops on a state of alert.[31] Hitler had a lot to think about. He spent four days, between 23 and 26 June, at the Berghof on the Obersalzberg contemplating his next move.[32] Meanwhile, back in Berlin, Himmler summoned all his senior SS leaders. Heydrich's staff had produced reports that suggested an SA-led putsch was imminent. They also claimed that Röhm was in contact with Gregor Strasser and General Kurt von Schleicher, the former chancellor. The time had come to strike a double blow against the SA leadership and the conservative reactionaries. Himmler and Heydrich drew up lists of those to be arrested.[33] On 27 June, Hitler met with Blomberg to assure himself of military support, and on 28 June Hitler ordered all senior SA leaders to the Pension Hanselbauer in Bad Wiessee for a mid-morning conference on 30 June.[34] Hitler was in Bad Godesberg, a small spa town on the edge of Bonn in North Rhine-Westphalia, when he gave the order late at night on 29/30 June to begin the purge. He was provoked into action by news of some 3,000 rowdy Brownshirts marauding in central Munich. Adolf Wagner, the Gauleiter of Bavaria, reported large groups of SA men rioting in the streets, and shouting 'the Reichswehr is against us!' and 'take to the streets, the Führer is no longer for us!'[35] Hitler flew to Munich with Lutze, Goebbels, and Sepp Dietrich, the commander of Hitler's personal bodyguard, the SS-Leibstandarte, landing at Oberwiesenfeld at 4.30 am.[36] Göring and Himmler were in command of operations in Berlin.

On arrival in Munich, Hitler summoned the city's two most senior SA-leaders, the SA-Obergruppenführer August Schneidhuber and the SA-Gruppenführer Wilhelm Schmidt. As soon as they appeared Hitler charged them with treason and tore off their epaulettes and party insignia. 'You are under arrest and will be shot,' Hitler shouted, before the two men were bundled off to Munich's Stadelheim prison. Impatient and unwilling to wait for his protection squad in the SS-Leibstandarte to arrive, Hitler ordered three cars to drive him and his entourage the one-hour journey to Tegernsee, to the Pension Hanselbauer in Bad Wiessee. Röhm and the other high-ranking SA leaders were still asleep when Hitler, Dietrich, Goebbels, Lutze, two armed detectives and several SS-adjutants including Wilhelm Brückner, Julius Schaub, and Hitler's chauffeur Erich Kempka stormed into the hotel around 6.30 am. Hitler had a night porter open the door to Röhm's room, number 21. 'Röhm, you are under arrest,' Hitler called out. Röhm, still half asleep, replied: 'Heil, Mein Führer.' Hitler shouted a second time, 'You are under arrest.'[37] Hitler then turned around and headed straight for Edmund Heines' room. Heines was still in bed with a young man when Brückner forced the door open and arrested him. Goebbels wrote of the incident in his diary: 'Heines is pathetic... caught with a boy of pleasure.'[38] Nazi propaganda later portrayed the SA's spa hotel in Bad Wiessee as a 'den of homosexual iniquity' that had to be cleansed by the most extreme measures. Dozens of other SA-leaders staying in the hotel were hustled out of their rooms, arrested, and locked up in the laundry room until they were herded into a chartered bus and driven to Stadelheim prison. A special SS-commando unit arrested a further 200 senior SA-leaders arriving for the conference that morning by car and by train at Munich's Hauptbahnhof.[39]

By late morning Hitler and his cortège of close associates and a few SS-men had returned to the Braunes Haus in Munich. Hitler appointed Lutze as the new SA chief of staff. After addressing a large number of party and SA leaders, Hitler spent much of the afternoon in conversations with Goebbels, Heß, Sepp Dietrich, and Theodor Eicke, the commandant of Dachau. The first the public knew of the day's tumultuous events was a 'Decree of the Führer' released by the DNB to the press at 3 pm. Röhm's dismissal and Lutze's appointment were confirmed, and all SA leaders and men were instructed to follow Lutze's orders otherwise they would be arrested and sentenced.[40] Early in the evening the public learnt that the two Munich SA leaders responsible for the riot the night before, the homosexual Heines, and three other high ranking SA leaders in the Röhm clique arrested at Bad Wiessee had been shot.[41] Many of the remaining SA men under arrest were transferred to Dachau where they were severely beaten by the SS guards. Several died later. Lists were also drawn up of other 'enemies of the regime' who lived in Munich and were to be arrested and shot. The former Bavarian Premier, Gustav von Kahr, was forcibly taken from his home, driven to Dachau, and tortured. Days later his body was found in a ditch not far from the camp, dead from a gunshot to the back of the head. Otto Ballerstedt, the Bavarian nationalist who had successfully prosecuted Hitler for beating him up in 1921, was arrested and shot in Dachau on 1 July. A similar fate befell Fritz Gerlich, the publisher and critic of the Nazi elite who had been languishing in Dachau since March 1933. Not only were the Nazis intent on murdering 'the traitors' they had singled out in the SA but they were eliminating hated rivals and settling old scores with those who had betrayed them. The purge widened across the country when Goebbels telephoned Berlin from the Braunes Haus and gave Göring the code word *Kolibri* (humming bird). This was the prearranged signal for Göring and Himmler to unleash the SS execution commandos. Herbert von Bose (Papen's secretary), Edgar Julius Jung (the man credited with writing Papen's Marburg speech), Gregor Strasser (the former party leader was tortured and killed in the basement of the new Gestapo headquarters in Berlin on Prinz-Albrecht-Straße), Erich Klausener (the 'Catholic Action' leader), Major General Kurt von Bredow (a fierce critic of the regime and close associate of General Schleicher), the former Chancellor, General Schleicher, and his wife (both were shot in their home in Neubabelsberg), are just some of the more prominent personalities the SS murdered.[42]

Hitler hesitated over what to do with Röhm. Both Amann and Heß offered to shoot him,[43] but Hitler was reluctant to sentence his old friend to death. Later that evening as Hitler left the Braunes Haus to return to Berlin he is purported to have told General von Epp that Röhm had been pardoned.[44] The next day, 1 July, Hitler changed his mind. Göring, Himmler, and the Reichswehr leadership implored Hitler to have Röhm killed. Accepting the logic of their arguments, Hitler telephoned Theodor Eicke and ordered him to take a revolver to Röhm's cell in Stadelheim prison. This way Röhm could have an honourable end. Eicke and Sturmbannführer Michael Lippert, the commander of the SS guards at Dachau, carried out Hitler's order. They told Röhm what was expected of him, placed a revolver loaded with a single bullet on his table, and stepped outside his cell. Approximately ten minutes later, when they had not heard a gunshot, they went back into the cell and shot him at point blank range. 'Mein Führer', Röhm gasped as he slumped to the floor, 'Mein Führer'. The DNB had already issued a bulletin that Röhm had been shot for treasonous deeds.[45]

The official death register listed eighty-three names but the actual number was at least twice as many.[46] Putzi Hanfstaengl bumped into Sepp Dietrich at the Chancellery on Monday 2 July. Hanfstaengl had been fending off foreign correspondents in Berlin 'buzzing around him like hornets' for a couple of days. They wanted answers for the blatant bloodthirstiness of the regime. He asked Dietrich 'what happened and was there a complete list of the people who have been killed?' 'The press people,' Hanfstaengl continued, 'are putting their own lists together and it is starting to look more like a thousand.' The journalists wanted to know who gave the orders, on whose authority, and who signed the execution warrants? Dietrich admitted that he had been in Bad Wiessee with Hitler, but he was not talking. 'You have no idea,' Dietrich replied solemnly, 'thank your lucky stars you were not around.' When Julius Schaub wandered over to join his two colleagues the conversation stopped. A conspiracy of silence had descended over the whole murderous affair.[47]

Christa Schroeder, Hitler's longest serving secretary, saw Hitler very late the night he returned from Munich. She was alone in the *SS-Begleitkommando* dining room at the Radziwill Palace, having gone to the kitchen in the Reich Chancellery for a snack. She had just sat down when Hitler came in and sat beside her. This brief and unexpected encounter in a part of the Chancellery Hitler seldom visited, she recalled, 'remains imprinted indelibly in my memory.' After taking a deep breath, Hitler said, 'I have bathed and feel as if newly born.' Schroeder could not help but notice how exhausted and troubled Hitler looked. He was 'like a person who, having gone through some dreadful experience, has to say: "Thank God" ...' Schroeder implicitly understood his 'newly born' comment: 'It was a sigh of relief and a lowering of his guard in front of someone he trusted, who was far removed from the particulars of the occurrence.'[48]

On Sunday morning, 1 July, after further discussions with Göring and Himmler, and a meeting with his friend the elderly General Litzmann, Hitler started to feel more confident that the previous day's events had been carried off successfully. His feelings were confirmed later in the afternoon when a company of the Berlin guard paraded down the Wilhelmstraße in goose-step to the Badenweiler March (Hitler's favourite military march) as he looked on from the Chancellery. The Reichswehr was paying homage to its leader. Blomberg, the Minister of Defence, had also issued a decree that praised Hitler for his 'exemplary courage in smashing the traitors and rebels' and further pledged 'devotion and loyalty' from the armed forces to the Führer. The following day, Hindenburg dispatched congratulatory telegrams to Hitler and Göring, which also appeared in the newspapers. The Reich President thanked Hitler for his 'brave personal intervention' and extended his appreciation to both men for their 'vigorous and successful action in crushing the attempt to commit high treason.'[49]

The army was pleased with the results of the purge, but explaining, not to mention justifying, the extra-judiciary killing spree to the German people and the wider international community was potentially more difficult. Hitler held an emergency Cabinet meeting on 3 July. Papen did not attend. Hitler outlined the extent of the plot against himself and the government, and how unforeseen circumstances had forced him to take swift and violent action. Imminent danger, Hitler asserted, necessitated the pre-emptive strike. The Cabinet not only accepted Hitler's explanation but they congratulated him for acting so expeditiously against the traitors. Franz Gürtner, the Reich Justice Minister, who was not even a National Socialist, declared the events of 30 June to 2 July an 'emergency defence of the state', which was already covered in the existing legislation.[50] Carl Schmitt, the brilliant constitutional lawyer, was tasked with drafting the legal interpretation for publication. Later that afternoon Hitler travelled to Neudeck. Hindenburg welcomed him warmly and reiterated his approval for the extreme measures taken to safeguard the state. 'That's the right way to go,' the Reich President declared, 'Nothing will happen without bloodshed.'[51] Hitler spent the remainder of the week addressing senior party officials on the suppression of the Röhm putsch before flying to Munich and then driving to the Obersalzberg for five days in the mountains.[52]

Goebbels was uneasy with Hitler's reluctance to speak about the purge publicly. The foreign press was highly critical, but Goebbels was mostly worried about negative domestic public opinion.[53] Goebbels, however, was unaware that while Hitler was at the Berghof he was writing a lengthy account of the Röhm-Schleicher conspiracy and legitimising his actions in its brutal suppression. Hitler returned to Berlin on Wednesday evening, 11 July, and two days later at 8 pm he addressed a special session of the Reichstag in the Kroll Opera House. SS guards were stationed next to the speaker's podium and throughout the building. The *Völkischer Beobachter* reported full attendance, but did not mention the Reichstag deputies who had either been killed in the purge or had 'recently retired' from politics. Hitler spoke late into the night. He insisted that his timely intervention had prevented the SA from plunging the country into a bloody uprising.[54] The members of the Reichstag signalled their approval with thunderous applause. Hermann Göring, the President of the Reichstag, stood up and declared: 'You have succeeded!' On behalf of the Reichstag he thanked Hitler for his statement and for 'his energetic and resolute salvation of the *Vaterland* from civil war and chaos'. Göring also elaborated on the complete trust the German people had in the Führer and warned foreign governments not to underestimate this trust. The German Volk, Göring emphasised, speaks as one: 'We will always approve everything our Führer does.'[55]

Goebbels need not have worried about German public opinion. The vast majority of Germans were relieved that the SA scourge was over. Despite the bloody excesses of the SS, Hitler had stopped the SA's politics of hooliganism. Not untypical was Luise Solmitz, a Hamburg school teacher, who told her friends how greatly she admired Hitler for 'the personal courage, the decisiveness and effectiveness he showed in Munich'.[56] The Führer's reputation grew in many parts of the country. In Upper Bavaria an SS security service report noted that in the aftermath of the Röhm purge Hitler was 'not only admired; he is deified'.[57]

Most ordinary citizens in Munich were of the opinion that Hitler had nothing to justify. They were glad that the drunken SA brawlers no longer terrorised their city's much-cherished beer gardens and beer halls.[58] On 1 August 1934, Schmitt published his legal argument supporting Hitler's handling of the purge in an article entitled '*Der Führer schützt das Recht*' ('The Führer Protects the Law'). Schmitt not only justified the killings as a form of higher justice, he argued that Hitler was the political sovereign authority when it came to protecting the law against abuse and if necessary creating new law in a moment of danger 'on the basis of his status as leader and supreme judge'.[59] Schmitt's opinion defined what was legal and as a consequence rationalised everything that happened in Nazi Germany till May 1945.

The end of the Röhm affair marked a significant turning point in Hitler's political career and the entrenchment of National Socialism in Germany. No longer was Hitler just an ethnic-chauvinist Bavarian politician from Munich. He was the incontestable ruler of Germany. The SS and the entire Nazi hierarchy moved with him to Berlin. Munich's prestige suffered. It ceased to be the centre of the party's power. Munich remained the headquarters of the SA, which had its origins in the city. The SA continued to function as one of the largest organizations in the party, but after it was further censured by the government for being 'depraved and thuggish' it never recovered its former standing. Restoring Munich's reputation was a huge challenge for the Lord Mayor Karl Fiehler and the Gauleiter of Bavaria Adolf Wagner, but they knew exactly how to proceed. They turned Munich into a shrine, a place of pilgrimage to the Movement.

The Cult of Nazism

Munich edged towards becoming a shrine to the Movement shortly after Hitler proclaimed the city the 'capital of art' on 15 October 1933. On 8 November Hitler flew from Berlin to Munich to lead commemorative activities marking the 10th anniversary of the 1923 Putsch. He greeted members of *Stoßtrupp Hitler* at the Braunes Haus and met with *Alten Kämpfer* at the Sterneckerbräu, the birthplace of the NSDAP, before going on to the Bürgerbräukeller where he delivered his first memorial speech.[1] He praised his comrades who marched with him ten years before 'on the dictates of a force majeure' not in rebellion against the Wehrmacht. They acted as they did 'to overcome the State of shame, the State of German misery, ... willing to commit and, if necessary, sacrifice their lives of their own free will for their goal', the salvation of their country. 'We know that this uprising of our Volk failed back then,' Hitler lamented, but it was 'the right decision,' he reassured them. 'It announced the Movement to the German people and it equipped us with the heroism we needed to succeed ten years later.'[2]

The next day, Hitler led the surviving members of the original Putsch in a re-enactment of the march along the exact route taken in 1923, from the Bürgerbräukeller to the Feldherrnhalle. Gauleiter Wagner and officers of both the Reichswehr and the Bavarian police were waiting for them. Hitler reciprocated their warm greetings before striding up the steps of the Feldherrnhalle to the podium from where he addressed the huge crowds gathered on the Odeonsplatz and down the surrounding side streets. Hitler's speech was full of emotion. He expressed grief over the loss of friends and colleagues on that fateful day ten years ago at the Feldherrnhalle, but their deaths, he stated confidently, had not been in vain. 'Were the dead of 9 November to rise again today they would shed tears of joy that the German Army and the awakening German Volk have now joined to form a single unit.' Hitler thanked all those who 'have faithfully fought for the German resurrection throughout all these long years,' and he welcomed those who 'came to join us in the end', especially the armed forces. 'In uniting the entire power of the nation today,' Hitler concluded, 'we are finally giving the dead eternal peace.' At the end of Hitler's speech a large bronze memorial plaque designed by Professor Troost, with the inscription 'And you have triumphed after all' and listing the names of the Nazis who died there, was unveiled on the east side of the memorial facing the Residenz. A smaller plaque mounted below commemorated the four policemen who were killed.[3]

Official receptions followed throughout the afternoon all across Munich, at the Braunes Haus, the Künstlerhaus at the southern end of Lenbachplatz, the Sterneckerbräu, and the Neues Rathaus (new city hall) at Marienplatz. Hitler had dinner with his sister Paula and Göring before he returned to the Feldherrnhalle later that evening for the final act in a long day of commemoration. Some 1,000 members of SS-Leibstandarte in their new, black, Hugo Boss dress uniforms along with 100 and 50 men respectively from the Göring and Röhm battalions of the SA assembled in front of the Feldherrnhalle to pledge *Treue bis in den Tod* (loyalty unto death) to their Führer. The oath swearing ceremony began at 9 pm with a chorale sung by Hitler's elite bodyguard regiment and music played by the SS-Musikkorps. Hitler led the men in reciting their oath, and impressed upon them that they were the heirs of the sixteen men who fell at this very spot ten years before. Against all odds, Hitler had achieved an improbable victory, and now his devoted followers had promised to give their blood and their lives for him. It was a triumphant spectacle.[4]

Hitler planned to make the commemoration of the 1923 Putsch a permanent occurrence, but after Röhm's execution and the suppression of the SA, the 1934 observance was decidedly low key. Hitler spoke to his 'old fighters' at the Bürgerbräukeller in the evening on 8 November. The next day he hosted a small reception at the Braunes Haus.[5] The following spring, Munich's city council, led by Oberbürgermeister Fiehler and Gauleiter Wagner, set out to reinstate the event and turn it into the most sacred ritual in the National Socialist calendar of holidays. The imminent completion of Troost's two imposing party buildings and the other alterations on the Königsplatz, which had turned the square into a National Socialist parade ground, gave them the perfect opportunity. Shortly after the Nazis gained power, a special Bureau for the Organization of Festivals had been set up in Berlin to create programmes for the 'celebration of the National Socialist Movement during the period of struggle'.[6] The bureau also established a fixed calendar of festivals, holidays, and special occasions. It began on 30 January with the anniversary of the Nazis' ascension to power, and ended on 9 November with the anniversary of the Munich Putsch. Munich was also the site for several other prominent celebrations, including the anniversaries of the birth of the NSDAP and the proclamation of the party programme on 24 February, Hitler's birthday on 20 April, and Oktoberfest (called the Wiesn by the people of Munich) in September. Oktoberfest was the largest of the *Volksfeste* (peoples' festivals) and to mark its 125th anniversary in 1935, Christian Weber, the chairman of the Munich city council, introduced an extravagant parade under the motto 'Proud City – Merry Land'. It showcased the beer and cultural traditions of Munich and Bavaria. The parade became a permanent feature at the beginning of Oktoberfest. No additional changes were made other than in 1936 when the *Weiß und Blau* flags of Bavaria were replaced by swastika flags.[7] Characteristic of all Nazi celebrations was grand spectacle. Parades with blaring bands and marching columns of soldiers, SA and SS men, dedications, roll calls, speeches, forests of flags, and torchlight processions were essential parts of the dramaturgy intended to create an almost mystical ecstasy amongst the people, stimulating popular imagination and rallying popular will into a unitary Volk. The most impressive of all these events were the NSDAP *Reichsparteitage* (Nazi Party rallies) in Nürnberg in early September. From 1933 to 1938 (the last year they were held), they epitomised the regime's glamour and power, and glorified Hitler, the man in charge, the Führer.[8]

Hauptstadt der Bewegung
(Capital of the Movement)

From the time Karl Fiehler became the first National Socialist mayor of Munich in March 1933, he referred to his city as the 'Capital of the Movement'. On Friday 2 August 1935 he spoke with Hitler in Berchtesgaden and obtained permission to use the title formally.[1] The city subsequently commissioned a new coat of arms that incorporated the Reich eagle and swastika. The city also contributed to a new museum in the Leiber Room in the Sterneckerbräu, where Hitler attended his first DAP meeting in 1919 and later established the NSDAP and its first headquarters. Commemorative plaques were erected on the front of the apartment buildings where Hitler had lived on Schleißheimer Straße and Thierschstraße, and in the beer halls where he had given major speeches, such as the Hofbräuhaus and the Bürgerbräukeller.[2] Over two days and nights on 8 and 9 November 1935, Munich's city officials staged a series of imposing ceremonies to mark the 12th anniversary of the 1923 Putsch. Everything was extravagant. All of the events were conducted with a great deal of pomp designed to expunge the bad memories of the Röhm affair the year before, and to restore Munich's prestige as the indispensable cradle of the Movement.[3]

Hitler arrived in Munich on Thursday 7 November. His first commitment was at the Feldherrnhalle, where troops of the Wehrmacht swore their allegiance to him. The following afternoon he attended a reception. City officials led by Fiehler and Wagner hosted the Nazi elite at the Bayerischer Hof, on the recently renamed Ritter von Epp Platz (formerly Promenadeplatz). At around 8 pm, Göring, Himmler, Heß, and other leading Nazi dignitaries including Winifred Wagner were chauffeured to the Bürgerbräukeller for Hitler's memorial address. The beer hall was overflowing with high-ranking party members, distinguished guests, and Munich's 'old fighters' and veterans of the putsch. Hitler began at 8.30 pm and finished some three hours later. His audience was entranced by his reminiscences of 'the early days of struggle' and the many challenges he and the party had overcome on their path to power. 'Fate was on our side,' he told them. Hitler finished his speech with a long tribute to the sixteen *Blutzeugen* (blood witnesses), the first martyrs of the Movement, and how their sacrifice for 'the idea' of a strong and united Germany was now 'the obligation of the entire Volk'. Coming generations, Hitler predicted, would draw strength 'from the sacrifices of the first fighters and will come forth with renewed strength to make sacrifices' for the Third Reich. Hitler then explained how these fallen heroes would be honoured in two *Ehrentempel* (Temples of Honour) on the eastern perimeter of the Königsplatz. 'Here they stand guard for Germany and watch over our Volk,' Hitler declared, 'as true witnesses of our Movement.' Hitler led his jubilant audience in a series of *Sieg Heil*s before departing for the Feldherrnhalle, where sixteen iron sarcophagi resting on biers, draped in swastika flags and surrounded by flaming braziers, lay in state.[4]

The caskets had been brought to the Feldherrnhalle in a solemn nocturnal procession down the Ludwigstraße, lit by fire bowls mounted on pylons. From Siegestor (Victory Arch) to the Odeonsplatz both sides of the street were lined by an SS honour guard. Hitler arrived just before midnight. He ascended the stairs alone, raised his right arm in the Nazi salute, and spent several minutes in contemplation before each coffin. Later he was joined by several 'old fighters' and the SS band played *Ich hatt' einen Kameraden* (I had a Comrade). The evening ceremony ended with 6,000 uniformed flag and standard bearers filing past the dead in silence. Hitler returned to his apartment on Prinzregentenplatz.[5]

Next morning Hitler was back at the Bürgerbräukeller to lead the memorial procession. Just as in 1923, it started at noon, following the same route. Behind Hitler and Göring in the front rank were three men carrying the Blood Flag, and they were followed by about one hundred veterans of the putsch dressed in the historic uniforms (canvas jacket, grey riding breeches, and 'model 23' ski cap) and all wearing the new *Blutorden* (Blood Order) medal Hitler had commissioned in March 1934.[6] The entire route was bedecked with banners and flags, and erected at regular intervals were black pylons, each one inscribed with the name of a fallen hero and a fire bowl on the top. When the parade passed one of the pylons, the sixteen names of the Movement's first martyrs were called out. Upon arrival at the Feldherrnhalle an artillery battery from the Seventh Army Corps (Munich) fired a sixteen-gun salute. Hitler laid a giant wreath beneath the memorial attached to the east side of the monument, dubbed 'Our Alter' by the *VB*, while the SS band played the two national anthems, 'Deutschland, Deutschland über Alles' and the Horst Wessel song. The sarcophagi were loaded onto horse-drawn gun carriages and the parade continued along the Brienner Straße to the Königsplatz, renamed the *Königlicher Platz* (Royal Square) in 1935, where more than ten thousand soldiers, SA and SS men, had assembled.[7]

The caskets were installed in the temples of honour with impressive pomp and circumstance. Gauleiter Wagner called out each martyr's name in a 'last roll call' and the crowd, as their proxies, answered 'Present'. The sea of flags on the square dipped in salute to the dead. When all the men had been interred, Hitler entered the temples alone and placed a wreath on each sarcophagus. The *Völkischer Beobachter* lauded Hitler for 'honouring his colleagues with the garlands of immortality'. Hitler spoke at length with the relatives of the sixteen men before the quasi-sacral ceremony came to an end. The last act in the three days of NS-ritual was another nocturnal ceremony at the Feldherrnhalle where SS recruits took their oath to the Führer. The following day, under the headline 'Resurrection and Eternity' the *VB* announced that the 'blood witnesses kept eternal watch as living sentinels in front of the Houses of the Movement in Munich' and through them 'the revolution's conscience beats on.' Munich's city leaders were overjoyed. They had accomplished their objective. 'The cult around the martyrs of the movement in the capital of the movement,' asserted the *VB*, 'represented the high point of the National Socialist festal programme.' This appraisal was echoed by the bureau for festivals in Berlin. The ceremony with Hitler's participation was repeated annually through to November 1943.[8]

Munich's *Oberbürgermeister Reichsleiter*, Karl Fiehler, acted quickly to capitalise on his city's renewed popularity as the town of Adolf Hitler and the birthplace of the Movement. He directed the city's culture department to produce a series of promotional brochures, pamphlets, and full-length books on the cultural and political history of the city for both German and overseas visitors. Published in four languages – German, English, Italian, and Spanish – these 'travel guides' served a dual purpose: showcase Munich's rich artistic past, and confirm its central role in the cultural reconstruction of Germany through National Socialism.[9] Collectively they portrayed Munich as the 'natural heir of a Germanic tradition of art and artists dating back centuries' and 'the first city in Germany to listen when Adolf Hitler came.'[10] Typical of most of the publications was an overstated romanticism. Munich, as one comprehensive guide book claims, stands out from all other cities and towns because in it 'grows and stirs a living soul.'[11] Whether one stood in the middle of the Marienplatz gazing at the towers of the Frauenkirche or watched the Knight's Tournament and the *Schäfflertanz* (an old Bavarian folk dance) on the clock tower of the Neues Rathaus, or walked through the tranquil gardens of the Nymphenburg palace, one could not help but 'feel the magic'. Munich, all the guide books emphasised, had 'a unique spirit that enabled it to develop in its own particular way into a real home for artists'.[12] Folklore tells of 'the wind that blew in turn from the South and the North, wafting fertile pollen over Munich' and transforming the city into a 'world-leading centre for art and an oasis for artists'.[13] Lavishly illustrated and replete with detailed itineraries on how to spend a day or even a week exploring Nazi Munich, the guide books are an engaging introduction to the architectural history of the city, the art galleries, the gardens and parks, the bierkellers and festivals, and *Gemütlichkeit*, the easygoing Bavarian love-of-life. 'Munich,' professed M. Reinhard, the director of the Culture Office, 'is not a place, but a condition.'[14] It was characterised by harmony, Reinhard explained, between the people and the princes who shared a deep appreciation of aesthetics and Germanic traditions, and most importantly a willingness to work together to build Munich into a spectacular jewel on the Isar. This was the unique Munich spirit. Furthermore, it was this spirit that encouraged and supported Hitler from the very beginning in his fight for Germany's regeneration. It was Munich, the city of German art, which embraced the vision of the Führer, an artist himself, and made the creation of National Socialist Germany possible.

Kunst ist kein Luxus (Art is not a Luxury)

'The opening of the "*Haus der Deutschen Kunst*" by the Führer', noted Fiehler in his introduction to the city's 1937 tourist guide, 'will tend to give the importance of Munich as the centre of German Art in the cultural reconstruction of the Nation, its truest meaning.'[1] On Sunday 18 July, the museum was officially opened on the last day of an extravagant three-day festival entitled *Tag der Deutschen Kunst*. Hitler arrived in Munich from the Obersalzberg on Friday afternoon 16 July and attended a command performance of *Tristan und Isolde* at Munich's Nationaltheater. Throughout the weekend there was an extensive artistic programme of concerts, theatre performances, street parties, and a marathon folk dance in the Englischer Garten. Gauleiter Adolf Wagner and his newly created '*Münchener Großveranstaltungen e.V.*' (Munich Large Events Association) – 300 men and women employed full-time to organize 'special National Socialist events' in the city aided by some 50,000 volunteers – spent months getting everything ready. Thousands of flag poles had been erected. A sea of 200 flags filled the square in front of the Hauptbahnhof. Public buildings and Hitler's apartment at Prinzregentenplatz were covered in opulent banners with golden laurel wreaths and swastikas. More banners and flags were hung on wires stretched across the main streets, and garlands decorated door frames and windows all across the city. At night, Munich's monuments were illuminated, and on Saturday evening every household burned ten candles in each of their windows. Goebbels was awestruck: 'Now Munich has put on her most festive robe. It is beautiful to behold.'[2]

On Sunday morning Hitler inaugurated the House of German Art and opened the first *Große Deutsche Kunstausstellung* (Great German Art Exhibition, GDK). His speech was an uncompromising assessment of what he believed was good 'German' art. Hitler explained that 'true art' emanated from 'the essential character of a people and was inherently eternal'. He rejected 'modern art' and the notion of 'an international experience' of art, which he characterised as *Kulturbolschewismus* (cultural Bolshevism) the product of talentless artists and promoted by Jews. 'These facile daubers in art who painted blue meadows and green skies or portrayed men and women as cretins and malformed cripples either set out to deceive the people with their work or they were insane.' Art, for Hitler, must accentuate the realistic ideal and ennoble the Volk; true art was not a chimera of changing fashions or a fleeting period of time. Hitler's single criterion for judging art was whether it was immortal, hence valuable, or transient and worthless. 'Art constitutes an immortal monument,' he claimed, which was 'anchored in the lives of the people whose immortality was assured as long as they prevailed.' The objective of National Socialism was to make 'German' art an eternal art.[3]

All ethnic German artists were eligible to submit their work for the 1937 exhibition. Some 25,000 works of art were registered and 15,000 were submitted, out of which 884 pieces by 556 artists were eventually selected.[4] Initially, a panel of three experts led by the painter Adolf Ziegler, *der Präsident der Reichskammer der Bildenden Künste* (the President of the Reich Chamber or Arts) and a professor at the Munich Academy, was tasked with choosing the art works. Ziegler was one of Hitler's artist friends from the *Kampfzeit*, the time of struggle in the early 1920s, and he had painted a good portrait of Hitler's niece, Geli.[5] Hitler had great faith in Ziegler's artistic judgement, but in May the group of selectors was increased to nine to cope with the sheer number of items that had to be evaluated. Gerdy Troost was one of the panel's new members. Six weeks before the exhibition, Hitler and Goebbels flew to Munich for a preview. 'The sculpture is not too bad, but some of the paintings are catastrophic. They've hung up works that really give you nightmares,' Goebbels wrote in his diary, 'this is what happens when you have a jury of artists.'[6] Hitler was furious. He dismissed the selection committee and appointed Heinrich Hoffmann, his friend and photographer, to salvage the situation. Hoffmann knew what Hitler liked. The paintings he approved were mostly in the Romantic tradition of the nineteenth century. Foremost among them were idyllic landscapes followed by pictures of animals, still lifes, portraits of workers, scenes of soldiers and peasant life, and plenty of female nudes extolling the fertility of German women. In sculpture, heroic and virile figures in the neoclassical style of Arno Breker and Joseph Thorak dominated. Hitler was not entirely satisfied with the overall quality of the exhibition, but he hoped that in the near future the House of German Art 'would house creations that were a worthy expression of our Volk's course of life' and 'inspire new generations of artists'.[7] The directive given to Germany's artists was carved in stone above the main entrance: '*Kunst ist eine erhabene und zum Fanatismus verpflichtende Mission*' ('Art is a sublime mission demanding fanatical devotion').

The festival concluded in the afternoon with a huge parade that celebrated 2,000 Years of German Culture. Stretching over three kilometres, 3,200 costumed participants and an equal number of soldiers and uniformed party sections trekked around the perimeter of the city centre. The pageant conveyed an overview of Germany's artistic heritage and cultural achievements from the ancient Germanic tribes to modern times, ending with a celebration of Richard Wagner and glorifying National Socialism. Marching bands were interspersed between the elaborately dressed groups, floats, and teams of horse riders that represented the heroic epochs of German history. Military units, SA and SS detachments completed the parade.[8] The *Völkischer Beobachter* hailed the spirited crowd, 'fellow Germans in the tens of thousands' who applauded the nation's new National Socialist warriors.[9] The idea that art was closely linked with the power of the state could not have been made any clearer.

When the GDK ended on 31 October, some 555,000 people had viewed the exhibition. More than 500 artworks were sold for a total sum of around 750,000 Reichsmark (RM). The Haus der Deutschen Kunst received ten per cent as its commission, in addition to the 500,000 RM it made from entrance and cloakroom fees, and the sales of catalogues, prints and postcards of the works on show, and other souvenirs. Goebbels declared the exhibition a great success, noting that the high sales figures were proof that the German people agreed with National Socialist art ideals. Hitler was equally pleased. The Day of German Art and the German Art Exhibition had increased Munich's fame as 'a truly artistic city'. Hitler enthusiastically added these two mega-events to the National Socialist calendar of holidays. Both were staged annually through 1939. The GDK continued throughout the war as a longer six-month exhibition, with the last one ending in the spring of 1945.[10]

Accompanied by Gerdy Troost, Hitler viewed the first GDK again on Monday 19 July. He returned a third time the following morning before driving back to the Obersalzberg. Two days in the mountains preceded a fortnight in Bayreuth where the Führer attended the Richard Wagner festival.[11]

Goebbels stayed in Munich to open *die Ausstellung 'Entartete Kunst'* (the 'Degenerate Art' Exhibition) in the Hofgarten-Arkaden, at Galeriestraße 4, on 19 July. Its purpose was to horrify the public with art that was the antithesis of the GDK. Modern art was deemed to be a cultural assault on German art and western values. Whole schools of modern art were condemned. Cubism, Dadaism, Expressionism, Futurism, Impressionism, and Surrealism were vilified as 'filth and rubbish' that threatened the 'noble, healthy, natural expression of life' characterised in true 'German' art.[12] The exhibition was organized in a matter of weeks before the GDK opened. Goebbels put Adolf Ziegler in charge of a committee tasked with selecting paintings and sculptures of a 'frightening and offensive nature that substantiated the undesirability of modern art'. Some 16,000 works had been confiscated from museums and private collections across Germany and around 650 were shown.[13] Among the artists classed as 'degenerate' were the pre-1914 Schwabing *Größenwahn-cafés* favourites Paul Klee, Wassily Kandinsky, and Franz Marc; the anti-war painters Otto Dix and Georg Grosz; and international stars Vincent van Gogh, Cézanne, Munch, Henri Matisse, and Pablo Picasso. Even Emil Nolde, a member of the Party and the Chamber of Culture, had hundreds of his works confiscated and burned. The definition of 'degenerate' was rather imprecise, but any artist whose work was seen to be incompatible with the ruling ideology risked being stigmatised as 'degenerate' and consequently banned from painting and exhibiting in Germany.[14]

The Degenerate Art exhibition was organized thematically and presented in nine dusty, poorly lit, storage rooms of the Archaeological Institute (today the Theatermuseum and Kunstverein). Exhibits were grouped into categories: demeaning of religion and women, 'Anarchist-Bolshevist Art', 'Jewish Art', and 'Primitive works' that were the products of 'sick minds'. Each room contained a haphazard mix of paintings and sculptures all crammed together. Paintings of various sizes were scattered about 'as if hung by fools or children'.[15] Large sculptures stood on pedestals while smaller ones were placed on the floor. Some objects had a sign placed beside them inviting visitors to guess whether it was 'the creation of a genius sculptor or an incurable lunatic?'[16] Explanatory notes, such as 'Christ as Adulteress', 'German woman as cretin and randy whore', 'German peasants from a Jewish perspective', and 'Thus do sick minds view Nature' were also scrawled on the walls to expose 'the harrowing cultural decay during the decades preceding the National Socialist government'.[17] Ziegler sought public affirmation for cleaning up 'bad art' and eliminating its malevolent political influence. 'Art,' in National Socialist Germany, 'must be easily understood by the great mass of the people, in order to reinforce the sure and healthy instinct of the Volk.'[18]

In many ways Ziegler and the organizers of the Degenerate Art exhibition had succeeded. Contemporary eyewitness reports confirm that the majority of visitors disliked it, and were highly critical of the 'so-called' art on display. While looking at paintings of the 'Primitive School' a woman from the Schwabing district in Munich laughingly told her friends: 'Anyone can slap on paint like that!' Another Bavarian man crudely joked with his companions: 'My four-year-old Sepp can make this kind of shit!' Two men looking at a seascape and a boat could not decide if it was a boat or something else. They both thought that the artist 'should go out to sea for a start to find out what it [the sea] looks like.' Some were very angry. One outraged visitor wrote in the gallery's guest book: 'The artists ought to be tied to their pictures so that every German can spit in their faces.'[19] Children were not allowed to see the 'Entartete Kunst' to protect them from 'the barbarous depravity on display'.[20] More than two million people viewed the exhibition in Munich before it closed on 30 November 1937. Many came to jeer, but others who were more reflective came to see art they would most likely never see again. The exhibition moved to Berlin and then on to ten more cities before the collections were sold to foreign buyers or burned. The Völkischer Beobachter praised the organizers for staging the exhibition at the same time as the GDK, triumphantly claiming that the cleansing of 'the temple', the moniker the *VB* gave to the House of German Art, had begun.[21]

Ziegler blamed International Jewry for the defilement of German art and culture. This was the theme of another exhibition '*Der ewige Jude*' (the Eternal Jew) at the Deutsches Museum in Munich from 8 November 1937 to 31 January 1938. It was organized by local Nazi propaganda officials in the city and from Upper Bavaria, assisted by Munich artists. Goebbels and Julius Streicher, two of the most virulent anti-Semites in the party, opened the exhibition to considerable fanfare, giving it the senior Nazi leadership's highest public approval. The exhibition was a vicious attack on the 'Jewish race'. It portrayed Jews as amoral and as an insidious threat to the German way of life. Jewish practices, such as circumcision and the methods used by kosher butchers to slaughter cattle, along with photographs of dwarfish, deformed, hook-nosed *Ostjuden* (Eastern European Jews) were used to illustrate cultural perversity and racial degeneracy. The political threat posed by Jewish-Bolshevism was also emphasised. Marx, Kurt Eisner, and the Jewish leaders of the two Bavarian Soviet Republics in 1919 were vilified, reinforcing the stereotype of a close connection between Communism and Jewishness, the theme of an earlier exposition, the 'Great Anti-Bolshevist Exhibit' held in the Deutsches Museum in November 1936. The Eternal Jew exhibition was heavily advertised. Classes of schoolchildren in Munich were given special tours. It attracted 412,300 visitors before it closed and travelled to other German cities.[22]

Munich, the city famous for *Gemütlichkeit*, became more intolerant and serious from the autumn of 1937 onwards. Mussolini's state visit in September was ostentatiously militaristic. The Munich Accords in September 1938 narrowly averted war over the Sudetenland and led to the partitioning of Czechoslovakia. And *Kristallnacht* (night of broken glass) or *Reichspogromnacht* on 9/10 November was a violent prelude to the unfathomable horrors yet to come in the Nazis' persecution of the Jews.

Slow March to War

J ust before 9 am on Saturday 25 September, Rudolf Heβ, the Deputy Führer, boarded Mussolini's train at the German border town of Kiefersfelden to greet *Il Duce* and ride with him to Munich for the start of a five-day state visit, his first to Nazi Germany. Uniformed boys and girls from the *Deutsches Jungvolk* (junior division of the Hitler Youth, DJV) and the *Bund Deutscher Mädel* (League of German Girls, BDM) lined the platforms of every station en route, cheering, waving, and giving the Führer's guest a very warm welcome. Hitler and a large entourage of senior military and party leaders, including Colonel-General Werner von Fritsch, General von Epp, Goebbels, Himmler, SA Chief Lutze, and Gauleiter Wagner, were waiting on the platform at 10 am when Mussolini's train arrived at the Hauptbahnhof. The two leaders greeted each other with the Fascist salute then shook hands. Hitler introduced Mussolini to the members of his welcoming party, and afterwards they inspected a mixed honour guard comprising companies drawn from the three armed services, the SA and the SS. Upon leaving the station they received a 21-gun salute. The *Bahnhofplatz* was a sea of flags, the swastika flag and the red, white, and green Italian flag, nested or artfully knotted together, while the station and the surrounding buildings were decorated with giant eagles, Roman fasces, swastikas, banners and garlands. A massed band of musicians from the Wehrmacht and the SS–Musikkorps played the 'Giovinezza' the Fascist hymn, before Hitler and Mussolini departed in an open-top Mercedes, cheered on by an enormous crowd shouting 'Heil Hitler!' and 'Duce, Duce!'[1]

Later that morning the two leaders had an informal chat in Hitler's apartment on Prinzregentenplatz. Mussolini spoke in German. The two men discussed containing Bolshevik Russia and weakening the position of Britain and France in Europe. The Berlin-Rome Axis, formalised earlier in the autumn of 1936, provided mutual support for expansionist foreign policies. Hitler recognised Italy's pre-eminence in the Mediterranean and Mussolini accepted Hitler's aspiration to unify Austria and all the other German-speaking regions in central Europe into a greater German Reich. Hitler and Mussolini restated their commitments to Franco's regime in Spain, and Hitler asked Mussolini to consider joining the Anti-Komintern Pact with Japan against the Soviet Union. At midday, Hitler and Mussolini laid wreaths at the Feldherrnhalle, the pantheon honouring the first martyrs in the National Socialist movement.

Hitler escorted Mussolini on a short tour of key Nazi sites in carnival-decorated central Munich, finishing up at the Königlicher Platz. They had lunch with members of the *Alten Kämpfer* in the Führerbau, and afterwards attended a large formal reception in the banquet hall before taking their places outside for a military parade on a special reviewing stand erected between the *Ehrentempel*. For over an hour Party and Wehrmacht formations goose-stepped past the two Fascist leaders. Mussolini was impressed. When he returned to Italy he introduced the goose step as the '*Passo Romano*' to the Italian armed forces. Following the parade, Hitler joined Mussolini at his luxurious guest-residence while in Munich, the *Prinz-Carl-Palais* (Prince Carl Palace), at the bottom of the Königstraβe, directly across the street from the Englischer Garten and the Haus der Deutschen Kunst. Hitler used the short break to present Mussolini with the Grand Cross of the Order of the German Eagle and the Golden Party Badge (which hitherto only Hitler was entitled to wear). Earlier Mussolini had made Hitler an 'Honorary Corporal in the Fascist Militia', the highest distinction bestowed by the Fascist Party of Italy. The last public function in the day's busy itinerary was at the Haus der Deutschen Kunst. Hitler and Mussolini had tea with Gerdy Troost in the Golden Bar, the chic café at the back of the museum. Afterwards there was a short reception with approximately a hundred celebrities invited from the worlds of German sport and entertainment, including Max Schmeling, the heavyweight boxing champion, and Leni Riefenstahl, actress and renowned film director of *Triumph des Willens* (*Triumph of the Will*) and *Olympia*, an artistic and award-winning documentary of the 1936 Olympic Games in Berlin. Before leaving the museum Hitler proudly showed Mussolini around, pointing out his favourite works. At around 7 pm they returned to the train station where they were met by an exuberant crowd and another guard of honour. The Führer and Il Duce left Munich separately on their own special trains. The German News Bureau (DNB) signed off: 'Thus ended the greatest day in the history of the Capital of the Movement.'[2]

Next morning the two leaders arrived in Lalendorf, a small village in Mecklenburg where they were met by the defence chiefs, General Werner von Blomberg (Defence Minister), Hermann Göring (Luftwaffe), Colonel-General Werner von Fritsch (army), and Admiral Erich Raeder (navy). Hitler and Mussolini spent the day touring in an open-top car observing a series of Wehrmacht manoeuvres. The following day they visited Essen and were escorted through the Krupp armament works. Mussolini's state visit ended in Berlin. Count Galeazzo Ciano, Mussolini's son-in-law and foreign minister, recalled that the welcome was 'Triumphal!' Berlin, similar to Munich, was fully decorated in German and Italian colours, flags, and party symbols. There were more gala receptions and military parades. When Mussolini returned to Italy on Wednesday 29 September he was fully aware of Germany's military power and his new role as Hitler's junior partner. He told his wife: 'The organization is fantastic, and the German people have an unusually great character. Hitler can dare to do anything!'[3]

From Hitler's perspective, the outcome of Mussolini's state visit could not have been better. The two leaders had grown closer together. Moreover they liked each other.[4] The Berlin-Rome Axis was stronger. Italy joined the Anti-Komintern Pact at the beginning of November. Hitler sent Mussolini a personal telegram thanking him for his support.[5]

Five months later, on 12 March, German troops entered Austria. General Heinz Guderian, who was with the main body of the 2nd Panzer Division heading toward Linz, 'felt that for both countries the *Anschluss* was an occasion of rejoicing'. His hunch was correct. 'The Austrian people saw that we came as friends, and we were everywhere joyfully received.'[6] Enormous crowds cheered the columns of German tanks and troops as they drove and marched towards Austria's main cities and towns. The Germans were greeted with shouts of Heil!, flowers were thrown onto the tanks, and women rushed forward to kiss a lucky soldier or two. Hitler crossed the border at Braunau am Inn, his birthplace, and slowly made his way to Linz. Everywhere he was greeted by jubilant crowds. He arrived in Vienna late in the afternoon on 14 March. The city was adorned with banners and swastika flags. When Hitler's motor cavalcade passed the Schönbrunn Palace the city's church bells chimed. A delirious crowd was waiting for him at his hotel, the Imperial, on Vienna's famous Ring. Next morning a quarter of a million people crammed the Heldenplatz to hear Hitler proclaim from the balcony of the Hofburg the unification of Austria and Germany. 'I now report to history that my homeland has joined the German Reich,' he concluded, prompting deafening chants of Heil Hitler! and '*Ein Volk, ein Reich, ein Führer*' (one people, one state, one leader) from the crowd that shouted itself hoarse.[7]

Hitler returned to Berlin on 16 March. He received a hero's welcome. The drive from Tempelhof Airport to the Chancellery took over an hour. Hundreds of thousands lined the streets creating a triumphal scene that the *Völkischer Beobachter* hailed as 'a victorious warlord coming home'.[8] At the Chancellery, Hitler addressed another large gathering of well-wishers from the balcony. '*Meinen Volksgenossen!*,' he began, sharing his joy with them over the recent events that had 'brought about the great consolidation of the German Volk'.[9] With the *Anschluss*, the unification of Austria with Germany, Hitler had achieved in his own words 'the greatest triumph' in his life. He had resolved the German problem by bringing the two German-speaking empires together in one German Reich. Mussolini, who was disappointed at not being told in advance, nevertheless congratulated Hitler for his bold action in 'solving the Austrian problem'.[10] Hitler received further praise on the evening of 18 March from the Reichstag. The Deputies had assembled in the Kroll Opera House to hear Hitler's account of the events in Austria. He also reminded them of President Wilson's 'right of self-determination of peoples' and the aim of his National Socialist government to procure the human rights not only of the German-Austrian *Volksgenossen* but the millions of German-speaking peoples in Czechoslovakia, Poland, Russia, and the Balkans. The Sudeten Germans were not mentioned by name but it was clear that addressing their cause was next on Hitler's agenda.[11]

Hitler had advised his generals back in November 1937 of his desire to annex the Sudetenland, the borderlands of Bohemia and Moravia with their 3.5 million Germans.[12] In the spring of 1938, Goebbels increased the pressure on Czechoslovakia. He mounted a full-on propaganda campaign against the Czech government, accusing it of abusing ethnic Germans and intolerable military posturing against Germany. The Czechs panicked. Over the weekend of 20–22 May, they mobilised the army and brought their military fortifications along the German border up to full strength. Some 1.5 million well equipped Czech soldiers were deployed in a near impregnable fortress line ready for operations. Hitler was furious. On 20 May he discussed the Wehrmacht's preparations for war against Czechoslovakia with General Wilhelm Keitel, the head of *Oberkommando der Wehrmacht* (High Command of the Armed Forces, OKW), and by the end of the month he approved the plan: *Fall Grün* (Case Green). The generals were given notice to be ready for action by 1 October.[13]

Hitler also pursued a political outcome to the crisis. He encouraged Konrad Henlein, the leader of the Sudeten Germans, to increase the pressure on the Czech government. Tensions continued to rise, and as the threat of war between Germany and Czechoslovakia escalated through the summer, Britain and France pressed the Czechs to accede to Henlein's demands. France was bound by treaty to defend Czechoslovakia, and both Britain and the Soviet Union had an agreement to support France.

Britain's Prime Minister, Neville Chamberlain, desperately wanted to avoid a war. He and most of his cabinet colleagues had no desire to 'spill British blood in a far-away country for people of whom we know nothing'.[14] On his own initiative Chamberlain contacted Hitler to arrange a meeting to resolve the crisis. Hitler accepted. Between 15 and 30 September, Chamberlain flew to Germany three times. This was quite an endeavour for a man who had never been on an aeroplane before and who was afraid of flying. Chamberlain's shuttle diplomacy looked promising. On 21 September he thought he had secured an agreement with the Czech government led by President Eduard Beneš and Prime Minister Milan Hodža to cede the German-speaking areas of Sudetenland to Germany. It collapsed immediately.

Hitler demanded that Czechoslovakia grant similar territorial concessions to Poland and Hungary. Self-determination was a legal right to which all the large enclaves of ethnic minorities were entitled, Hitler argued. Chamberlain objected. Hitler countered by threatening war: 'The oppression of the Sudeten Germans and the terror instigated by Beneš against them allow no further delay.'[15]

The injustices perpetrated by the illegitimate state of Czechoslovakia, an abomination created out of the Versailles diktat in 1919, were themes that Hitler elaborated on during a long and fiery speech at the Berlin Sportpalast on 26 September.[16] The following afternoon Hitler reviewed the 2nd Motorised Division as it paraded down the Wilhelmstrasse en route to Saxony and its deployment on the border with Czechoslovakia.

Britain responded by mobilising the Royal Navy. Chamberlain also sent his close adviser Sir Horace Wilson to warn Hitler that Britain and France would honour their commitment to defend Czechoslovakia if attacked. French reserve troops were taking up their positions in the Maginot Line. Wilson tempered his warning by telling Hitler that Britain would guarantee the Czechs ceded the Sudetenland to Germany if Hitler eschewed war.

France and the United States also urged Hitler to pursue a diplomatic outcome. André François-Poncet, the French ambassador in Berlin, one of the few foreign diplomats Hitler respected and whose opinions he valued, told Hitler that he could achieve all of his fundamental demands without recourse to war. Attacking Czechoslovakia, François-Poncet cautioned, 'will set all of Europe aflame'.[17] President Roosevelt concurred. On 26 and 27 September he sent two personal telegrams to Hitler expressing his and the American peoples' desire for a peaceful negotiated settlement rather than another world war. The breakthrough finally came when Mussolini accepted Chamberlain's request to act as a mediator.

On 28 September, a mere two hours before Germany mobilised its armed forces, invitations were sent out to the leaders of the four powers – Britain, France, Italy, and Germany – to come to Munich the next day for an international conference to 'find a peaceful solution to the Sudeten crisis'. The Czechs were not invited, but it was agreed later that they should send two 'observers' to Munich. Before Göring left Berlin for the conference, he chaired a small committee of German foreign office officials who drafted a detailed memorandum of the German demands. The document, which included a map illustrating the territory to be ceded to Germany, was cabled to Mussolini at his request. He wanted to read it on the train when he left Rome in the morning. Hitler travelled to Munich overnight in his personal train.[18]

Hitler met Mussolini's train at Kufstein and the two leaders travelled together to Munich on Hitler's *Sonderzug* (special train). En route the two friends conversed at leisure and they also agreed a joint negotiating strategy. Chamberlain and French Prime Minister Édouard Daladier arrived in Munich separately by plane at Oberwiesenfeld airport. They found the city awash with colour, stylishly decorated with banners and the flags of the four powers. Munich's citizens gave all the leaders a warm welcome. Thousands lined the streets and showered the official motorcades with ovations as they drove to the Königsplatz where another large crowd cheered the statesmen as they entered the Führerbau. The conference took place in Hitler's study on the first floor, what is now Room 105 on the west side overlooking the Königsplatz. A seating area comprising a large sofa and comfortable chairs had been arranged for the leaders in front of the green marble fireplace, above which hung a portrait of Bismarck by Franz Lenbach. Additional paintings by Defregger, Spitzweg, and a portrait of Frederick the Great by Menzel supported Hitler's presentation of himself as a connoisseur of art. The carpets, chandelier, and furniture were also designed and coordinated to give the room aesthetic distinction.[19]

The conference began at 12.30 pm with the four leaders stating their positions. They all expressed their desire to reach a peaceful solution, and overall the atmosphere was amicable. At 3 pm they stopped their deliberations for lunch. After the recess the discussion was somewhat haphazard and laborious. Paul Schmidt, Hitler's translator, recalled that there was no agenda to guide the debate and there were long delays to accommodate translation. Only Mussolini was conversant in a foreign language, and his knowledge of German, English and French made him the de facto chairman of the conference. The leaders took a second break at 8 pm for the formal banquet held in the Führerbau's opulent dining room. There was some discomfiture when the British and French delegations decided not to attend and returned to their respective hotels, but the Germans and the Italians stayed and enjoyed a sumptuous dinner. The talks resumed at 10 pm. Weary but eager to reach an agreement, Chamberlain and Daladier accepted a proposal put forward by Mussolini as the basis of the Munich Accord. The terms were essentially the same as the German demands set out in the memorandum Göring had sent Mussolini the previous evening along with a British and French declaration to guarantee the integrity of Czechoslovakia's remaining territory. Once the text of the agreement had been translated into four languages and approved, the documents were signed in the early hours of 30 September. The Czechs were to leave the Sudetenland immediately, and over ten days from 1 to 10 October the ceded territory would be occupied by German troops.[20] Hitler concluded the conference with a short speech. He thanked the three leaders for coming to Munich and praised their commitment to the preservation of peace in Europe.[21]

It was left to Chamberlain and Daladier to break the news to the two Czech observers, anxiously waiting in another room in the Führerbau. Chamberlain explained what had happened while Daladier handed them a copy of the agreement. The Czechs were distraught. Britain and France had abandoned their ally. Later that morning, the Czech government accepted the full terms of the Munich settlement. Hermann Göring summed up the whole affair: 'Neither Chamberlain nor Daladier was the least bit interested in sacrificing or risking anything to save Czechoslovakia … We got everything we wanted, just like that.'[22] Hitler was in a buoyant mood when he said goodbye to Mussolini at the Hauptbahnhof just before 2 am. He returned to his apartment on Prinzregentenplatz exhausted but satisfied.

Next morning Hitler was more circumspect. He was aware that by signing the agreement he had either limited his territorial expansion in Eastern Europe or he would have to break an international agreement to build his new greater German Reich. Hitler's mood had worsened by early afternoon when he received Chamberlain in his private apartment. In contrast, the British prime minister was more optimistic than he was the night before at the Führerbau. Chamberlain cheerfully talked about a new era of cooperation and friendship between Britain and Germany. Hitler, for the most part, sat still and listened. Paul Schmidt thought that he was distracted and uncharacteristically compliant.[23] Just before Chamberlain left he produced a short document in which both leaders pledged to recognise the importance of the Anglo–German relationship and 'the desire of our two peoples never to go to war with one another again'. They also resolved to consult with one another 'to remove possible sources of difference, and contribute to the peace of Europe'.[24] Again, Schmidt recalled that Hitler was irritated with Chamberlain and displeased with the declaration placed before him, but he signed it anyway. This was the paper Chamberlain waved before a cheering crowd at Heston Airport (London Heathrow today) on his return from Munich, a stunt that was seized upon by the British media as 'peace in our time'.[25]

On 1 October, German troops entered the Sudetenland unopposed. Scenes reminiscent of the *Anschluss* were repeated as ethnic Germans lined the streets and cheered the German soldiers as they marched past. In Munich the people were relieved that war had been avoided rather than joyous that the German territories in Czechoslovakia had been repatriated. Similar feelings of relief were evident across Germany. SS Security Service reports noted that 'a war psychosis' had gripped much of the population until the Munich Agreement had been signed.[26] Hitler was irked by this news. His generals had lacked an appetite for war and so had the German people. Added to this was the widely shared popular opinion that severe economic problems would accompany the Sudetenland's incorporation into the German Reich. Needing a quick fix that emphasised the benefits of securing his most recent foreign policy triumph without bloodshed, Hitler commissioned a commemorative medal. On one side were the profiles of the four leaders and on the other the Führerbau and the city crest of Munich with the date 29.IX.1938 and inscription '*Die Münchener Abmachungen im Führerhaus*' (the Munich Agreement in the Führer's House). Hitler presented André François-Poncet with one when he visited the Berghof on 18 October.[27]

Kristallnacht (Night of Broken Glass)

Hitler returned to Munich on 8 November for the 1923 putsch anniversary, the most symbolic and triumphal ritual in the Nazi calendar of events. The 1938 commemorations should have been conspicuously triumphant after the Führer's recent foreign policy achievements, but the city teetered on a knife's edge. The previous day in Paris, Ernst von Rath, a Foreign Ministry official at the German embassy, was shot and mortally wounded by Herschel Grynszpan, a 17-year-old Polish-German Jew. Grynszpan's attack was an extreme protest against the hostile environment towards Jews in Germany. Discrimination against German Jews had increased steadily since the Nazis came to power in 1933. The passage of the Nürnberg Laws in September 1935 made Jews 'subjects of the state' without any political rights and stripped them of their citizenship. In October 1938 the SS forcibly sent 17,000 Polish Jews back to an equally antisemitic Poland. Among the deported were Grynszpan's parents and siblings.[1] Reprisals and random acts of violence against Jews were reported in Kassel, Hannover, and Berlin. In Munich, on 8 November, the *Münchener Neueste Nachrichten* and the *Völkischer Beobachter* condemned Grynszpan's cowardly act and claimed that the shooting was indicative of 'the murderous criminals of international Jewry'. Both papers called for a pogrom to solve the Jewish problem once and for all.[2] Curiously, later that evening, Hitler refrained from making any reference to the assassination attempt in his annual putsch-anniversary speech to his old fighters and party officials at the Bürgerbräukeller. His only recorded comment was the publication of a telegram he sent to von Rath's parents, in which he expressed his condolences on the death of their son.[3]

Hitler left it to his Propaganda Minister Joseph Goebbels to orchestrate the response to von Rath's murder. Late in the evening on 9 November, Goebbels unleashed the *Reichspogromnacht* (Night of Pogroms) in Munich and across the country. He delivered an incendiary anti-Semitic speech at the end of the gala commemorative dinner hosted by Munich's *Oberbürgermeister* Karl Fiehler at the *Altes Rathaus* (Munich's Old City Hall at Marienplatz 15). 'The Jews must feel the people's anger,' Goebbels declared, while at the same time he predicted that 'spontaneous anti-Jewish riots should be expected.' Goebbels' speech received 'frenetic applause' from the putsch veterans and party members at the dinner.[4] The ballroom emptied quickly, and soon after, the sound of glass shattering could be heard throughout the city. SA men ransacked Jewish businesses and shops. The Uhlfelder Department Store at Rosental 16 was completely destroyed. It was the second largest department store in Munich in the 1930s, with 7,000 square metres of retail space and steady employment for 1,000 people. More than forty other Jewish businesses in the old city centre, including Sigmund Koch's music store at Neuhauser Straße 50 and Heinrich Rothschild's hat and finery store at Sendlinger Straße 38, had their doors and windows smashed and were looted. The local police and the SS did nothing. Himmler had ordered them not to participate in the pogrom. Munich's fire brigades only intervened to prevent burning Jewish properties spreading fire to neighbouring buildings.[5]

SA storm troopers set fire to the Ohel Jakob Synagogue in Herzog-Rudolf-Straße (two blocks east of the Vier Jahreszeiten Hotel on Maximilianstraße) and ransacked another on Reichenbachstraße. Munich's main synagogue on Herzog-Max-Straße across the street from the Künstlerhaus on Lenbachplatz was demolished in June to make way for a park, part of architect Hermann Giesler's plans for a massive reconfiguration of the 'Capital of the Movement'. On 9/10 November more than 1,400 synagogues were burned to the ground across Germany. Some 400 Jews were murdered and another 400 died of their wounds in the days that followed. Heydrich ordered that Jews around the country be brought into 'protective custody'. Some 30,000 were arrested out of which 25,000 were sent to concentration camps. In Munich, over 1,000 Jewish men were taken to Dachau, where 30 were beaten to death and another 185 did not survive three weeks of internment.[6]

Kristallnacht was the worst outbreak of anti-Semitic violence in Germany since the Middle Ages, and was widely condemned in the international press. President Roosevelt recalled the American ambassador in protest. Many Germans were also horrified by the destruction of property and the brutal hooliganism of the SA. Some felt sympathy for the Jewish victims, and even party leaders were appalled by the inhumanity. Over lunch at the Osteria Bavaria on 10 November, Hitler told Goebbels to halt the pogrom. German radio immediately broadcast the message: 'the German people are to desist from all further demonstrations and acts of retribution in any form against Jewry.' Next day the newspapers published Goebbels' promise to protect the German people from the Jewish threat through 'legislation and ordinances'.[7] Pressure was put on Jews to emigrate. Those who stayed had their economic existence plundered. They were forced to hand over all their valuables to the state. A flurry of laws was also passed before the end of the year preventing Jews from running their own businesses, owning or even driving a vehicle, and from attending cultural and sporting events. Jewish children were forbidden to attend German schools, and Jews were banned from public and university libraries. Adding to their misery, Göring levied a tax of one billion Reichsmarks on all German Jews to cover the cost of the destruction and clean-up and pay for the overtime worked by the police and fire service. 'I would not want to be a Jew in Germany,' Göring told the government ministers he assembled to deal with the Jewish question.[8]

Hitler remained exempt from most of the criticism. While others dealt with the fallout from the pogrom he read the newspapers at Café Heck and visited his friends Gerdy Troost and Hermann Giesler at their respective *Ateliers* (architecture studios). His strategy to remain above the domestic turmoil and concentrate on international diplomacy had worked. On 10 November, Hitler invited the German press to an evening reception at the Führerbau. Journalists and publishers representing some 400 papers attended. Officially, Hitler hosted the event to thank the press for its coverage of the Sudeten Crisis, but he also used it to enlist their help in preparing the German people for more difficult challenges ahead. The task, Hitler stressed, was to prepare the nation for war. He spoke for nearly an hour, confirming his desire for peace but emphasising that a nation's future cannot always be secured by peaceful means. Referring to the decision between peace and war, Hitler told the journalists that the people feel confident and secure when the leadership and the press speak as one. 'To this end, it is imperative that the press pledge itself to one principle: The leadership acts correctly!', Hitler demanded. 'It is this that makes the people happy! That is what they want!' By working together, Hitler counselled, we 'will make the German Volk great and mighty' and they 'will lead the German nation onwards toward a bright future'.[9]

Diplomatic Intrigues, Ultimatums, and War

Before the end of November, Hitler instructed his generals to review contingency plans for the military occupation of Czechoslovakia. In January he began discussions with Poland over the Free City of Danzig and the Polish Corridor that separated East Prussia from the rest of the Reich. 'Danzig is German, will always remain German, and sooner or later will come to Germany,' Hitler told Józef Beck, Poland's Foreign Minister. He proffered that it was in both countries' interests to find a solution, and urged 'the use of completely new methods' to find one.[1] To entice the Poles, Hitler dangled the prospect of an alliance against the Soviet Union. Beck was noncommittal on all counts.

Political instability worsened in Eastern Europe throughout the winter. On 14 March 1939, Slovakia, strongly encouraged by Hitler, proclaimed its independence from Czechoslovakia. On the following day German troops occupied the rest of the country. The Czech government was incapable of governing its rebellious ethnic minorities, and both Poland and Hungary had massed troops on the border threatening to invade. Hitler issued a proclamation on 16 March, dissolving Czechoslovakia and establishing the Protectorate of Bohemia and Moravia. 'For a millennium,' Hitler asserted, these territories have 'belonged to the *Lebensraum* of the German people.'[2] The puppet state of Slovakia also fell under Hitler's control. Eight days later, on 23 March, Memel Territory was reunited with the Reich. Hitler arrived in the port of Memel on the battleship *Deutschland*, and at 2 pm he delivered a short speech from the balcony of the city's main theatre to an enthusiastic mass crowd below. He welcomed 'Our old German racial comrades as the newest citizens of our Greater German Empire.'[3] Britain and France condemned Hitler's aggressive expansionism and on 31 March they issued a joint statement guaranteeing the independence of Poland.[4]

The Nazi leadership did not take the protests from London and Paris seriously. Many ordinary Germans, however, were worried. Increasing international criticism of Germany's foreign policy made them anxious and fearful of another war. They did not blame Hitler. Rather, they worshipped him like a god.[5] The people believed in him. He had made Germany great again, and despite his risky manoeuvres they trusted him to maintain peace. Historian and Hitler biographer Joachim Fest has implied that had Hitler died at the end of 1938 many people, not just Germans, would have called him 'one of the greatest of German statesmen, the consummator of Germany's history'.[6] Hitler had re-established much of the German empire of Charlemagne, and he did so without recourse to war. On 20 April 1939, Hitler celebrated his fiftieth birthday. Berlin marked the occasion with two days of lavish festivities. The city was decorated with Swastika banners and flags, and the main streets were lined with tall pylons topped with either a golden Reich Eagle or a golden Swastika. All the public reception rooms in the Old Chancellery were filled with presents for the Führer. The entire Nazi leadership, some 1,600 senior officials, patiently queued to shake Hitler's hand and offer their congratulations in the Mosaic Hall in Albert Speer's monumental New Reich Chancellery on Voβ-straβe. There were concerts, a torchlight parade down the Wilhelmstrasse, a military tattoo, receptions with foreign dignitaries and the diplomatic corps, and a spectacular military parade on Speer's newly completed East-West Axis through the centre of the city. Goebbels called it 'a celebration without compare'.[7] 'The Führer was celebrated by the people as no mortal man before him has ever been celebrated,' he wrote in his diary at the end of the festivities.[8]

In Munich many residents welcomed the arrival of summer in their city's famous beer gardens. Bavarian brass bands played on Saturday and Sunday afternoons at the Chinesischer Turm in the Englischer Garten. The Hirschgarten, Munich's largest beer garden, located in a small corner of the palatial grounds surrounding the Nymphenburg Palace, regularly served 8,000 guests on a warm day. Evening crowds packed the Augustiner-Keller near the Hauptbahnhof and the Groβgastwirtschaft Münchner-Kindl-Keller on Rosenheimer Straβe east of the Isar River in the brewery district of Au-Haidhausen. On Friday 14 July, Hitler arrived in Munich for the three days of festivities to mark the opening of the annual Great German Art Exhibition. On Saturday morning he visited the Deutsches Museum with Eva Braun and had a late lunch at the Osteria Bavaria before attending a performance of *Tannhäuser* in the evening. Sunday began with an early drive up to the Nordfriedhof, Munich's north cemetery, where Hitler laid a wreath on Paul Troost's grave. At 10 am he arrived at the Haus der Deutschen Kunst to open the exhibition.[9]

It was a clear beautiful day in Munich. The locals called it '*Führer Wetter*' (Hitler weather). Munich's cultural society turned out en masse, glamorously dressed. The Day of German Art was also political. Many Nazi leaders attended. The most senior present included Himmler, Goebbels, Speer, Heβ, Robert Ley, Julius Streicher, Gauleiter Adolf Wagner, and the Nazi mayor of Munich Karl Fiehler. A large official delegation from Italy attended, as did 650 journalists, nearly half representing foreign newspapers.[10] Hitler was dressed in his brown party uniform, but his speech was all about art: 'The primary goal of our artistic work in Germany has no doubt already been attained today.' He praised

Professor Troost's contribution before emphasising his own role in the rebirth of German art. 'Just as the campaign for architectural recovery had its beginnings in this city, Munich, a cleansing of the perhaps even more devastated field of sculpture and painting was launched here three years ago.' Hitler was satisfied that 'a decent standard had been achieved ... and that ever-more stringent criteria could be applied when selecting works of art for the current and future exhibitions.' He also urged artists both amateur and professional to 'approach their work with holy zeal' and use their 'truly creative genius' to record the great events in the current epoch of German history.[11] Unbeknown to Hitler at the time, this was his last speech on art and culture. After opening the 1939 exhibition he quickly walked through the gallery with Gerdy Troost, who was strikingly dressed from head to toe in white. Hitler had lunch at the Osteria Bavaria, and later in the afternoon watched the grand parade, '2000 Years of German Culture', from the Führer's reviewing stand set up at the Odeonsplatz. British journalist Isabel Hilton wrote, 'the success of the Day was testimony to the power of Nazi mythology.'[12]

Hitler spent most of the summer on the Obersalzberg. When he left his mountain it was to attend a cultural event. From 25 July through 3 August he was in Bayreuth for the annual Wagner festival. He saw the full cycle of music dramas, which in 1939 included the *Ring*.[13] Diana and Unity Mitford were also in Bayreuth for the festival and they had dinner with Hitler each evening. Hitler visited the Wagner family regularly and on Friday 28 July he took the Mitford sisters with him to Wahnfried for lunch. Hitler told them that he believed war between Britain and Germany was becoming more likely. This upset the women, particularly Unity. Later, on Wednesday 2 August, after the sisters had seen *Götterdämmerung*, Diana wrote in her diary, 'Never had the glorious music seemed to me so doom-laden.' She thought that she would never see Hitler again and that 'the future held only tragedy and war.' Unity was even more melancholy. After the opera she told her sister that she 'would not live to see a war.'[14]

On 3 August Hitler spent the day in Nürnberg visiting the *Reichsparteitagsgeländes* (Nazi Party Rally Grounds) where he was shown the preparations for the upcoming rally in early September. The following day he had lunch with Unity back in Munich. They went to the Osteria Bavaria, the restaurant where they first met on 9 February 1935.[15] Unity had returned to Munich from Bayreuth to set up her new apartment on Agnesstraße 26. While redecorating kept her busy, she was lonely and depressed. She hated the thought of the two countries she loved going to war against each other. All she wanted was to be the Führer's wife and to have his children. Another woman in Munich, Eva Braun, shared similar dreams. Both would suffer for their love, and ultimately they also shared a fate not too dissimilar to Wagner's heroine Brünnhilde at the end of *Götterdämmerung*.

Hitler returned to the Obersalzberg and remained there until Thursday 24 August when he suddenly flew back to Berlin. The Chancellery had been a hive of diplomatic activity for weeks. In the very early hours of the same morning in Moscow, Joachim von Ribbentrop and Vyacheslav Molotov, the Foreign Ministers of Nazi Germany and the Soviet Union, signed a Non-Aggression Pact. A secret protocol established the terms by which Hitler and Stalin would eliminate Poland and divide the spoils.[16] The alliance caught many by surprise, not least the German and Russian people who had heard their respective governments vilify each other for the past six years. Hitler wrote to Mussolini on Friday 25 August to explain why he had concluded a pact with Stalin. Mussolini replied that Italy was not ready for war. Over the weekend the two fascist leaders discussed German industrial and military support for Italy and Italian diplomatic support for Germany's action against Poland. Hitler also continued to negotiate with Britain and France, as well as Poland, but these discussions were half-hearted at best and none of the parties was willing to compromise. The British and French reiterated their pledge to Poland, and the Poles refused to negotiate away their territory as had the Czechs a year earlier. General mobilisation was declared by the Polish government. News of Poland's military escalation of the crisis swept through Berlin in the middle of the afternoon on Wednesday 30 August. Hitler ordered Reich Marshal Hermann Göring to set up and chair an emergency Council for the Defence of the Reich, and meetings were held with the senior commanders of the three armed services. The next day at 12.40 pm Hitler issued the Wehrmacht with 'Directive No. 1' for the conduct of war, to begin the following morning in accordance with the preparations for 'Case White'. The war plan, which had been drawn up in the spring, called for an overwhelming air and land offensive against Poland, while on Germany's western frontier 'the greatest possible restraint was to be observed' even if the British and French opened hostilities. Hitler's objective was to crush Poland in a limited war, not start a wider European war with the western powers.[17]

On 1 September, German troops crossed the Polish border at 4.45 am. It was a sunny late-summer's day in Munich. Generally in Munich, as in other German cities, there was little enthusiasm for the war. The public response was calm. There were serious looks on people's faces as they clustered around loudspeakers and radios, eager to hear the periodic announcements on the progress of the fighting. During the preceding weeks many Münchners probably had sensed that a new war was likely. On 27 August Hitler cancelled the annual Reich Party Congress in Nürnberg. During the last weeks of August city officials had also run a series of air raid drills. One took place just down the road from Hitler's apartment, in the Hochbunkers (air raid shelters) attached at opposite ends of a massive experimental housing estate on Prinzregentenstraße. Munich's National Socialist councillors wanted to build a *Neue Südstadt* (New Southern

City) adding 14,500 apartments to the city's housing stock between Ramersdorf and Giesing, emphasising a close connection between living-space and shelter. Only the experimental estate on Prinzregentenstraße was completed when the war began, but an additional thirty air raid bunkers were built around the city before the end of 1942. Built above ground with 1.3 metre walls and a 2-metre thick roof, they were also designed to blend in with the surrounding buildings. The average shelter could accommodate 750 people comfortably and safely.[18]

Also on 1 September, the British government ordered 'the complete mobilisation of the Royal Navy, Army and Royal Air Force'.[19] Later that evening Chamberlain told the House of Commons that the imminent war was Hitler's fault. Should Nazi Germany not renounce the use of force and restore the status quo in Poland, Chamberlain warned, Britain with the support of the Dominions and the British Empire would lead the struggle to rid Europe of Hitler and his regime. Both the British and French ambassadors in Berlin presented Ribbentrop with protest notes that demanded the immediate cessation of military operations and the withdrawal of the Wehrmacht from Poland. Germany had until 12 noon (CET) to comply otherwise the two western powers would fulfil their obligations to Poland.[20]

Unity Mitford was still in Munich when the war began. She was angry and distraught. On 2 September she wrote a letter to her sister Diana back in England. She blamed the war on Chamberlain and his fellow 'criminals' in the cabinet and proposed that all of them 'should be hanged'. She mentioned that telephone calls to England were no longer allowed and that a blackout was enforced at night. Unity was particularly distressed by her fear that she 'shan't see the Führer again'. Her letter ended with a strong hint of suicide: 'If anything should happen to me, & the English press try to make some untrue story out of it,' she pleaded, 'you will see to it that the truth is known won't you.' She also asked Diana to rescue her dog, a Great Dane named Boy, and bring him back to England.[21]

The next morning Unity went to the British Consul in Munich where she left her letter to Diana and another one addressed to her parents. She visited a few friends and Gauleiter Wagner. At midday, Britain and France declared war on Germany. Shortly afterwards, Unity visited Wagner a second time at his office. She was pleased to learn that she was not considered to be an enemy alien, and she gave him an envelope. Her next destination was the Englischer Garten, where she shot herself in the head.[22]

V

Munich During the War, 1939–45

Munich's First Casualty of the War

Obergefreiter Erwin Wincenty and a tourist named Emil Knobloch found Unity Mitford seriously wounded but still alive. They did not know who she was, but they helped the police secure the area and saw the young woman taken away in an ambulance. At the hospital the renowned Munich surgeon Professor Magnus and his team from the university saved Mitford's life, but removing the bullet from her brain was too risky. Earlier, Gauleiter Wagner had opened the envelope Unity had given him. Inside was her swastika party badge engraved with Hitler's signature and a framed photograph of the Führer. Wagner assumed the worst, and after a frantic twenty-four-hour search he found Unity in hospital, late in the afternoon on 4 September. She was unconscious but stable. Her attempted suicide inflicted irreversible damage, most noticeably limited speech and partial paralysis. Several weeks passed before she recognised Wagner, or Julius Schaub and his wife, who had watched over her in hospital on Hitler's instructions.[1]

There were no flags and no flowers for the soldiers as they marched to Munich's main railway stations en route to the front. When Britain and France declared war on Germany a sense of resignation weighed down many Münchners, who recalled the 'bad times' of the Great War. One reporter for the *Münchner Neueste Nachrichten* noted that several people he had interviewed regarded the new war as 'disastrous for Germany and the world'. Food rationing cards were issued before the end of August. Once the war began, Munich's restaurants were urged to serve an inexpensive vegetable stew and on two days a week not serve any meat dishes. New taxes were added onto the price of beer and tobacco products. A much anticipated international football match between Germany and Sweden was cancelled, as was the Oktoberfest. The beer tents and amusements that had only just been set up on the Theresienwiese were taken down. Petrol was restricted to 'war essential vehicles' that displayed special red number plates. One aspect of life in Munich that continued despite the onset of war was appreciation for art. Some 400,000 visitors passed through the Haus der Deutschen Kunst to see the 1939 exhibition.[2]

On 17 September, the Red Army invaded eastern Poland. German forces had already occupied most of the western half of the country and had surrounded Warsaw. The Polish capital surrendered eleven days later on 28 September. On the same day at a military conference in Berlin, Hitler told his senior generals that he wanted to begin operations in the West against England and France as soon as possible.[3] His generals were not enthusiastic. The rapid conclusion of the Polish campaign was impressive but victory had come at a cost. Some 11,000 German soldiers had been killed and another 30,000 wounded with a further 3,400 listed as missing in action. The Luftwaffe had lost approximately 25 per cent of the aircraft it committed to the campaign, and the army's losses in guns and tanks were 5 and 10 per cent respectively.[4] The Wehrmacht needed time to regenerate.

Ribbentrop flew to Moscow. On 28 September he agreed the final details for the partition of Poland and signed the German–Soviet 'boundary and friendship treaty'. A week later Hitler flew to Warsaw for the victory parade. He was greeted by his generals before reviewing the Eighth Army as it marched down Aleje Ujazdowskie (Ujazdów Avenue). In the afternoon Hitler toured the Belvedere Castle, and then flew back to Berlin where he received another hero's welcome.[5] In Munich, Goebbels presided over the victory celebrations. Flags and banners fluttered once more in the Capital of the Movement as the returning troops marched through the city, cheered on by large and appreciative crowds. Seven of Munich's cinemas screened the film *Der Westwall* to capacity audiences.[6] Directed by Fritz Hippler, head of the film department in the Ministry of Propaganda, the film glorified the Siegfried Line, a series of fortifications and obstacles around the German border with France, Belgium, Luxembourg and the Netherlands. The apprehensions about 'another war' that many Münchners had harboured just a few weeks earlier had been swept away and replaced by a renewed sense of confidence in the Führer and an outburst of national pride.

Hitler was in good spirits when he arrived in Munich mid-morning on 8 November 1939. He had travelled overnight from Berlin on his special train for the annual commemoration of the November 1923 Putsch. His first engagement was at the clinic on Nußbaumstraße where Unity Mitford was convalescing. Afterwards he visited his friends Gerdy Troost and Hermann Giesler at their respective studios, before having a late lunch at the Osteria Bavaria. Hitler met with his old fighters at the Bürgerbräukeller, left for a brief visit to Café Heck, and returned to the beer hall to give his customary speech at 8.10 pm, twenty minutes earlier than the historically accurate time.[7] 'I have come to join you for a few hours to relive in your midst the memory of a day which has become of supreme significance to us, to the Movement, and hence to the entire German Volk,' Hitler began.[8] He skimmed over the party's achievements from the early years to the present, emphasising the regeneration of German culture since 1933 and the restoration of the greater German Reich. The rest of his speech was a vicious attack on Great Britain, and the duplicity of its war policy. 'England does not want peace!', Hitler announced, citing as proof Chamberlain's contemptuous rejection of his peace offer in October.[9] He further mocked the

British Prime Minister's claim that England was fighting a war for freedom, justice and civilisation – the very things the English would not countenance for some 480 million subjugated people across the British Empire never mind other foreign nations. The English are the masters at dressing up their selfish goals in altruistic terms and grandiose language, Hitler counselled. 'British statesmen are doing today what they do whenever it suits their ends and programmes.' The British Empire, he asserted, is the product of nearly 300 years of world conquest. Today, as in 1914, the same old warmongers, Winston Churchill chief among them, supported by Jewish and other 'international' banking barons, agitate for war because they hate what Germany has achieved. 'Lord Halifax,' Hitler continued, 'declared himself a champion of the arts and culture; and because of this Germany had to be destroyed!' Hitler scoffed: 'Halifax had no inkling of the term… Within the last six years more had been done for culture in Germany than in England within the last 100 years.… The English cannot tell us Germans anything about culture: our music, our poetry, our architecture, our paintings, our sculptures can more than stand a comparison to the English arts. I believe that a single German, let us say Beethoven, achieved more in the realm of music than all Englishmen of the past and present together! And we take care of this culture better than the English are capable of doing.'[10]

Hitler characterised the war as a crusade to defend German culture against 'English civilisation' (exemplified by English exceptionalism and materialism). He regretted that France, like Poland before, had been duped into the service of 'these British warmongers'. He thanked his followers for their loyalty over the years and, without revealing to them that he had instructed his generals to begin the campaign in the west on 12 November, he told them: 'We National Socialists have always been fighters. This is a great time. And in it, we shall prove ourselves all the more as fighters.' Wild acclaim and applause interrupted Hitler's speech. When the ovation abated, he concluded: '*Sieg Heil* – to our Party Comrades of the National Socialist Movement, to our German Volk, and above all to our victorious Wehrmacht!'[11] It was 9.07 pm. Hitler left the Bürgerbräukeller immediately. His private train departed from the Hauptbahnhof at 9.31, squeezed into the train timetable because heavy fog prevented air travel. Hitler had to be in Berlin early the next morning to deal with 'urgent state business'.[12]

A Bomb in the Bürgerbräukeller

Goebbels predicted that Hitler's speech in Munich would be 'a world sensation'.[1] He was right, but not for the reasons he expected. At 9.20 pm a bomb exploded just behind the speaker's rostrum in the grand Festsaal where Hitler had been standing thirteen minutes earlier. The blast brought the roof down and buried the area around the lectern under metres of rubble. Eight party members were killed and another 63 were wounded, 17 of them seriously.[2] Eva Braun's father Friedrich was one of the injured and he required treatment in a nearby hospital. Shortly after midnight, Hitler's train was stopped in Nürnberg, and he was told of the assassination attempt. On 10 November the headline in *Völkischer Beobachter* proclaimed, 'The wonderful salvation of the Führer.'[3] Goebbels recorded in his diary that 'providence had spared the Führer so that he could complete his glorious mission.'[4]

When Hitler arrived in Berlin the next morning, he was greeted by Göring and Hans Heinrich Lammers, head of the Reich Chancellery, who congratulated him on his miraculous escape. Hitler seemed indifferent. His focus was fixed solely on the impending offensive in the west. General Brauchitsch told him that the army was not ready. Frustrated and irritable, Hitler reluctantly agreed to postpone the attack, something he would do twenty-nine times before the campaign began on 10 May 1940.[5]

Late in the morning on 9 November, Hitler instructed Himmler to start an investigation into the bomb attack at the Bürgerbräukeller. A special commission under the command of Arthur Nebe, chief of the Reich Criminal Police Office, a division of the Reich Security Main Office under Heydrich's control, was set up in Munich at the Gestapo Headquarters located in the former Wittelsbacher Palais on Brienner Straße.[6] Initially the investigation failed to uncover any information on the perpetrators or the assassination attempt. Rumours persisted that it was the work of British secret agents, or possibly disgruntled Bavarian monarchists. There was even a suggestion that the SS or the Gestapo may have been involved. The breakthrough came unexpectedly when Georg Elser, a Swabian cabinet maker arrested in Konstanz for trying to cross the Swiss border illegally, was sent to Munich for interrogation. The customs officers who stopped Elser on the night of 8 November, found in his possession sketches of exploding devices and fuses, detonator parts and firing pins, wire cutters, and a postcard of the interior of the Bürgerbräukeller bearing an official seal of the Nazi Party.[7] Soon after Elser was transferred to Munich, Maria Strobl, a waitress at the Bürgerbräu, identified him. Several other women from the beer hall also recognised Elser as a regular customer a week or so immediately before the bomb attack. 'He was usually poorly dressed, ate the regular worker's meal for sixty pfennings, and – this was suspicious – he never ordered anything to drink.'[8] On the night of 13 November, Elser confessed to the crime after several 'intensified interrogations', euphemistic Gestapo language for brutal beatings and torture sessions. Next morning Elser was transferred to Berlin for further interrogations. He was held as a special prisoner in Sachsenhausen concentration camp until late 1944 when he was sent back to Munich and held as a 'privileged prisoner' at Dachau. On 5 April 1945, Himmler ordered Elser's execution. Four days later, on 9 April at around 10 am, Franz Böttger marched Elser behind the crematorium and shot him.[9]

Before Elser planted his bomb in the Bürgerbräukeller he had spent time in Dachau for being a Communist sympathiser. He had long been an opponent of the Nazis. After his release from the concentration camp he stayed in Munich and became a tenant of Alfons and Rosa Lehmann in Türkenstraße 94. He also obtained a small workshop in Türkenstraße 59, where he built his bomb and a sophisticated timing device. Elser saw Hitler's annual speech to mark the anniversary of the putsch as an ideal opportunity to kill the Führer and several senior leaders in the Nazi Party. Working for almost a month late at night after the beer hall had closed he meticulously carved a hole inside a pillar immediately behind the speaker's rostrum and fitted a secret door that blended seamlessly into the panelling. He smuggled the debris out in a small suitcase when he left undetected in the morning. On 1 November, he began to install the explosive device, and on the night of 7 November he attached the self-made timer and armed the bomb. Based on Hitler's previous anniversary speeches he set the timer for 9.20 pm. Elser's assassination attempt failed because Hitler started his speech twenty minutes early and left without socialising with his *Alten Kämpfer*, thirteen minutes before the explosion, much earlier than he normally did on these occasions.[10]

On 11 November 1939, Hitler flew back to Munich for the state funeral of the victims of the bomb attack. The caskets were set out in front of the Feldherrnhalle draped in Swastika flags. Rudolf Heß called out each victim's name and addressed the thousands of mourners. Hitler did not speak, but shook hands with the relatives of the deceased and marched at the head of the long procession up the Ludwigstraße through the Siegestor (Victory Arch) and along Leopoldstraße to the Nordfriedhof (Northern Cemetery). Hitler also visited his injured followers in hospital and inspected the half-destroyed beer hall before he flew back to Berlin late that afternoon. At the end of November, Hitler returned to Munich for the fourth time that month. He spent the weekend of

25/26 November relaxing at his favourite haunts, attending a birthday party, and visiting the few remaining victims still recuperating in hospital from the injuries they suffered at the Bürgerbräukeller.[11]

Hitler was not a frequent visitor to Munich once the war had begun. He returned to the city mostly to deliver his annual speeches commemorating the founding of the Party in the Hofbräuhaus on 24 February and the anniversary of the 1923 Putsch on 8/9 November. After 1939, and the destruction of the Bürgerbräukeller, Hitler addressed his *Alten Kämpfer* in the Löwenbräukeller at Stiglmaierplatz, not far from where he had first lived in Munich in 1913, in a room he rented from Anna and Joseph Popp above their tailor shop on Schleißheimer Straße. Hitler also used these official occasions to see Eva Braun and longstanding friends, and relax at a favourite café or restaurant. His visits to Atelier Giesler and Atelier Troost were welcome diversions from politics and the war. When he was with his architect friends he immersed himself in their new designs and projects. Hitler also remembered his earliest and most devoted benefactors. He visited Elsa Bruckmann on 23 February 1941 to wish her a happy 75th birthday.[12] When time permitted, Hitler went to the Haus der Deutschen Kunst or the Deutsches Museum to see a new exhibition, have tea at Café Heck, or a meal at the Osteria Bavaria. An unannounced visit to the Braunes Haus or the Führerbau boosted the morale of local party officials. Otherwise Munich was a transit point he passed through when travelling to his mountain home, the Berghof, on the Obersalzberg.

The 1940 festivities in Munich to commemorate the 1923 Putsch began with Hitler's speech at the Löwenbräukeller. Hitler was in a bullish mood. When he arrived in Munich two days earlier on 6 November, his publisher told him that the 6,500,000th copy of *Mein Kampf* had just been sold.[13] Hitler regaled his old fighters and party leaders with a lengthy narrative on the party's struggle and how the victory achieved then over internal opponents would be repeated in the fight against Germany's external enemies. 'I am convinced that this battle will end not a whit differently from the battle I once waged internally,' Hitler assured his appreciative audience. Under his leadership, he reminded them, Germany erased the shame of 1918–19. 'A year ago the Wehrmacht crushed Poland in eighteen days, and more recently it crushed the entire west within a few weeks.'[14] National Socialism, Hitler emphasised, had given the German Volk purpose and strength, and created the moral, physical, and conceptual conditions for victory. 'Every soldier knows it and must know that the armies which today march beneath our banner are the revolutionary armies of the Third Reich!' The spirits of the sixteen men who fell in front of the Feldherrnhalle in 1923, he told them, now live in the entire German Volk who 'carry in their hearts not only a faith in a Germany as it once was, but the faith in an even better Reich in which the great goals of our national and social Movement shall be realised.'[15]

Munich Adjusts to the Demands of War

While Hitler was delivering his speech in Munich, the RAF was dropping bombs on Berlin. Six nights later, on 14 November, and on Hitler's orders, the Luftwaffe retaliated with an attack on Coventry.[1] RAF bombers attacked Munich for the first time in June 1940 and carried out another ten small raids before the end of the year. Early in the war Munich was at the outer edge of Bomber Command's range. This made the Bavarian capital a relatively safe place for the expansion of war industries. Munich also possessed a highly developed infrastructure. Two of the leading armaments firms were the *Bayerische Motorenwerke* (Bavarian Engine Factory, BMW) in Milbertshofen, north-central Munich, and Krauss-Maffei in Allach, north-west Munich. BMW was founded in 1913 as an aircraft engine company. At the end of the Great War and with the ban imposed on German military aviation by the Versailles treaty in 1919, BMW converted production to motorcycles, and after 1928 added automobiles. BMW returned to aviation when the Luftwaffe was created, and soon Munich's largest private employer of skilled labour became the largest producer of aircraft engines in Germany. Krauss-Maffei was a heavy machine works specialising in locomotives and later armoured vehicles. Other companies including the aircraft manufacturers Dornier and Junkers and the multi-faceted conglomerate IG Farben also set up large-scale factories in and around Munich.[2]

A dramatic expansion of arms production demanded a dramatic increase of the work force. Voluntary recruitment did not meet the demand. By the end of 1940, Nazi bureaucrats responsible for labour and munitions looked to foreign labour to meet their needs. Czechs and Poles were the first to be 'conscripted' followed by people from virtually all the countries of Eastern Europe. Following the invasion of the Soviet Union on 22 June 1941, Ukrainians were recruited for 'work duty' and, starting in November 1941, millions of Russian prisoners-of-war were used as slave labour in German factories and to support agriculture across the Reich. More than 13 million people were brought in to work for the German war economy, many against their will.[3] The man responsible for labour deployment was Fritz Sauckel. By November 1942 he had added 1.5 million foreign civilians, many of them highly skilled, to the German labour force. Goebbels was impressed by Sauckel's achievement, and on 21 June (a year to the day since Germany invaded the Soviet Union) he wrote in his diary: 'if you put a task, no matter how difficult, in the hands of a true, energetic, and focused National Socialist, it is as good as done.'⁴ By the end of 1944, BMW employed over 16,000 foreign workers in its two main factories in Munich.⁵

All these extra workers in Munich needed places to live. Initially the confiscated homes of the city's Jews provided additional accommodation. In the spring of 1941, a Jewish Housing Estate was built on Knorrstraße, not far from the BMW factory in Milbertshofen. This was the first camp of its kind in Germany. It housed some 11,000 evicted Jews in eighteen wooden barracks, which had been built by the people forced to live in them. A second camp was set up in a Catholic convent requisitioned by the SS, the *Kloster der Barmherzigen Schwestern* (Abbey of the Merciful Sisters) in the district of Berg am Laim. Both camps were holding-centres for Jews waiting to be 'evacuated' to other parts of the Reich. In reality, most were sent to the extermination camps in occupied Poland. The first deportation train left Munich on 20 November 1941. On board were 998 Jewish men, women, and children from Milbertshofen. They were transported to Kaunas in Lithuania where an SS death squad shot them. There were a further forty-two trains that took Jews from Munich to Theresienstadt near Prague, and Piaski or Auschwitz (both in Poland) where they were murdered. On 30 June 1943, Hans Wegner, the Director of the *Arisierungsstelle* (Office of Aryanisation) in Widenmayerstraße 27, informed Himmler that 'Munich is free of Jews'. In 1933, when the Nazis came to power, 19,000 Jews lived in Munich. At the end of the war only eighty-four lived there.⁶

Once all the Jews had been deported from Milbertshofen, the camp was leased by BMW for its foreign workers. By 1942, an extensive network of camps and other holding centres had been built across Munich to house a virtual army of foreign labour. Many of the housing facilities were little more than dilapidated barracks with a communal infrastructure, surrounded by barbed wire. There were 286 camps and hostels for civilian workers and another 120 small camps to hold mainly Russian prisoners of war. In April 1943 the Swiss Consul General in Munich noted in his monthly report: 'You can hear every European language on the streets save German.'⁷ Some 120,000 foreigners, a third of them women, were doing forced labour in and around Munich in 1944. Foreign workers were also compelled to clear damage from air raids, and afterwards repair roads, rail lines, and utilities. Treatment of foreign workers ranged between small acts of kindness and humanity from some German worker colleagues to institutionalised brutality. Foreign workers caught stealing or committing acts of sabotage faced the death penalty. 'Eastern Workers' from Poland and the Soviet Union received the worst treatment. They were forced to wear racial identification badges similar to Jews, and all social contact with Germans was forbidden. Romantic relationships between foreign workers and

German women were against the law. Eastern European men caught being intimate with German women were usually executed and the women sent to a concentration camp. Conditions for foreign workers generally improved after the German army's shock defeat at Stalingrad in February 1943. Both Nazi officials and company executives conceded that better treatment often increased productivity. As defeat loomed in the spring of 1945, several companies and many individual Germans were thankful for having dissociated themselves even slightly from the brutality of the Nazi regime.[8]

By the autumn of 1942, the war was no longer going to Hitler's plan. Stalemate in Russia was accompanied by defeats in North Africa and the Battle of the Atlantic, while German cities suffered under the increasing weight of the strategic bomber offensive carried out by Anglo-American air forces flying out of England. Germany's enemies had turned the tide. Under this foreboding cloud Hitler left his military headquarters at the Führerhauptquartier Wolfsschanze on 7 November. He travelled overnight on his special train to Munich to give his annual speech commemorating the 1923 Putsch. His train arrived at Munich's Hauptbahnhof shortly before 4 pm the following afternoon. He received an update on the American and British landings in Morocco and Algeria and discussed the likely reaction of Vichy France with his generals, Keitel and Jodl. At 6 pm he began his speech at the Löwenbräukeller: 'My German Volksgenossen! Party Comrades! …' There was little enthusiasm in the beer hall. His followers were polite rather than boisterous as they usually were on these occasions. They were preoccupied with the day's events. The Allied landings in North Africa earlier that morning had shocked them, but even more troubling were their impulsive thoughts on the terrible consequences likely to come from more active American involvement in the war.[9]

Hitler addressed all the recent setbacks before reassuring his audience that Germany would emerge from the war stronger and victorious. 'It is understandable,' he counselled, 'that in such a worldwide struggle as the present one you cannot expect to score a new success every week. That is impossible.' What was important and 'what is decisive in this war,' he asserted, 'is who lands the final blow. And you can be assured that it will be us!'[10] The war to eliminate the conspiracy of Jews, capitalists, and Bolsheviks, Hitler reiterated, was necessary to preserve German and by extension European culture. Success, he confirmed, hard fought as it was, had been achieved. Stalingrad, the essential transportation hub for grain and oil necessary to sustain the Russian war effort, had been cut off. 'No ship comes up the Volga anymore. That is what is decisive!'[11] Hitler attempted a bit of humour characterising Churchill as a fool and Roosevelt as an *Oberstrolch* (first-class rascal) before he called upon his comrades to stay strong and to trust in their National Socialist values. He ended his speech with a plea: 'Without exception, man and woman, always remember that this war will decide life and death for our Volk.'[12] On this sombre note, Hitler left the Löwenbräukeller with Himmler and Munich's new Gauleiter, Paul Giesler, brother of Hermann Giesler, Hitler's close artist friend. The three Nazi leaders drove the short distance to the Führerbau where they ate a late dinner and talked about declining morale in Munich.[13]

Die Weiße Rose (the White Rose)

Asmall resistance group acting under the name *Weiße Rose* had formed at the Ludwig-Maximilians-Universität (LMU) in the spring of 1942. All the members of the group came from conservative middle class backgrounds. They rejected the criminal brutality of the Nazi regime and saw it as their 'moral duty' to work towards abolishing Hitler's evil state. They were motivated and united in their cause by strong Christian beliefs and humanistic values. Two medical students, Hans Scholl and Alexander Schmorell, provided the initial inspiration for action. Together they wrote and distributed four leaflets in June and early July 1942, before they were posted to the Eastern Front, serving in a casualty clearing centre south-west of Moscow near Gshatsk, a relatively quiet sector controlled by Army Group Centre. Scholl and Schmorell, along with Willi Graf, who later joined the inner circle of the opposition group, were members of a medical Students' Company, serving a three-month tour in between academic terms.[1]

The leaflets written by Scholl and Schmorell were intended to shake people's belief in Hitler and expose the full horror of the Nazi state and its monstrous war. 'Abominable crimes' perpetrated in the name of all Germans, had taken 'frightful subhumanity' to an extraordinary level, the second leaflet proclaimed. The Nazis were responsible for crimes 'unworthy of the human race' including the murder of 'three hundred thousand' German Jews since the war began, 'the most terrifying crime against human dignity and a crime that is unparalleled in the entire history of mankind'.[2] Mistreatment of Slavic peoples from the occupied countries and the mass murder of Poles, Russians, and Eastern European Jews were also condemned. Cities all across Europe had been bombed into ruin. Terror begat more terror, the leaflets warned, and must be stopped. Acknowledging that there was little any one individual could do, the *Weiße Rose* called for passive resistance on a grand scale to topple the regime.[3] Hitler's war machine, the young activists recognised, could only be defeated 'by military means … on the smoking battlefields,' but they wanted the German people to admit their guilt and stop being accomplices as the first step to healing the 'severely wounded German spirit'.[4]

Every leaflet ended with a request: 'Please copy and distribute'. Each leaflet was composed on a typewriter and duplicated on a hectograph machine. Hundreds were printed. A few trusted members put them in people's mail boxes around the university, and the remaining leaflets were posted to addresses around the city, selected at random out of the telephone directory. On 30 October 1942, the medical students returned to Munich to resume their studies. Galvanised by what they experienced in Russia, Scholl, Schmorell, and Graf intensified their resistance. The inner circle of the group also expanded, and included Christoph Probst (a close friend of Schmorell since school days), Sophie Scholl (Hans's younger sister), Traute Lafrenz, and one of their tutors, Professor Kurt Huber, the only university lecturer to be a member of the *Weiße Rose*.[5] The fifth leaflet, which Huber co-authored, dispensed with the idealism and poetry of the earlier leaflets. There were no quotations from Goethe, Friedrich Schiller, Lao-Tzu, and Aristotle. Rather the 'Appeal to all Germans!' forewarned that Hitler was leading them into the abyss. 'Hitler cannot win the war; he can only prolong it. … and just retribution comes closer and closer.'[6]

By the end of November 1942, the German 6th Army was surrounded in Stalingrad. Students at LMU openly criticised the Nazis and the war. A mass student protest broke out at the Deutsches Museum on 13 January after Gauleiter Giesler made a crass request to female students during his speech to commemorate the 470th anniversary of the University of Munich. Giesler urged the young women listening in the Congress Hall to suspend their studies and 'bear a son and future soldier for the Führer'. Deluded by his apparent wit Giesler compounded his initial insult by offering to help the less attractive women find SS men who would gladly get them pregnant. The hundreds of students in the audience, both men and women, were outraged and shouted the Gauleiter down. Giesler was forced to break off his speech and had to be escorted from the hall. Outside the protest turned violent when the police were called to disperse the crowd. On several nights students defaced public buildings, writing slogans – 'Down with Hitler' and 'Freedom' – on the walls. Even the Feldherrnhalle bore the graffiti of the amateur activists.[7]

Encouraged by the student protests, the *Weiße Rose* addressed the next leaflet directly to them: 'Fellow Students!' Huber wrote the sixth, and last, leaflet after the fall of Stalingrad was announced in early February 1943. He sarcastically thanked the Führer for the senseless death and destruction concomitant with his criminal war. 'Do we want to sacrifice the rest of German youth to the base ambitions of a Party clique?' he asked rhetorically, and immediately answered, 'No, never!' The leaflet concluded with a plea to Munich's students to rise up and shake off the yoke of Nazism: 'The dead of Stalingrad implore us to take action! Rise up … rebel against the National Socialist enslavement of Europe in a devout new breakthrough of freedom and honour!'[8] Some 3,000 copies were printed. Graf took on the task of expanding the protest beyond Munich and posted leaflets to his friends in Saarbrücken, Cologne, Bonn, Freiburg, and Ulm. Leaflets soon appeared in Frankfurt and Berlin, and even in Austria, in Linz,

Salzburg and Vienna.[9] Leaflets were deposited in the mailboxes of students who lived close to the university and posted to others further away having obtained their addresses from a student register. Late at night handfuls of leaflets were left at the bus and tram stops on Karlsplatz (Stachus) and Sendlingertor Platz. On Thursday 18 February, the same day Goebbels gave his 'Total War' speech in Berlin's Sportpalast, Hans and Sophie Scholl went to the university and left stacks of leaflets in the corridors beside classroom doors a few minutes before lectures ended. Sophie threw her remaining leaflets into the air and watched them flutter down into the Atrium from the second floor. Jakob Schmid, a porter at the university, watched. Perturbed by their behaviour, he took both Hans and Sophie to see the Dean. Once the significance of their actions became apparent, the Scholl siblings were handed over to the Gestapo.[10]

At first the Gestapo thought that Hans and Sophie had just got caught up in a tasteless prank, but after Hans was caught trying to eat a draft copy of another leaflet the interviews became more serious. Two days later, on 20 February, Probst was arrested in Innsbruck and returned to Munich. Gauleiter Giesler wanted all three executed and called for a public hanging on the Odeonsplatz to send a stern message to any other wayward students. News of the students' protest spread fast and even reached inmates of the Dachau concentration camp.[11] At this point the Reichsführer-SS Heinrich Himmler took charge. He banned newspapers from reporting on the student resistance group and ordered a closed trial. Roland Freisler, the fanatical President of the People's Court, was rushed from Berlin to preside. On Monday morning at 10 am the trial began in Courtroom 216 (now 253) in the Justizpalast (Palace of Justice) on Elisenstraße 1a. Freisler did not conduct an impartial trial. He repeatedly shouted insults at the defendants, and at 1.30 pm, after berating them one last time for their seditious acts, he sentenced them to death. Hans and Sophie Scholl, and Christoph Probst were taken to Munich's Stadelheim Prison where at 5 pm they were executed by guillotine.[12] The three friends are buried beside each other in the Friedhof am Perlacher Forst (Perlacher Forest Cemetery), Stadelheimer Straße 24, south Munich.[13]

Further arrests and trials in Munich followed. On 19 April 1943, fourteen members of the *Weiße Rose* stood in front of Roland Freisler in the Justizpalast. The trial began at 9 am and carried on for fourteen hours. Willi Graf, Alexander Schmorell, and Kurt Huber received death sentences. Ten other defendants, including Traute Lafrenz and Franz Josef Müller, were sentenced to long terms of imprisonment. Somewhat surprisingly, one of the accused, Falk Harnack, was acquitted.[14] Huber and Schmorell were executed by guillotine at Stadelheim Prison on 13 July 1943. Graf suffered the same fate later on 12 October, after months of interrogations aimed at extracting the names of *Weiße Rose* members operating outside Munich. Hans Leipelt was the seventh and last member of the group to be executed at Stadelheim. His crime was collecting money for Huber's widow Clara and her two children. He was denounced and imprisoned in October 1943, and murdered on 29 January 1945.[15]

Despite Himmler's efforts to dismiss the *Weiße Rose* as small and insignificant, their courageous defiance inspired other anti-Hitler resistance groups both inside and outside Germany. Helmuth James Graf von Moltke, an international lawyer and head of the Kreisau resistance circle in East Prussia, smuggled a copy of the sixth leaflet to his contacts in Scandinavia, who forwarded it to British intelligence in England. During the summer and autumn of 1943, RAF Bomber Command dropped some 5 million copies of 'A German Leaflet – Manifesto of the Students of Munich' all across Germany. Thomas Mann also hailed the students of the White Rose in his regular BBC broadcast to Germany. On 23 June 1943 he expressed his hope that 'a revolution of a thoroughly purifying nature' led by German students 'will enable the country to find its reunion with the future world commonwealth of nations'.[16]

British and American Bombs Rain Down on Munich

On the night of 2/3 October 1943, the RAF returned to Munich carrying bombs not leaflets. 294 Lancasters attacked the city killing 191 people and injuring another 748. A Munich police report listed 339 buildings destroyed and many more severely damaged, including the Braunes Haus.[1] Most of the debris had been cleared by 8 November when Hitler arrived late in the afternoon for the annual commemoration of the 1923 Putsch. He stopped briefly at the Führerbau to greet the staff before going to the Löwenbräukeller where at 5 pm he started his speech. He spoke for nearly an hour, recounting the 'party narrative' on the Putsch, and how overcoming the struggles of the past had made the National Socialist Movement and later the German Reich strong. Europe's future, he stated, now depended on the Wehrmacht winning the war in the East, a colossal life or death struggle against Jewish-Bolshevism, 'the most difficult that the German Volk has ever had to fight'. He urged his listeners to make every sacrifice, 'the fate of our entire Volk, our women and children, our entire future depends on forcing the decision in our favour by a supreme effort.' He acknowledged that 'too many sacrifices had already been made' and that many more may be required, but he assured them that 'with fanatical confidence and fanatical faith there can be nothing other than our victory.' In a veiled reference to the *Weiße Rose* he warned, 'rascals who agitate for an Allied victory, if any still exist … would lose their heads.' He also announced retribution against the British and Americans for the 'air terror' they had inflicted on the German homeland, and promised, 'we will rebuild our cities to be more beautiful than ever before.'[2]

Hitler's speech was recorded, and broadcast nationally later that evening. It was the last time he spoke to the German people. He spent the night in his private apartment at Prinzregentenplatz, an ordinary activity which, unbeknown to him, he did for the last time. The following morning after a late breakfast with Eva Braun, he visited Atelier Troost. He had lunch at Osteria Bavaria, spent the afternoon with Eva back at his apartment, and met up with his friend Heinrich Hoffmann for a late dinner before boarding his special train for the overnight journey back to the Führerhauptquartier Wolfsschanze, his military headquarters.[3]

Munich was the target of several heavy air attacks in 1944 and early 1945. The USAAF bombed during the day and the RAF at night. One of the largest joint raids took place on 24/25 April 1944. Over seven hundred bombers from the 8th and 9th US army air forces escorted by 800 fighter aircraft attacked the German aircraft factories in Allach, north-west Munich, and the Dornier factory in east Munich. Later that night 234 Lancasters from RAF Bomber Command hit the city centre. They were directed by low-level target marking, which increased the concentration of the attack and contributed to extensive damage. Some 1,104 buildings were destroyed and another 1,367 were badly damaged, including the Löwenbräukeller, the Frauenkirche, and the Neues Rathaus. Both of the city's large railway stations, the Hauptbahnhof and the Ostbahnhof (Munich East) were destroyed. The Munich police reported 88 people killed, 2,945 injured, and another 30,000 made homeless.[4] Later in November and December the RAF struck Munich again with a similar number of heavy bombers. On the night of 7/8 January 1945, Bomber Command conducted its largest and last major raid on Munich, attacking the city with 645 Lancasters and nine Mosquito bombers. Several 'nuisance' raids flown by a few fast Mosquito bombers in April 1945 set off the air raid sirens and forced people to run to their shelters. Overall, seventy-four air raids on Munich killed 6,632 people and injured 15,800. Approximately 81,500 homes were destroyed and more than 300,000 people made homeless. An estimated 3.5 million incendiary and 61,000 high-explosive bombs destroyed most of the *Altstadt* (old city centre) and roughly 45 per cent of the city. The amount of rubble created by the bombardment was 12 million tonnes, about five million cubic metres.[5]

Götterdämmerung (Twilight of the Gods)

Hitler came to Munich for the last time in April 1944. On 17 April he arrived by car from the Obersalzberg to attend Adolf Wagner's funeral. The putsch veteran, horse racing aficionado, and former Gauleiter of Munich died of complications from a stroke he had suffered in July 1942. He received a state funeral in the Congress Hall of the Deutsches Museum. Goebbels delivered the eulogy. As Wagner was interred in the northern pantheon of the *Ehrentempel* at the *Königlicher Platz* the orchestra of the Bavarian State Opera played *Siegfrieds Tod und Trauermarsch* (Siegfried's Death and Funeral March) from Wagner's *Götterdämmerung*. Hitler laid a wreath with the inscription: 'Commander of the Guard on duty at the Eternal Guard'. A short reception followed in the Führerbau. Before Hitler left he addressed all the Gauleiters and Reichleiters. He returned to the Berghof on the Obersalzberg later that evening.[1] After spending a week with Eva Braun at his mountain retreat, he returned to Munich to take the train to Berlin. He was in the city for only a few hours before his special train left the Hauptbahnhof for the overnight journey.[2] Almost thirty-one years earlier, as a young aspiring artist eager to make his mark on the world, Hitler arrived in Munich, by train, for the first time. He was excited to live in this German city renowned for its art and architecture around the world. When Hitler's train departed on 24 April 1944, he was the Führer, but his favourite city, upon which he had bestowed the title Capital of Art in 1933, was a bombed out smouldering ruin. He would never return.

No arrangements had been made to commemorate the 1923 Putsch in November 1944. Hitler was ensconced in his military headquarters, the Wolfsschanze in East Prussia, and the Löwenbräukeller had been converted into a food warehouse, having been severely damaged in an air raid back in April. After discussions with Goebbels and Himmler on 10 November, Hitler agreed to write a statement to mark the event and send the Reichsführer-SS to Munich. A small rally was held on 12 November in the Zirkus Krone, and Himmler read out Hitler's proclamation.[3] It was a lengthy address. Hitler started off by explaining how 'the requirements for waging total war' had compelled him 'to postpone the anniversary celebration to the next available Sunday', and that his absence was because 'work at the headquarters does not allow me to leave it even for a few days.' The war against Bolshevism, he cautioned, was at a critical juncture, but the German people had embraced the spirit of 9

November, formed the *Volkssturm* (the civilian army) and defied the 20 July criminals (the army officers who tried to assassinate Hitler). He said he saw in 'the loyal following of the German Volk' hope for the future. He was confident that the Volk together with the Wehrmacht and Waffen-SS 'will successfully survive this time of trial and our efforts will finally be crowned by success.' Himmler added his own appeal for more volunteers, and then he read Hitler's concluding words: 'The goal of our struggle is no different from what we fought for in the year 1923 ... to safeguard the future of our Volk and the Greater German Reich!'[4]

By 24 February 1945, Hitler had abandoned his field headquarters and returned to the Reich Chancellery. He wrote another message to be read at the Hofbräuhaus to mark the 25th anniversary of the founding of the party. This time it was his friend from the earliest days of the struggle, Hermann Esser, who delivered his proclamation.[5] Again, Hitler began by emphasising his sense of duty, directing the battle against 'the unnatural alliance of exploiting capitalism and misanthropic Bolshevism in the service of international Jewry', which had prevented him from being in Munich. 'The stake was and is the existence of our German Volk!' Esser read Hitler's address on the ground floor of the Hofbräuhaus to a much smaller gathering of the party faithful than was customary at these occasions. The Festsaal, where Hitler announced the 25 points of the NSDAP, had been destroyed months ago during an air attack. Hitler acknowledged in his message how difficult the war had been and how many sacrifices had been made, but he also warned of the dire consequences that were sure to follow should Germany lose the war to such 'merciless enemies'. He urged the front and the homeland to continue to show courage and resolve, and together reap the reward of a great German victory. 'My party comrades! Twenty-five years ago I announced the victory of the movement. Today, I prophesy – as always inspired by my faith in our Volk – the final victory of the German Reich!'[6] Hitler's *Alten Kämpfer* and party loyalists wanted to believe him, but as they shuffled out of the Hofbräuhaus into the gloomy surroundings, few did. The time for Nazi celebrations in Munich was over.

Gauleiter Paul Giesler prepared for the *Endsieg*. He aimed to turn Munich and its mountainous hinterland into an 'alpine fortress'. He called on all 'loyal fighters' to converge on the Capital of the Movement, where National Socialism had begun, and where its fanatical followers would make their last stand. Giesler even envisaged himself leading the decisive battle in front of the Feldherrnhalle, the Blood Flag in his hand, reminiscent of the 'Ninth of the Eleventh' in November 1923, but this time to preserve the spark for future generations. In March 1945, all boys in the last two years of school were enlisted in the *Volkssturm*. Hitler created the 'People's militia' in September 1944, calling up all able-bodied men between 16 and 60 years of age who were not already serving in the army. The *Volkssturm* was ill-prepared to stave off defeat. All but the most fanatical Nazis just wanted to survive and the war to end. Murder and terror maintained the regime's control until the final days in Munich. Giesler used the police and the SS to deal with dissident citizens, punishing even the most minor infractions with death. Anyone showing signs of 'defeatism' or 'corrosion of defensive morale' was shot.[7]

By the end of April, the 42nd ('Rainbow') and 45th ('Thunderbird') Divisions of the US Seventh Army were in the far western suburbs of Munich. On 28 April, a Southern Bavarian resistance group called the *Freiheitsaktion Bayern* (Freedom Action Bavaria, FAB) attempted to take the city from the Nazis and hand it over to the Americans without further bloodshed. A FAB detachment of 440 ex-soldiers and civilians wearing Bavarian blue and white armbands, supported by a few tanks, succeeded in reaching the city centre and taking two radio stations in Freimann and Erding, in north and north-eastern Munich. FAB broadcast repeated announcements that they had taken over the government, and called on the people to rise up and rid the city of its Nazi oppressors. Major Günther Caracciola-Delbrück, a FAB commander and decorated army officer, attempted to arrest Gauleiter Giesler. The rebellion failed. The people of Munich did not rise up, and the SS rounded up and murdered most of the rebels. Giesler ordered that the leaders of the rebellion, including Caracciola-Delbrück, be shot. Nine were shot in the courtyard of the Central Ministry on Ludwigstraβe, and many more were executed in the Perlach Forest.[8] On 29 April Giesler used the radio to summon the people of Munich to defend their city. Just as they did the previous day, the vast majority of Münchners ignored the Gauleiter's call and waited for the Americans to liberate them. Giesler fled the city before the American troops arrived. He committed suicide near Berchtesgaden on 8 May 1945.[9]

Elements of both the 42nd and 45th Infantry Divisions liberated the Dachau concentration camp on 29 April. Accompanied by a group of journalists, Brigadier General Henning Linden (42nd Div) officially accepted the surrender of the camp from acting commandant Lieutenant Heinrich Wicker. The Americans were sickened by what they saw inside. Some 32,000 half-starved inmates, many infected with typhus, were in urgent need of medical care. Soldiers in the 157th Infantry Regiment, of the 45th Division, found an abandoned train of open box cars to the west of the camp. They were filled with dead bodies. Some of the American soldiers were so enraged by their discovery that they lined up the captured SS camp guards against a wall and machine-gunned them. More than fifty SS men were killed before Felix L. Sparks, the commanding officer, stopped the executions.[10] 'The violence of Dachau,' historian David Clay Large has insightfully noted, 'had a way of implicating all, even the liberators.'[11]

On 30 April, the daily communiqué issued by Supreme Headquarters of the Allied Expeditionary Force (SHAEF) stated: 'Our armor entered the outskirts of MUNICH.'[12] Elements of the 20th Armored Division entered Munich from the north-west, driving down Dachauer Strasse to the city centre. Other armoured units drove into the city through Herrsching in the south. They encountered very limited resistance. Thousands of white flags fluttered from windows and the streets were littered with discarded photographs of Hitler. SS and Wehrmacht units based in the city had retreated the previous day. Only a few 'ideologically blinded Hitler Youth' and *Volkssturm* put up an occasional token fight. By late afternoon the Americans were in the Marienplatz. The Swastika flag was removed from the clock tower of the Neues Rathaus. At approximately the same time, Hitler and his new wife Eva Hitler (née Braun) committed suicide in the Führerbunker in Berlin.[13] The following day SHAEF announced that 'Organized resistance in all of MUNICH west of the Isar river has ceased. This is more than three-fourths of the city.'[14]

Some Münchners saw the occupation of their city as a bitter defeat. Many greeted the Americans as liberators. The Americans moved swiftly and rigorously to establish their control. The US Army set up its headquarters in the Neues Rathaus. Denazification started immediately with the removal of Nazi symbols from buildings and public spaces, the restoration of old street names and the destruction of National Socialist monuments. Party buildings on and around the Königsplatz were used for a variety of 'US Occupation' functions, and both the Führerbau and its twin administration building served as collection points for 'looted art'. The Americans also used buildings formerly revered by the Nazis for their own entertainment and recreation. A baseball ground was set up on the Königsplatz, the Haus der Deutschen Kunst was converted into an officers' casino, and the Bürgerbräukeller was closed to the public and used as a Red Cross Club. Many of the Americans serving in the 'occupation force' confiscated the surviving villas in the fashionable district of Bogenhausen, on the east side of the Isar River, for their living quarters. Lee Miller, an American journalist with the US army, took up residence in Hitler's apartment in Prinzregentenplatz. She had her colleague, David Scherman, take a photo of her lying naked in Hitler's bath with a framed picture of the Führer propped up on the edge of the tub.[15] Not all Americans were as benign in their victory celebrations. Physical and verbal abuse, looting, murder, and the rape of German women were crimes American soldiers frequently committed in Munich and throughout Bavaria. Little was done to punish the perpetrators. A heightened sense of the victors' entitlement and in some cases a desire for retribution was sufficient justification for brutal behaviour and common theft.[16]

Klaus Mann, who was working as an interpreter for the US army and as a correspondent for the American military newspaper *The Stars and Stripes*, returned to his native city in early May, a few days before the official German surrender. 'What a strange, nightmarish experience!' he recalled, 'to walk through those once-familiar streets, now reduced to masses of ruins and rubble.'[17] When he finally found his family home beside the Isar River on Poschingerstrasse 1 (now Herzogpark off Thomas-Mann-Allee) it appeared to be okay but 'it turned out to be an empty shell, with its inside all burnt out, its roof destroyed, its staircase in pieces.' A sense of melancholy overwhelmed him. He had been away for twelve years, and he 'felt like a stranger in his former fatherland'.[18] Munich had paid a heavy price for supporting Hitler. Fewer than three per cent of all buildings in Munich had escaped damage and ninety per cent of the historic city centre had been destroyed. Most of the characteristic landmarks were missing. The total number of people now living in Munich was 470,000, down from 824,000 at the start of the war. Some 20,000 inhabitants had died fighting in the SS and the Wehrmacht, more than 11,000 were officially listed as 'missing', 6,700 died in the air raids including 2,966 women and 425 children, and 3,000 Jewish residents had been murdered in the Holocaust.[19] Despite these losses, Klaus Mann was worried that many of the survivors in the city of his birth, and Germans in general, still 'adored their Führer'.[20]

One of these survivors was Traudl Junge. She was 26 and a widow when she returned to Munich in April 1946. Her husband had been killed in Normandy in August 1944.[21] She had also been one of Hitler's private secretaries for two and a half years, beginning in November 1942. 'I was fascinated by Adolf Hitler, thought him an agreeable employer, paternal and friendly.' Confronting her time with the Führer in the mid-1960s, she acknowledged, 'I enjoyed working for him almost to the bitter end. After the revelation of his crimes, I shall always live with a sense that I must share the guilt.' Traudl Junge wrote her memoir in 1947–48 while her recollections were 'still very vivid', but delayed publication until 2002, shortly before she died. She feared that her account would either be trivialised or, worse, receive 'approval from the wrong quarters'.[22] What she produced is an honest exposé of daily life, often spectacularly ordinary life, inside Hitler's inner circle during the last years of the Second World War. It is also a human story of a young woman coming to terms with her own and her country's past. One of the most insightful passages in her memoir is her instant reaction to the confirmation of Hitler's death while she was still inside the bunker in Berlin:

Suddenly I feel something like hatred and helpless anger rise in me. I'm angry with the dead Führer. I'm surprised by that myself, because after all, I knew he was going to leave us. But he's left us in such a state of emptiness and helplessness! He's simply gone away, and with him the hypnotic compulsion under which we were living has gone too.[23]

Traudl Junge's immediate thoughts provide an obvious explanation why there was no fanatical last stand in front of the Feldherrnhalle in Munich. She, like so many Germans, looked to Hitler to provide answers to their own as well as the nation's problems. They trusted the Führer to look after them. That trust was irrevocably broken when he committed suicide. Hitler was dead. The Movement died with him.

Epilogue

In a small square off Türkenstraße is an art installation in memory of Georg Elser. The artist, Silke Wagner, won a competition in 2009 held by the Department of Arts and Culture in Munich to commemorate Elser's audacious attempt to blow up Hitler in the Bürgerbräukeller. The award winning design is mounted on the street-facing wall of a school. It is a circular set of red neon tubes that light up for one minute each night at 9.20 pm, the exact time of the explosion, illuminating the historic date, 8 November 1939. The square was renamed Georg-Elser-Platz in 1997; it is directly across the street from Elser's former workshop and the restaurant Alter Simpl still frequented today by artists, students, and writers, and where the anti-authoritarian satirical magazine *Simplicissimus* was produced. Close by, at the university, are several memorials to the White Rose and a foundation (*Weiße Rose Stiftung e.V.*) that maintains a permanent museum and promotes scholarship on the life and work of the resistance group. One of the most poignant memorials is a set of ceramic tiles embedded in the pavement at the entrance of the university. The tiles depict the leaflets and portrait photos of the student resistance fighters. They are also made to look as if they were dropped accidentally by someone in a hurry, similar to Hans and Sophie Scholl before she launched a handful of leaflets into the air in the Atrium on the day she and her brother were arrested. Another important monument of atonement is the memorial stone located on Herzog-Maz-Straße near Karlsplatz (Stachus) commemorating Munich's former main synagogue and the destruction of Jewish life under the Nazis. Every year on 9 November, the anniversary of *Kristallnacht*, prominent members of Munich society and the Jewish community and ordinary citizens all gather at the memorial stone where they spend several hours listening to a roll call of the names of Munich's Jewish citizens murdered in the Holocaust. Many more monuments, memorials, and commemorative plaques throughout the city testify to Munich's efforts to acknowledge and remember its role in the history of National Socialism.

Munich's road back from the Nazi era has been long and hard. Addressing the city's National Socialist past was difficult, but through a combination of initiatives by citizens, city and Bavarian officials, business leaders and corporate support, much has been done to influence Munich's memorial landscape and to face up to the crimes committed by the Nazis. Münchners have embraced a duty to remember and to engage with their city's past. The

NS-Dokumentationszentrum München (Munich Documentation Centre for the History of National Socialism) opened on 30 April 2015, seventy years to the day since the Americans freed the city from the Nazi regime. This centre is the ideal place to start your study of Hitler and National Socialism in Munich when you visit the city. Winfried Nerdinger, the first director of the Documentation Centre, is resolute in his belief that dealing with Munich's toxic history honestly and openly is the best and only way forward. The guiding maxim of the centre is a quotation by Primo Levi: 'It happened, and thus it can happen again.'[1] Our duty, as Nerdinger sees it, is to be informed, to demand an ongoing engagement with the past, and to remember. The message he wants you to take away after your visit to the Documentation Centre is that Hitler and National Socialism intrinsically have something to do with every ordinary person anywhere and anytime. Populist politics feed on fear, prejudice, and uncertainty, particularly in times of crisis. Hitler was a charismatic leader who knew how to speak to the 'common people'. His anti-establishment sentiments and his ethnic-chauvinist nationalism struck a chord with the people of Munich during a time of unprecedented economic, political and social strife in the city. The 'Movement' offered a quick fix to these problems. Over time it became very seductive for many in Munich and across Germany. Guarding against intolerance and rejecting the fanaticism of exclusionary politics is essential for the survival of democracy and, most importantly, the essence of our humanity. As such, please embrace the task set for us by Nerdinger and the Documentation Centre: 'We all carry the responsibility of ensuring that what started in Munich and ended in the Holocaust never happens again.'[2]

Notes

Austrian Beginnings

1. The Gasthaus was sold to Joseph Pommer in 1912. See: *The Hitler Pages*, Braunau am Inn (hitlerpages.com).
2. Adolf Hitler, *Mein Kampf* trans. Ralph Manheim (Boston: Houghton Mifflin Company, 1971) p.3.
3. *Mein Kampf*, p.123; Volker Ullrich, *Hitler. Ascent 1889–1939* (2016), p.17; Werner Maser, *Hitler* (1973) p.25; and Gaab, *Munich* (2008) p.64.
4. Gustav (1885–87); Ida (1886–88); and Otto (1887 – shortly after birth).
5. Ullrich (2016), pp.18–19; Maser, pp.24–5.
6. *Mein Kampf*, p.6.
7. Franz Jetzinger, *Hitler's Youth* (1958) p.57.
8. John Toland, *Hitler* (1997) p.9.
9. *Mein Kampf*, p.6.
10. Ibid, p.7.
11. Bundesarchiv (BA) Berlin-Lichterfelde, Bestand NS 26 (principal NSDAP archive). Johann Weinberger, NS 26/17a; Maser, p.28.
12. Ullrich (2016), pp.20–21; Toland, p.14; and Maser, p.33.
13. *Mein Kampf*, pp.15, 17.
14. BA Berlin-Lichterfelde, 'Unser Führer Adolf Hitler als Student in Steyr von seinem einstigen Lehrer Gregor Goldbacher Prof. i. R', NS 26/17a.
15. Hitler's school report, 16 September 1905; and Heinrich Heim Report, 1942 as cited by Werner Maser. See Maser, p.35, fn.50 and 51.
16. Toland, p.19.
17. BA Berlin-Lichterfelde, Gregor Goldbacher NS 26/17a.
18. Anton Schmidt to Werner Maser, 1969. See Maser, p.37, fn.57.
19. Ulrich (2016), p 22.

Young Hitler in Linz

1. *Mein Kampf*, p.18.
2. August Kubizek, *The Young Hitler I Knew* (2006) p.30; and Brigitte Hamann, *Hitler's Vienna* (1999) pp.21–3.
3. Kubizek, p.23.
4. Kubizek, p.105; and Toland, p.24.
5. Kubizek, p.34.
6. Ibid, p.86.
7. Thomas Mann, 'Versuch über das Theater' in *Essays I: 1883–1914* (2002) p.139.
8. *Mein Kampf*, p.17.
9. Kubizek, pp.76, and 84.
10. Kubizek, p.118; and Ben Novak, 'Hitler's *Rienzi* Experience: Factuality', *Revista de Historia Actual* Vol.5, No.5 (2007) pp.106–7.
11. Novak, pp.105–16; Speer, *Spandau* (1976) p.96;
12. Kubizek, p.85.
13. Hamann (1999), pp.26–7.

14. Ibid, pp.21–2.
15. Sandner, *Hitler*, Band I: 1889–1927 (2016) pp.80–81; and Kubizek, p.125.
16. Toland, pp.24–5; and Kubizek, pp.30, 38, and 127.
17. Maser, pp.39–41; Toland, pp.25–6.
18. Kubizek, p.135.
19. BA Berlin-Lichterfelde, Eduard Bloch, 'Erinnerungen an den Führer und dessen verewigte Mutter' (Nov. 1938) NS 26/65; Ullrich, p.27.
20. Sandner, p.84; and Eduard Bloch, 'My Patient Hitler' in *Collier's Weekly* (15 and 22 March 1941).
21. Hamann (1999), pp.41–2. See also Sandner, p.85.

Vienna
1. Kubizek, p.151.
2. Kubizek, pp.185, 196–7; and Toland, pp.32–3.
3. Karl Kraus as quoted in Ullrich, pp.31–2. See Herre, *Jahrhundertwende 1900* (1998) p.190.
4. *Mein Kampf*, p.123.
5. Hamann (1999), p.274; and Ian Kershaw, *Hitler. 1889-1936: Hubris* (1998) p.41.
6. *Mein Kampf*, pp.76, 92.
7. Hamann (1999), pp.12–13.
8. Hamann (1999), pp.274–5, 302; and Ullrich (2016), pp.35–6.
9. *Mein Kampf*, pp.21, 125.
10. Hamann (1999), pp.404–5; and Timothy W. Ryback, *Hitler's Private Library* (2008) pp.38–9.
11. Kubizek, p.164.
12. Kubizek, pp.160–1, 163
13. Ibid, pp.204–5.
14. Toland, p.36.
15. Hamann (1999), pp.133–4.
16. US Army Military History Research Collection, Carlisle Barracks, Pennsylvania. CIC-agent interview with Paula Hitler, 5 June 1946. Quoted in Toland, p.38.
17. *Mein Kampf*, pp.22; Hamann, p.134.
18. Hitler, *Hitler's Table Talk 1941–1945*. ed. H. Trevor-Roper (2000) p.333, entry on 22–3 February 1942.
19. Hitler, *Table Talk 1941–1945*, p.97 (29 October 1941).
20. Marie Fellinger (née Rinke) as cited in Toland, p.39.
21. Kubizek, pp.239–40; and Sandner, pp.88–9.
22. Toland, pp.40–42; and Kershaw (1998), pp.52–3.
23. Hamann (1999), pp.170–74; and Ullrich (2016), pp.39–42.
24. Karl Honisch as cited in Ullrich (2016), pp.42, and 771 fn.70; Joachimsthaler, *Korrektur* (1989) pp.54–7.
25. Facsimile of the Court report in Maser, *Sturm auf die Republik* (1994) pp.81–3; and Hamann, p.397.
26. *Mein Kampf*, p.125.

Munich
1. Wheatley, *Munich* (2010) p.60.
2. Maxse, *Bavaria in a nutshell* (1910) pp.75–6.

Hitler's Early Years in Munich
1. Heinz, *Germany's Hitler* (1934) p.55; Grammbitter and Lauterbach, *The NSDAP Centre in Munich* (2015) p.25.
2. Heinz, pp.55–6; Maser, pp.51–2; and Joachimsthaler, *Korrektur*, pp.14–17 including a copy of Hitler's police registration form.

3. Nerdinger ed., *Architekturführer* (2002) p.123.
4. *Mein Kampf*, pp.126–7, 163.
5. Linz Police File as quoted in Ullrich (2016), p.48.
6. For Hitler's avoidance of military service in Austria see the description and documents in Franz Jetzinger, *Hitler Jugend: Phantasien, Lügen und Wahrheit* (1956) pp.253–65.
7. Maser, p.52.
8. Wheatley, p.72; Toland, pp.53–54; Ullrich (2016), p.47; and Kershaw (1998), pp.81–2.
9. Kershaw (1998), pp.84–5.
10. Sandner, p.99; and Ullrich (2016), p.49.
11. Arthur Schopenhauer as quoted in Maser, p.59.
12. Richard Wagner, *My Life* (2007) pp.415–16.
13. Thomas Mann, 'Bruder Hitler', *Das Neue Tagebuch*, 25 March 1939.
14. Sandner, p.98.
15. Heinz, p.58; and Maser, p.52.
16. Joachimsthaler, *Hitlers Weg* (2000) p.89; and Maser, p. 71.
17. Joachimsthaler, *Hitlers Weg*, pp.83–6.
18. Sandner, p.99.
19. Gaab, pp.47–8.
20. Jetzinger, *Hitlers Jugend*, p.265.
21. Heinz, p.58.
22. The concept of Volk (people, ethnic community, and nation) had been an underlying idea in German history since the early nineteenth century. It refers to a unique German culture, folklore, people in an ethnic sense, and the German nation.
23. *Mein Kampf*, p.158.
24. Heinz, p.68.
25. *Mein Kampf*, pp.158–9.
26. Sandner, p.106.
27. Thomas Mann, *Reflections of a Nonpolitical Man* (1983) pp.150–5.
28. Toland, p.57.
29. *Mein Kampf*, p.161.
30. Stefan Zweig, *Die Welt von gestern* (1942) p.254.
31. Thomas Mann, 'Gedanken im Kriege', in *Essays II: 1914–1916* ed. Hermann Kurzke (2002) p.32; and Ullrich (2016), p.52.

The Artist Goes to War
1. *Mein Kampf*, p.163.
2. Heinz, pp. 97–8, 110–11.
3. Sandner, pp.107–13; and Toland, pp.58–9.
4. Heinz, p.59.
5. Hitler to Anna Popp, 20 October 1914 in Adolf Hitler *Sämtliche Aufzeichnungen 1905–1924* ed. Eberhard Jäckel with Axel Kuhn (Stuttgart, 1980) no. 24, p.59; and Ullrich (2016), p.53.
6. Sandner, pp.113–15; and Heinz, pp.71–2.
7. Ignaz Westenkirchner as cited in Heinz, p.71.
8. *Mein Kampf*, p.164.
9. Westenkirchner as cited in Heinz, p.73; and Ullrich (2016), pp.54–5.
10. Hitler to Ernst Hepp, 5 February 1915, as cited in Ullrich (2016), p.57; and Maser, pp.78–83.
11. *Mein Kampf*, p.165.
12. Max Amann and Fritz Wiedenmann as cited in Joachimsthaler, *Korrektur*, pp.159–60; and Kershaw (1998), p.91.
13. Hitler to Joseph Popp, 3 December 1914, as cited in Sandner, p.122; Ullrich (2016), p.57; and Maser, pp.83–4.
14. Maser, p.83.

15. Heinz, pp.81–2, and 99.
16. *Mein Kampf*, pp.192–3.
17. Fritz Wiedemann, *Der Mann der Feldherr warden wollte* (1964) p.30.
18. Sandner, p.170.
19. Westenkirchner as cited in Heinz, p.85.
20. *Mein Kampf*, pp.193–200.
21. Wiedemann as cited in Toland, p.66; and Amann as cited in Joachimsthaler, *Korrektur*, p.159. See also Kershaw (1998), pp.92–4.
22. Sandner, p.180.
23. Postcard Hitler sent to Ernst Schmidt, 5 October 1917, as quoted in Jäckel, p.82.
24. Sandner, pp.191 and 197.
25. Wiedemann, pp. 25, 85; and BA Koblenz, N 1720/4. See also Toland, pp.69–70; and Maser, pp.87–8.
26. Sandner, pp.197–200.
27. Hitler, *Table Talk 1941–1945*, p.81 (21/22 October 1941). See also Weber, *Hitler's First War* (2010) pp.218–19.
28. *Mein Kampf*, p.204.
29. Sandner, pp.200–3.

The Soldier Returns
1. Sandner, p.203.
2. Kurt Eisner as cited in Ullrich (2016), p.74. See also Grau, *Kurt Eisner* (2001) pp.343–5.
3. *Mein Kampf*, p.207.
4. Heinz, pp.102–103; Sandner, pp.205–7; Toland, p.74; and Maser, pp.95–6.
5. *Mein Kampf*, p.206.
6. Hauner, *Hitler. A Chronology of his Life and Time* (2008) Entry for 19 November 1918, p.16.
7. Ullrich (2016), p.72; and Ernst Deuerlein, *Hitler* (1969) p.40.

Revolutionary Munich
1. Mark Jones, 'The Crowd in the German November Revolution 1918', Klaus Weinhauer, Anthony McElligott, and Kirsten Heinsohn (eds.), *Germany 1916–23: A Revolution in Context* (2015) p.51.
2. Mitchell, *Revolutions in Bavaria* (1965) p.95; and Grunberger, *Red Rising in Bavaria* (1973) p.33.
3. Fechenbach, *Der Revolutionär Kurt Eisner* (1929) pp.40–42; Buchner, *Revolutionsdokumente* (1921), I:364, and as cited in Large, *Where Ghosts Walked* (1997) p.77.
4. Graf, *Wir sind Gefangene* (1927) pp.551–6, and as cited in Large, p.78.
5. Mitchell, p.96.
6. Ibid., p.98.
7. Grunberger, p.34; and Mitchell, p.99.
8. Fechenbach, pp.43–4; and Fritz Wahl, 'Rätezeit in München', *Gegenwart* (1956) pp.15–16.
9. Grunberger, pp.33–5; and Mitchell, p.100.

Kurt Eisner and the Bavarian Republic
1. Mitchell, p.106.
2. Large, p.84; and Toland, p.78.
3. Nerdinger (ed.), *Munich and National Socialism* (2015) p.19.
4. Mitchell, pp.127–9.
5. Large, pp.85–6; Mitchell, pp.132–3; Luhrssen, *Hammer of the Gods* (2012) p.106; and Ullrich (2016), p.75.
6. *Vorwärts* as cited in Hanser, *Putsch* (1970) p.143.
7. Nettl, *Rosa Luxemburg* vol.1 (1966) p.21.

8. Ullrich (2016), p.74; Mitchell, p.118; Large, pp.84–6; and Luhrssen, p.107.
9. Mitchell, pp. 165, and 255.
10. Thomas Mann, *Diaries 1918–1939* (1984) pp.19–20.
11. Sterling Fishman, 'Prophets, Poets and Priests: A Study of the Men and Ideas that made the Munich Revolution of 1918/19' PhD Dissertation, University of Wisconsin, Madison, 1960) pp.101–2.
12. David Ian Hall, 'Wagner, Hitler, and Germany's Rebirth after the First World War', *War in History* Vol.24, No.2, 2017, pp.170–1; Georg Franz, 'Munich: Birthplace and Centre of the National Socialist German Workers' Party', *Journal of Modern History* Vol.29 (1957) p.326; and Luhrssen, pp.107–11.
13. Nerdinger (2015), p.32; Luhrssen, pp. 98, 154–5; and Large, p.88.
14. Approximately 3,410,000 ballots were cast. See Mitchell, p.217.
15. Mitchell, pp.212–20; and Large, p.89.
16. *Bayerische Kurier*, 'Kurt Eisner' 16 January 1919; *Das Bayerische Vaterland*, 'Ist Herr Eisner Bolschewist?' 23 January 1919.
17. Erich Mühsam as cited in Mitchell, p.246. See Bayerisches Hauptstaatsarchiv (BHS), München. Akten betref. Arbeiter- und Soldatenräte (ASR). 25. Sozialistische Arbeitsgemeinschaft, Sitzungsberichte, 1919. Sitzung der linkssozialistischen Arbeitsgemeinschaft des MAR im Finanzausschusszimmer am Samstage den 11.1.19.
18. Mitchell, pp.270–1.

Eisner's Assassination and the Second Revolution
1. Grunberger, p.84.
2. Large, pp.90–1; Luhrssen, p.114; and Mitchell pp. 271–2.
3. Hanser, p.162.
4. Müller-Meiningen, *Aus Bayerns schwersten Tagen* (1924) pp.122–7.
5. Nerdinger (2015), p.19.
6. Mitchell, pp.278–80.
7. Toland, 78; and Large, 103.
8. Luhrssen, p.117.
9. Sebottendorff, *Bevor Hitler kam* (1933) pp.82–4.
10. Fishmann, p.112.
11. Sebottendorff, p.83.
12. Mitchell, pp.282–3.
13. Kurt Eisner Special Exhibition, Münchner-Stadtmuseum (2017).
14. Sandner, p.208.
15. Grunberger, p.83.
16. Heinrich Mann, *'Kurt Eisner'* (1989) pp.169–70.
17. Grunberger, p.90.
18. Mitchell, pp.283–6; Large, p.104–5.
19. Johannes Hoffmann as cited in Mitchell, p.289.

The Hoffmann Interregnum and the Bavarian Soviet Republics
1. Toland, pp.78–9.
2. Mitchell, pp.301–3.

The First Bavarian Soviet Republic
1. Grunberger pp.94–5; and Large, pp.107–8.
2. Mitchell, p.314.
3. Max Gerstl, 'Die Münchener Räterepublik', *Politische Zeitfragen* (1919) p.340; and Luhrssen, p.119.
4. Sebottendorff, pp.95–6, 102; Luhrssen, pp.118, 122–3; and Grunberger, pp.111–12.

5. Sebottendorff, pp.110–11.
6. Grunberger, pp.112–13; Mitchell, pp.317–18; and Siegert, *Aus Münchens schwerster Zeit* (1928) pp.53–4.
7. Mitchell, pp.318–19; and Grunberger, pp.113–14.

The Second Bavarian Soviet Republic

1. Hayman, *Thomas Mann* (1995) pp.310–11.
2. Luhrssen, pp.132–3; and Large, pp.114–15.
3. Grunberger, pp.124–5; Mitchell, pp.325–6.
4. Large, p.116.
5. Ernst Röhm, *Die Geschichte eines Hochverräters* (1934) pp.100–1.
6. Direktive des Reichswehrministers Noske für die Truppenführung im Kampf um München', *Darstellungen aus den Nachkriegskämpfen deutscher Truppen und Freikorps*, IV: *Die Niederwerfung der Räteherrschaft in Bayern*. (Berlin: *Kriegsgeschichtliche Forschungsanstalt des Heeres*, 1939) pp.213–15.
7. Luhrssen, pp. 130, 135–7.
8. Ernst Toller as cited in Grunberger, p.130.
9. Mitchell, pp.325–7; and Large, 117–18.
10. Salomon, *Das Buch vom deutschen Freikorpskämpfer* (1938) p.101.
11. The ten hostages executed at the Luitpold-Gymnasium were two Hussars, Walter Hindorf and Fritz Linnenbrügger, Art Professor Ernst Berger, and seven Thulists: Franz Karl Freiherr Baron von Teuckert, Walter Nauhaus, Friedrich Wilhelm von Seidlitz, Anton Daumenlang, Walter Deike, Gräfin Haila von Westarp, and Gustav Franz Maria Prince von Thurn und Taxis. The death notice taken out by the Thule Society for members massacred at the Luitpold, and published on 8 May 1919 in the Bayerische Staatszeitung, does not name Thurn und Taxis but lists Karl Stecher of Munich instead as the seventh member killed. See Nerdinger (2015), p.25.
12. Salomon, p.101.
13. Mitchell, p.329.
14. Wollenberg ms. p.202, Erich Wollenberg Papers, Box 1, Hoover Institution. See Large, p.119.
15. Grunberger, pp.137, 144.
16. Large, pp.119–20; and Nerdinger (2015), p.25.
17. Nerdinger (2015), pp.23–4; and Friedrich Wilhelm von Örtzen, *Die deutschen Freikorps 1918–1923* 5 ed. (1939) p.346.
18. Hanser, p.176; Grunberger, pp.144–5; and Large, p.121.
19. Sebottendorff, pp.133–4.
20. Mitchell, p.331; Grunberger, pp.157–8; and Luhrssen, p.143.
21. Lukacs, *The Hitler of History* (2002) p.65.

Hitler Finds his Political Voice in Munich

1. Ernst Schmidt as cited in Heinz, pp.102–3.
2. Ullrich (2016), pp.78–9.
3. Hitler as quoted in Toland, p.80.
4. Kershaw (1998), p.120.
5. Ernst Schmidt as quoted in Heinz, p.110.
6. Quoted in Joachimsthaler, *Korrektur*, p.214; and Ullrich (2016), p.80, fn.28.
7. *Mein Kampf*, p.208.
8. Karl Alexander von Müller, *Mars und Venus. Erinnerungen 1914–1919* (1954) pp.338–9; and Grunberger, pp.152–3.
9. Maser, p.105.
10. *Mein Kampf*, p.215.
11. Ullrich (2016), p.81; and Kershaw (1998), p.123.

12. Toland, p.84.
13. Sandner, 219–20; and Plöckinger, *Unter Soldaten und Agitatoren* (2013), pp.108–10.
14. Toland, pp.84–5.
15. Maser, pp.107–8; Ullrich (2016), 82–3; Kershaw (1998), p.124; Plöckinger (2013), p.128; and Deuerlein, 'Hitlers Eintritt', docs.7&9, pp.199–200.
16. Plöckinger (2013), p.330.
17. Deuerlein, 'Hitlers Eintritt', pp.185, 202–5; Joachimsthaler, *Korrektur*, pp.243–9; Plöckinger (2013), p.257, 334f; and Hauner, p.18. See also Houston Stewart Chamberlain, *Die Zuversicht: Zweite Auflage* (1915) and *Arische Weltanschauung* (1916).
18. Ullrich (2016), p.85; and Deuerlein, 'Hitlers Eintritt', doc.11, p.202f.

Hitler Joins the *Deutsche Arbeiterpartei* (DAP)

1. Richard Evans, *The Coming of the Third Reich* (2004) p.170; and Kershaw (1998), p.125.
2. *Mein Kampf*, p.217.
3. Plöckinger (2013), pp.144, 147–51.
4. Anton Drexler as quoted in Heinz, pp.123–4. See also *Mein Kampf*, pp.218–19.
5. *Mein Kampf*, p.220.
6. Ibid, p.222.
7. Sandner, pp.222–3.
8. *Mein Kampf*, p.224.
9. Sandner 222; and Tyson (2008) p.333.
10. Ullrich (2016), p.88.
11. Maser, p.72.
12. *Mein Kampf*, p.355; Sandner, p.224; Hauner, p.18.
13. *Mein Kampf*, p.355, 358; Sandner, p.224; Hauner, p.18; and Deuerlein, 'Hitlers Eintritt', doc. 14, pp.205–7.
14. *Münchener Beobachter*, 19 November 1919.
15. Hauner, p.18; and Luhrssen, p.160.
16. Heiden, *Adolf Hitler* (1944) pp. 57–8; and Luhrssen, p.173.
17. Large, pp.155–6; and Evans, p.178.
18. Luhrssen, p.173; and Tyson, p.335.
19. Deuerlein, 'Hitlers Eintritt', doc. 16, pp.209–10; and Ullrich (2016), p. 89.
20. *Mein Kampf*, pp.358–9, 365; and Ullrich (2016), p.89.
21. *Mein Kampf*, p.591; Hauner, p.19; Toland, pp.95–6; and Kershaw (1998), p.141, and 644 fn.85.

The Birth of the *Nationalsozialistische Deutsche Arbeiterpartei* (National Socialist German Workers' Party, NSDAP)

1. Heinz, pp.160–1.
2. *Mein Kampf*, pp.368–9, 382–5; and Evans (2004), p.173.
3. Heinz, p.161; and Luhrssen, p.175.
4. Sandner, p.234.
5. *Mein Kampf*, pp.369–70.
6. Hauner, p.20; Evans (2004), pp.179–80; and Ernst Deuerlein (ed.), *Der Aufstieg der NSDAP in Augenzeugenberichten* (1974) pp.108–12.
7. Hans Frank, *Im Angesicht des Galgens: Deutung Hitlers und seiner Zeit auf Grund eigener Erlebnisse und Erkenntnisse* (1953) pp. 39, 52; and Toland, pp.97–8.
8. Heinz, p.162.
9. *Mein Kampf*, p.370.
10. *Völkischer Beobachter*, 28 February 1920.
11. Hauner, p.21; Large, pp.135–139; and Toland, pp.99–101.
12. Nerdinger (2015), pp.29–30; Kershaw, p.171.

13. Sandner, p.236.
14. Hauner, p.21.
15. John Dornberg, *Munich 1923. The Story of Hitler's First Grab for Power* (1982) pp.12, 73; Large, p.140; and Ullrich (2016), p.94.
16. Nerdinger (2015), p.33; and Kershaw (1998), p.171.
17. Large, p.140.
18. Ernst Röhm, *The Memoirs of Ernst Röhm* intro. Eleanor Hancock, trans. Geoffrey Brooks (2012) pp. ix and 38.

Hitler Leaves the Army and Returns to Civilian Life

1. Sandner, pp.238–40; Hauner, p.21; Anton Joachimsthaler, *Hitlers Liste: Ein Dokument persönlicher Beziehungen* (2003) p.219; and Ullrich (2016), p.119.
2. Ernst Hanfstaengl, *The Unknown Hitler: Notes from the Young Nazi Party* (2005) pp.51–2.
3. Sandner, p.240; and Kopleck (2010), p.23.
4. Heinz, pp.131–3; Sandner, p.242.
5. Nerdinger (2015), p.56. For the social composition of the early party membership see Paul Madden, 'Some Social Characteristics of Early Nazi Party Members, 1919–23', *Central European History* v.15, no.1 (March 1982) pp.34–56.
6. *Mein Kampf*, pp.478–9. *Als Suchender* – a Wagnerian term for one who searches for greater fulfilment in life and spiritual redemption, that Hitler was determined to use.
7. Ibid, 491–2.
8. Sandner, p.243; and Brian Deming and Ted Iliff, *Hitler and Munich* (n.d.) p.18.
9. Toland, pp.103–4; Ullrich (2016), p.129; Hall, pp.165–6; and *Mein Kampf*, pp.98–9.
10. Nerdinger (2015), pp.54–5; Sandner, pp.250–7; and Heinz, p.163.
11. Detlef Mühlberger, *Hitler's Voice. The Völkischer Beobachter, 1920–1933* Vol.I Organization & Development of the Nazi Party (2004) pp.20–22, 30 fn.24; Kershaw (1998), pp.155–6; Luhrssen, p.191–2; Toland, p.108; Sandner, 260–26; and Hauner, p.25.
12. Sandner, p.261.
13. *Völkischer Beobachter*, (henceforth *VB*), Nos. 1/2, 6 January 1921; Sandner, p.262; and Hauner, pp.25–6.
14. In April 1921, the Reparations Commission reduced the payment to 132 billion gold marks, which Hitler later referred to as 'the insane sum of a hundred billion gold marks' in *Mein Kampf*. See: Kershaw, pp.157, 652 fn.128; and *Mein Kampf*, pp.497–8.
15. *Mein Kampf*, pp.498–500; and Toland pp.109–10.
16. *Mein Kampf*, pp.500–501.
17. Ullrich (2016), p.122.
18. *Mein Kampf*, p.501; and Toland, p.110.
19. Ernst Deuerlein ed., *Der Aufstieg*, p.131.
20. *VB*, No.16, 3 March 1921.
21. Julius Streicher joined the NSDAP in Munich on Friday 20 October 1922. He also published the crude anti-Semitic newspaper *Der Stürmer* from 1923 to 1945. See Sandner, p.306; and Mühlberger, p.71, fn.104.
22. Sandner, p.274; and Ullrich (2016), pp.109–11.

Hitler Takes Control of the NSDAP

1. Hauner, pp.29–30; Sandner, p.274; and Kershaw (1998), p.163.
2. Deuerlein, *Der Aufstieg*, pp.138–40; Sandner, pp.274–5; Hauner, p.30; Mühlberger, p.28.
3. Deuerlein, *Der Aufstieg*, 136–41; Hauner, p.30; and Sandner, p.275.
4. Article 5 of the new party statutes. See Jeremy Noakes and Geoffrey Pridham (eds.) *Nazism 1919–1945 Vol.1: The Rise to Power 1919–1934* (1983) pp.21–2.

5. For the full terms of the NSDAP's new charter of 29 July 1921 see Albrecht Tyrell, *Vom 'Trommler' zum Führer: Der Wandel von Hitlers Selbstverständnis zwischen 1919 und 1924 und die Entwicklung der NSDAP* (1975) pp.132–50; and *Mein Kampf*, pp.349–50.

6. Sandner, p.275; Hauner, p.31; Mühlberger, p.29; Ullrich (2016), p.113; Toland, pp.111–12; and Kershaw (1998), p.164.

7. *VB*, No.60, 31 July 1921.

8. Heβ joined the NSDAP in 1920, was a fanatical admirer of Hitler, and Deputy *Führer* from 1933–41. See Dietrich Orlow, 'Rudolf Hess: Deputy *Führer*', in Ronald Smelser and Rainer Zitelmann (eds.), *The Nazi Elite* (1993) pp.74–84.

9. Heβ quoted in Werner Maser, *Die Frühgeschichte der NSDAP: Hitlers Weg bis 1924* (1965) p.281.

Hitler Builds the Party

1. 'To our German Youth!' in *VB*, No.64, 14 August 1921. See also Mühlberger, pp.30–31, and document 14, pp.54–5.

2. Deuerlein, *Der Aufstieg*, p.46; Sandner, pp.278, 280; Evans (2004), pp.180–81; and Ullrich (2016), p.115.

3. Sandner, p.280; and Evans (2004), p.183. For a comprehensive history of the SA see Daniel Siemens, *Stormtroopers. A New History of Hitler's Brownshirts* (2017).

4. *Mein Kampf*, pp.502–6; Siemens, p.13; and Heinz, pp134–8.

5. *Mein Kampf*, p.505.

6. Magdalena Schweyer as cited in Heinz, p.137–8.

7. Hauner, p.33; Sandner, p.281; Siemens, p.13; and *Mein Kampf*, p.506.

8. *VB*, Nos.84&85, 5&9 November 1921.

9. *VB*, No.85, 9 November 1921; and *Mein Kampf*, p.591.

10. Nerdinger (2015), p.55.

11. *Mein Kampf*, pp.496–7.

12. See *National Socialism in Munich*, City of Munich-Stadtarchiv, 2008, p.25.

13. Hauner p.34; and Sandner, p.285.

14. *VB* No. 19, 8 March 1920 and No.70, 18 April 1923. See also Mühlberger, pp.31–2, and Docs. 15 & 16, pp.55–7.

15. Sandner, pp.287–8, 291–3, and 296.

16. Toland, pp.116–17; Kershaw (1998), p.174; Large, pp.141–2; and Norman H. Baynes (ed.), *The Speeches of Adolf Hitler April 1922–August 1939* Vol.1 (1942) pp.21–41.

17. Baynes, pp.40–41.

18. *Mein Kampf*, p.547–8; and Kurt G.W. Ludecke, *I Knew Hitler* ed. Bob Carruthers (2013) pp.19–20.

19. Coburg, the former co-capital of the Duchy of Saxony-Coburg-Gotha, was a separate administrative entity up to 1920 when it became part of Bavaria. See: *Mein Kampf*, pp.548–52; Toland, pp.119–21; and Ullrich (2016), p.116.

20. *Mein Kampf*, pp.549–50.

21. Ibid., p.551.

22. Hauner, p.36; and Mühlberger, p.71.

23. Hauner, p.37; Sandner, p.309; Hanfstaengl, p.28 and introduction by Richard Evans, p. 17; and Nerdinger (2015), p.58.

24. Sandner, p.309; Nerdinger (2015), p.78; Mühlberger, p.410; and Ullrich (2016), p.121.

25. Mühlberger, p.150; and Ullrich (2016), p.210.

26. Ludecke, p.21.

27. Kershaw (1998), pp.247–50.

28. The Hitler Pages, 'Hitler's Favourite Bars and Restaurants', p.5; Ullrich (2016), pp.120–21; and Large, pp.154–5.

29. Jäckel (1991), p.727.

30. Kershaw (1998), pp.158–9; Sandner, p.308; and Nerdinger (2015), pp.42–5.
31. Nerdinger (2015), pp.51, 55; Sandner, pp.309 and 310. On 30 November, Hitler spoke at the Hofbräuhaus, the Löwenbräukeller, the Bürgerbräukeller, the Schwabingerbräu, and the Thomasbräukeller. On 13 December he spoke at the Hofbräuhaus, the Franziskanerkeller on Residenzstraße 9 and Weinstraße 5, the Salvatorkeller, the Löwenbräukeller, the Hackerbräukeller at Theresienhöhe 4, the Bürgerbräukeller, the Hofbräukeller, the Gasthaus 'Großer Wirt' at Hohensalzaer Straße 1, the Restaurant 'Zur Blüte' at Blütenstraße 18, and the Hirschbräukeller at Herbststraße 11.

1923 – the Beer Hall Putsch

1. On Armistice Day 1918, the Mark was 7.45 to the US dollar. See Toland, p.131.
2. Nerdinger (2015), p.66; Steven Lehrer, *Hitler Sites* (2002) p.67.
3. Sandner, p.313; Eberhard Jäckel and Axel Kuhn (eds.), *Hitler. Sämtliche Aufzeichnungen 1905–1924* (1980) pp.783–5; and Large, p.162.
4. Ullrich (2016), pp.134–5; and Large, pp. 163–4.
5. Karl Alexander von Müller as quoted in Toland, p.132.
6. *Mein Kampf*, p.552; and Siemens, p.41.
7. Hauner, pp.38–9.
8. *Mein Kampf*, pp.552–3; and Mühlberger, p.30.
9. Sandner p.327; Kopleck, p.64; Hatheway (1999) p.15; Joseph Berchtold, an original member of the *Stoßtrupp Hitler* as cited in Heinz, p.172; and von Halasz (2007) p.41.
10. Sandner, p.325; Hauner, p.40; and *Mein Kampf*, pp.677–82.
11. Sandner, pp.325–6; and Ulrich Chaussy (2005) pp.26–30, 61–4.
12. Siemens, pp.20–22; Sandner, p.328.
13. Sandner, pp.328–36; Hauner, pp.40–1; Hitler, Table Talk 1941–1945, pp.164–5 (2/3 January 1942); and Geoffrey R. Walden, *Hitler's Berchtesgaden. A Guide to Third Reich Sites in the Berchtesgaden and Obersalzberg Area* (2014).
14. Hauner, p.42; Ullrich (2016), pp.140–14 ; and Evans (2004), p.190.
15. Nerdinger (2015), p.66; Eric D. Weitz, *Weimar Germany. Promise and Tragedy* (2007) pp.140–1.
16. Ullrich (2016), p.143.
17. Heinz, pp.173–5; Evans (2004), p.192; Noakes and Pridham (eds.), *Nazism* Vol.1 (1983), pp.26–7.
18. *Oberfränkische Zeitung* (*OfZ*), 1 Oktober 1923.
19. Alexander Spring, 'Siegfried Wagner. Zur 70. Wiederkehr seines Geburtstages', *Bayreuther Festspielführer* 1939, p.22.
20. Nationalarchiv der Richard-Wagner-Stiftung, Bayreuth (NRWB). Chamberlain, Briefe 3, ii.124–5, letter from Houston Stewart Chamberlain to Adolf Hitler, 7 October 1923.
21. *VB*, 3 October, 1923. See also Brigitte Hamann, *Winifred Wagner. A Life at the Heart of Hitler's Bayreuth* trans. Alan Bance (2005) pp.56–61; and David Ian Hall, 'Wagner, Hitler, and Germany's Rebirth after the First World War', *War in History* Vol.24, No.2 (2017) pp.154–75.
22. Harold J. Gordon, *Hitler and the Beer Hall Putsch* (1972) pp.243–4.
23. Dornberg, pp.31, 46; Gordon, pp.270–3.
24. Hauner, p.44; Dornberg, pp.47–8.
25. Hanfstaengl, p.94.
26. Sandner, p.360; Hauner, p.44; Toland, pp.152–3; Ullrich (2016), p.146; and Large, pp.174–5.
27. Hanfstaengl, pp.93–4.
28. Dornberg, p.51; and Large, p.175.
29. Hanfstaengl as quoted in Toland, p.153.
30. Dornberg, pp.19, 25–6, 49–50.
31. Hauner, p.45.
32. Ullrich (2016), p.148; and Dornberg, p.89.

33. Göring as cited in Dornberg, p.92; and Large, p.177.

34. Professor Müller as quoted in Large, pp.177–8.

35. Dornberg, pp.95–6.

36. Dornberg, pp.102–8; and Ullrich (2016), p.150.

37. Dornberg, pp.85–6, 129–31.

38. Large, pp.178–9; Ullrich (2016), p.151; and Toland, p.161.

39. Toland, p.164; Ullrich (2016), p.154; Nerdinger (2015), p.55.

From the Bürgerbräukeller to the Feldherrnhalle

1. Hitler as quoted in Large, p.183.

2. Joseph Berchtold in Heinz, pp.181–4.

3. Hans Hinkel, *Einer unter Hunderttausend* (1938) p.107.

4. Hamann (2005), p.64; and Large, pp.183–6.

5. Joseph Berchtold in Heinz, p.185; and Dornberg, pp.294–6.

6. Baker (1931) p.36.

7. Helene Hanfstaengl as quoted in Ullrich (2016), p.155.

8. Sandner, pp.361–3; Heinz, p.188; Dornberg, p.304, 313–14.

9. General von Lossow's telegram to General von Seeckt in Heinz, p.188.

10. *Mein Kampf*, pp.595; and Nerdinger (2015), p.69.

11. Stefan Zweig, 'Incipit Hitler' in *The World of Yesterday. Memoirs of a European* trans. Anthea Bell (2011) pp.386.

12. Karl Arnold, '*Der Münchner*', *Simplicissimus*, Nr.36, München, 3 Dezember 1923.

Hitler in Prison

1. Sandner, p.363; Franz Hemmrich in Heinz, pp.194–6; and Institut für Zeitgeschichte München (IfZ) Franz Hemmrich, 'Erinnerungen eines Gefängnisbeamten', ED 153–1, pp.6–8; and Lurker, *Hitler hinter Festungsmauern* (1933) p.6.

2. Die Regierung von Oberbayern an das Generalstaatskommissariat, 13 November 1923, Ernst Deuerlein (ed.), *Der Hitler-Putsch. Bayerische Dokumente zum 8/9 November 1923* (1962), Nr. 118, p.373.

3. Anton Drexler as cited in Heinz, p.189.

4. IfZ Franz Hemmrich ED 153–1 p.20; and Heinz 189–90.

5. Anton Drexler as cited in Toland, p.182.

6. Hans Knirsch as cited in Toland, p.183; and Ullrich (2016), p.158; and King, *The Trial of Adolf Hitler. The Beer Hall Putsch and the Rise of Nazi Germany* (2017) pp.131–2.

7. Sandner, p.364; and Heinz, p.190.

8. Sandner, p.365; King, pp.137–138; and Toland, pp.183–4.

9. Hamann (2005), p.71.

10. King, p.136.

11. Angela Raubal as cited in Toland, p.184.

12. Sandner, p.365.

The Trial

1. Nerdinger (2015), p.70; David Clay Large, pp.191–2; and King, pp.139–41.

2. Ullrich (2016), p.159; Deuerlein, *Aufstieg*, p.205; King, pp.143, 149–50; and Gritschneder, *Bewährungsfrist* (1990) p.63.

3. *New York Times*, 27 February 1924.

4. *Das Bayerische Vaterland*, 27 February 1924.

5. King, p.148; and Range, *1924: The Year That Made Hitler* (2016) p.126.

6. Sandner, pp.367–70.

7. *Völkischer Kurier*, 27 February 1924.

8. King, p.151.

9. *Münchner Neueste Nachrichten*, 27 February 1924; *Münchener Post* , 27 February 1924; and *Reichspost (Wein)* 28 February 1924; Range, p.132; and *Hitler-Prozess (Antsgericht München*, trial transcript) p.3.
10. King, pp.152–3; and *Hitler-Prozess*, pp.24–5.
11. Range, pp.133–4; Gritschneder, *Der Hitler-Prozess* (2001) p.65.
12. Deuerlein, *Aufstieg*, p.215; Gordon, p.480; and Nerdinger (2015), p.70.
13. Kershaw (1998), p.217; Large, p.192.
14. *Der Hitler-Prozess* as cited in Ullrich (2016), p.160, fn.116.
15. *Amtsgericht München* transcript of the trial, National Archives, Washington, DC. NA T84 EAP 105/7, 120–2 as cited in King, p163; and Range, p.143.
16. Trial transcript. NA T84 EAP 105/7, 127 as cited in King.
17. *Das Bayerische Vaterland*, 27 February 1924; and *Markt Grafinger Wochenblatt*, 29 February 1924.
18. *Vossische Zeitung, Morgen Ausgabe* (Morning Edition) 27 February 1924.
19. *Vancouver Sun*, 27 February 1924; and the *Daily Express*, 27 February 1924.
20. *Münchener Post*, 29 February 1924.
21. *Münchener Neueste Nachrichten* as cited in Bauer and Piper, *München* (1993) p.324.
22. Sackett, *Popular Entertainment, Class, and Politics in Munich, 1900–1923* (1982) pp.99–100; Sabine Sünwoldt, *Weiß Ferdl. Eine Weiss-Blaue Karriere* (1983) pp.77–85; and Gaab, p.67.
23. Range, p.144.
24. Sandner, p.369; and King, pp.231–2.
25. *Völkischer Kurier*, 14 March 1924.
26. *Allgemeine Rundschau*, 20 March 1924.
27. *Vorwärts*, 28 March 1924.
28. Trial transcript. NA T84/2 EAP 105/7, 2869–2870 as cited in King, pp.276–8.
29. Trial transcript. NA T84/2 EAP 105/7, 2897–2916 as cited in King, pp.279–85; *Der Hitler-Prozess* as cited in Ullrich (2016), p.161; Toland, pp.191–192.
30. Sandner, pp.370–1; and King, pp.288–9.

The Verdict
1. Gritschneder (1990), pp.92–4; Range, pp.177–80; and Toland, pp.192–3.
2. King, pp.294–5; *Vorwärts*, 2 April 1924; and 'All Fools Day' in the *Times* of London, 2 April, 1924.
3. Deuerlein, *Aufstieg*, pp.225–7; and Kershaw (1998), p.216.
4. Range, p.181.
5. Hanser, p.396.
6. The NSDAP was the third largest party in Bavaria (17.1% of the vote), behind the BVP (32.8%) and the SPD (17.2%). Jablonski, *The Nazi Party in Dissolution* (1989) pp.82–3; Geoffrey Pridham, *Hitler's Rise to Power* (1973) p.18; and Large, p.194.
7. *Simplicissimus*, Nr.51, München, 17 März 1924.
8. Thacker, *Goebbels* (2009) pp.33–4; Peter Longerich, *Goebbels* (2015) pp.36–7; and Fest, *Hitler* (1974) p.200.

Back in Landsberg Prison
1. King, pp.304–5.
2. Hemmrich as cited in Heinz, p.197; Fest, p.199.
3. Ludecke, p.177.
4. Kershaw (1998), pp.211, 225; and Evans (2004), p.199.
5. *Abschrift. Besuche für den Festungsgefangenen Adolf Hitler* reproduced in Nerdinger (2015), p.73; Hanfstaengl, pp.120–1; and King, pp.310–11.
6. Sandner, p.377; and King, pp.314–15.
7. From Elsa Bruckmann's essay 'My First Trip to the Führer' written in 1933, as cited in Ullrich (2016), pp.166–7.

8. Hanfstaengl, p.121.
9. Lurker, p.20; Franz Hemmrich's memoirs, IfZ München, ED 153–1, pp.46–7; Hemmrich as cited in Heinz, p.198.
10. Ullrich (2016), pp.170–1.
11. Drexler as cited in Frank, pp.48–9; and Toland, p.196.
12. Röhm, *Memoirs*, pp.210–11; Ludecke, pp.181, 184–6.
13. *Völkischer Kurier*, 7 and 29 July 1924; Deuerlein, *Aufstieg*, pp.235–6; and Jablonski, pp.96–8. (and Ullrich (2016), p.172; Toland, p196, 200; King, p.318).

Mein Kampf
1. Plöckinger, *Geschichte eines Buches* (2011) pp.11–15; King, p.320; and Range, p.188.
2. Franz Hemmrich's memoirs, IfZ München, ED 153–1, p.35; Plöckinger, pp.21–6; Hauner, pp.47–8; Range, pp.188–91; and Evans (2004), p.197; (and Ullrich (2016), p.173)
3. Evans (2004), p.196.
4. Fest, p.202.
5. Ullrich (2016), p.176.
6. Letter König Ludwig II to Wagner, 28 May 1865. Otto Strobel, ed., *König Ludwig II und Richard Wagner: Briefwechsel* 5 vols (1936–39).
7. Stewart Spencer, 'Autobiographical Writings', in Barry Millington, ed., *The Wagner Compendium* (1992) pp.183–6.
8. Florian Beierl und Othmar Plöckinger, 'Neue Dokumente zu Hitlers Buch "*Mein Kampf*"' *Vierteljahrshefte für Zeitgeschichte* 57, nr.2 (2009) pp.261–79.
9. Deuerlein, *Aufstieg*, p.238. Otto Leybold's report, 15 September 1924.
10. Rudolf Heß to Ilsa Pröhl, 23 July 1924 in Rudolf Heß, *Briefe 1908–1933* ed. Wolf Rüdiger Heß (1987) p.347; Hemmrich as cited in Heinz, p.213; and Ullrich (2016), p.174.
11. Ilse Heß to John Toland, 1971 interview. See Toland, p.199.
12. *Mein Kampf*, p.v. The 'blood witnesses' as Hitler called them were, in alphabetical order: Felix Alfarth, Andreas Bauriedl, Theodor Casella, Wilhelm Ehrlich, Martin Faust, Anton Hechenberger, Oskar Körner, Karl Kuhn, Karl Laforce, Kurt Neubauer, Claus von Pape, Theodor von der Pfordten, Johann Rickmers, Dr Max Erwin von Scheubner-Richter, Lorenz Ritter von Stransky, and Wilhelm Wolf.
13. Plöckinger (2011), pp.76–8, 86–9, 177–82; Ullrich (2016), pp.174–175; and King, pp.322–3.
14. Plöckinger (2011), p.406; and Range, p.197.

Parole Postponed
1. Toland, pp.200–1; and Deuerlein, *Aufstieg*, pp.238–9.
2. Gritschneder (1990), pp.101–7.
3. Ullrich (2016), pp.181–2; Fest, pp.218–19; Kershaw (1998), pp.235–7; King, pp.325–7; and Gritschneder (1990), pp.116–18.
4. Lurker, p.63; Gritschneder (1990), pp.128–30; and Hauner, p.49.
5. Ullrich (2016), p.182; Deuerlein, *Aufstieg*, pp.239–40; and D.C. Watt, '*Die bayerischen Bemühungen um Ausweisung Hitlers 1924*' *Vierteljahrshefte für Zeitgeschichte*, 6 (1958) pp.270–80.
6. Otto Leybold cited in Jäckel, p.1247; and Hauner, p.49
7. Hemmrich as cited in Heinz, pp.222–4; and Hoffmann, *Hitler was my Friend* (2011) p.61.
8. Fest, p.219; Toland, p.203.
9. Evans (2004), p.199.
10. Otto Leybold to Franz Hemmrich as cited in Heinz, p.224.
11. Hoffmann, pp.60–1; Hitler, *Table Talk 1941–1945*, pp.285–6 (3 February 1942).
12. Hoffmann, p.61; and Heß, *Briefe*, (20 December 1924), p.260.
13. Sandner, p.385; and Fest, p.223.
14. Nerdinger (2015), p.58.
15. Hanfstaengl, pp.127–8; and Toland, pp.203–4.

Rebuilding the Party

1. Jochmann (ed.), *Nationalsozialismus* (1963) pp.193–4; and Kershaw (1998), p.262.
2. Held as cited in Clemens Vollnhals, 'Der Aufstieg ser NSDAP in München 1925 bis 1933: Forderer und Gegner', Bauer (ed.), *München* (2002) p.157; and Toland, p.206.
3. Mühlberger, p.105; and Hauner, p.50.
4. '*Die Bewegung ist wieder frei!*', *Völkischer Beobachter*, 1 Ausgabe, München, Donnerstag, 26 February 1925.
5. Adolf Hitler, '*Zum Wiedererstehen unserer Bewegung!*', *VB*, 26 February 1925, p.1; and Mühlberger, Doc.43, pp.121–3.
6. '*Grundfäßliche Richtlinien für die Neuaufstellung der Nationalsozialistischen Deutschen Arbeiter-Partei*', *VB*, 26 February 1925, p.2; and Mühlberger, Doc.44, pp.124–5.
7. Toland, pp.207–8.
8. Large, p.203; and Institut für Zeitgeschichte (ed.), *Hitler Reden, Schriften, Anordnungen. Februar 1925 bis Januar 1933* (1992) vol.I, pp.14–16.
9. Max Amann as cited in Fest, p.227.
10. Hermann Esser as cited in Heinz, p.228.
11. *VB*, Nr.2, 7 March 1925. This was the second issue of the *VB*, and it contained a lengthy report of the meeting. Rosenberg returned as the editor-in-chief, and the paper appeared as a daily again from 4 April 1925. See also Mühlberger, pp.107–8, fn.18; and Hauner, pp.50–51.
12. Sandner, pp.391–2; and Toland, p.208.
13. Evans (2004), pp.202–3; Large, pp.204–5; Ludecke, pp.206–8; Dietrich Orlow, *The History of the Nazi Party*, Vol.I: 1919–1933 (1971) pp.66–7; and Stachura, *Gregor Strasser* (1983).
14. Fest, p.224; and Noakes and Pridham, vol.1, pp.40–41.
15. Evans (2004), p.81; Kershaw (1998), p.267; Hauner, p.51; Large, p.203; and Hermann Esser as cited in Heinz, p.228.

The Charismatic Führer

1. d'Almeida, *High Society in the Third Reich* (2008) p.28; Toland, p.209; and Rees, *The Dark Charisma of Adolf Hitler* (2012).
2. Fest, pp.264–5; Ullrich (2016), p.211; and Heß, *Briefe*, (27 April 1927), p.380.
3. Nerdinger (2015), p.58.
4. Stratigakos, *Hitler at Home* (2015) pp.109–10.
5. Wistrich, *Weekend in Munich* (1995) pp.33–5; Kopleck, *Munich 1933–1945*, p.11.
6. The four operas that make up *The Ring* are: *Das Rheingold*, *Die Walküre*, *Siegfried*, and *Götterdämmerung*.
7. Adolf Hitler as cited in Hamann (2005), pp.108; and Adolf Hitler, *Monologe im Führerhauptquartier 1941–1944* ed. Jochmann (1980) 24/25 January 1942, pp.224–5.
8. Hitler, *Table Talk 1941–1945*, pp.348–9 (28 February-1 March 1942).
9. Sandner, pp.416–20.
10. Kershaw (1998), pp.259–61; Mühlberger, pp.108–10; *VB*, No.19, 19–20 April 1925; and Kershaw, *The 'Hitler Myth'* (1987) pp.25–47.
11. Hauner, 51; Evans (2004), pp.201–2; Kershaw (1998), pp.268–9; and *VB*, No.12, 10 April 1925, and No.25, 26–27 April 1925.
12. Röhm, *Memoirs*, p.231.
13. Ibid., pp.232–3.
14. Evans (2004), p.201; and Kershaw (1998), p.265.
15. Noakes and Pridham, vol.1, pp.40–46; Jochmann, pp.207–9, 212–13.
16. Goebbels, *The Early Goebbels Diaries: 1925–1926* ed. H. Heiber (1962) pp.66–7.
17. Noakes and Pridham, vol.1, pp.47–8; Ullrich (2016), pp.196–9.
18. After Röhm refused to accept Hitler's terms for the reconstituted *Sturmabteilung* (SA), Hitler created a new elite organization, the *Schutzstaffel* (SS) out of his personal bodyguard,

the *Stoßtrupp Adolf Hitler*, in April 1925. See Koehl, *The Black Corps* (1983) pp.21–5; and Höhne, *The Order of the Death's Head* (1980) pp.23–5.

19. Goebbels, *Tagebücher*, part I, vol.1/2, p.103 (6 July 1926); Hitler, *Reden, Schriften, Anordnungen*, vol.2, part I, doc. 3–7, pp.4–25; and Ullrich (2016), p.199.
20. Sandner, 482–485; Hauner, p.55; Evans (2004), p.206; Toland, p.219.

Creation of the Party Cadre and National Organization

1. Hoffmann, p.61.
2. Kopleck, *Munich 1933–1945*, pp.44–5; and Ullrich (2016), p.209.
3. Adolf Hitler as cited in Toland, p.210.
4. Mühlberger, p.112, 116; Noakes and Pridham, vol.1, p.40; and Kershaw (1998), p.276.
5. Noakes and Pridham, vol.1, pp.48–9; and Evans (2004), pp.207.
6. Mühlberger, pp117–18; and Hoffmann, p.130.
7. From Frank's speech to the BNSDJ at the Nürnberg Rally in 1929, *VB*, No.180, 6 August 1929; and Mühlberger, pp291–2.
8. *VB*, No.9, 11 January 1929; and Mühlberger, p292, and Doc.140, A 'Combat League for German Culture'!, p.346.
9. Nerdinger (2015), p.86.
10. Mühlberger, p292.
11. *VB*, No. 150, 3 July and No. 156, 10 July 1926; Mühlberger, p234–5; and Evans (2004), pp.212–13.
12. Evans (2004), pp.211, 215–16; Mühlberger, p.431; Nerdinger (2015), p.76; and Tyrell (ed.), *Führer befiehl* (1969) p.352, Doc.147.
13. Evans (2004), p.217.
14. Görtemaker, *Eva Braun* (2012) pp.66–9; Thamer, *Der Nationalsozialismus* (2002) pp.66–8; and Klabunde, *Magda Goebbels* (1999).
15. Kershaw (1998), p.260.
16. The twelve central 'tenets' of Nazi ideology in no particular order are: Arierkult, Führerprinzip, Völkischer Nationalismus, Rassismus, Xenophobie, Eugenik, Antisemitismus, Sozialdarwinismus, Arbeit und Brot, Anti-Marxismus, Lebensraum, and Geschlechterordnung. See the mind-maps illustrating the flexible structure of Nazi ideology in Nerdinger (2015), pp.62–3.

Erholung (Rest and Recovery)

1. Hitler as cited in Ludecke, p.206.
2. Hanfstaengl, p.142; Görtemaker, p.15; Large, p.224; and von Halasz, pp.17–18, 65.
3. Heß, *Briefe*, (24 October 1926) p.371.
4. Goebbels, *Tagebücher*, part I, vol. 2/2, p.210 (3 February 1932).
5. Ullrich (2016), p.404.
6. Beierl, *Geschichte des Kehlsteins* (1994/2001) p.7; Joachimsthatler, *Hitlers Liste*, pp.285, 288–9; Chaussy, pp.45–48, gives the wrong date spring 1927; Stratigakos, p.13; Kershaw (1998), p.283; Ullrich (2016), p.214.
7. Ilse Heß as cited in Toland, p.229; Sigmund, *Des Führers bester Freund* (2003) pp.154, 159; and Ullrich (2016), p.278.
8. Goebbels, *Tagebücher*, part I, vol. 2/2 pp.135 and 154 (27 October and 22 November 1931); and Hoffmann, p.148–51, 156–9.
9. Goebbels, *Tagebücher*, part I, vol.1/3 p.295 (2 August 1929); and Hauner, p.64.
10. Fest, pp.266, 322; Stratigakos, pp.19–20; and Joachimsthatler, *Hitlers Liste*, p.324.
11. Beierl, p.7; Joachimsthatler, *Hitlers Liste*, pp.294–6, 299; and Le Tissier, *The Third Reich* (2005) pp.40–3.
12. Kopleck, *Munich 1933–1945*, p.26; and Stratigakos, pp.14–18.
13. Hilmes, *Cosima Wagner* (2010) p.271; Hamann (2005), p.141; and Stratigakos, pp.61–2.

14. Hauner, p.64; Stratigakos, pp.48–9; and Ullrich (2016), p.279.
15. Görtemaker, p.16; and Gun, *Eva Braun-Hitler* (1969) pp.42–3, 49–50.
16. Sandner, p.712, 862–3; Hoffmann, p.155; Görtemaker, pp.12–13; Gun, pp.52–3; and Large, pp.225–6.
17. Hamann (2005), p.165.
18. Statements to the police from Georg and Anni Winter, Maria Reichert, and Anna Kirmair in Sigmund, 'Geli Raubal' (1998) pp.148–9. See also Hoffmann, p.152; Sigmund, *Des Führers bester Freund*, pp.171–3; and Ullrich (2016), p.281.
19. Hitler's statement to the police on 19 September 1931 is reprinted in Sigmund, *Des Führers bester Freund*, pp.175–6. See also Hoffmann, pp. 152–5; Sigmund, 'Geli Raubal', pp.150, 154; and Ullrich (2016), p.281.
20. *Münchener Post*, ('A Mysterious Affair: Suicide of Hitler's Niece'), 21 September 1931; and the retraction '*Rätselhafte Affäre*'), 22 September 1931.
21. See *Fränkische Tagespost*, ('Suicide in Hitler's apartment'), 21 September 1931; *Freistaat*, ('Hitler's family drama'), 22 September 1931; and *Regensburger Echo*, ('Tragedy in Munich's Bogenhause'), 25 September 1931; and *Die Fanfare*, ('Hitler's Lover Commits Suicide: Bachelors and Homosexuals as Nazi Leaders'), 2 October 1931 in *BA Berlin-Lichterfelde*, NS 26/13. See also Ullrich (2016), p.831 fn.78; and Stratigakos, pp.20–1.
22. Hans Frank, pp.90–1.
23. Stratigakos, pp.21, 23.
24. Ullrich (2016), pp.267–8; Maser, pp.194–208; and Kershaw, *The 'Hitler Myth'*, pp.43–6; Kershaw (1998), pp.351–5. Two examples of puerile innuendo masquerading as history are Pope, *Munich Playground* (2015/1941) and Sayer and Botting, *The Women Who Knew Hitler* (2004). See the bibliographies of both these books for more examples in this genre of dubious history on Hitler's personal life.
25. Anni Winter to Werner Maser, 1969 interview. See Maser, p.203, fn.53.
26. Görtemaker, p.51.
27. Hauner, pp.85, 109; and Maser, pp.198, 202–3.
28. Schroeder, *He Was My Chief* (2009) pp.133, 141–3; Joachimsthaler, *Hitlers Liste*, pp.441–2; and Ullrich (2016), pp.288–9.
29. Traudl Junge, *Until the Final Hour* (2003) pp.58, 75–7, 100; and Görtemaker, pp.100, 173.
30. Wagener, *Hitler aus nächster Nähe* (1978) p.99; and Ullrich (2016), p.287.
31. Junge, p.107.
32. Hitler, *Table Talk* (16/17 January 1942), p.218.
33. Hoffmann, p.159; Schroeder, p.133; and Large, p.225.
34. Ullrich (2016), pp.287–8.

The Path to Power

1. 'Table on the percentages of votes cast in favour of the NSDAP', 20.v.28, as cited in Noakes and Pridham, vol.1, p.83; Dieter Nohlen and Philip Stöver, *Elections in Europe. A data handbook* (…) pp.777, 790; and Large, p.221.
2. Hermann Esser as cited in Heinz, p.231.
3. SA leader from 1 November 1926, Pfeffer dropped the Jewish-sounding 'Solomon' and called himself Franz von Pfeffer. See Mühlberger, p.114.
4. Straumann, *1931 – Debt, Crisis, and the Rise of Hitler* (2019) p.8.
5. Noakes and Pridham, vol.1, p.58; Evans (2004), pp.234–5; and Kershaw (1998), p.318.
6. Evans (2004), p.233.
7. 'Reich Propaganda Department directives to all *Gaue* and all *Gau* Propaganda Departments, March–April 1932, as cited in Noakes and Pridham, vol.1, p.73.
8. Kopleck, *Munich 1933–1945*, p.7.
9. Grammbitter and Lauterbach, pp.10–11; and Sandner, p.750.
10. Kopleck, *Munich 1933–1945*, p.7; Hauner, p.67; Sandner, pp.759, 789; and Grammbitter and Lauterbach, pp.11–12.

11. Ullrich (2016), pp.249–50; Heusler, *Das Braune Haus* (2008) pp.156–7; Grammbitter and Lauterbach, p.12; and Hermann Esser as cited in Heinz, p.231.

The Breakthrough
1. Nerdinger (2015), pp.92, 94; Sandner, p.782; and Hauner, p.68.
2. Hermann Esser as cited in Heinz, p.233; and *The Times* and the *Daily Mail* as cited in Hauner, p.68.
3. Dietrich, *The Hitler I Knew* (2010) p.15.
4. Goebbels, *Tagebücher*, part I, vol. 2/2, p.241 (13 March 1932); and Ullrich (2016), p.299.
5. Goebbels, *Tagebücher*, part I, vol. 2/2, pp.241–2 (14 March 1932); Large, p.227; and Ullrich (2016), p.299. Hindenburg secured 19,300,000 votes (53%) and Hitler received 13,400,000 (36.8%). See Sandner, pp.913, 924: Hauner, p.80.
6. Hauner, pp.83–4; Large, pp.228–9; Sandner, pp.976, 982–3; and Ullrich (2016), pp.316–27.
7. Hermann Esser as cited in Heinz, p.232.
8. Sandner, p.938; Hitler as cited by Vollnhals, 'Der Aufstieg ser NSDAP' in *München – 'Hauptstadt der Bewegung'*, p.165; and Large, p.229.
9. Nerdinger (2015), p.94; and Ullrich (2016), p.331.
10. Hauner, p.85; and Domarus, *Hitler. Speeches* Vol.I (1990) pp.172–3.
11. Sösemann, *Das Ende der Weimarer Republik* (1976) p.164; and Ullrich (2016), p.331.
12. Hauner, p.86; von Papen, *Der Wahrheit eine Gasse* (1952) p.250; Ullrich (2016), pp.338–9.
13. Hall, *'Furor Teutonicus'* (2012) p.116; and Wheeler-Bennett, *The Nemesis of Power* (1967) pp.315–6.
14. Sandner, p.1013–14.
15. Sandner, p.1015; and Hanfstaengl, pp.209–11. Joining Hitler and Eva Braun at the opera were Heinrich Hoffmann and his girlfriend Erna Gröbke (whom he later married), Wilhelm Brückner and his girlfriend Sophie Stork, Julius Schaub, Heß and his wife Ilse, and Ingeborg Groen.
16. Sandner, p.1016; Hauner, pp.88–9; and Noakes and Pridham, vol.1, pp.115–16, and 121–2 for the composition of Hitler's first Reich Cabinet.
17. Frau Solmitz diary entry 30 January 1933 as cited in Noakes and Pridham, vol.1, pp.129–30.
18. Sandner, p.1030; and Adolf Hitler's Radio Address: 'Appeal to the German People', 31 January 1933 (Winchester: The Tomahawk Films Archive, 1999).
19. Noakes and Pridham, vol.1, pp.120–2, 126–7.
20. Nerdinger (2015), p.94; and Hauner, p.91.
21. Evans (2004), pp.328–33; Noakes and Pridham, vol.1, pp.139–42.
22. Hauner, pp.91–2; and Noakes and Pridham, vol.1, pp.161–3.
23. Goebbels, *Vom Kaiserhof* (1934) p.302. See also Goebbels, *Tagebücher*, part I, vol. 2/3, p.172 (22 April 1933); and Hauner, p.93.

Consolidation of Power
1. Ullrich (2016), pp.426–427; Fest, p.400; and Broszat, *Der Staat Hitlers* (1969) pp135–7.
2. Kollmeier (ed.) (2008) p.9; Large, p.236; and Toland, pp.304–5.
3. Hitler's speech in the *Flugplatz*, Munich's Oberwiesenfeld airport, 12 March 1933. Baynes, vol.1, pp.269–70; Domarus, pp.266–7; and Sandner, pp.1038–9.
4. Baynes, vol.1, p.270.
5. Domarus, vol.1, p.267.
6. Large, p.247.
7. Preis, *München unterm Hakenkreuz* (1989) p.9; and Large, p.237.
8. Weale, pp.84–5.
9. *VB*, No.80, 21 März 1933.
10. Distel (ed.), *Dachau* (2005) pp.62, 67; Nerdinger (2015), p.119; and Large, pp.238–9.
11. Fest, pp.401–2.

12. Nerdinger (2015), p.119; and Kollmeier (ed.), p.55.
13. Hauner, p.91; and Domarus, p.269.
14. Nerdinger (2015), p.129.
15. *Simpl* editorial cited in Large, p.244. See: Ernst Piper, 'Nationalsozialistische Kulturpolitik und ihre Profiteure', in *'Niemand war dabei und keiner hat's gewußt': Die deutsche Öffentlichkeit und die Judenverfolgung* (ed.) Jörg Wollenberg (1989) p.152.

Bringing German Society into Line
1. Ullrich (2016), p.441.
2. Kershaw, *Popular Opinion* (1984) pp.247, 189; and Georg Denzler, 'Ein Gebetssturm für den Führer', Björn Mensing und Friedrich Prinz (eds.), *Irrlicht im leuchtenden München? Der Nationalsozialismus in der "Hauptstadt der Bewegung"* (1991) p.127. (and Large, p.248)
3. Kollmeier (ed.), p.59, 83–4; Nerdinger (2015), pp.127, 130; Kopleck, *Berlin* (2005) p.25; and Large, p.245.
4. Kuhn, *Nuremberg* (2007) p.62.
5. FC Bayern Munich Erlebniswelt (museum); and Wheatley, pp.196–8.
6. Fest, p.402.
7. Ullrich (2016), pp.445–6; and Jahn (ed.), (1988) doc. 197, pp.881–2.
8. Kollmeier (ed.), pp.55–6; Nerdinger (2015), pp.128–9; Jahn, doc. 206, pp.898–900; and Smelser, *Robert Ley* (1989) pp.134–6.
9. Ullrich (2016), pp.536–41.
10. Domarus, vol.1, p.305.
11. Nerdinger (2015), p.134.
12. Kollmeier (ed.), p.56.

Hauptstadt der Deutschen Kunst **(Capital of German Art)**
1. Domarus, 22 April 1933, vol.1, p.308.
2. Schlenker, *Hitler's Salon* (2007) pp.33–41.
3. Kurt Schmid-Ehmen designed party emblems for virtually all public buildings in Munich.
4. Brantl, *Haus der Kunst* (2017) pp.51–5.
5. Walther Schwerdtfeger writing about Paul Ludwig Troost, *Neues Münchener Tageblatte*, 18 August 1938.
6. Karl Friedrich Schinkel (1781–1841) was Prussia's most famous architect. He designed both neoclassical and neogothic buildings. His most famous buildings are found in and around Berlin.
7. Brantl, pp.28–35; Nerdinger (2015), pp.109–110; Grammbitter and Lauterbach, pp.37–40; and Schlenker, pp.57–9.
8. Grammbitter and Lauterbach, pp.13–16.
9. 'München rüstet zum Tag der Deutschen Kunst', in *Münchner Neueste Nachrichten*, 15 September 1933.
10. Brantl, pp.71–2; and Schlenker, pp.48–50.
11. Domarus, 15 October 1933, vol.1, pp.376–8; and Baynes, vol.1, pp.603–4.
12. Domarus, 15 October 1933, vol.1, p.378.
13. Brantl, p.74; Schlenker, p.50; Preis, pp.67–8; and Toland, p.414.
14. *VB* No.290, 17 Oktober 1933; Baynes, vol.1, p.604. See also *Mein Kampf*, p.126. 'Not only has one not seen Germany if one does not know Munich – no, above all, one does not know German art if one has not seen Munich.'
15. Drechsel, *The Temple of German Art* (1934); and Brantl, pp.73–4.
16. Gellately, *Backing Hitler* (2001) pp.257–63; Large, p.259.
17. Fest, p.427; and Hans Jürgen Koehler, *Inside Information* (1940) pp.67–8.

Dissent and Resistance to the New Nazi Regime in Munich

1. Thomas Mann, 'What We Must Demand [An Appeal to the Reich Government]' in the *Berliner Tageblatt*, 8 August 1932 as cited in Nerdinger (2015), p.101.
2. Thomas Mann, *Pro and Contra Wagner* (1985) p.91; *VB*, Nos.43/44, 12/13 Februar 1933.
3. Klaus Mann, *The Turning Point* (1984) pp.263–5.
4. *Münchner Neueste Nachrichten*, 16/17 April 1933; and Thomas Mann, *Diaries 1918–1939* (1983) Entry for Wednesday, 19 April 1933, Lugano. pp.151–2.
5. Mann, *Pro and Contra Wagner*, pp.149–51; Nerdinger (2015), p.194; Kopleck, *Munich*, p.32; and Evans, *The Third Reich in Power* (2006), p.521.
6. Haub and Sudbrack, *Father Rupert Mayer* (2008) pp.6–7; and Deming and Iliff, pp.83–4.
7. Deming and Iliff, pp.83–84; and Lehrer, pp.38–9.
8. Father Mayer as cited in Haub and Sudbrack, p.26.
9. Evans (2006), p.244.
10. Father Mayer as cited in Haub and Sudbrack, p.28.
11. Haub and Sudbrack, p.16; Evans (2006), p.244; and Kollmeier (ed.), pp.71–3.
12. Father Mayer as cited in Haub and Sudbrack, p.7–8, 16. In 1988 a commemorative plaque for Pater Rupert Mayer was mounted in the foyer of the Justizpalast. See Brantl, *Places of Remembrance* (2010) pp.44–6; and Deming and Iliff, pp.84–6.
13. Haub and Sudbrack, pp.8–9; Deming and Iliff, p.86; and Lehrer, p.39. See also Father Rupert Mayer SJ Crypt and Museum, Lower church hall, Bürgersaal, Neuhauser Straβe 14.

Ernst Röhm and 'The Night of the Long Knives'

1. Ernst Röhm as cited in Large, p.250. See also Large, *Between Two Fires* (1990) pp.101–37.
2. Heiden, *The Führer* (2002/1944) p.467.
3. Broszat, (1969) pp.251–2; Evans (2006), p.21; Bessel, *Political Violence* (1984) p.126; and Toland, pp.329–30.
4. Large, p.251; and Gaab, pp.74–5.
5. Siemens, pp.155–6; Longerich, *Die braunen Bataillone* (1989) pp.183–4.
6. Ullrich (2016), p.459; Evans (2006), p.22; Longerich (1989), p.184; and Bessel, p.97.
7. Hitler's 'New Year's Proclamation to the National Socialists and Party Comrades', published in the *VB*, No.1/2, 1/2 January 1934. See also Domarus, 1 January 1934, vol.1, pp.411–12.
8. Domarus, 1 January 1934, vol.1, pp.411–13; and Evans (2006), p.25.
9. Hitler's letter to Ernst Röhm, 1 January 1934, published in the *VB*, No.1/2, 1/2 January 1934. See also Baynes, vol.1, p.289.
10. Longerich (1989), p.204.
11. Toland, p.330; Evans (2006), pp.24–5; Ullrich (2016), p.461; and Schäfer, *Werner von Blomberg* (2006) pp.123–4.
12. Ullrich (2016), p.461; and Evans (2006), p.25.
13. Domarus, 19 February 1934, vol.1, p.435; and Hauner, p.100.
14. Decree of the Reich President, 12 March 1933. Domarus, vol.1, p.265.
15. Alan Bullock, *Hitler. A Study in Tyranny* rev. ed. (1962) pp.288–9; Domarus, 21 February 1934, vol.1, p.435; and Sandner, p.1162.
16. The street was renamed Stauffenbergstraβe in 1955. Cf. Brian Ladd, *The Ghosts of Berlin* (1997) pp.149–50.
17. Domarus, 28 February 1934, vol.1, pp.437–8; Schäfer, pp.136–7; Siemens, pp.159–160; and Sandner, pp.1163–5.
18. Röhm as cited in Höhne, *The Order of the Death's Head* p.88; and Hauner, p.101.
19. Fest, p.455; Sandner, pp.1169–70; Ullrich (2016), p.462; Kershaw (1998), p.502; and O'Neill, *The German Army and the Nazi Party 1933–1939* (1966) pp.38–42.
20. Max Heydebreck as cited in Bessel, pp.130–2; and Evans (2006), p.26.
21. *VB*, No.106, 16 April 1934; Sandner, pp.1172–3; Domarus, 11–15 April 1934, vol.1, p.447; and Bullock, p.290.

22. *VB*, No.109, 19 April 1934; Sandner, p.1173; Domarus, 17 April 1934, vol.1, p.448.

23. Toland, pp.331–2; and Siemens, p.173. For a list of other homosexual SA leaders see Reichardt (2009) pp.679–80.

24. Domarus, 4–8 June 1934, vol.1, pp.457–9; and Ullrich (2016), p.463.

25. Toland, p.332; Sandner, p.1189; and Hauner, p.102

26. Sandner, pp.1190–1191; Domarus, 14–16 June 1934, vol.1, pp.460–3; Fest, p.458; and Tanner, *Wagner* (2010) pp.78–9.

27. Sandner, p.1193; Domarus, 17 June 1934, vol.1, pp.463–5; Siemens, pp.160–2: and Kershaw (1998), p.509.

28. Fest, p.459.

29. Ullrich (2016), p.464; Evans (2006), p.28; and Toland, p.333.

30. Sandner, p.1195; Ullrich (2016), p.465; Fest, 460; Kershaw (1998), p. 511; Evans (2006), p.31; and Wheeler-Bennett (1953) pp.319–20.

31. Hauner, p.103.

32. Sandner, pp.1205–6.

33. Ullrich (2016), pp.465–6; Fest, p.460; and Kershaw (1998), p.511.

34. Hauner, p.103; and Sandner, p.1196.

35. Höhne, p.112; Evans (2006), p.31; and Toland, p.337.

36. Sandner, p.1199.

37. Hitler as quoted in a report written by Erich Kempka and cited at length in Evans (2006), p.32

38. Goebbels, Tagebücher, part I, vol. 3/1 p.72 (1 July 1934).

39. Domarus, 30 June 1934, vol.1, pp.469–70; Longerich (1989), pp.216–17; Ullrich (2016), pp.466–7; Evans (2006), pp.31–2; Fest, p463; and Hauner, p.103.

40. Domarus, 30 June 1934, vol.1, pp.471.

41. Sepp Dietrich was in charge of the SS firing squads that executed the SA leaders at Stadelheim Prison in Munich. The first six to be shot were Obergruppenführer August Schneidhuber, Munich; Obergruppenführer Edmund Heines, Silesia; Gruppenführer Wilhelm Schmidt, Munich; Gruppenführer Hans Hayn, Saxony; Gruppenführer Hans Peter von Heydebreck, Pomerania; and Standartenführer Hans Erwin Graf Spreti, Munich. Their deaths were announced immediately by the Reich Press Office of the NSDAP. See Domarus, 30 June 1934, vol.1, pp.477–8, and fn.142 p..

42. Evans (2006), pp.33–4; Ullrich (2016), pp.467–8; Domarus, 30 June 1934, vol.1, pp.470–1; Fest, 465; Toland pp.341–2; and Nerdinger (2015), p.104.

43. Kershaw (1998), p p.515.

44. General von Epp account 'Judgment on Josef Dietrich (Munich, 14 May 1957) p.61, as cited in Toland, p.343.

45. Domarus, 1 July 1934, vol.1, p.479; Evans (2006), p.33; Large, p.254; and Toland, p.345.

46. Hauner, p.103. Volker Ullrich cites 90 as the official number killed. See Ullrich (2016), p.468.

47. Hanfstaengl, p.272.

48. Schroeder (2009) pp.29–30.

49. Domarus, 1–2 July 1934, vol.1, pp.478–80; and Fest, p.470.

50. Domarus, 3 July 1934, vol.1, pp.481; and Hauner, p.103.

51. Hindenburg as cited in Ullrich (2016), p.470. See Memorandum by Wilhelm Brückner, 28 May 1949, IfZ München, ED 10/43.

52. Sandner, pp.1205–6.

53. Goebbels, Tagebücher, part I, vol. 3/1 p.76 (7 July 1934); and Ullrich (2016), p.471.

54. Domarus, 13 July 1934, vol.1, pp.495. For Hitler's full speech see pp.486–501. Hitler used the phrase 'The Night of the Long Knives' in his speech, turning around the SA's own words for their planned purge of the NSDAP leadership including Hitler if necessary.

55. Göring as cited in Domarus, 13 July 1934, vol.1, pp.501–2.

56. Solmitz as cited in Evans (2006), pp.38–9.

57. Ullrich (2016), p.471; and Kershaw, *The 'Hitler Myth'*, pp.85–7.
58. Large, p.255.
59. Carl Schmitt, 'Der Führer schützt das Recht', *Deutsche Juristen Zeitung* (1 August 1934) pp.945–50; Ullrich (2016), p.472; and Siemens, p.177.

The Cult of Nazism
1. Sandner, pp.1120–21.
2. *VB*, No.313, 9 November 1933. See also Domarus, 8 November 1933, vol.1, pp.388–9.
3. *VB*, No.314, 10 November 1933. See also Domarus, 9 November 1933, vol.1, pp.389–91; and Kopleck, p.3.
4. Sandner, p.1123; Domarus, 9 November 1933, vol.1, pp.391–2; and Matthews, *Military Music of the Third Reich* (2002) pp.41 and 58.
5. Sandner, p.1245.
6. Fest, p.516.
7. Oktoberfest was not held between 1939 and 1945 because of the Second World War. See '1933–1938 The Oktoberfest under National Socialist Rule' in *The Oktoberfest 1810–2010: Kultur Geschichte Bayern*, published by Landesstelle für die Nichtstaatlichen Museen in Bayern and the Münchner Stadtmuseum (2010).
8. Ullrich (2016), p.523; and Fest, pp.512–17. See also Schmeer, *Die Regie* (1956) pp.68–116.

Hauptstadt der Bewegung (**Capital of the Movement**)
1. Sandner, p.1315.
2. Kollmeier (ed.), pp.9–10; Preis, p.51; Kopleck, 22–3; and Large, pp.231–2.
3. Domarus, 8 November 1935, vol.2, p.723. See also 'Munich: *Der Neunte Elfte*' (Munich: the ninth of the eleventh), *After the Battle* (No.66, 1989) pp.8–21; and Le Tissier, 'The Feldherrnhalle 16 – 'Die Neunte Elfte', pp. 134–51.
4. *VB*, No.315, 11 November 1935; Domarus, 8 November 1935, vol.2, pp.723–8; Sandner, p.1342.
5. Domarus, 8 November 1935, vol.2, p.728; and Fest, p.513.
6. The Blood Order was a silver medal with a matt finish measuring 4 cm in diameter. The front displayed an eagle clutching a wreath with the date '9. Nov.' in the centre. On the reverse side was the Feldherrnhalle bathed in sunrays emanating from a Swastika above, and an inscription: *Und ihr habt doch gesiegt!* (But you still have triumphed!).
7. Domarus, 9 November 1935, vol.2, p.729; Sandner, p.1344; Fest, pp.513–14; and Large, pp.256–7.
8. Sandner, pp.1343–4; *VB*, No.314, 10 November 1935; Grammbitter and Lauterbach, pp.19–24; and Krause, *No.12 Arcisstraße* (2010) pp.35–7.
9. Two examples of these 'tourist guides' published in English are: *München Hauptstadt der Bewegung* (Munich, 1937) reproduced by Robin Saikia and Joachim von Halasz (eds.), *Hitler's Munich: A Third Reich Tourist Guide* (2008); and *Munich: The spirit of a German City* (Munich: Culture Department of the Capital of the National Movement, 1939).
10. P. Wolfrum, 'A Week in Munich', in Saikia and Halasz (eds.), *Hitler's Munich*, p.24; and Hanns Wiedmann, 'Under the open sky' in *Munich: The spirit of a German City*, p.4
11. Ernst Hoferichter, 'The soul of a town is an experience ...' in *Munich: The spirit of a German City*, p.15.
12. Jorg Lampe, 'The Artist's Town' in *Munich: The spirit of a German City*, p.22.
13. Hoferichter, p.17; and Lampe, p.23.
14. M. Reinhard, 'Munich' in Saikia and Halasz (eds.), *Hitler's Munich*, p.45.

Kunst ist kein Luxus (**Art is not a Luxury**)
1. Karl Fiehler, the Lord Mayor's forward to *München Hauptstadt der Bewegung*, reproduced in Saikia and Halasz (eds.), *Hitler's Munich*, p.10.

2. Goebbels, Tagebücher, part I, vol. 3, p.205 (18 July 1937); Sandner, p.1456; Brantl, pp.74–7; and Schlenker, pp.62–4, 67.

3. Baynes, vol.1, pp.584–92; *VB*, No.200, 19 July 1937; and Domarus, 19 July 1937, vol.2, pp.909–15. (Domarus wrongly states that Hitler's speech was on 19 July).

4. Schlenker, pp.78–9.

5. Ibid., p.211.

6. Sandner, p.1446; and Goebbels, Tagebücher, part I, vol. 3, p.167 (5 June 1937)

7. Domarus, 19 July 1937, vol.2, p.915; Hoffmann, pp.170–171; and Brantl, pp.85–6.

8. Brantl, pp.77–9; and Schlenker, pp.67–9.

9. *VB*, No.201, 20 July 1937. See *Tag der Deutschen Kunst 1937, 16. Bis 18. Juli zu München*, Leitung des Tages der Deutschen Kunst (ed.), Munich 1937.

10. Goebbels, Tagebücher, part I, vol. 3, p.209 (22 July 1937); and Schlenker, pp.76, 82–3.

11. Sandner, pp.1457–61.

12. Willrich, *Die Säuberung des Kunsttempels* (1937) introduction, Eng. trans. 37–70; and Kaiser, *Entartete 'Kunst'* (1937/2012) pp.1–3.

13. Preis, pp.84–5; and Kopleck, *Munich*, p.36.

14. Brantl, pp.89–90; and Nicholas, *The Rape of Europe* (1995) pp.13–14. See also Schuster (ed.) *Nationalsozialismus* (1987).

15. Paul Ortwin Rave, Curator at the Berlin National Gallery as cited in Brantl, p.92.

16. Kaiser, *Entartete 'Kunst'*, p.67.

17. Kaiser, *Entartete 'Kunst'*, p.40; Nerdinger (2015), p.197.

18. Baynes, vol.1, p.592.

19. Public reactions to the exhibition as cited in Brantl, p.95; Toland, p.416; and Large, p.265. See also Wulf, *Die bildenden Künste* (1963) p.363.

20. Nicholas, p.22.

21. *VB*, No.201, 20 July 1937.

22. *'Der ewige Jude'* show, p.409 and *Große antibolschewistische Schau*, pp.387–8 in Bauer *et. al.*, München – 'Hauptstadt der Bewegung'; Nerdinger (2015), p.178; Kopleck, *Munich*, p.25; and Large, pp.266–7.

Slow March to War

1. Sandner, p.1473; Bauer *et. al.*, *München – 'Hauptstadt der Bewegung'*, p.390; and Le Tissier, p.50, 162.

2. Hauner, p.123; Sandner, p.1474; Domarus, 25 September 1937, vol.2, pp.944–5; and *VB*, No.271, 28 September 1937.

3. Mussolini as cited in Ullrich (2016), p.695. See also Domarus, 26–29 September 1937, vol.2, pp.946–51; Sandner, pp.1476–8; and Hauner, pp.123–4.

4. Goebbels, Tagebücher, part I, vol. 4, p.329 (26 September 1937).

5. Hauner, p.125.

6. Guderian, *Panzer Leader* (1952) pp.50–1.

7. Domarus, 15 March 1938, vol.2, pp.1056–7; Sandner, pp. 1503–11; Ullrich (2016), pp.716–18; Evans (2006), p.652–3; and Wallner, *Der Österreich-Anschluß* (2003).

8. *VB*, Nos.76 and 78, 17 and 19 März 1938.

9. Domarus, 16 March 1938, vol.2, pp.1059–60.

10. Telegram from Mussolini to Hitler, Sunday 13 March 1938 as cited in Toland, p.453.

11. Hitler's speech to the Reichstag, Domarus, 18 March 1938, vol.2, pp.1060–68.

12. Hauner, pp.124–5.

13. Hauner, pp.130–1; Sandner, pp.1545, 1550; and Lehrer, pp.47–53.

14. Harold Nicolson as cited in Lehrer, p.48.

15. Domarus, 22 September 1938, vol.2, p.1172.

16. Extensive excerpts of Hitler's speech can be read in Domarus, 26 September 1938, vol.2, pp.1183–94.

17. French ambassador André François-Poncet as cited in Ullrich (2016), p.742. See also Schmidt, *Statist auf diplomatischer Bühne* (1949) p.411; and André François-Poncet, *Als Botschafter in Berlin 1931–1938* (Mainz, 1949) p.333; and Schäfer, *André François-Poncet* (2004) pp.309–10.
18. Sandner, p.1595; and Karel Margry, '50 Years Ago: The Munich Crisis', *After the Battle* (No. 62, 1988) pp.34–5.
19. Nerdinger (2015), pp.200–1; Krause, p.39; Grammbitter and Lauterbach, pp.53–4; Deming and Iliff, p.46; and Le Tissier, p.52.
20. For the full text of the Munich Agreement see Domarus, 29 September 1938, vol.2, pp.1207–8.
21. Deming and Iliff, p.48; Schmidt, p.414; Ullrich (2016), pp.743–4; and Margry, p.38.
22. Göring as cited in Lehrer, p.51.
23. Schmidt, p.417; and Domarus, 30 September 1938, vol.2, pp.1210–11.
24. The joint declaration signed by Chamberlain and Hitler is reproduced in Domarus, 30 September 1938, vol.2, pp.1211.
25. Fest, p.567; and Toland, p.493.
26. Evans (2006), pp.674, 678.
27. Krause, p.46; and Sandner, p.1614.

Kristallnacht (Night of Broken Glass)

1. Domarus, 8 November 1938, vol.2, p.1240; Ullrich, p.668; and Evans (2006), pp.543–6.
2. *VB*, No.312, 8 November 1938; and Hanke, *Zur Geschichte der Juden* (1967) p.211.
3. Hitler's telegram to Herr und Frau von Rath was sent late in the afternoon on 9 November. See *VB*, No.314, 10 November 1938; and Domarus, 8–9 November 1938, vol.2, pp.1240–2.
4. Goebbels, Tagebücher, part I, vol. 6, p.180 (10 November 1938).
5. Kopleck, *Munich*, p.18; Nerdinger (2015), pp.210–11; and Ullrich (2016), pp.670–1.
6. Nerdinger (2015), pp.208–9; and Sandner, p.1627.
7. Ullrich (2016), p.672.
8. Evans (2006), pp.593–7; Nerdinger (2015), pp.206–8; and Toland, pp.503–7.
9. Domarus, pp.1254–5; and Sandner, pp.1626–8. For Hitler's speech in full see Domarus, 10 November 1938, vol.2, pp.1244–55.

Diplomatic Intrigues, Ultimatums, and War

1. Baynes, vol.2, p.1565. See also Hauner, p.139.
2. Baynes, vol.2, p.1586.
3. Domarus, 23 March 1939, vol.3, p.1516. For the full text of the treaty reuniting Memel with Germany see pp.1512–14, and for Hitler's full speech see pp.1515–16. See also Eberle and Uhl (eds.) (2005) pp.37–41.
4. Sandner, pp.1664, 1667; and Nerdinger (2015), p.214.
5. Klemperer, *Ich will Zeugnis ablegen* (1995) p.469 (20 April 1939).
6. Fest, p.9.
7. Goebbels, *Tagebücher*, part I, vol. 6 p.322 (20 April 1939); and Ullrich, *Geburtstags-Parade* (2004).
8. Goebbels, *Tagebücher*, part I, vol. 6, p.323 (21 April 1939).
9. Sandner, p.1711.
10. Wistrich, *Weekend in Munich* (1995) pp.70–1.
11. Domarus, 16 July 1939, vol.3, pp.1644–5. For Hitler's full speech see pp.1643–5.
12. Isabel Hilton as cited in Brantl, p.80; and Sandner, pp.1711–12.
13. Sandner, pp.1715–17.
14. Diana Mitford Mosley, *A Life of Contrasts* (1977) p.160.
15. Sandner, pp.1718 and 1261.
16. Ibid., pp.1722–4. For the text of the agreement plus the secret protocol see Domarus, 23 August 1939, vol.3, pp.1682–4.
17. Maier et al, *Germany and the Second World War* Vol.II (1991) pp.75–80.
18. Maier et.al, p.101; Sandner, p.1724; and Kopleck, *Munich*, pp.32 and 21.

19. Domarus, 1 September 1939, vol.3, p.1763.
20. Ibid., pp.1766–8.
21. Charlotte Mosley (ed.), *The Mitfords* (2008) pp.138–9.
22. Kathryn Steinhaus, 'Valkyrie: Gender, Class, European Relations, and Unity Mitford's Passion for Fascism', PhD Thesis, McGill University, Montreal, December 2011, p.305.

Munich's First Casualty of the War
1. Steinhaus, pp.306–9; and Mosley, p.143.
2. Preis, pp.130–5.
3. Hauner, p.149; and Halder, *Kriegstagebuch 1939–1942* (1962–4) v.1 p.90.
4. Maier, pp.101 and 124. For the official German history narrative of the campaign against Poland see pp.101–26.
5. Domarus, 5 October 1939, vol.3, pp.1827–8.
6. Preis, p.134. The Siegfried Line was a military defence system spread over 630 km on Germany's western border. It ran from Kleve on the Dutch border southward to Grenzach-Wyhlen on the Swiss border. Built between 1938 and 1940, it incorporated 18,000 bunkers, tunnels, countless trenches, and tank barriers.
7. Sandner, pp.1757–8; and Haasis, *Bombing Hitler* (2013) p.3.
8. Domarus, 8 November 1939, vol.3, p.1865. For the full text of Hitler's speech at the Bürgerbräukeller see pp.1865–75.
9. Ibid, p.1872. On 6 October, immediately after Hitler returned from Warsaw, he made public his peace offer to Britain. 'I believe even today that there can only be real peace in Europe and throughout the world if Germany and England come to an understanding.' Under inexorable pressure from the conservative press and warmongers in his party, Chamberlain rejected Hitler's offer six days later on 12 October. See Bullock, p.556; Hauner, p.149; and Lukacs, *The Duel* (1991).
10. Domarus, pp.1866, 1869–70.
11. Ibid., p.1875.
12. Sandner, pp.1758–60; and Haasis, pp.3 and 10.

A Bomb in the Bürgerbräukeller
1. Goebbels, *Tagebücher*, part I, vol.7, p.184 (7 November 1939).
2. Sandner, p.1759.
3. *VB*, No.314, 10 November 1939.
4. Goebbels, *Tagebücher*, part I, vol.7, p.188 (9 November 1939).
5. See Maier, pp.278–326 for the official German history narrative of the campaign in the west.
6. Ullrich, *Hitler. Downfall* (2020) p.80.
7. Report written by Xaver Rieger, one of the border-patrol officers who arrested Elser. See Haasis, pp.15–16.
8. Haasis, p.53.
9. Ortner, *The Lone Assassin* (2012) pp.176–7; and Haasis, p.204..
10. Kopleck, *Munich*, pp.42–4; Nerdinger (2015), p.216; and Large, pp.314–15.
11. Domarus, 11 November 1939, vol.3, p.1878; Sandner, pp.1760–3; and Le Tissier, pp.368–71. Le Tissier's timings of Hitler's speech and the explosion on 8 November are incorrect, but the photographs of the damage in the Bürgerbräukeller and of the funeral ceremonies on 11 November are very useful.
12. Sandner, p.1898.
13. Ibid., p.1879.
14. Domarus, 8 November 1940, vol.3, p.2115. For the full text of Hitler's speech see pp.2113–20.
15. Ibid., p.2119.

Munich Adjusts to the Demands of War
1. Sandner, p.1880; and Domarus, 14 November 1940, vol.3, p.2133.
2. Nerdinger (2015), p.262; and Kopleck, *Munich*, pp.57, 63–4, and 76–8.
3. Nerdinger (2015), p.259.
4. Goebbels, *Tagebücher*, part II, vol.4, p.567 (21 June 1942).
5. Evans, *The Third Reich at War* (2008), pp.348–51.
6. Nerdinger (2015), p.228; Kopleck, *Munich*, pp.19 and 65; and Tooze, *Wages of Destruction* (2006) p.519.
7. Nerdinger (2015), p.260; Bajohr and Strupp (eds.), *Fremde Blicke* (2011) p.571; Ullrich (2020), p.359.
8. Nerdinger (2015), pp.258–9 and 264; Ullrich (2020), pp.359–60; Evans (2008), p.351; and Herbert, *Hitler's Foreign Workers* (1997).
9. Sandner, p.2037–8; and Domarus, 8 November 1942, vol.4, pp.2694–5. For the full text of Hitler's speech see pp.2696–708.
10. Domarus, 8 November 1942, vol.4, pp.2702–3.
11. Ibid., p.2701.
12. Ibid., p.2708.
13. Sandner, p.2038.

***Die Weiße Rose* (the White Rose)**
1. Kershaw, *Nemesis* (2000), p.552; and Müller (ed.), *The White Rose* (2006), p.54. See also Kopleck, *Munich*, pp.39–42; and Lloyd (ed.), *The White Rose* (2019).
2. Leaflet of the White Rose II reprinted in Müller, *The White Rose*, pp.62–4.
3. Leaflet of the White Rose III reprinted in Müller, *The White Rose*, pp.65–7.
4. Leaflet of the White Rose IV reprinted in Müller, *The White Rose*, pp.68–9.
5. Müller, *The White Rose*, pp.54–6; and Nerdinger (2015), p.278.
6. Leaflet of the White Rose V reprinted in Müller, *The White Rose*, p.70.
7. Kopleck, *Munich*, p.25; and Müller, *The White Rose*, pp.3 and 16; and Large, pp.329–30.
8. Leaflet of the White Rose VI reprinted in Müller, *The White Rose*, pp.71–2.
9. Müller, *The White Rose*, pp.20 and 57; and Kopleck, *Munich*, p.40.
10. Sandner, p.2055; and Willi Graf, Gestapo interrogation protocol, 1943 in Müller, *The White Rose*, pp.56–8.
11. Müller, *The White Rose*, p.3.
12. Ibid., pp76–7; Kopleck, *Munich*, pp.15–16, 40; and Nerdinger (2015), pp.279–80.
13. The graves of Hans and Sophie Scholl and Christoph Probst are located at 73-1-18/19. Alexander Schmorell's grave is at 76-1-26.
14. Müller, *The White Rose*, pp.76 and 80; Benz and Pehle (eds.), *Lexikon* (1994) pp. 318–19; and Kershaw (2000), p.552.
15. Nerdinger (2015), p.280.
16. Thomas Mann as cited in Large, p.333. See also Müller, *The White Rose*, p.56; and Nerdinger (2015), p.281.

British and American Bombs Rain Down on Munich
1. Middlebrook and Everitt, *The Bomber Command War Diaries* (1985) p.435; and Sandner, p.2152.
2. Domarus, 8 November 1943, vol.4, pp.2832–43 for the full text of Hitler's speech.
3. Sandner, pp.271–3.
4. Middlebrook and Everitt, p.499.
5. Middlebrook and Everitt, pp.692–7; Nerdinger (2015), p.249; Kopleck, *Munich*, p. 58; Preis, p.219; and Deming and Iliff, p.93.

Götterdämmerung (Twilight of the Gods)

1. Sandner, p.2210; Domarus, 17 April 1944, vol.4, p.2889; Large, pp.325 and 340; and Hauner, p.193.
2. Sandner, p.2215.
3. Sandner, pp.2267–9; and Le Tissier, p.391.
4. Domarus, 8 November 1944, vol.4, p.2971. For the full text of Hitler's speech see pp.2964–71.
5. Sandner, p.2320.
6. Domarus, 24 February 1945, vol.4, p.3019. For the full text of Hitler's speech see pp.3014–19.
7. Nerdinger (2015), p.291 and 296; Kopleck, *Munich*, p. 59; and Large, pp.343–4.
8. Preis, pp.204–12; Nerdinger (2015), pp.294 and 297.
9. Nerdinger (2015), p.296; and Kopleck, *Munich*, pp. 59–60.
10. Distel (ed.), (2015), p.299. See also Andrew Mollo, 'Dachau', *After the Battle* (no.27, 1980) pp.1–33.
11. Large, p.345. See also Abzug, *Inside the Vicious Heart* (1985) p.93.
12. SHAEF Communiqué Number 387, 30 April 1945 in Ramsey (ed.), *The Defeat* (2015) p.482.
13. Nerdinger (2015), p.299; Sandner, p.2350; Hauner, p.208.
14. SHAEF Communiqué Number 388, 1 May 1945 in Winston Ramsey, p.486.
15. Winfried Nerdinger, 'Dealing with Munich's Tattered Past' in Nerdinger (2015), pp.541–2; and Deming and Iliff, p.97.
16. Gebhardt, *Crimes Unspoken* (2017) chapter 3 'South Germany – who will protect us from the Americans?'
17. Klaus Mann, *Turning Point*, p.368.
18. Ibid., p.372.
19. Preis, p.219; Kopleck, *Munich*, p. 61. See also Deming and Iliff, p.93; and Large, p.346 for slightly different numbers.
20. Klaus Mann, p.367.
21. Hans Junge was an SS-Obersturmführer in the 12th SS Hitler Youth Panzer Division when he was killed near Dreux in Normandy in August 1944. He is burred in the German Military Cemetery at Champigny St-Andre in Normandy (block 6, grave no.1816). See Junge, *Until the Final Hour*, pp.197–8 fn.10, and 210 fn.82.
22. Junge, pp.1–2.
23. Ibid., p.188.

Epilogue

1. Primo Levi, *Die Untergegangenen und die Geretteten* (1990).
2. Nerdinger (2015), p.12.

Bibliography and Sources

Archives and Libraries
Bayerisches Hauptstaatarchiv, (BHS) Munich
Bayerische Staatsbibliothek (BSB), Munich
Bodleian Library
British Library
Bundesarchiv (BA) Berlin-Lichterfelde
Bundesarchiv (BA) Koblenz
Institut für Zeitgeschicthe (IfZ) Munich
Monacensia im Hildebrandhaus, Munich
Münchner Stadtmuseum
Richard Wagner Museum mit Nationalarchiv der Richard-Wagner-Stiftung
Obersalzberg-Institut, Berchtesgaden
DenkStätte Weiße Rose (The White Rose exhibition), Ludwig-Maximilians-Universität, München
National Archives of the United States, College Park Maryland and Washington, DC
The National Archives, Kew, London, UK
Tomahawk Films Archive

Newspapers and Magazines
Allgemeine Rundschau
Auf gut Deutsch, München
Collier's Weekly
Bayerische Kurier
Bayreuther Festspielführer
Daily Express
Daily Mail
Das Bayerische Vaterland
Deutsche Allgemeine Zeitung, Berlin
Deutsches Adelsbtatt, Berlin
Die Rote Fahne, Berlin
Die Fanfare
Die Zeit
Fränkische Tagespost
Frankfurter Allgemeine Zeitung
Grossdeutsche Zeitung, München
Illustrierter Beobachter, München
Markt Grafinger Wochenblatt
Münchener Beobachter
Münchner Neueste Nachrichten
Münchener Post
New York Times
Oberfränkische Zeitung (OfZ)
Regensburger Echo
Reichspost (Wein)
Simplicissimus

The Times (London)
Vancouver Sun
Völkischer Beobachter (VB), München
Völkischer Kurier, München
Vossische Zeitung, Berlin
Vorwärts, Berlin

Books

Abzug, Robert. *Inside the Vicious Heart: Americans and the Liberation of Nazi Concentration Camps* (New York: Oxford University Press, 1985)

Bajohr, Frank and Christoph Strupp (eds.), *Fremde Blicke auf das 'Dritte Reich': Berichte ausländischer Diplomaten über Herrschafte und Gesellschafte in Deutschland 1933–1945* (Göttingen: Wallstein, 2011)

Baker, Suzanne St. Barbe. *A Wayfarer in Bavaria* 2nd ed. (London: Methuen, 1931)

Bauer, Reinhard and Ernst Piper, *München: Die Geschichte einer Stadt* (München: Piper, 1993)

Bauer, Richard (ed.). *München – 'Hauptstadt der Bewegung'. Bayerns Metropole und der Nationalsozialismus* (Münchner Stadtmuseum, Edition Minerva, 2002)

Baynes, Norman H. (ed.). *The Speeches of Adolf Hitler April 1922 – August 1939* Vol.1 (Oxford: Oxford University Press, 1942)

Beierl, Florian M. *Geschichte des Kehlsteins* (Berchtesgaden: Plenk Verlag, 1994) English ed., *History of the Eagles Nest* 3rd ed. (Berchtesgaden: Plenk Verlag, 2001)

Benz, Wolfgang and Walter Pehle (eds.), *Lexikon des deutschen Widerstandes* (Frankfurt am Main: Fischer, 1994)

Bessel, Richard. *Political Violence and the Rise of Nazism: The Storm Troopers in Eastern Germany 1925–1934* (London: Yale University Press, 1984)

Brantl, Sabine. *Haus der Kunst, Munich. A Locality and its History in National Socialism* (Munich: Alliteria, 2017)

Brantl, Sabine. *Places of Remembrance and Commemoration. National Socialism in Munich* trans. Melanie Newton (City of Munich-Stadtarchiv, 2010)

Broszat, Martin. *Der Staat Hitlers: Grundlegung und Entwicklung seiner inneren Verfassung* (München: Deutscher Taschenbuch Verlag, 1969)

Buchner, Eberhard. *Revolutionsdokumente: Im Zeichen der roten Fahne* (Berlin: Deutsche Verlagsgesellschaft für Politik und Geschichte, 1921)

Bullock, Alan. *Hitler: A Study in Tyranny* (London: Odhams Press, 1964)

Chamberlain, Houston Stewart. *Arische Weltanschauung* (München: Bruckmann, 1916)

Chamberlain, Houston Stewart. *Die Zuversicht: Zweite Auflage* (München: Bruckmann, 1915)

Chamberlain, Houston Steward. *Richard Wagner* trans. G. Ainslie Hight (München: Verlagsanstalt F. Bruckmann, 1987)

Chaussy, Ulrich. *Nachbar Hitler. Führerkult und Heimatzerstörung am Obersalzberg* (Berlin: Ch. Links, 2005)

d'Almeida, Fabrice. *High Society in the Third Reich* trans. Steven Rendall (Cambridge: Polity Press, 2008)

Deming, Brian and Ted Iliff, *Hitler and Munich* (Berchtesgaden: Verlag Anton Plenk KG, n.d.)

Denzler, Georg. 'Ein Gebetssturm für den Führer', Björn Mensing und Friedrich Prinz (eds.), *Irrlicht im leuchtenden München? Der Nationalsozialismus in der 'Hauptstadt der Bewegung'* (Regensburg: F. Pustet, 1991)

Deuerlein, Ernst (ed.), *Der Aufstieg der NSDAP in Augenzeugenberichten* (München: Deutscher Taschenbuch Verlag, 1974)

Deuerlein, Ernst. *Hitler: eine politische Biographie* (München: List, 1969)

Deuerlein, Ernst (ed.). *Der Hitler-Putsch. Bayerische Dokumente zum 8/9 November 1923* (Stuttgart: Deutsche Verlags-Anstalt, 1962)

Dietrich, Otto. *The Hitler I Knew. Memoirs of the Third Reich's Press Chief* (New York: Skyhorse Publishing, 2010)

Distel, Barbara (ed.). *The Dachau Concentration Camp, 1933–1945* (Munich: Karl M. Lipp, 2005)

Domarus, Max. *Hitler. Speeches and Proclamations 1932–1945* 4 vols. trans. Mary Fran Gilbert (Wauconda, Il., USA: Bolchazy-Carducci Publishers, 1990)

Dornberg, John. *Munich 1923. The Story of Hitler's First Grab for Power* (New York: Harper & Row, 1982)

Drechsel, Karl. *The Temple of German Art. Das Haus der Deutschen Kunst, The New Glass Palace* (München: Bruckmann, 1934)

Eberle, Henrik and Matthias Uhl (eds.), *The Hitler Book* trans. Giles MacDonogh (London: John Murray, 2005)

Evans, Richard. *The Third Reich at War* (London: Penguin, 2008)

Evans, Richard. *The Third Reich in Power* (London: Penguin, 2006)

Evans, Richard. *The Coming of the Third Reich* (London: Penguin, 2004)

Fechenbach, Felix. *Der Revolutionär Kurt Eisner aus persönlichen Erlebnissen* (Berlin: Dietz, 1929)

Fest, Joachim C. *Hitler* trans. Richard and Clara Winston (London: Penguin, 1974)

François-Poncet, Andreé. *Als Botschafter in Berlin 1931–1938* (Mainz: Kupferberg, 1949)

Frank, Hans. *Im Angesicht des Galgens: Deutung Hitlers und seiner Zeit auf Grund eigener Erlebnisse und Erkenntnisse* (München: Beck, 1953)

Gaab, Jeffrey S. *Munich. Hofbräuhaus & History – Beer, Culture, & Politics* (New York: Peter Lang, 2008)

Gebhardt, Miriam. *Crimes Unspoken: The Rape of German Women at the End of the Second World War* trans. Nick Somers (Malden, MA: Polity, 2017)

Gellately, Robert. *Backing Hitler: Consent and Coercion in Nazi Germany* (Oxford: Oxford University Press, 2001)

Goebbels, Joseph. *Die Tagebücher von Joseph Goebbels*, ed. Elke Fröhlich, Part 1: *Aufzeichnungen 1923–1942* 9 vols in 14 parts (Munich: Saur, 1998–2006); Part 2: Diktate 1941–1945, 15 vols (Munich: Saur, 1993–98)

Goebbels, Joseph. The *Early Goebbels Diaries: 1925–1926* ed. Helmut Heiber (London: Weidenfeld and Nicolson, 1962)

Goebbels, Joseph. *Vom Kaiserhof zur Reichskanzlei 1932–1933* (München: Eher, 1934)

Gordon, Harold J. *Hitler and the Beer Hall Putsch* (Princeton: Princeton University Press, 1972)

Görtemaker, Heike B. *Eva Braun. Life With Hitler* trans. Damion Searls (London: Penguin, 2012)

Graf, Oskar Maria. *Wir sind Gefangene* (Munich: Drei-Masken-Verlag, 1927)

Grammbitter, Ulrike and Iris Lauterbach, *The NSDAP Centre in Munich* (Berlin-München: Deutscher Kunstverlag, 2015)

Grau, Bernhard. *Kurt Eisner 1867–1919: Eine Biographie* (München: Beck, 2001)

Gritschneder, Otto. *Der Hitler-Prozess und sein Richter Georg Neithardt: Skandalurteil von 1924 ebnet Hitler den Weg* (München: Beck, 2001)

Gritschneder, Otto. *Bewährungsfrist für den Terroristen Adolf H. Der Hitler-Putsch und die bayerische Justiz* (München: Beck, 1990)

Grunberger, Richard. *Red Rising in Bavaria* (London: Arthur Barker, 1973)

Guderian, Heinz. *Panzer Leader* (London: Michael Joseph, 1952)

Gun, Nerin E. *Eva Braun-Hitler: Leben und Schicksal* (Velbert und Kettwig: Blick & Bild Verlag, 1968) English ed., *Eva Braun: Hitler's Mistress* (London: Leslie Frewin, 1969)

Haasis, Hellmut G. *Bombing Hitler. The Story of the Man who almost assassinated the Führer* trans. William Odom (New York: Skyhorse Publishing, 2013)

Halasz, Joachim von. *Hitler's Munich* (London: Foxley Books, 2007)

Halder, Franz. *Kriegstagebuch 1939–1942* 3 vols. (Stuttgart: Kohlhammer, 1962–4)

Hamann, Brigitte. *Winifred Wagner. A Life at the Heart of Hitler's Bayreuth* trans. Alan Bance (London: Granta, 2005)

Hamann, Brigitte. *Hitler's Vienna. A Dictator's Apprenticeship* trans. Thomas Thornton (Oxford: Oxford University Press, 1999)

Hanfstaengl, Ernst. *The Unknown Hitler: Notes from the Young Nazi Party* (London: Gibson Square Books, 2005)

Hanke, Peter. *Zur Geschichte der Juden in München zwischen 1933 und 1945* (München: Bauknecht, Wölfle, 1967)

Hanser, Richard. *Putsch: How Hitler Made Revolution* (New York: Wyden, 1970)

Hatheway, Jay. *In Perfect Formation. SS Ideology and the SS-Junkerschule-Tölz* (Atglen, PA: Schiffer Military History, 1999)

Haub, Rita and Josef Sudbrack. *Father Rupert Mayer SJ. Apostle of Munich* trans. Oliver Lobschat and Niall Leahy (Munich: INIGO Medien, 2008)

Hauner, Milan. *Hitler. A Chronology of his Life and Time* 2nd revised edition (Basingstoke, Hampshire: Palgrave Macmillan, 2008)

Hayman, Ronald. *Thomas Mann: A Biography* (New York: Scribner, 1995)

Heiden, Konrad. *The Führer* trans. Ralph Manheim (Edison, NJ: Castle Books, 2002; first US edition 1944)

Heinz, Heinz A. *Germany's Hitler* (London: Hurst & Blackett, 1934)

Herbert, Ulrich. *Hitler's Foreign Workers: Enforced Foreign Labor in Germany under the Third Reich* (Cambridge: Cambridge University Press, 1997)

Herre, Franz. *Jahrhundertwende 1900: Untergangsstimmung und Fortschrittsglauben* (Stuttgart: Deutsche Verlags-Anstalt, 1998)

Heß, Rudolf. *Briefe 1908–1933* ed. Wolf Rüdiger Heß (München: Langen–Müller, 1987)

Heusler, Andreas. *Das Braune Haus: Wie München zur 'Hauptstadt der Bewegung' wurde* (München: Deutsche Verlags-Anstalt, 2008)

Hilmes, Oliver. *Cosima Wagner. The Lady of Bayreuth* trans. Stewart Spencer (London: Yale University Press, 2010)

Hinkel, Hans. *Einer unter Hunderttausend* (München: Knorr & Hirth, 1938)

Hitler, Adolf. *Mein Kampf* trans. Ralph Manheim (Boston: Houghton Mifflin, 1971)

Hitler, Adolf. *Hitler's Table Talk 1941–1945. His Private Conversations* ed. H.R. Trevor-Roper, trans. Norman Cameron and R.H. Stevens (New York: Enigma Books, 2000)

Hitler, Adolf. *Monologe im Führerhauptquartier 1941–1944* ed. Werner Jochmann (Hamburg: Albrecht Knaus Verlag, 1980)

Hitler, Adolf. *Sämtliche Aufzeichnungen 1905–1924* ed. Eberhard Jäckel with Axel Kuhn (Stuttgart: Oldenbourg Wissenschaftsverlag, 1980)

Hoffmann, Heinrich. *Hitler was my Friend. The Memoirs of Hitler's Photographer* trans. R.H. Stevens (Barnsley, Yorkshire: Frontline Books, Pen & Sword, 2011)

Höhne, Heinz. *The Order of the Death's Head. The Story of Hitler's SS* (London: Nationwide Book Service, 1980)

Howitt, Anna Mary. *An Art-Student in Munich* (London: Longman, Brown, Green, and Longmans, 1853)

Institut für Zeitgeschichte (ed.). *Hitler Reden, Schriften, Anordnungen. Februar 1925 bis Januar 1933* (München: Saur, 1992)

Jablonski, David. *The Nazi Party in Dissolution: Hitler and the Verbotszeit 1923–1925* (London: Frank Cass, 1989)

Jäckel, Eberhard. *Hitlers Weltanschauung. Entwurf einer Herrschaft* (Tübingen, 1969; 4th ed., Stuttgart: Deutsche Verlags-Anstalt, 1991)

Jäckel, Eberhard and Axel Kuhn (eds.). *Hitler. Sämtliche Aufzeichnungen 1905–1924* (Stuttgart: Oldenbourg Wissenschaftsverlag, 1980)

Jahn, Peter (ed.). *Die Gewerkschaften in der Endphase der Republik 1930–1933* (Köln: Bund-Verl., 1988)

Jetzinger, Franz. *Hitler's Youth* (London: Hutchinson, 1958)

Jetzinger, Franz. *Hitler Jugend: Phantasien, Lügen und Wahrheit* (Vienna: Europa-Verl., 1956)

Joachimsthaler, Anton. *Hitlers Liste: ein Dokument persönlicher Beziehungen* (München: Herbig, 2003)

Joachimsthaler, Anton. *Hitlers Weg begann in München 1913–1923* (München: Herbig, 2000)

Joachimsthaler, Anton. *Korrektur. Einer Biographie Adolf Hitler 1908–1920* (München: Herbig, 1989)

Jochmann, Werner (ed.). *Nationalsozialismus und Revolution* (Frankfurt am Main: Europäische Verl.-Anst., 1963)

Junge, Traudl. *Until the Final Hour. Hitler's Last Secretary* ed. Melissa Müller, trans. Anthea Bell (London: Weidenfeld & Nicolson, 2003)

Kershaw, Ian. *Hitler. 1936–1945: Nemesis* (London: Penguin, 2000)

Kershaw, Ian. *Hitler. 1889–1936: Hubris* (London: Penguin, 1998)

Kershaw, Ian. *The 'Hitler Myth'. Image and Reality in the Third Reich* (Oxford: Oxford University Press, 1987)

Kershaw, Ian. *Popular Opinion and Political Dissent in the Third Reich: Bavaria 1933–1945* (Oxford: Clarendon Press, 1984)

King, David. *The Trial of Adolf Hitler. The Beer Hall Putsch and the Rise of Nazi Germany* (London: Macmillan, 2017)

Klabunde, Anja. *Magda Goebbels. Annäherung an ein Leben* (München: Bertelsmann, 1999)

Klemperer, Victor. *Ich will Zeugnis ablegen bis zum letzten: Tagebücher 1933–1941* ed. Walter Nowojski (Berlin: Aufbau-Verl., 1995)

Koehl, Robert L. *The Black Corps. The Structure and Power Struggles of the Nazi SS* (Madison: University of Wisconsin Press, 1983)

Koehler, Hans Jürgen. *Inside Information* (London: Pallas, 1940)

Kollmeier, Kathrin (ed.). *National Socialism in Munich* trans. Melanie Newton (City of Munich-Stadtarchiv, 2008)

Kopleck, Maik. *Munich 1933–1945* 2nd ed., trans. Adelheid Korpp (Berlin: Ch. Links, 2010)

Kopleck, Maik. *München 1933–1945* (Berlin: Christoph Links, 2006)

Kopleck, Maik. *Berlin 1933–1945* (Berlin: Christoph Links, 2005)

Krause, Alexander. *No.12 Arcisstraße* (Munich: Allitera, 2010)

Kubizek, August. *The Young Hitler I Knew* trans. Geoffrey Brooks (London: Greenhill Books, 2006)

Kuhn, Robert. *Nuremberg* (Düsseldorf: Pastfinder Limited, HK, 2007)

Large, David Clay. *Between Two Fires: Europe's Path in the 1930s* (New York: W.W. Norton, 1990)

Large, David Clay. *Where Ghosts Walked: Munich's Road to the Third Reich* (New York: W.W. Norton, 1997)

Le Tissier, Tony. *The Third Reich Then and Now* (London: Battle of Britain International, 2005)

Lehrer, Steven. *Hitler Sites* (Jefferson, North Carolina: McFarland, 2002)

Levi, Primo. *Die Untergegangenen und die Geretteten* (München: Hanser, 1990)

Lloyd, Alexandra (ed.). *The White Rose. Reading, Writing, Resistance* (Oxford: Taylor Institution Library, 2019)

Longerich, Peter. *Goebbels: A Biography* trans. Alan Bance, Jeremy Noakes, and Lesley Sharpe (London: Bodley Head, 2015)

Longerich, Peter. *Die braunen Bataillone: Geschichte der SA* (München: Beck, 1989)

Ludecke, Kurt G.W. *I Knew Hitler* ed. Bob Carruthers (Barnsley: Pen & Sword, 2013)

Luhrssen, David. *Hammer of the Gods: the Thule Society and the birth of Nazism* (Washington, DC: Potomac Books, 2012)

Lukacs, John. The Hitler of History (London: Phoenix Press, 2002)

Lukacs, John. *The Duel, 10 May–31 July 1940: The Eighty-Day Struggle Between Churchill and Hitler* (New York: Ticknor and Fields, 1991)

Lurker, Otto. *Hitler hinter Festungsmauern: Ein Bild aus trüben Tagen* (Berlin: E.S. Mittler & Sohn, 1933)

Maier, Klaus A., Horst Rohde, Bernd Stegemann, and Hans Umbreit. *Germany and the Second World War* Vol.II Germany's Initial Conquests in Europe, trans. Dean S. McMurry and Ewald Osers (Oxford: Clarendon Press, 1991)

Mann, Heinrich. *'Kurt Eisner' Macht und Menschen* (Frankfurt, 1989)

Mann, Klaus. *The Turning Point. The Autobiography of Klaus Mann* (London: Oswald Wolff, 1984)

Mann, Thomas. 'Versuch über das Theater' in *Essays I: 1883–1914* ed. Hermann Kurzke (Frankfurt am Main: S. Fischer, 2002)

Mann, Thomas. 'Gedanken im Kriege', in *Essays II: 1914–1916* ed. Hermann Kurzke (Frankfurt am Main: S. Fischer, 2002)

Mann, Thomas. *Pro and Contra Wagner.* ed. Patrick Carnegy, trans. Allan Blunden (London: Faber and Faber, 1985)

Mann, Thomas. *Diaries 1918–1939* trans. Richard and Clara Winston (London: André Deutsch, 1983)

Mann, Thomas. *Reflections of a Nonpolitical Man*, trans. Walter D Morris (New York: Frederick Ungar Publishing, 1983)

Maser, Werner. *Sturm auf die Republik* (Düsseldorf: Econ, 1994)

Maser, Werner. *Hitler* trans. Peter and Betty Ross (London: Allen Lane, 1973)

Maser, Werner. *Die Frühgeschichte der NSDAP: Hitlers Weg bis 1924* (Frankfurt am Main: Athenäum-Verl., 1965)

Matthews, Brian. *The Military Music & Bandsmen of Adolf Hitler's Third Reich 1933–1945* (Winchester, Hampshire: Tomahawk Films, 2002)

Maxse, Reginald. *Bavaria in a nutshell* (München: J. Lindauersche Buchhandlung, 1910)

Metzger, Rainer. *Munich Its Golden Age of Art and Culture 1890–1920* (London: Thames and Hudson, 2009)

Middlebrook, Martin and Chris Everitt. *The Bomber Command War Diaries. An Operational Reference Book, 1939–1945* (Harmondsworth, Middlesex: Viking, Penguin Books, 1985)

Millington, Barry (ed.). *The Wagner Compendium* (London: Thames and Hudson, 1992)

Mitchell, Allan. Revolutions in Bavaria, 1918–1919. The Eisner Regime and the Soviet Republic (Princeton, New Jersey: Princeton University Press, 1965)

Mitford Mosley, Diana. *A Life of Contrasts: The Autobiography of Diana Mitford Mosley* (New York: New York Times Books, 1977)

Mosley, Charlotte (ed.). *The Mitfords. Letters Between Six Sisters* (London: Harper Perennial, 2008)

Mühlberger, Detlef. *Hitler's Voice. The Völkischer Beobachter, 1920–1933* Vol.I Organization & Development of the Nazi Party (Oxford: Peter Lang, 2004)

Müller, Franz Josef (ed.). *The White Rose* (Munich: Weiße Rose Stiftung, 2006),

Müller, Karl Alexander von. *Mars und Venus. Erinnerungen 1914–1919* (Stuttgart: Kilpper, 1954)

Müller-Meiningen, Ernst. *Aus Bayerns schwersten Tagen* (Berlin: de Gruyter, 1924)

Nerdinger, Winfried (ed.). *Munich and National Socialism* (Munich: Beck, 2015)

Nerdinger, Winfried (ed.). *Architekturführer München/Architectural Guide to Munich* (Berlin: Dietrich Reimer, 2002)

Nettl, J.P. *Rosa Luxemburg* vol.1 (London: Oxford University Press, 1966)

Nicholas, Lynn H. *The Rape of Europe* (London: Papermac, 1995)

Noakes, Jeremy and Geoffrey Pridham (eds.) *Nazism 1919–1945 Vol.1: The Rise to Power 1919–1934.* (Exeter: University of Exeter Press, 1983)

O'Neill, R.J. *The German Army and the Nazi Party 1933–1939* (London: Cassell, 1966)

Orlow, Dietrich. *The History of the Nazi Party*, Vol.I: 1919–1933 (Newton Abbot: David & Charles, 1971)

Ortner, Helmut. *The Lone Assassin. The Epic True Story of the Man Who Almost Killed Hitler* trans. Ross Benjamin (New York: Skyhorse Publishing, 2012)

Örtzen, Friedrich Wilhelm von. *Die deutschen Freikorps 1918–1923* 5 ed. (München: Bruckmann, 1939)

Papen, Franz von. *Der Wahrheit eine Gasse* (München: List, 1952)

Plöckinger, Othmar. *Unter Soldaten und Agitatoren: Hitlers prägende Jahre im deutschen Militär 1918–1920* (Paderborn : Ferdinanc Schöningh, 2013)

Plöckinger, Othmar. *Geschichte eines Buches: Adolf Hitlers 'Mein Kampf' 1922–1945* rev.ed. (München: Oldenbourg, 2011)

Pope, Ernest R. *Munich Playground. The Nazi Leadership at Rest and Play* (London: Fonthill, 2015, originally published 1941)

Preis, Kurt. München unterm Hakenkreuz (München: Herbig, 1989)

Pridham, Geoffrey. *Hitler's Rise to Power: The Nazi Movement in Bavaria 1923–1933* (London: Hart-Davis, MacGibbon, 1973)

Ramsey, Winston (ed.). *The Defeat of Germany*. Then and Now. After the Battle (Old Harlow, Essex: Battle of Britain International, 2015)

Range, Peter Ross. *1924: The Year That Made Hitler* (New York: Little, Brown, 2016)

Rees, Laurence. *The Dark Charisma of Adolf Hitler* (London: Ebury Press, 2012)

Reichardt, Sven. *Faschistische Kampfbünde: Gewalt und Gemeinschaft im italienischen Squadrismus und in der deutschen SA* (Köln: Böhlau, 2009)

Röhm, Ernst. *The Memoirs of Ernst Röhm* intro. Eleanor Hancock, trans. Geoffrey Brooks (London: Frontline, 2012)

Röhm, Ernst. *Die Geschichte eines Hochverräters* (München: Eher, 1934)

Ryback, Timothy W. *Hitler's Private Library* (New York: Alfred A. Knopf, 2008)

Sackett, Robert Eben. *Popular Entertainment, Class, and Politics in Munich, 1900–1923* (Cambridge, Massachusetts: Harvard University Press, 1982)

Saikia, Robin and Joachim von Halasz (eds.). *Hitler's Munich: A Third Reich Tourist Guide* (London: World Propaganda Classics, 2008)

Salomon, Ernst von. *Das Buch vom Deutschen Freikorpskämpfer* (Berlin: Wilhelm Lempert, 1938)

Sandner, Harald. *Hitler. Das Itinerar. Aufenthaltsorte und Reisen von 1889 bis 1945.* Band I-IV (Berlin: Berlin Story Verlag, 2016)

Sayer, Ian and Douglas Botting. *The Women Who Knew Hitler. The Private Life of Adolf Hitler* (London: Constable, 2004)

Schäfer, Claus W. *André François-Poncet als Botschafter in Berlin 1931–1938* (München: Oldenbourg Wissenschafts-Verlag, 2004)

Schäfer, Kirstin A. *Werner von Blomberg: Hitlers erster Feldmarschall. Eine Biographie* (Paderborn: Schöningh, 2006)

Schlenker, Ines. *Hitler's Salon. The Große Deutsche Kunstausstellung at the Haus der Deutschen Kunst in Munich 1937–1944* (Oxford: Peter Lang, 2007)

Schmeer, Karlheinz. *Die Regie des öffentlichen Lebens im Dritten Reich* (München: Pohl, 1956)

Schmidt, Paul. *Statist auf diplomatischer Bühne 1923–45: Erlebnisse des Chefdolmetschers im Auswärtigen Amt mit den Staatsmännern Europas* (Bonn: Athenäum-Verl., 1949)

Schroeder, Christa. *He Was My Chief. The Memoirs of Adolf Hitler's Secretary* trans. Geoffrey Brooks (London: Frontline, 2009)

Schuster, Peter-Klaus (ed.). *Nationalsozialismus und 'Entartete Kunst'. Die 'Kunststadt' München 1937* (Munich: Prestel-Verlag, 1987)

Sebottendorff, Rudolf von. *Bevor Hitler kam* (München: Deukula Verlag Grassinger, 1933)

Siegert, Max. *Aus Münchens schwerster Zeit: Erinnerungen aus dem Münchener Hauptbahnhof während der Revolutions- und Rätezeit* (München: Manz, 1928)

Siemens, Daniel. *Stormtroopers. A New History of Hitler's Brownshirts* (London: Yale University Press, 2017)

Sigmund, Anna Maria. *Des Führers bester Freund: Adolf Hitler, seine Nichte Geli Raubal und der 'Ehrenarier' Emil Maurice, eine Dreiecksbeziehung* (München: Heyne, 2003)

Smelser, Ronald. *Robert Ley: Hitlers Mann an der 'Arbeitsfront'* (Paderborn: Schöningh, 1989)

Sösemann, Bernd. *Das Ende der Weimarer Republik in der Kritik demokratischer Publizisten* (Berlin: Colloquium-Verl., 1976)

Speer, Albert. *Spandau: The Prison Diaries* trans. Richard and Clara Winston (New York: Macmillan, 1976)

Stachura, Peter D. *Gregor Strasser and the Rise of Nazism* (London: Allen & Unwin, 1983).

Stratigakos, Despina. *Hitler at Home* (New Haven: Yale University Press, 2015)

Straumann, Tobias. *1931 – Debt, Crisis, and the Rise of Hitler* (Oxford: Oxford University Press, 2019)

Strobel, Otto (ed.). *König Ludwig II und Richard Wagner: Briefwechsel* 5 vols (Karlsruhe: Braun, 1936–39)

Sünwoldt, Sabine. *Weiß Ferdl. Eine Weiss-Blaue Karriere* (München: Heinrich Hugendubel, 1983)

Tanner, Michael. *Wagner* (London: Faber and Faber, 2010)

Thacker, Toby. *Joseph Goebbels: Life and Death* (Basingstoke, Hampshire: Palgrave Macmillan, 2009)

Thamer, Hans-Ulrich. *Der Nationalsozialismus* (Stuttgart: Reclam, 2002)

Toland, John. *Hitler* (Hertfordshire: Wordsworth Editions, 1997)

Tooze, Adam. *Wages of Destruction: The Making and Breaking of the Nazi Economy* (London: Allen Lane, 2006)

Tyrell, Albrecht. *Vom "Trommler" zum "Führer": der Wandel von Hitlers Selbstverständnis zwischen 1919 und 1924 und die Entwicklung der NSDAP* (München: Fink, 1975)

Tyrell, Albrecht (ed.). *Führer befiehl … Selbstzeugnisse aus der 'Kampfzeit' der NSDAP. Dokumentation und Analyse* (Düsseldorf: Droste, 1969)

Tyson, Joseph Howard. *Hitler's Mentor: Dietrich Eckart, His Life, Times, & Milieu* (New York: iUniverse, 2008)

Ullrich, Viktor. *Geburtstags-Parade 20. April 1939 Berlin* (Kiel: ARNDT-Verlag, 2004)

Ullrich, Volker. *Hitler. Downfall 1939–1945* trans. Jefferson Chase (London: Bodley Head, 2020)

Ullrich, Volker. *Hitler. Ascent 1889–1939* trans. Jefferson Chase (London: Bodley Head, 2016)

Wagener, Otto. *Hitler aus nächster Nähe: Aufzeichnungen eines Vertrauten 1929–1932* ed. Henry A. Turner (Frankfurt am Main: Ullstein, 1978)

Wagner, Richard. *My Life* (Teddington, Middlesex: The Echo Library, 2007)

Wahl, Fritz. 'Rätezeit in München', *Gegenwart* (Frankfurt a.M., 1956)

Walden, Geoffrey R. *Hitler's Berchtesgaden. A Guide to Third Reich Sites in the Berchtesgaden and Obersalzberg Area* (Stroud: Fonthill Media, 2014)

Wallner, Franz. *Der Österreich-Anschluß 1938* (Kiel: ARNDT-Verlag, 2003)

Weber, Thomas. *Hitler's First War: Adolf Hitler, the Men of the List Regiment, and the First World War* (Oxford: Oxford University Press, 2010)

Weitz, Eric D. *Weimar Germany. Promise and Tragedy* (Princeton: Princeton University Press, 2007)

Wheatley, Paul. *Munich: From Monks to Modernity* (München: Volk Verlag München, 2010)

Wheeler-Bennett, John. *The Nemesis of Power* (London: Macmillan, 1967)

Wiedemann, Fritz. *Der Mann der Feldherr warden wollte* (Velbert: Blick & Bild Verl., 1964)

Wistrich, Robert S. *Weekend in Munich. Art, Propaganda and Terror in the Third Reich* (London: Pavilion Books, 1995)

Wulf, Joseph. *Die bildenden Künste im Dritten Reich. Eine Dokumentation* (Gütersloh: Mohn, 1963)

Zweig, Stefan. *Die Welt von gestern: Erinnerungen eines Europäers* (Stockholm: Bermann-Fischer, 1942)

Articles, Chapters, Essays, Pamphlets, and Theses

Arnold, Karl. '*Der Münchner*', *Simplicissimus*, Nr.36, München, 3 Dezember 1923.

Beierl, Florian und Othmar Plöckinger. 'Neue Dokumente zu Hitlers Buch "*Mein Kampf*"', *Vierteljahrshefte für Zeitgeschichte* 57, nr.2 (2009)

Bloch, Eduard. 'My Patient Hitler' in *Collier's Weekly* (15 and 22 March 1941)

Deuerlein, Ernst. 'Hitlers Eintritt in die Politik und die Reichswehr', *Vierteljahrshefte für Zeitgeschichte*, Vol.7, Nr.2 (1959).

Fishman, Sterling. 'Prophets, Poets and Priests: A Study of the Men and Ideas that made the Munich Revolution of 1918/19' PhD Dissertation, University of Wisconsin, Madison, 1960.

Franz, Georg. 'Munich: Birthplace and Centre of the National Socialist German Workers' Party', *Journal of Modern History* Vol.29 (1957)

Gerstl, Max. 'Die Münchener Räterepublik', *Politische Zeitfragen*, 1919.

Hall, David Ian. 'Wagner, Hitler, and Germany's Rebirth after the First World War', *War in History* Vol.24, No.2 (2017)

Hall, David Ian. '*Furor Teutonicus*: the Regeneration of the German Armed Forces after the Great War', ed. Stuart Griffin, *Extended Readiness and Capabiltiy Re-Generation: Lessons from History* (Ministry of Defence: DSTL, 2012)

Hitler, Adolf. Radio Address: 'Appeal to the German People', 31 January 1933 (Winchester: The Tomahawk Films Archive, 1999)

Jones, Mark. 'The Crowd in the German November Revolution 1918', Klaus Weinhauer, Anthony McElligott, and Kirsten Heinsohn (eds.), *Germany 1916–23: A Revolution in Context* (Bielefeld, transcript Verlag, 2015)

Kaiser, Fritz. *Entartete 'Kunst'. Degenerate Art: The Exhibition Catalogue Guide in German and English* (Berlin, 1937; This edition Ostara Publications, 2012)

Mann, Thomas. 'Versuch über das Theater' in *Essays I: 1883–1914* ed. Hermann Kurzke (Frankfurt am Main, 2002)

Mann, Thomas. 'Gedanken im Kriege', in *Essays II: 1914–1916* ed. Hermann Kurzke (Frankfurt am Main, 2002)

Mann, Thomas. 'Bruder Hitler', *Das Neue Tagebuch*, 25 March 1939.

Margry, Karel. '50 Years Ago: The Munich Crisis', *After the Battle* (No. 62, 1988)

Mollo, Andrew. 'Dachau', *After the Battle* (no.27, 1980)

München Hauptstadt der Bewegung (Munich, 1937)

'Munich: *Der Neunte Elfte*' (Munich: the ninth of the eleventh), *After the Battle* (No.66, 1989)

Munich: The spirit of a German City (Munich: Culture Department of the Capital of the National Movement, 1939)

Novak, Ben. Hitler's *Rienzi* Experience: Factuality', *Revista de Historia* Actual Vol.5, No.5 (2007)

The Oktoberfest 1810–2010: Kultur Geschichte Bayern, published by Landesstelle für die Nichtstaatlichen Museen in Bayern and the Münchner Stadtmuseum (München: P.medien, 2010)

Orlow, Dietrich. 'Rudolf Hess: Deputy *Führer*', in Ronald Smelser and Rainer Zitelmann (eds.), *The Nazi Elite* (Basingstoke, 1993)

Piper, Ernst. 'Nationalsozialistische Kulturpolitik und ihre Profiteure', in *'Niemand war dabei und keiner hat's gewußt': Die deutsche Öffentlichkeit und die Judenverfolgung* (ed.) Jörg Wollenberg (München, 1989)

Schmitt, Carl. 'Der Führer schützt das Recht', *Deutsche Juristen Zeitung* (1 August 1934)

Sigmund, Anna Maria. 'Geli Raubal' in *Die Frauen der Nazis: Die drei Bestseller vollständig aktualisiert in einem Band* vol.I (Vienna, 1998)

Steinhaus, Kathryn. 'Valkyrie: Gender, Class, European Relations, and Unity Mitford's Passion for Fascism', PhD Thesis McGill University, Montreal, December 2011.

Tag der Deutschen Kunst 1937, 16. Bis 18. Juli zu München, Leitung des Tages der Deutschen Kunst (ed.), Munich 1937.

Vollnhals, Clemens. 'Der Aufstieg ser NSDAP in München 1925 bis 1933: Forderer und Gegner', Richard Bauer (ed.), *München – 'Hauptstadt der Bewegung'. Bayerns Metropole und der Nationalsozialismus* (Münchner Stadtmuseum, Edition Minerva, 2002)

Watt, D.C. '*Die bayerischen Bemühungen um Ausweisung Hitlers 1924*' *Vierteljahrshefte für Zeitgeschichte*, 6 (1958)

Willrich, Wolfgang. *Die Säuberung des Kunsttempels. Eine kunstpolitische Kampfschrift zur Gesundung deutscher Kunst im mordischen Geist* (Munich/Berlin, 1937)

Zweig, Stefan. 'Incipit Hitler' in *The World of Yesterday. Memoirs of a European* trans. Anthea Bell (London: Pushkin Press, 2011)

Websites

NS-Dokumentationszentrum – Documentation Centre for the History of National Socialism (ns-dokuzentrum-muenchen.de)

Münchner Stadtmuseum – Munich City Museum (muenchner-stadtmuseum.de)
  1. Kurt Eisner Special Exhibition (2017)
  2. Permanent Exhibition on National Socialism

Landeshauptstadt München Kulturreferat (muenchen.de/kulturreferat)

City of Munich-Culture and Historic Walks
  1. ThemenGeschichtsPfad (National Socialism in Munich) (muenchen.de/kgp)
  2. ThemenGeschichtsPfad (Places of Remembrance and Commemoration – National Socialism in Munich) (muenchen.de/tgp)
  3. Georg Elser (georg-elser.de)

Haus der Kunst, München (hausderkunst.de)

Jüdisches Museum München (Jewish Museum Munich) (juedisches-museum-muenchen.de)

Weiße Rose Stiftung (White Rose Foundation) (weisse-rose-stiftung.de)

Valentin Karlstadt Musäum (Karl Valentin and Liesl Karlstadt Museum) (valentin-musaeum.de)

FC Bayern Erlebniswelt (FC Bayern Munich Museum – Allianz Arena) (fcbayern.com/museum/de)

Richard Wagner Bayreuther Festspiele (bayreuther-festspiele.de)

Dokumentation Obersalzberg (obersalzberg.de)

The Hitler Pages (hitlerpages.com)

The Third Reich in Ruins (thirdreichruins.com)

Acknowledgements

The idea for this book came from the students who took my seminar in Hitler Studies at the Joint Services Command and Staff College as part of their MA in Defence Studies, King's College London. I am fortunate to have worked at the UK Defence Academy in Shrivenham where I have been surrounded by academics and military officers who provide continuous encouragement and intellectual stimulation. I am sincerely grateful for having worked in this challenging and engaging environment and with people who have always been incredibly supportive of my scholarship.

Many people have helped with the writing and publication of this book. First, the team at Pen and Sword have been brilliant. I sincerely thank Henry Wilson, my commissioning editor, for his enthusiasm and encouragement throughout the project. Matt Jones, the production manager, and his exceptional group of designers and editors have produced a book that I am enormously proud to have on my bookshelf. Barnaby Blacker's keen eye and light touch as copy editor and Tony Williams' proof reading saved me from many embarrassing inconsistencies and typing errors. Jon Wilkinson designed the striking dust jacket, Saravanan Jayaraman (SJ as he is affectionately known at Pen & Sword) drew the maps, and Mat Blurton designed the book. Tara Moran and Rosie Croft handled the marketing despite all the challenges brought on by the coronavirus pandemic, and Lori Jones in the central office has always been cheerful and helpful. At Shrivenham I received invaluable advice and encouragement from several colleagues and friends. Special thanks are owed to Dr Nick Lloyd (who also accompanied me on an enjoyable research trip to Munich), Dr William Mitchinson, Dr Saul Kelly, Dr Robert Foley, Squadron Leader Jason Murdock (RAF), and Aaron Cripps, now the Library Manager for Central Swindon North Parish Council. Professors Mary Kathryn Barbier and Dee Dee Baldwin at Mississippi State University kindly helped me navigate the internet and obtain historical photographs that are freely available in the public domain. Over several years Florian Beierl, my good friend and historian colleague in Berchtesgaden, has guided me through the finer details of Hitler's years on the Obersalzberg.

This book would not have been completed without access to the holdings of many archives and libraries. I am very grateful to the staff members who helped me at the Institut für Zeitgeschichte (IfZ) München; the NS-Dokumentationszentrum München; the Bayerisches Hauptstaatarchiv (BHS) München; the Bayerische Staatsbibliothek (BSB) München; the Monacensia im Hildebrandhaus Literaturarchiv und Bibliothek, München; the Münchner Stadtmuseum; the Weiße Rose Stiftung, München; the Nationalarchiv der Richard-Wagner-Stiftung, Bayreuth; the National Archives, Kew; the Bundesarchiv in Berlin-Lichterfelde and Koblenz; the National Archives of the United States in College Park Maryland and Washington, DC; the newspaper archive at the British Library; the Bodleian Library; the Hobson Library at the JSCSC; and the Obersalzberg-Institut in Berchtesgaden.

I am also grateful to my family for their unflagging interest in my research and my innumerable trips to Munich and elsewhere in Bavaria. My father and my brother have always been my greatest supporters. At home, Kathryn has learnt more about Hitler and his time in Munich than she ever imagined. She read draft after draft of the manuscript, corrected my German spelling, and provided insightful observations on how to make the book better. And Sissi, our German Shepherd, did not complained too much at missing out on a walk or fußball in the garden. I am thankful to them all for their love and support. All the interpretations and opinions expressed in the following pages are my responsibility alone and do not necessarily reflect the views of those who have assisted this project.

David Ian Hall

November 2020

Image and Photograph Credits

The images, numbered below, appear sequentially in the book.

1. *Simplicissimus*, Thomas Theodor Heine (author's collection)
2. Alter Simpl Interior, Türkenstraße (D. I. Hall)
3. Print of Café Stefanie, unknown (author's collection)
4. Print of 'Der Alter Hof' by Adolf Hitler (author's collection)
5. Main Gate, Türkenstraße Barracks (D. I. Hall)
6. Statue of Bavaria, Theresienwiese (D. I. Hall)
7. Friedensengel, Maximilian Park (D. I. Hall)
8. Kurt Eisner Memorial, Ostfriedhof (D. I. Hall)
9. Thule-Gesellschaft logo, unknown (author's collection)
10. Haus (Café) Neumayr, (D. I. Hall)
11. Hofbräukeller, Innere Wiener Straße (D. I. Hall)
12. Hofbräuhaus, Am Platzl (D. I. Hall)
13. Hofbräuhaus Festsaal (D. I. Hall)
14. Feldherrnhalle, Odeonsplatz (D. I. Hall)
15. Hitler's 2nd private residence, Thierschstraße (D. I. Hall)
16. Hitler-Ludendorff Prozess, 1924 Trial (Bundesarchiv, Heinrich Hoffmann, public domain)
17. 'Munich Man' *Simplicissimus*, Karl Arnold (author's collection)
18. Hoffmann Photographic Studio / 4th NSDAP HQ, Schellingstraße (D. I. Hall)
19. Newspaper Wagon, *Völkischer Beobachter* (D. I. Hall)
20. Neues Rathaus, Marienplatz (D. I. Hall)
21. Braunes Haus, Brienner Straße (Bundesarchiv, unknown, public domain)
22. Hitler at his desk, Braunes Haus (Bundesarchiv, Heinrich Hoffmann, public domain)
23. Postcard of 1923 Putsch Commemoration, Feldherrnhalle (author's collection)
24. Ehrentempel, Königsplatz (Bundesarchiv, unknown, public domain)
25. Polizeipräsidium, Ettstraße (D. I. Hall)
26. Haus der Deutschen Kunst, Prinzregentenstraße (Bundesarchiv, unknown, public domain)
27. 'Bolshevism' Exhibition 1936, Poster (D. I. Hall)
28. Hitler opens the first Große Deutsche Kunstausstellung (Great German Art Exhibition), 18 July 1937 (Bundesarchiv, unknown, public domain)
29. Der ewige Jude (The Eternal Jew) Exhibition 1937, Poster (author's collection)
30. Art Exhibition Programmes 1937 (author's collection)
31. Haus der Deutschen Kunst (Bundesarchiv, unknown, public domain)
32. Hitler and Mussolini, September 1938 (Bundesarchiv, unknown, public domain)
33. Führerbau, Munich Conference, September 1938 (Bundesarchiv, unknown, public domain)
34. Altes Rathaus, Marienplatz (D. I. Hall)
35. Hitler's 3rd private residence, Prinzregentenplatz (D. I. Hall)
36. Prinzregenten Theater, Prinzregentenplatz (D. I. Hall)
37. NS-Housing Estate and Air Raid Bunker, Prinzregentenstraße (D. I. Hall)
38. Hitler and Eva Braun at the Berghof, Obersalzberg (Bundesarchiv, unknown, public domain)
39. Air Raid Bunker, Blumenstraße (D. I. Hall)
40. Bürgerbräukeller damaged by Elser's bomb, 9 November 1939 (Bundesarchiv, Wagner, public domain)

41. Funeral for the victims of the Bürgerbräukeller bombing, 11 November 1939 (Bundesarchiv, Wagner, public domain)
42. Siegestor (Victory Gate), Ludwigstraβe (D. I. Hall)
43. Justizpalast, Karlsplatz (Stachus) (D. I. Hall)
44. Weiβe Rose Court Room 253, Justizpalast (D. I. Hall)
45. Löwenbräukeller, Stiglmaierplatz (D. I. Hall)
46. City Centre in Ruins, May 1945 (Bundesarchiv, unknown, public domain)
47. Elser Memorial Art, Georg-Elser-Platz (D. I. Hall)
48. Elser Memorial, Illuminated (D. I. Hall)

All the images in the book come from either the author's personal collection or Wikimedia Commons, the free media repository in the public domain. We have made our best efforts to credit the original photographer and publishers and to do this accurately from the information available and have credited the rights holders where appropriate and possible.

Index